AF804954

THE RISE OF INVESTOR–STATE ARBITRATION

The Rise of Investor–State Arbitration

Politics, Law, and Unintended Consequences

TAYLOR ST JOHN

OXFORD
UNIVERSITY PRESS

OXFORD
UNIVERSITY PRESS

Great Clarendon Street, Oxford, OX2 6DP,
United Kingdom

Oxford University Press is a department of the University of Oxford. It furthers the University's objective of excellence in research, scholarship, and education by publishing worldwide. Oxford is a registered trade mark of Oxford University Press in the UK and in certain other countries

© Taylor St John 2018

The moral rights of the author have been asserted

First Edition published in 2018

Impression: 1

All rights reserved. No part of this publication may be reproduced, stored in a retrieval system, or transmitted, in any form or by any means, without the prior permission in writing of Oxford University Press, or as expressly permitted by law, by licence or under terms agreed with the appropriate reprographics rights organization. Enquiries concerning reproduction outside the scope of the above should be sent to the Rights Department, Oxford University Press, at the address above

You must not circulate this work in any other form and you must impose this same condition on any acquirer

Published in the United States of America by Oxford University Press
198 Madison Avenue, New York, NY 10016, United States of America

British Library Cataloguing in Publication Data
Data available

Library of Congress Control Number: 2017951760

ISBN 978–0–19–878991–8

Printed and bound by
CPI Group (UK) Ltd, Croydon, CR0 4YY

Links to third party websites are provided by Oxford in good faith and for information only. Oxford disclaims any responsibility for the materials contained in any third party website referenced in this work.

To my Mother

Acknowledgments

It has been ten years since I stumbled across ICSID while researching another part of the World Bank. I could not quite believe investor–state arbitration was real, and could not stop wondering how it was created. My initial speculations were dead wrong, but with help and guidance from hundreds of people, I slowly travelled from those speculations to this book. As Aron Broches once said, sometimes you need to "take the show on the road." Although on a much smaller scale than Broches, I have had the chance to explain my ideas to, and learn from, arbitrators, negotiators, officials, practicing lawyers, legal scholars, political science scholars, and my students. To all of them, even those that do not appear here by name, I express my heartfelt gratitude.

Meg Kinnear, Milanka Kostadinova, Martina Polasek, and others at the ICSID Secretariat were welcoming, and I thank them for incisive feedback. Conversations with Antonio Parra enriched this book greatly; his knowledge, generosity, and warmth are unparalleled. I am grateful to the officials from twenty-five countries who were willing to make long trips to join closed-door workshops in Oxford and Santiago and then be frank about the challenges they face. I am also indebted to the officials and others who made time to answer my questions in other contexts; these interviews and conversations were invaluable.

Many scholars, officials, colleagues, and friends have provided comments on drafts related to this book, asked thought-provoking questions, or happily discussed issues with me. I have benefited greatly from discussions with Faisal Ahmed, Todd Allee, Wolfgang Alschner, Freya Baetens, Axel Berger, Ketevan Bolkvadze, Dominique Bruhn, Jansen Calamita, Yuliya Chernykh, Joel Dahlquist, Andreas Føllesdal, Susan Franck, Christopher Gandrud, Bryant Garth, David Gaukrodger, Julia Gray, Yoram Haftel, Andreas Hofmann, Rainer Hofmann, Lise Johnson, Noel Johnston, Mareike Kleine, Jan Kleinheisterkamp, Tori Loven Kirkebø, Olof Larsson, Hannes Lenk, Katerina Linos, Andrew Lugg, Kate Miles, Alex Mills, James Morrison, Natalya Naqvi, Federico Ortino, Stefano Pagliari, Martins Paparinskis, Clint Peinhardt, Mona Pinchis-Paulsen, Sergio Puig, Catherine Rogers, Love Rönnelid, Sudhanshu Roy, Stephan Schill, Øyvind Stiansen, Szilárd Gáspár-Szilágyi, Christian Tams, Alexander Thompson, Todd Tucker, Elisabeth Tuerk, Geir Ulfstein, Güneş Ünüvar, Pierre-Hughes Verdier, Michael Waibel, Todd Weiler, Rachel Wellhausen, Simon Williams, Zoe Williams, Steve Woolcock, Jason Yackee, and Alain Zysset.

A number of institutions have supported this project, which began as a doctorate at the University of Oxford. My time at Oxford was made possible by the Marshall Scholarship, Marshall-Oxford Scholarship, and subsequently by the Global Economic Governance (GEG) Programme. My supervisors, Ngaire Woods and Valpy FitzGerald, transformed not only my writing and approach to scholarship—they transformed my life. I cannot possibly express the extent of my gratitude to them. My examiners, Joost Pauwelyn and John Toye, as well as Adeel Malik, Diego Sánchez-Ancochea, Duncan Snidal, and Adrian Wood, my examiners at earlier stages, clarified and deepened everything they read. I also learned an immense amount from my colleagues and friends in the Loft at Queen Elizabeth House, at St Antony's College, and at GEG (especially Emily Jones, Reija Fanous, and Alexa Zeitz). I've lost count of how many discussions I've had with Geoff Gertz, Tom Hale, and Lauge Poulsen about arbitration, but their insights, both theoretical and empirical, have sharpened my own immeasurably. When I moved to the London School of Economics to teach, the ideas in this manuscript often crept into seminar discussions; I am grateful to my students for entertaining and improving these ideas.

The manuscript then came with me to PluriCourts, where I found expert colleagues ready to challenge and improve it: my thanks in particular to Daniel Behn, Tarald Laudal Berge, Ole Kristian Fauchald, Daniel Naurin, Theresa Squatrito, and Maxim Usynin. This work was partly supported by the Research Council of Norway through its Centres of Excellence funding scheme, project number 223274. Daniel Naurin and Ole Kristian Fauchald suggested and then provided the resources for a book workshop, and I am indebted to them and all attendees at that workshop, especially Mark Pollack, Nicole De Silva, and Tom Hale, for making this a much better book. I thank Dominic Byatt at Oxford University Press for believing in this book, as well as Sarah Parker, Olivia Wells, Vijaya Manimaran, and Phil Dines for making it a reality with such skill.

I was fortunate to have assistance from the supremely capable Yannick Stiller, whose appreciation for the nuance and sparkle of archival documents brought long-dead officials back to life. My partner, Henning Tamm, nurtured and strengthened each idea in this book; his skills as a sympathetic interlocutor and his unwavering commitment always illuminate what matters. Finally, my sister and my mother's exuberance and encouragement sustained me and this project every step of the way.

Contents

List of Tables

List of Archive Abbreviations

AVL	Axis Victims League
CH	Bundesarchiv Bern (Swiss Federal Archive)
DE	Bundesarchiv Koblenz (German Federal Archive)
IFZ	Institut für Zeitgeschichte (Institute for Contemporary History)
NZ	National Archives of New Zealand
UK FCO	National Archives of the United Kingdom, Foreign and Commonwealth Office
UK T	National Archives of the United Kingdom, Treasury
US	United States National Archives, Department of State
US LA	United States National Archives, Center for Legislative Archives
US BPL	United States National Archives, Bush Presidential Library
US CPL	United States National Archives, Clinton Presidential Library
US FBI	United States National Archives, Federal Bureau of Investigation
US TPL	United States National Archives, Truman Presidential Library
WB	World Bank Group Archives

Selected Abbreviations

AIOC	Anglo-Iranian Oil Company
APPI	Association for the Promotion and Protection of Private Foreign Investments
BIT	bilateral investment treaty
DAC	Development Assistance Committee (OECD)
ECLA	United Nations Economic Commission for Latin America
ECOSOC	United Nations Economic and Social Council
FDI	foreign direct investment
IBRD	International Bank for Reconstruction and Development
ICC	International Chamber of Commerce
ICJ	International Court of Justice
ICSID	International Centre for Settlement of Investment Disputes
IDA	International Development Association
IFC	International Finance Corporation
ILA	International Law Association
ILM	International Legal Materials
IPPA	Investment Promotion and Protection Agreement
LDC	least developed country
NFTC	National Foreign Trade Council
OECD	Organisation for Economic Co-operation and Development
OEEC	Organisation for European Economic Co-operation
OPIC	Overseas Private Investment Corporation
PCA	Permanent Court of Arbitration
PCIJ	Permanent Court of International Justice
SCC	Arbitration Institute of the Stockholm Chamber of Commerce
UNCITRAL	United Nations Commission on International Trade Law
UNCTAD	United Nations Conference on Trade and Development
USTR	United States Trade Representative

Introduction

On June 19 2008, Viorel and Ioan Micula, Romanian-born brothers with Swedish citizenship, attended a hearing at the World Bank's Paris office. Three years earlier, the Miculas had filed a claim requesting over 450 million euros in compensation from the Romanian government. The claim was being heard at the International Centre for Settlement of Investment Disputes (ICSID), a small arm of the World Bank that arranges arbitrations between foreign investors and states. The arbitration tribunal had three members: one appointed by the Miculas, one appointed by Romania, and the third by agreement of the parties. In that hearing room in Paris, there were thirty lawyers, but no one from the Romanian government, Swedish government, or the European Commission.[1]

The Miculas' counsel argued that when Romania partially withdrew investment incentives to disfavored regions, it violated the Fair and Equitable Treatment clause in the Sweden–Romania bilateral investment treaty (BIT).[2] Romania's counsel argued that these incentives had to be partially withdrawn as a condition of Romania acceding to the European Union (EU)—a position the European Commission confirmed in an amicus submission.[3]

The ICSID tribunal found that Romania had violated the Sweden–Romania BIT by prematurely repealing the economic incentives and by failing to inform the Miculas promptly about the repeal. The arbitrator appointed by Romania dissented here, noting that "situations of two parts of government speaking at cross-purposes, as well as hesitation or wavering, are usual occurrences, particularly in times of rapid (and rather disorderly) change. They can happen in the best of governments." The arbitrator also observed that the Romanian government had no intention to deceive; rather, this was merely "a case of

[1] *Micula v Romania* (Decision on Jurisdiction 2008): 8–15.

[2] *Micula v Romania* (Decision on Jurisdiction 2008): 8–15.

[3] *Micula v Romania* (Award 2013): 15, 93, 97. In 2016, the Commission filed an amicus with the US Court of Appeals for the Second Circuit (New York), where the Miculas sought to enforce the award against Romanian assets in the US. In 2015, the Commission concluded that payment of the award itself would violate EU rules on state aid, and ordered the Miculas to pay back all amounts already received (Commission Decision 2015/1470 of March 30 2015 on State Aid).

failure of communication and... coordination between different parts of government."[4]

The award sparked outrage in Romania: no property had been taken from the Miculas—they had lost only their expectation of not having to pay a particular tax for four more years. Their claim to Swedish citizenship was tenuous, their primary residence was Romania, the "disfavored region" was their hometown, and the Miculas were well-known as some of Romania's wealthiest men.[5] The award, to be paid by Romanian taxpayers, would cost more than 30 euros for every working person in Romania—about 10 percent of the average Romanian monthly salary.[6]

The Swedish government remained silent throughout the Micula case. If investment dispute resolution were a state–state system, like trade dispute resolution, would the Swedish government have taken up the case, brought a claim against Romania, and antagonized the European Commission?

That question could also be asked about another case involving a Swedish investor. The German government decided to phase out nuclear energy after the 2011 Fukushima disaster. Phasing out nuclear energy is a complex process, and the utility companies affected argued that the decision was taken hastily and saddled them with losses from earlier-than-planned shutdowns. The affected companies filed complaints with the German Constitutional Court. Most of the companies were German and their only legal recourse was to German courts. One of the companies, Vattenfall, was a Swedish state-owned firm. Swedish nationality gave Vattenfall the ability to bring two claims against the German government at ICSID, alleging violation of the Energy Charter Treaty. The Vattenfall cases surprised German officials and citizens—in the German press, there was a sense of incredulity that a foreign corporation could challenge German environmental regulations before an international tribunal, which might award billions of euros in compensation to the foreign firm.[7] Here again, would the Swedish government—aware of Sweden's own tumultuous political history with nuclear phase-out[8]—have taken up the case against the German government?

[4] Dissent of Georges Abi-Saab (2013): 5.

[5] The Miculas are frequently covered in the Romanian press, including articles on their extravagant lifestyles. For instance, Victor Micula's son is known for landing a helicopter at a Black Sea resort and for refusing to comply with police while driving his Ferrari (Bonchiş 2015).

[6] Romania was ordered to pay the award of RON 376,433,229 (84.5 million euros), plus interest, plus half the cost of the arbitration, plus their legal fees (11.5 million euros). The Miculas were ordered to pay their own legal fees, which totaled 18.4 million euros, and half the cost of the arbitration. *Micula v Romania* (Award 2013): 366–7. The average Romanian monthly salary in January 2013 was 1548 lei (351 euros). Institutul National de Statistica 2017.

[7] In a *Frankfurter Rundschau* article, for instance, Vattenfall's claim at ICSID is described with outrage while its parallel claim in German courts is not (Schlandt 2013).

[8] Phasing out nuclear power has long been a salient, even a defining issue in Swedish politics. Sweden held an advisory referendum on nuclear power in 1980 (after the Three Mile Island

It is difficult to imagine the Swedish government—or any other government—taking up these cases. So why did governments create a special system in which foreign investors are able to bring their cases directly against states? In other words, what explains the rise of investor–state arbitration? These questions motivate this book. The chapters that follow probe the intellectual, political, and economic forces behind the rise of investor–state arbitration.

The corporations and law firms that dominate investor–state arbitration today were not present at its creation. It did not emerge through corporate greed or investor lobbying. In fact, there was almost no demand from investors for this type of arbitration. Nor did powerful states have a strong preference for it, compared with other options available to them for investment protection. Nor was it created because there was evidence that it facilitated investment or improved the climate for investment—there was no such evidence. Most investors and officials believed investment insurance was far more effective at facilitating investment. So why, and how, did it emerge?

International officials with peacebuilding and development aims drove the rise of investor–state arbitration. They saw themselves forging a lowest common denominator solution for investment protection, something that most of their member states could ratify in the short run, which could also facilitate the growth of international law related to foreign investment in the long run. While these international officials were able to anticipate many developments—including an enormous caseload from investment treaties—they certainly did not set out to create a system so loathed that the European Trade Commissioner recently called ISDS, another abbreviation for this type of arbitration,[9] "the most toxic acronym in Europe."[10] They did not intend to create a system that embodies the worst fears of those concerned about runaway globalization. If they had been alive to read it, they would have been horrified by how *The Economist* introduced ISDS in 2014:

> If you wanted to convince the public that international trade agreements are a way to let multinational companies get rich at the expense of ordinary people, this is what you would do: give foreign firms a special right to apply to a secretive tribunal of highly paid corporate lawyers for compensation whenever a government

accident), which led to a nuclear phase-out policy. This policy was then reversed in 2009, but Sweden now has a tax on nuclear power, and decisions to close older reactors are pending (World Nuclear Association 2017).

[9] Investor–state dispute settlement (ISDS) and investor–state arbitration are interchangeable in contemporary parlance, and I follow that usage. Where possible, I prefer investor–state arbitration, because it is a more precise term. Technically, it is a subset of ISDS, which includes mediation, conciliation, and other forms of dispute resolution.

[10] Commissioner Cecilia Malmström said this in Washington DC (Palmer 2015) and at the European Parliament (Ardhe 2015).

> passes a law to, say, discourage smoking, protect the environment or prevent a nuclear catastrophe.[11]

Foreign firms would not have that special right without the actions of those officials in the 1960s. This book uses thousands of archival documents to elaborate and illustrate this argument, tracing investor–state arbitration from their initial ideas to contemporary realities. This book provides a new explanation for the rise of investor–state arbitration, split into two phases. In the first phase, several institutional options for investment protection were discussed, and I argue that the intensity of involvement from international officials determined which institutional framework emerged. The creation of this institutional framework, ICSID, kicked off the second phase, which is a process of gradual institutional development that led to contemporary investor–state arbitration. It was ICSID Secretariat officials who encouraged states to provide access to investor–state arbitration in their investment treaties. Only after treaties with investor–state arbitration existed did a constituency of law firms and investors begin developing a preference for it, based on the revenue and prestige they received from it. While this constituency was developing, the institution of investor–state arbitration was being put to new purposes. Institutions do not determine the purposes to which they may be put. Analyzing gradual institutional change helps to explain how unintended consequences emerge and why institutions persist even when they generate unintended consequences.

The international officials who developed investor–state arbitration had all fled the Second World War and were drawn to the idea of ISDS because they believed in the power of law to resolve disputes peacefully and believed that rich societies had an imperative to use law to facilitate development in poorer societies.[12] Yet it is their actions, stabilized through decades of path-dependent institutional development, that created today's investor–state arbitration system—a system which many observers, like *The Economist*, perceive as working against ordinary people and against development.

[11] *The Economist* 2014.

[12] For instance, in a speech to the International Law Association in 1973, ICSID Secretary General Aron Broches ([1973] 1995: 514) chastised the international legal community for not doing enough to improve the quality of life in poor states: "We failed to meet adequately the moral obligations accepted in all civilized societies since the beginning of time, the obligations of the strong to help the weak. These moral obligations toward which international law is moving, however slowly and painfully, to recognize as legal obligations, exist not only between rich and poor societies, but also between any given society and its poor members." Later in the same speech, Broches ([1973] 1995: 516) challenged his audience, "to help create the conditions for economic and social progress, with dignity and in freedom, remembering that the ultimate object of law is the welfare of mankind."

THE PUZZLE: WHAT EXPLAINS THE RISE OF INVESTOR–STATE ARBITRATION?

Providing individual investors with standing against states is a fundamental revision in the nature of sovereignty. Governments moved from a state-based international investment order to one in which individuals were accorded equal standing. Why? This is the central puzzle. This development is related to momentous transformations in human rights that occurred after the Second World War—specifically, individuals being endowed with rights under international law—and some of the same legal minds were involved, but in investment, the dynamics were different.[13] In investment, a muffled plea of "never again" came from German bankers who found the uncompensated expropriation of their assets (largely by the American and Soviet governments) during and after the Second World War unconscionable.

This transformation of sovereignty took decades. Rather than one moment of institutional design, the institution of investor–state arbitration developed incrementally—a transformative political change that occurred in small steps. Since the end of the Second World War, ISDS has been transformed from a vague idea into an expansive, decentralized legal architecture in which bilateral treaties, contracts, and domestic law all provide access to arbitration that is backed up by robust enforcement. I argue that the crucial period to explain the rise of investor–state arbitration is roughly 1954 to 1994, long before it attracted much public or scholarly attention. Actions taken during these years of neglect and near-invisibility laid the foundations for the subsequent explosion in investment arbitration.

The explosion in the investor–state caseload occurred largely after 2000. During its first twenty-five years, between 1966 and 1991, ICSID (the only investor–state arbitration organization that releases its caseload) registered one case per year, on average.[14] In 2015 alone, ICSID registered fifty-two cases.[15] Individual cases are an engine of legal reasoning that push forward the development of investor–state arbitration. As a growing proportion of the caseload becomes publicly available, it has become possible to write a history of ICSID by "presenting the landmark cases that have been decided under its auspices."[16] Analyzing cases is the domain of the lawyer, and a profusion of

[13] Elihu Lauterpacht is perhaps the best known of the legal thinkers involved with individual standing in both investment and human rights (see Chernykh forthcoming).

[14] During this period, there were twenty-six cases registered (ICSID 2016).

[15] ICSID 2016.

[16] Kinnear et al. 2015. As more decisions become public, it also becomes possible for tribunals to rely heavily on past decisions, despite the absence of formal precedent in ISDS. Commission (2007: 151) finds that tribunals now routinely discuss the role played by "ICSID's case law." Fauchald (2008) finds tribunals increasingly cite other instruments of international law. The average jumped to between eleven and thirteen previous awards per decision during 2004–6.

legal scholarship analyzes the interpretive innovations that drive this field of practice. The focus of this book is different. It seeks to explain the earlier, political decisions that made this caseload possible.

This book splits these early decisions into two phases: creating the ICSID Convention, and eliciting state consent for ISDS. I argue that without the actions taken during these two phases, it is unlikely that contemporary investor–state arbitration would exist. Each of these phases can also be considered a manifestation of an institutional design puzzle familiar to international relations scholars: the creation of a new international organization on the basis of a multilateral treaty and the delegation of dispute resolution.

First Phase: Creating the ICSID Convention

The ICSID Convention is a multilateral treaty that sets out procedural rules and enforcement provisions for the resolution of disputes between foreign investors and states through arbitration or conciliation. It is the closest thing to a founding treaty for investor–state arbitration. Ratifying the Convention formally recognizes that individuals—natural or otherwise—have the legal standing to bring a claim directly against a state under international law. When the Convention came into force in 1966, and for decades afterwards, it was synonymous with the idea of investor–state arbitration. Although there are historical antecedents, for many governments around the world, the idea of equal standing between individual investors and states was radical.

Technically, it was possible for individual investors to face a state in arbitration prior to the ICSID Convention. By 1966, the International Chamber of Commerce (ICC) in Paris had decades of experience as the global headquarters of commercial arbitration, and it was possible, and perhaps common, to include recourse to ICC arbitration in contracts between foreign investors and states.[17] The Permanent Court of Arbitration (PCA) in The Hague, established in 1899, was able to administer disputes between investors and states—a fact the PCA Secretariat advertised in the late 1950s and that the British government raised during the creation of ICSID.[18]

Guillaume (2011: 7), a former president of the International Court of Justice (ICJ), argues that of all types of arbitration, ICSID decisions refer to precedent the most. In his words, "they do this . . . with rather excessive zeal."

[17] Records of ICC arbitrations between investors and states are not public so there is no authoritative count, but government officials discussed them in the 1960s as though they were common. For instance, British officials noted: "When contracts are being negotiated between Western industrialised countries, there is normally no difficulty about arbitration since the accepted thing is to provide for ICC arbitration." Letter from Hester Boothroyd to Mr. Mitchell entitled "IBRD and Arbitration," February 6 1962. UK T 312/251.

[18] Letter from Hester Boothroyd to Peter Reilly, October 4 1961. UK T 312/251.

If investor–state arbitration was already possible, why did states go to the trouble of drafting a new treaty? The ICSID Convention is distinct because it emerged at the World Bank, and, unlike any previous treaty, is an intergovernmental convention dedicated to investor–state arbitration. The involvement of the World Bank changed investor–state arbitration in several ways. First, the idea of investor–state arbitration was reframed to fit within the Bank's mission of facilitating investment and improving investment climates. Second, the World Bank's involvement meant that appealing to capital-importing countries became a central concern. Arbitration could not disrupt the World Bank's main business—lending to capital-importing states, many of them newly independent—and the World Bank's special relationship with its borrowers underlay the entire drafting and ratification process.[19] The initiative would have been fundamentally different, and likely a failure, without the World Bank's backing.

The ICSID Convention included many legal and technical innovations, but the reason it matters in this account is because it rebranded arbitration, put the World Bank's reputation behind it, and introduced it to new audiences. It created an intergovernmental framework and set in motion dynamics that would eventually lead to contemporary ISDS. The ICSID Convention also created a new international organization, known as the ICSID Secretariat, which, as an arm of the World Bank, has direct, privileged lines of communication to governments.

The patterns of state ratification for the ICSID Convention reflect the Bank's focus on newly independent countries, and suggest a relationship between investor–state arbitration and foreign investment policymaking generally. Fifteen of the first twenty ratifications were from sub-Saharan African states. During the first six years that the Convention was open for ratification, only forty-seven states ratified out of the 102 eligible to do so. During the 1970s and 1980s, few additional states ratified. Then in the early 1990s, the number of ratifications rose sharply, in line with changing ideas toward foreign investment, especially in former Soviet and Latin American states. Today there are 153 member states, out of 189 World Bank member states. While other arms of the World Bank have near-universal membership, many large countries remain outside ICSID today, including Brazil, Ethiopia, India, Mexico, Poland, Russia, South Africa, and Thailand.[20]

[19] Gwynn (2016) conceptualizes the World Bank's position and advocacy for investment arbitration and treaties using Susan Strange's concept of structural power. Although I recognize that the special relationship between the World Bank and its borrowers was vital for ICSID's emergence, I do not use the term structural power because it obfuscates underlying dynamics, and these underlying dynamics are important for the rise of ISDS. Without structural power, I can better interrogate the arguments and relationships cultivated by individual officials, and gain more analytical insight into the relations between different arms of the World Bank.

[20] The comparable arms of the World Bank Group are the International Finance Corporation (IFC) (184 member states) and the Multilateral Investment Guarantee Agency (181 member states).

When a state ratifies the ICSID Convention, that ratification does not enable investors to bring cases against them. Ratification is an official, public recognition of the principle that investors *could* have the legal standing to bring cases against them. The ICSID Convention's unique double-consent formulation requires that a state provide its consent in two places before an investor can bring a claim.[21] In order for ICSID to have any cases, states must provide their consent in a second instrument.

Second Phase: Eliciting State Consent to ISDS

The actual delegation of dispute resolution authority occurs with the second consent, when states write access to arbitration into their treaties, contracts, or domestic laws. State officials specify the substantive law to be applied: in a treaty arbitration, it is the text of the treaty; in a contract arbitration, it is the text of the contract; and when domestic law provides the basis for jurisdiction, specified host country laws are the relevant substantive law.[22] In theory, this gives state officials discretion to tailor the substantive legal standards or exempt sensitive sectors. It also means that states could, in theory, remain members of ICSID but revoke their delegation to ICSID arbitration by exiting or rewriting their treaties, contracts, and domestic laws to remove access to arbitration.

Despite receiving the majority of the scholarly attention, especially in the field of political science, BITs have provided the basis for only 60 percent of ICSID's caseload to date. Investment contracts have provided the basis of consent for nearly 17 percent of cases, regional or sectoral agreements for 13 percent, and domestic laws for nearly 10 percent.[23] Table 1.1 details how different instruments delegate dispute resolution to ICSID, including multilateral agreements, several of which have been negotiated, although none have come into force.

This table makes clear that investor–state arbitration and BITs are analytically distinct phenomena. None of the first BITs provided access, and not all of the BITs in force today provide access.[24] All instruments of consent—contracts, domestic laws, and every type of treaty—are important, historically and possibly in the future. It is the decentralization of consent that makes ISDS

[21] Report of the Executive Directors 1965; Schreuer et al. 2009. The jurisdiction of ICSID is a topic of extensive legal scholarship, in part because of its unique double-consent requirement. Schreuer's commentary on the ICSID Convention devotes 340 pages to ICSID's jurisdiction.

[22] These are simplifications; in any particular arbitration, there may be other sources of applicable law and Most Favoured Nation clauses that can make other instruments relevant.

[23] ICSID 2016: 10.

[24] UNCTAD (2016) finds 1683 out of 1959 mapped treaties include provisions that mention ICSID.

Table 1.1. How Consent Operates in Different Types of Investment Agreements

Type of investment agreement	How consent to ICSID operates	Examples
Individual investment contracts	Consent to ICSID is written into individual contracts between investors and host states	Contracts are private, but discussed in contract-based cases, like *Société Générale de Surveillance (SGS) v Pakistan*
Domestic law	Consent to ICSID is written into domestic legal frameworks on foreign investment	Albania's Foreign Investment Law of 1993
BITs	Consent to ICSID is written into a bilateral treaty between two states	Thousands in force; for example, Argentina–France BIT
Bilateral free trade agreements, with investment chapters	Consent to ICSID is written into the investment chapter of a trade treaty	US–Chile Free Trade Agreement
Regional investment (or trade) agreements	Consent to ICSID is written into treaties negotiated at a regional level or for a specific issue area	North American Free Trade Agreement, Energy Charter Treaty
Multilateral investment agreements	Consent to ICSID is written into multilateral treaties with global aims or scope	Multilateral agreement on investment (not in force; negotiations discontinued in 1998)

resilient.[25] Even if, for instance, investor–state arbitration were removed from all European investment treaties, its survival would not be in doubt. Thousands of contracts, dozens of domestic laws, and hundreds of treaties would still be in force that provide investors with standing. In other words, ISDS is bigger than BITs.

An explanation of why states provided consent to ISDS must include why, for instance, nearly forty governments have inserted clauses into their *domestic law*, enabling foreign investors to bypass their national courts and instead take them, the government, directly to international arbitration. This is a unilateral concession of sovereignty, inherently more puzzling than taking the same action in a bilateral negotiation. Who elicited this consent from governments, and why did governments agree to provide it? This is what the puzzle looks like in the second phase, eliciting consent for ISDS.

This book is structured to examine the two phases sequentially. Chapters two to five focus on the creation of the ICSID Convention. Chapters six to eight evaluate how consent was elicited from states in domestic laws, contracts, and all varieties of treaty.

[25] Pauwelyn (2014) frames contemporary ISDS as the result of thousands of different decisions made by many actors, making it stable and dynamic. Puig (2013) observes that ISDS, and ICSID in particular, is more resilient than typically assumed.

CONVENTIONAL ACCOUNTS: LOBBYING AND INTERGOVERNMENTAL BARGAINING

Beth Simmons observes that "the private right to sue a government for damages and to choose the forum in which to do so constitutes the most revolutionary aspect of the international law relating to foreign investment in the past half-century."[26] Remarkably, despite a substantial political science research program on investment treaties, the rise of ISDS—the most revolutionary aspect of these treaties—has not been the subject of political science scholarship.

Decades of conventional wisdom assume that investors drove the creation of investor–state arbitration, and dominant scholarly explanations rely on this assumption. It is investors that gain from having the standing to bring claims directly and it is therefore reasonable to expect that investors sought this standing.[27] Firms may request ICSID access from two governments. First, they can ask host governments directly, for instance in contract negotiations.[28] Second, and more importantly, they can ask their home governments. Domestic lobbying channels are well-developed pathways and there is every reason to expect that firms lobbied for their preferred ISDS policy and that their governments translated this lobbying into a state preference for access to arbitration.[29] Capital-exporting states, therefore, are assumed to have an *ex ante* preference for investor–state arbitration.[30] This is classic liberal intergovernmental preference formation, familiar across many issue areas.

In conventional accounts, when capital-exporting states negotiated treaties that provide their investors with standing, they were acting on their investors' preferences. Capital-exporting states largely determine the content of BIT dispute resolution clauses in these accounts. As their relative bargaining power increases, so does the likelihood of their investors having direct access

[26] Simmons 2014: 17.

[27] This standing strengthens the bargaining position of an investor, even before they file a case; negotiation that occurs in the shadow of arbitration is likely to reach a different conclusion than similar negotiation without the shadow of arbitration.

[28] Wells and Ahmed (2007: 72, 134–5, 259) provide examples of ICSID in contract discussions.

[29] In line with scholarship on firm lobbying in other areas, such as trade. See Milner 1997, chapter 2; Mansfield and Milner 2012, chapters 2 and 3.

[30] For instance, Allee and Peinhardt (2014: 62–3) observe: "In terms of preferences, all else equal, home-state governments will prefer BITs to include multiple, strong options for enforcing the treaties ... The best way to do this is to include in the treaty elements such as preconsent clauses, multiple options for enforcement, and the ability to utilize institutionalized arbitration venues." They find real-world evidence of these preferences in the model BITs of OECD countries, which "reveal their preferences and serve as a template for treaty bargaining. These model treaties typically include advanced consent to arbitration and provide for arbitration through permanent arbitration institutions" (Allee and Peinhardt 2014: 63).

to arbitration.[31] Given their wish to attract foreign investment, host countries "are 'price-takers' with respect to the terms of these treaties."[32] The dispute resolution clause is particularly important for attracting investment: influential scholars argue that capital-importing states accept arbitration clauses because it makes their commitments more credible, and that additional credibility is expected to attract additional investment.[33] A series of large-N studies connect "strong" dispute resolution clauses to additional investment.[34]

Existing accounts provide an intuitive explanation for the two phases examined in this book. With regard to the first phase, creating the ICSID Convention, conventional explanations generate clear expectations. First, firms develop a strong preference for investor–state arbitration machinery. Then, governments of capital-exporting states (likely led by the US government, as the largest exporter and largest shareholder of the World Bank) draft and push a new proposal for an investor–state arbitration convention. Conventional accounts also expect firms and home governments to lead in eliciting state consent, the second phase.

These accounts assume that firms articulate a clear preference for ISDS to be included in the investment treaties signed by their home governments. The more active domestic industry groups are, the likelier it is that a government will insert ISDS into its treaties. Firms also articulate a clear preference for ISDS in contracts and domestic laws, and demand ISDS from their host states. The governments of capital-importing states are presented with contracts and treaties that include investor–state arbitration by foreign firms and capital-exporting states, and they make the decision to provide access to arbitration as part of a trade-off for more

[31] Allee and Peinhardt 2014: 72–3. Coding the dispute resolution provisions of BITs is a detailed, legal exercise, and the measure used by Allee and Peinhardt raises serious doubts about validity. What matters for the enforceability of an award is whether the relevant treaty includes enforcement through the New York Convention or the ICSID Convention. Their indicator does not measure this. Instead, Allee and Peinhardt (2014: 54) create a composite indicator called "treaty enforceability" from three underlying indicators: (i) preconsent to international arbitration; (ii) how many venues for arbitration are provided in the treaty; and (iii) the degree to which the available arbitration venues are institutionalized.

[32] Elkins, Guzman, and Simmons 2006: 822.

[33] Guzman (1998) first put forward this logic in an influential article, later expanded and tested by Elkins, Simmons, and Guzman 2006; Büthe and Milner 2008, 2014; Allee and Peinhardt 2010, 2014; Simmons 2014.

[34] Büthe and Milner (2014), for instance, analyze investment flows into 125 developing countries from 1971 to 2007, and show that more investment is induced by trade agreements that include stronger mechanisms for credible commitment. Allee and Peinhardt (2011) find that investment treaties with stronger dispute resolution provisions attract more investment. Many studies have examined the impact of BITs (or BITs with ISDS access) on investment flows, yet problems like missing and poor quality data (Kerner 2014), endogeneity (Aisbett 2009), and the need to distinguish between sectors (Colen, Persyn, and Guariso 2016) suggest caution in drawing strong conclusions from these results. In addition, studies come to contradictory results; some (Hallward-Driemeier 2003; Rose-Ackerman and Tobin 2005; Yackee 2007) find that BITs have no effect on investment flows, while others (Neumayer and Spess 2005; Salacuse and Sullivan 2005; Büthe and Milner 2008, 2014) find an effect.

Table 1.2. Empirical Expectations from Existing Explanations

Expectations about preferences
1. Firms articulate a coherent preference for new investor–state arbitration machinery. 2. Governments of capital-exporting states respond to the lobbying from firms by developing a preference for, and advancing proposals for, investor–state arbitration.
Expectations about the drafting of the ICSID Convention
1. Governments of capital-exporting states (likely led by the US) draft and push a new proposal for an investor–state arbitration convention.
Expectations about ISDS clauses appearing in investment treaties
1. Firms articulate a coherent preference for the insertion of access to investor–state arbitration in investment treaties. 2. The governments of capital-exporting states respond to the lobbying from firms by inserting investor–state arbitration into investment treaties. The more active domestic industry groups are and the more concerned they are with investment treaties, the more likely we are to see demands for arbitration. 3. The governments of capital-importing states are presented with contracts and treaties with investor–state arbitration by investors and capital-exporting states. This is their first exposure to arbitration. 4. By implication, international officials do not influence the content of bilateral treaties, contracts, or domestic laws.
Expectations about gradual institutional change
1. Investor and state preferences are stable, but to the extent there is change in investor preferences, it is driven by exogenous factors. 2. If ISDS no longer aligns with state preferences, governments use control or corrective mechanisms to realign the institution with their new preferences.

foreign investment. Finally, if ISDS no longer aligns with state preferences, governments use control or corrective mechanisms to realign the institution of ISDS with their new preferences. These expectations are summarized in Table 1.2.

These conventional explanations leave important questions unanswered. For instance, why did investors and governments select this particular form of dispute resolution? Was ad hoc arbitration truly what they considered optimal? What explains the timing? If investors lobbied for arbitration, why did it take them so long to bring cases?

THE ARGUMENT: INTERNATIONAL OFFICIALS AND INCREMENTAL CHANGE

This book puts forward a new explanation for the rise of ISDS, applying the tools of historical institutionalism. In short, my explanation is that international officials backed one institutional framework, and the creation of this institutional framework kicked off a process of gradual institutional development that led to contemporary investor–state arbitration and established a pro-ISDS constituency along the way.

This explanation starts by presenting the mid-1950s to the late 1960s as a critical juncture, a period in which actors faced "a broader than normal range of feasible options."[35] These years were relatively open to new multilateral cooperation on investment dispute settlement for several reasons. First, the post-war years were conducive to multilateral institution building generally.[36] Second, the end of colonial rule opened up new conversations about how investment disputes should be resolved, with both colonizers and former colonies turning to multilateral cooperation for a better way forward. In the early 1960s, government officials saw three viable paths for multilateral cooperation: intergovernmental discussions were held about a proposal for a substantive convention, a proposal for investment insurance, and an arbitration convention.

I argue that the intensity of involvement of international officials—which varied between the three paths—is the primary reason why only one of these possible institutions emerged, and why the arbitration convention (ICSID) was what emerged. Investor demand or investor preferences were, if anything, likely to be much stronger for the other two proposals—but that is an empirical question. My explanation starts with no assumptions about investor or state preferences for investor–state arbitration. Imputing preferences backward from who benefits today obscures the process through which preferences for ISDS actually emerged. The reasons behind an institution's creation cannot be inferred from its effects; they are "a wide-open terrain for systematic research."[37]

While not assuming preferences, this explanation does expect antecedent conditions—that is, actors' experiences before the critical juncture—to matter for outcomes. Antecedent conditions can vary in importance.[38] Given the charged nature of expropriation, I expect previous experiences to be influential, even capable of overpowering considerations of optimal design at times. Lingering disagreements and distrust between governments can compromise their ability to cooperate and find technical solutions. Officials active in the 1960s had lived through the Second World War, with its many expropriations (by the American, British, German, and Soviet governments, among others), as well as the expropriations associated with decolonization. These experiences are likely to have influenced officials' views and potentially inhibited cooperation between governments.

[35] Capoccia 2016: 92.
[36] Hale, Held, and Young 2013: 4–9.
[37] Pierson 2004: 130.
[38] Slater and Simmons 2010.

Intergovernmental disagreements create openings for international officials to enter the institutional design process.[39] In the early 1960s, a small group of expert international officials—with their own personal and institutional experiences of expropriation—had strong motivation, sufficient resources, and enough autonomy from states to influence investment protection. These officials had two motivations: advancing policy goals and ensuring organizational survival.[40] They worked within the Legal Department of the World Bank, and therefore had considerable resources in terms of funding and time, but even more importantly, they had unparalleled resources in the form of specialized expertise, access to privileged information, and a formidable reputation.[41]

I argue that this group of international officials used agenda-setting and brokering to facilitate the creation of the ICSID Convention. "Agenda-setting" is defined here as inventing institutional options or policy proposals—which they must match to problems perceived by government officials.[42] To foreshadow the findings of Chapter four, these officials set the agenda by drafting the proposal for ICSID: the Convention emerged nearly fully formed out of the World Bank's Legal Department. Brokering is the ability to construct coalitions and work around disagreements skillfully. To foreshadow Chapter five, these officials brokered the ICSID Convention into existence by introducing their proposal to governments slowly, quietly, and refining the proposal as needed to secure the widest possible support.

Once the Convention came into force, these officials had a strategic interest in making ICSID a success. One of the first tasks they faced after the Convention came into force (and they had become ICSID Secretariat officials) was to elicit consent from states. ICSID needed cases to survive, and it needed consent from states in order to have cases. Therefore, I argue these officials used agenda-setting and brokering to elicit consent from states. As Chapter six demonstrates, ICSID officials did set the agenda, by drafting model clauses that show government officials how to provide advance consent to investor–state arbitration. Then, ICSID officials brokered these clauses into existence by disseminating them widely and meeting government officials to discuss how these model clauses could be adapted into domestic law, contracts, and treaties. I argue that investor–state clauses were layered into treaties: they were added with little fanfare, alongside state–state clauses, but over time supplanted the state–state system entirely. The centralized starting point for investor–state clauses in treaties was the ICSID Secretariat: without the Secretariat's actions, it is doubtful that governments would have added clauses giving individuals standing in their treaties.

[39] Johnson 2014.

[40] While these motivations have roots in competing approaches (the first ideational [Barnett and Coleman 2005] and second material [Vaubel 2006]), they may be intertwined in reality.

[41] Beach (2004) and Tallberg (2010) elaborate resources available to international officials to influence outcomes.

[42] Pollack 2003: 50.

I theorize the subsequent trajectory as a process of gradual institutional development propelled by positive feedback, which slowly builds a constituency for investor–state arbitration, while other forms of gradual institutional change keep operating in the background. Positive feedback encourages actors (in this instance, governments, law firms, and other actors) to make commitments that stabilize investor–state arbitration and make a reversal of course more difficult.[43] As law firms and investors receive positive feedback in the form of prestige and revenue, they adapt their practices, take actions that stabilize the institution, and develop a preference for investor–state arbitration. As positive feedback accumulates, constituencies and preferences develop. In other words, preferences—including investor preferences—are endogenous.[44] This means that I argue investors to develop a preference for investor–state arbitration slowly, and only *after* large awards and expansive interpretations became public, which occurred in the 1990s.

At the same time that positive feedback is building a constituency, the purposes that institutions are called to meet can change dramatically over time. Conversion is a form of gradual institutional change that calls attention to the process by which actors put an institution to a new purpose. I apply conversion to the actions of government officials when they negotiated investment treaties. Have the purposes of ISDS within investment treaties changed over time? I answer this question by examining a place where conversion is least likely to occur: the American investment treaty program, widely perceived as the most consistent (in terms of treaty text) and the most closely managed in the world. To foreshadow Chapter seven, the purposes of the American treaty program have changed over time, and the purpose of ISDS changed alongside this broader change: officials drafting the initial US model treaty saw it as a way to protect investment, but a decade later, investment treaties were reimagined as tools to lock in domestic liberalization reforms in former Soviet or Latin American states.

Once granted, a right is difficult to revoke. The "dead weight of previous institutional and policy decisions" limits the ability of governments and other actors to change course.[45] Governments seeking to change or exit investor–state arbitration today face thousands of treaties, contracts, and laws, and even more importantly, they face a constituency that has developed with an interest in the maintenance of ISDS. Even when an institution generates unintended consequences, governments face many obstacles to exit. Chapter eight explores these obstacles as well as the related question of who determines the uses to which an institution is put.

Empirical expectations generated by my explanation are summarized in Table 1.3 below.

[43] Pierson 1996: 146. [44] Fioretos 2011: 376.
[45] Pierson 1996: 146–7.

Table 1.3. Empirical Expectations from My Explanation

Expectations about preferences
1. No assumption about firm preferences regarding investor–state arbitration. 2. No assumption about government preferences, but previous expropriation experience may influence government officials.
Expectations about the drafting of the ICSID Convention
1. World Bank officials lead the creation of an investor–state arbitration convention, relying on agenda-setting and brokering.
Expectations about ISDS clauses appearing in investment treaties
1. Lobbying from firms about investor–state arbitration in investment treaties is weak or absent. 2. Governments of capital-exporting states (not being lobbied by investors) are ambivalent and/or have not considered the idea of adding investor–state arbitration to investment treaties, until information from international organizations reaches them. 3. Governments of capital-importing states are "educated" by international organization officials about investor–state arbitration. 4. International officials draft and disseminate model clauses for use in bilateral treaties and contracts. They do so to generate a caseload.
Expectations about gradual institutional change
1. Investors and capital-exporting states slowly and endogenously develop a preference for arbitration. 2. Governments find it costly and difficult to use control or corrective mechanisms, even when officials believe that ISDS does not align with their preferences.

THE RESEARCH APPROACH: SOURCES AND METHODS

Chapters two to eight adjudicate between the two explanations for the rise of investor–state arbitration. To do so, these chapters draw on over 30,000 pages of primary materials, almost none of which have been used in previous scholarship. Where copyright permits, every archival document cited in this book is available in the Qualitative Data Repository (https://qdr.syr.edu/). The repository also contains a document with all translated quotations in this book, first with the English translation used here and then with the text in its original language.

The most revealing materials were internal deliberations and confidential letters and memos sent within the ministries of capital-exporting states. Instead of assuming or speculating about what these officials were thinking as they inserted their first ISDS clause, it is possible to go back and look.[46] I looked at all declassified files related to ICSID in the national archives of Germany, New Zealand, Switzerland, the UK, and the US.[47] I also looked at all files related to multilateral investment conventions, investment insurance, and investment treaties during the relevant years.

Importantly, I drew upon files from multiple ministries or branches of government, which provide multiple perspectives and sharper insight into internal debates. For instance, in the UK, both the Treasury and the Foreign Office kept folders related to ICSID, and these parallel sets of records show that these ministries at times had different concerns. In the US, the State Department, the United States Trade Representative (USTR), and the Senate Committee on Foreign Relations records are kept not just in separate folders but in different cities, which made me especially aware of the differences in their views toward investor–state arbitration.

Primary sources from a forty-year period, 1954 to 1994, were accessed, and the changes over time vividly illustrate the reality that to understand a phenomenon like ISDS, one needs analysis that provides a "moving picture" instead of a "snapshot."[48] Government views change over time: the US moved from opposition to support of the OECD Draft Convention within a five-year period, while the Swiss government moved in the opposite direction during the same five years. Priorities and influence shift with changes in the party in power: for instance, German banker Hermann Abs had exceptional access to government while Konrad Adenauer was Chancellor, but that influence diminished after Adenauer left office, and diminished still further when the first Social Democratic Chancellor, Willy Brandt, took office. The records also show that historical memories and beliefs, correct or not, can endure for decades in a government: even in the late 1960s, German officials believed that the US government did not support the OECD Draft because they saw it as an attempt to receive compensation for German property seized in America during the Second World War.

The perspectives from national archives were compared with archived documents from international organizations. The ICSID Secretariat does not have public archives, but the World Bank Group archives contain personal papers from officials that worked for ICSID, including papers from Aron Broches, Georges Delaume, and Paul Szasz, as well as papers belonging to the World Bank Presidents but relating to ICSID. Many of these World Bank officials also recorded oral histories before they died; these are an invaluable source, brimming with personality, wit, and frank reflections. As with

[46] The admonition to "go back and look" comes from Pierson (2004: 47).
[47] Yannick Stiller provided superlative assistance with files written in French and German.
[48] Pierson 2004: 2.

governments, the World Bank changes over time in its ideological outlook and priorities, and these wider changes affect ISDS. For instance, after Robert McNamara became World Bank President in 1968, Aron Broches was left with the title of General Counsel but few of the responsibilities of the post, because McNamara preferred to rely upon an American lawyer, Lester Nurick—giving Broches time and other resources to devote to ICSID.

I also located publications from the ICSID Secretariat in university libraries and personal collections: *Annual Reports*, *News from ICSID*, *Foreign Investment Laws of the World*, and a few miscellaneous publications. Many of these publications, and the four-volume *History of the ICSID Convention*, which is the *travaux préparatoires* for the Convention, have recently become available online through the ICSID Secretariat website. During the years that I spent researching this book, it became substantially easier to access documents related to ICSID, thanks to the efforts of ICSID's current Secretary General, Meg Kinnear, to increase transparency and to the pioneering scholarship of former ICSID Deputy Secretary General Antonio Parra.

I also interviewed thirty-six current and former officials in governments and international organizations involved with ISDS. These interviews provided deep background and help me triangulate findings that emerged from archival documents. Many of the interviews were conducted off the record, so to ensure consistency and total confidentiality, none of the interviews are cited in this book. Archival documents were found that expressed all the interview assertions that appear in this book, except for two comments. One appears in a footnote in Chapter seven and the other in Chapter eight; ancillary evidence supports both assertions and the relevant archive files have not been declassified yet.

The method used in this book is based on counterfactual reasoning—analyzing what happened in the context of what could have happened.[49] Counterfactuals are central to King, Keohane, and Verba's definition of causality,[50] and they are fundamental to much political science research: as Tetlock and Belkin observe, "the alternative to an open counterfactual model is a concealed one."[51] This book heeds Fearon's prescription that researchers using counterfactual argument "should be methodologically aware of what they are doing and should make their counterfactual arguments as explicit and defensible as they can."[52] The chapters in this book are structured as a series of counterfactual arguments, and these counterfactual arguments are defended on the basis that they all follow the "minimal rewrite of history rule," which instructs scholars to avoid counterfactuals that require undoing events.[53]

[49] Capoccia and Kelemen (2007: 355) use this description, quoting Isaiah Berlin.
[50] King, Keohane, and Verba 1994: 77–9.
[51] Tetlock and Belkin 1996: 4.
[52] Fearon 1991: 170.
[53] Tetlock and Belkin 1996: 7.

This book's overarching counterfactual is based on three actual proposals discussed in intergovernmental negotiations.[54] This counterfactual does not require undoing any events: it merely brings back how officials viewed their options during these years.[55] In Chapters four and five, the counterfactual revolves around the presence or absence of a specific causal factor: in the absence of World Bank agenda-setting and brokering, would the ICSID Convention have emerged? Chapter six has a similar counterfactual: would investor–state arbitration clauses have been inserted into investment treaties in the absence of ICSID agenda-setting and brokering? These counterfactual framings enable a more rigorous isolation and examination of the World Bank's influence. Chapters seven and eight do not pose counterfactuals; rather, they illuminate how earlier events shaped the choices available in later periods.

This book presents its findings as a structured, theory-guided narrative. The main theoretical expectations are set out in the tables above. "The extent to which a historical narrative is transformed into a theoretical explanation can vary," George and Bennett observe, and note that an explanation "may be deliberately selective, focusing on what are thought to be particularly important parts of an adequate or parsimonious explanation."[56] In many places, my explanation deliberately focuses on the strategy of World Bank officials. One shortcoming of theory-guided narratives is that researchers focus on supporting the argument that interests them most, while giving little attention to evidence that supports alternative explanations.[57] Identifying specific empirical expectations for an explanation other than my own counteracts this tendency, as does the alternation of focus in the chapters. Chapters three, five, and seven focus on the actions of government officials, while Chapters four, six, and eight focus on the actions of international officials and other non-state actors. This chapter structure helps to guard against an explanation that assumes that if the Bank was the dominant actor in one stage, it was always dominant: indeed, later chapters find that the role of Bank officials and the importance of the Bank's involvement vary considerably over time and in different countries.

At its core, this book analyzes decision-making by officials under conditions of uncertainty and often incomplete information. It seeks to understand why, facing the world they faced, with the information they had, officials made the decisions that created the architecture for ISDS.[58] The methods adopted "should therefore reconstruct, in a systematic and rigorous fashion, each step of the decision-making process, identify which decisions were most

[54] As mentioned previously, three proposals for new multilateral organizations related to investment were discussed in the 1960s: a substantive convention, an investment insurance organization, and an arbitration convention.

[55] This counterfactual echoes Lebow's (2000: 551) observation that "counterfactual analysis is not always based solely on speculation."

[56] George and Bennett 2005: 211.

[57] George and Bennett 2005: 217.

[58] This approach echoes how Jupille, Mattli, and Snidal (2013) frame institutional choice.

influential and what options were available and viable to the actors who took them, and clarify both their impact and their connection to other important decisions."[59] Subsequent chapters follow this advice, by taking particular care to elaborate the institutional paths available but not taken and to reconstruct each step of the decision-making process.

The rise of investor–state arbitration is a complex, decentralized phenomenon that unfolded over several decades. This complex process does not lend itself to easy operationalization in a single dependent variable. There are many possible observable, discrete indicators along the way: ratification of the ICSID Convention, insertion of access to ISDS in domestic law, and insertion of access to ISDS in investment treaties, for instance. These indicators appear in subsequent chapters, with the knowledge that each of these indicators captures only a small piece of the broader phenomenon. They are all part of the larger rise of ISDS, which is analyzed here as a single process over time, split into two phases.

FINDINGS

There are four main findings of my analysis, which are previewed here and then developed further in subsequent chapters.

1. Investor preferences for access to ISDS developed slowly over time. There was little initial demand from investors.

Only 16 percent of foreign investment firms surveyed by the ICC in 1962 believed that access to arbitration "affected the investment climate" of a country.[60] This is striking: the overwhelming majority of firms responding to an ICC survey—the most likely group to care about arbitration—thought it did not affect the investment climate. In 1976, a survey of the top legal counsel within Fortune 1000 firms found that only 15 percent of respondents were "familiar with" ICSID.[61] Ten years after it was created, 85 percent of the top lawyers at the largest international firms had not even heard of ICSID. This is

[59] Capoccia and Kelemen 2007: 355.

[60] Figure cited by a German official in 1962 (noting that no German firms that responded thought the investment climate would be improved by the creation of an arbitration tribunal.) Internal Note from Dr. Berger, March 8, 1962, subject: "Vermittlungs- und Schiedsgerichtstätigkeit unter dem Schutze der Weltbank (Mediation and Arbitration Activities under the Protection of the World Bank)." DE B102/48464.

[61] Ryans and Baker (1976: 70) asked, "Are you familiar with the Convention on the Settlement of Investment Disputes?" Apart from the 15 percent of respondents that were familiar with it, 81 percent reported that they were not and the rest did not give an answer.

the picture that emerges from the archives, too: investors were largely uninformed and uninterested.[62]

The finding of lackluster investor demand matters because it shows that the core assumption of dominant accounts of ISDS is untenable. The inaccuracy of this core assumption hampers existing theories' ability to explain—an *ex ante* assumption of investor demand obfuscates many puzzles related to ISDS.

2. The ICSID Convention did not emerge as an optimal institutional solution.

Institutional design is the art of the possible, not the optimal. The ICSID Convention did not emerge because relevant government officials believed it to be the best way to protect investment: by and large, they did not believe it was. It did not emerge because relevant officials believed it to be the most effective way to facilitate additional investment: most officials did not believe it would do so. As a British official wrote, "we do not expect the existence of the Centre to give any major stimulus to new investment at a rate in the short term."[63] Nor did officials believe it was the most direct way to develop or improve international investment law: a substantive multilateral treaty would have done this more directly. The ICSID Convention emerged because it was a lowest common denominator solution, inoffensive and ineffective enough to be possible.

3. Historically, the ICSID Secretariat was a highly autonomous actor. ICSID officials influenced states' decisions to delegate in their investment treaties.

ICSID Secretariat officials wrote and disseminated the model clauses that showed states and investors how to provide advance consent in their treaties. ICSID officials understood the ramifications of this, too: in 1984, before the first investment treaty case was filed, an ICSID official remarked that consents in investment treaties created an "enormous potential clientele."[64] Early events in a path-dependent process often matter more than later events,[65] and the Secretariat's actions in the late 1960s created the practice of inserting ISDS access in treaties, which was then reproduced thousands of times throughout the 1980s, 1990s, and 2000s. Yet without a moving picture approach, the Secretariat's influence disappears. The influence of the ICSID Secretariat has been forgotten

[62] In corporatist states like Switzerland and Germany, where the government held top-down consultations with industry groups about investment protection initiatives, firms were better informed. Yet they were still not particularly interested in arbitration. Elaborated in Chapter three.

[63] Letter from W. S. Ryrie to J. M. Stevens, January 1967, "International Centre for Settlement of Investment Disputes." UK FCO 48/145.

[64] Aron Broches (the World Bank's General Counsel from 1959 to 1979 and Secretary General of ICSID from 1966 to 1979) acknowledged the enormous potential clientele in 1984, though the first investment treaty arbitration was not filed until 1987. Broches 1984 (May): 44–5. *Asian Agricultural Products Ltd. v Republic of Sri Lanka*, ICSID Case No. ARB/87/3.

[65] Fioretos, Falleti, and Sheingate 2016: 11.

because investment treaty negotiations have been studied by examining only the moment of interstate bargaining. At any one time, the diplomatic maneuvering among states looms large, but seen as a historical process, the influence of other actors and the cumulative constraints of previous decisions come through.

No previous study has conceptualized the ICSID Secretariat with autonomy or the ability to influence events. Even Schill's insightful study, which emphasizes that arbitration is vital for turning bilateral investment treaties into a multilateral regime, does not take account of the special role the ICSID Secretariat played in facilitating the growth of arbitration.[66] Neither does Parra's otherwise exhaustive *The History of ICSID*.[67] Yet without the Secretariat's dissemination of model clauses, it is unlikely that ISDS clauses would have been inserted into investment treaties when they were, and perhaps ever.

4. Exiting from ISDS is hard: it is costly and difficult to rescind a right given to individuals once it has been created.

Once states provide a new right, individuals make commitments given the existence of this right, which over time has made exiting or reforming ISDS more difficult. Over time, a constituency of law firms and investors developed with a vested interest in the maintenance of ISDS. This constituency developed as law firms and investors received positive feedback in the form of revenue and prestige; the positive feedback stabilized investor–state arbitration and led this constituency to develop a preference for it. The commitments that are most important for stabilizing ISDS may not be actual foreign investments—they likely take the form of law firms building large practices devoted to international arbitration or government ministries negotiating dozens of bilateral treaties with ISDS. The accumulation of commitments and development of a constituency make a reversal of course difficult for governments. Even though states remain masters of their treaties, the obstacles to governments exercising control grow over time. The hurdles to realignment vary by country: while the institution of ISDS is sticky but malleable for officials in powerful countries, the institution of ISDS is stuck and viewed as unchangeable by officials in smaller countries.

STRUCTURE OF THE BOOK

Chapter one elaborates the theoretical argument. Then Chapters two to eight proceed chronologically, with each chapter pulling the reader forward toward the present. Chapters two to five study the first phase, the creation of the ICSID Convention, and then the second half of the book turns to the second

[66] Schill 2009(a). [67] Parra 2012, 2017.

phase, the eliciting of consent from states. Chapter two is a short chapter, serving only to identify historical antecedents and permissive conditions that were brought together in the ICSID Convention. Chapter three analyzes intergovernmental bargaining on investment protection in the 1950s and early 1960s, and focuses on the two multilateral paths not taken: a substantive convention and an insurance agency. Chapter four focuses on the World Bank's agenda-setting and brokering regarding the ICSID Convention, and why the Bank became involved with investment protection. Chapter five evaluates how states responded to the Bank's proposal for the ICSID Convention.

Chapter six documents how arbitration clauses were integrated into investment treaties and the forgotten role of international officials in this process. ICSID did not have a single case for eight years, but many advance consents to investor–state arbitration were provided in those early years, creating a lasting institutional infrastructure. Chapter seven charts the evolution of US government thinking on arbitration from 1966 to 1993, as investment treaties became instruments of foreign policy as well as devices to reward and reinforce liberalization reforms. Access to arbitration was a key US demand in negotiations with Argentina, Poland, Russia, and Turkey, but strong opposition from these middle-income countries spurred US negotiators to redraft arbitration provisions, and make refinements in the US model that were key milestones on the road to NAFTA. Chapter eight is another short chapter, which briefly probes why exiting from ISDS is so difficult, even after governments express a desire to exit. The conclusion examines two visions for the future of investor–state arbitration (one fully private and one fully public), and discusses the political prerequisites for either of these visions to become realities.

Readers familiar with international investment law may wish to go straight to Chapter three, which, along with Chapters four and five, provides new insight into the drafting of the ICSID Convention. Readers interested in international relations theory and international political economy scholarship will want to begin with Chapter one, and look at Chapters six and seven, which refute existing scholarship on investment treaties most directly. Readers interested in contemporary challenges will find Chapter eight and the conclusion of interest.

1

International Officials and the Rise of ISDS

A Historical Institutionalist Account

This chapter builds a new explanation for the rise of ISDS, drawing on the theoretical tradition of historical institutionalism. The explanation's central insight is: new policies create a new politics.[1] That is, a new policy or institution can cause the development of a constituency or client group with an incentive to push for the institution's maintenance and expansion. The new politics of investor–state arbitration is that investors, law firms, and related interest groups now have a strong preference for access to arbitration. The preference emerged after several decades of institutional development. This preference does not precede the institution; instead, in this explanation, the existence of investor–state arbitration created a constituency that, over many decades, realized it had a strong incentive in the maintenance of arbitration.

If investors did not advocate for the creation of investor–state arbitration, then its creation needs to be theorized (and examined empirically) with fresh eyes. The motivations, resources, constraints, and strategies of the actors involved in the creation of investor–state arbitration need to be identified. In order to do this, I frame the period in which the ICSID Convention emerged as a critical juncture in investment protection. This allows me to analyze this moment of enhanced possibility in depth. Of the various institutional paths that were available, I argue that the intensity of involvement from international officials determined which path emerged from the critical juncture. National governments faced collective action problems, and I argue that international officials had the motivation and resources to become involved—even if they lacked a formal mandate to do so. The agenda-setting and brokering of these officials led to the ICSID Convention, which created an institutional framework for

[1] Schattschneider's 1935 observation that "new policies create a new politics" is at the center of much historical institutionalist scholarship. Hacker and Pierson (2014) discuss Schattschneider's analysis at length.

investor–state arbitration. This institutional framework, and other early steps taken by international officials, often in conjunction with member states, set in motion the dynamics that led to contemporary ISDS.

This chapter elaborates this explanation in four sections. The first section briefly sets out the foundations of historical institutionalism as a theoretical tradition. The second articulates the theoretical concepts of critical juncture, agenda-setting, and brokering, as well as the motivations and resources of international officials, and then applies these concepts to the rise of investor–state arbitration. This section generates expectations for the creation of the ICSID Convention, which are examined in Chapters two to five. The third section discusses several mechanisms of gradual institutional development, including feedback (the development of a constituency with incentives to push for an institution's maintenance), as well as layering and conversion. This section generates expectations about how the ICSID Convention led to the contemporary ISDS caseload; these are examined in Chapters six to eight. The final section compares the arguments of this historical institutionalist explanation with those generated by conventional accounts and other theoretical perspectives.

ANALYZING POLITICS IN TIME: THE PROMISE OF HISTORICAL INSTITUTIONALISM

Historical institutionalism is a theoretical tradition distinguished by the primacy it accords to "temporality—the notion that the timing and sequence of events shape political processes."[2] It emerged in part as a reaction to theories that conceptualized each decision as a fresh roll of the dice. Instead, historical institutionalists present a picture of policymaking that is "much more structured by past decisions."[3] Decisions in the present are shaped by what has come before, especially when previous decisions have created institutions: "rather than treat each policy battle as one in which all alternatives are equally plausible, these accounts show that conflicts over policy are structured by the interests and institutions created by earlier decisions. This past confers advantages on some policies even as it rules others out of serious consideration."[4] Historical institutionalism engages with history not to draw lessons or document the past; it engages with history to identify "the conditions under which and mechanisms by which the past affects the present and the future."[5]

[2] Fioretos 2011: 371. [3] Weir 2006: 171.
[4] Weir 2006: 171. [5] Fioretos 2011: 383.

Historical institutionalism provides a rich toolbox to explain institutional and political development. These tools have been applied for decades in the fields of American political development and comparative politics. In recent years, a number of scholars have brought the tools of historical institutionalism into international relations[6] and even into international political economy[7] and the study of international courts[8] specifically. I have chosen a few of these tools to explain aspects of the rise of investor–state arbitration that previous accounts fail to explain. This means the theoretical discussion in this chapter is selective; it focuses on elaborating critical junctures, feedback effects, layering, and conversion, in ways that demonstrate the usefulness of these concepts for world politics. These historical institutionalist concepts hold promise for advancing our understanding of outcomes and phenomena at the international and transnational levels. This book proceeds in the belief that for the promise of these concepts to be realized, they must be introduced fully, not as adjustments to existing theories.[9]

One critique of historical institutionalism is that while it is useful for explaining stability, it is less useful for explaining change. In the last decade, historical institutionalist scholars have created a number of concepts that refine understandings of gradual institutional change.[10] In this second generation of historical institutionalism, many scholars are moving beyond the traditional framing of a critical juncture followed by a path-dependent trajectory. As Thelen observed in her study of vocational training institutions,

> If one told this purely as a tale of critical juncture and positive feedback, however, one would miss much of what is in fact interesting and important about the way in which these institutions were transformed through political re-alignments and specifically through the incorporation of groups whose role in the system was unanticipated at the time of their creation.[11]

[6] For instance, Fioretos's (2011) influential review essay in *International Organization*, Fioretos's (2017) edited volume, and Rixen, Viola, and Zürn's (2016) edited volume, all of which tackle historical institutionalism in international relations.

[7] For instance, Farrell and Newman's (2010) special issue of the *Review of International Political Economy* and Moschella and Tsingou's (2013) edited book on incremental change after the financial crisis.

[8] Alter, Helfer, and McAllister (2013) use conversion, a mode of gradual institutional change first theorized in the context of domestic institutions.

[9] Zürn (2016) sees historical institutionalism as a bridge between rational choice and sociological institutionalism; Jupille, Mattli, and Snidal (2013) integrate tenets from all three institutionalisms, while Fioretos (2011; 2017) argues that historical institutionalism has distinct micro-foundations.

[10] In particular, see the edited collections from Streeck and Thelen (2005) and Mahoney and Thelen (2009; 2015).

[11] Thelen 2004: 34.

The tools of historical institutionalism provide analytical insight into these gradual transformations, identifying conditions under which change is likely to be transformative or when institutional stability is likely to emerge.[12]

In this book, I retain the concept of critical juncture as a device to put additional emphasis on the dynamics leading to the emergence of the key institutional framework, the ICSID Convention. The critical juncture was a period of enhanced agency relative to other periods, but was not the only moment in which change occurred. In fact, as the Thelen quotation above suggests, some of the most interesting and important changes occurred later. In order to analyze and articulate these changes, I do not use path dependence as a central concept in this book. Although I believe that path dependence is occurring (insofar as the institutional framework that emerged from the critical juncture set developments along a particular path, and feedback effects pulled developments further and further along this path), for analytical clarity, I focus on the actual mechanism of reproduction—feedback effects. Positive feedback, I argue, can tell us a great deal about how key actors—investors, law firms, and related interest groups—became interested in arbitration and how the institution grew. Yet these self-reinforcing processes occur alongside other mechanisms, some of which encourage institutional stability and others that generate change, sometimes even transformative change. I do not draw a line between institutional reproduction and change. As Thelen argues, for any institution that endures over long periods of time, "the story of institutional reproduction is likely to be strongly laced with elements of institutional transformation."[13]

I focus on two areas where the expectations of a historical institutionalist explanation provide the starkest contrast with those of conventional accounts—preferences and unintended consequences. In conventional accounts, preferences are "analytically prior to politics" and individuals assumed to "define their material and ideational interests independently of politics and then advance those interests through political exchange and collective action."[14] In historical institutional accounts, preferences do not precede politics: individuals and groups may develop or adjust their preferences in response to existing institutional frameworks. Actors' preferences are "shaped heavily by their investments in existing and past designs, especially when these are the source of increasing returns and positive externalities."[15] This means that "a historical institutional approach to state preferences is not as parsimonious as approaches that stress strong logics of consequence or appropriateness" but

[12] For instance, Capoccia (2016) focusing on how actors can enhance institutional stability or Hanrieder and Zürn (2017) focusing on reactive sequences that lead to institutional destabilization, not reproduction.

[13] Thelen 2004: 35. [14] Moravcsik 1997: 517. [15] Fioretos 2011: 384.

that this approach "holds a valuable key to theorizing finer variations" and is able to provide "more nuanced and more comprehensive explanations."[16]

Similarly, historical institutionalism provides a less parsimonious but more insightful approach to unintended consequences in world politics. While unintended consequences are anomalies in conventional accounts, historical institutionalists expect them to be relatively common. They are often considered the result of cognitive limitations in conventional accounts, but historical institutionalists argue they may be evident even "when states have complete information, act transparently, and do not face major time constraints."[17] It is difficult to predict or make generalizable statements about unintended consequences, but articulating unintended consequences as a possible, even likely, outcome liberates researchers from misleading assumptions that current institutional outcomes represent their framers' intentions. This matters for theory and for research generally because if explanations for unintended consequences "turn less on identifying chance events, cognitive limitations, or bureaucratic pathologies" then it invites researchers to look seriously at what officials were thinking at particular moments—to undertake "a careful analysis of what the historical archive reveals about the actual preferences of and constraints faced by those most directly involved in negotiations over international designs."[18] Careful analysis of officials' actual preferences and constraints, using original materials, is the project that unfolds throughout this entire book. The next section begins by framing the 1960s as a critical juncture for investment protection.

CRITICAL JUNCTURES AND THE EMERGENCE OF AN INSTITUTIONAL FRAMEWORK

Critical junctures are brief periods in which actors face "a broader than normal range of feasible options" and their choices among these options "are likely to have a significant impact on the path-dependent development of an institution."[19] These junctures are defined in relative terms: an institution or issue area is *relatively* open for agency, compared to the periods before and after. In their volume analyzing reforms to financial regulation after the 2008 financial crisis—a time period which seems a strong contender to be labeled a critical juncture—Moschella and Tsingou eschew the language of critical junctures.

[16] Fioretos 2011: 386. [17] Fioretos 2011: 380.

[18] Fioretos 2011: 381. Other approaches also welcome this analysis, which can help to distinguish between officials taking calculated risks, ignoring consequences that could have been foreseen, or truly generating unintended consequences.

[19] Capoccia 2016: 92.

Instead they argue that major transformations in financial regulation are associated with incremental, endogenously driven dynamics, not exogenous shocks; they find that "radical transformations are not solely the result of... exogenously driven punctuated equilibrium" models.[20] The way that critical junctures are conceptualized here is compatible with an understanding that radical transformation may result from the cumulative effects of small incremental changes. That is, the term critical juncture does not imply that major, transformative change can emerge only from a critical juncture with an exogenous shock. "Critical juncture" remains an analytically useful term here because it draws heightened attention to a particular period of time when officials were actively considering several institutional paths forward.

Analyzing a critical juncture requires reconstructing the context, establishing who the key decision-makers were, and what choices were historically available to them.[21] Chapter two reconstructs the historical context of the key actors and identifies antecedents that were meaningful for those actors. Antecedent conditions structure the options available, usually limiting what is possible.[22] The range of options available to actors is broader than normal during a critical juncture, but not infinite. Antecedent conditions vary in importance: certain critical junctures can entail considerable discretion while in others "the presumed choice appears deeply embedded in antecedent conditions."[23] Slater and Simmons argue that some antecedent conditions are "critical," that is, they have causal force, albeit indirectly and in combination with other factors.[24] Chapter two argues that unresolved, contentious questions stemming from the long history of investment dispute settlement were a set of critical antecedents. These unresolved questions made various institutional options more or less politically viable in the 1960s. For officials making decisions during the 1960s critical juncture in investment, these unresolved questions constrained their choices, but did not determine them.

Critical junctures are defined in relative terms, so how do we know one when we see it? Soifer focuses our attention on the loosening of constraints.[25] Constraints become looser at the beginning of a critical juncture, perhaps because of an exogenous shock like a financial crisis, and then become tighter again, perhaps after the subsequent recession is declared over. When these constraints are loosened, it becomes possible for the productive condition, the

[20] Moschella and Tsingou 2013: 4. [21] Capoccia and Kelemen 2007: 355.

[22] Specifying antecedent conditions makes clear that in this account, the events and circumstances predating the critical juncture are expected to matter. While many analyses situate critical junctures at the point of an exogenous shock, Falleti and Lynch (2009: 1155) observe that the most widely read, classic examples of critical junctures analysis "embed critical junctures in a richly detailed context." Here I use antecedent conditions to bring structure and clarity to the claim that context matters.

[23] Collier and Collier 1991: 27. [24] Slater and Simmons 2010: 889.

[25] Soifer 2012.

factor that actually produces the outcome of the critical juncture, to operate.[26] In other words, the loosening of constraints opens a window of opportunity.[27] As discussed in Chapter two, in investment dispute settlement, the end of the Second World War and the end of colonial rule created a context in which multilateral investment governance institutions could emerge—these events gradually opened a critical juncture. Large-scale nationalizations in the 1950s drew attention to how investment disputes were resolved, and created space for politicians and officials to propose new institutional solutions. The critical juncture for investment dispute settlement started to close in the late 1960s and shut entirely with the breakdown of the Bretton Woods system in 1971.

The concept of critical juncture invites scholars to consider the institutional path taken alongside "the paths not taken, although plausible at the time."[28] This is both analytically and methodologically useful, because it supports the use of counterfactuals. The main counterfactual of the book is three institutional proposals discussed during the 1960s: a new multilateral investment insurance organization, a new multilateral treaty with substantive legal standards, and a new multilateral procedural convention without substantive standards. These are not just plausible or historically available choices: all three proposals were the subject of formal intergovernmental discussions. Governments and international organizations devoted resources to developing and discussing all the proposals. All of them were feasible, and all three could have emerged, or two, any one alone, or none. The critical juncture opened up a possibility that any of these institutions might emerge, but nothing was inevitable. The questions explored in the next section are: Why did only one of these proposals succeed during the early 1960s? What determined which one?

The Productive Condition: Involvement by International Officials

The intensity of involvement from international officials varied between the three institutional options mentioned above. I argue that this is why one of the institutional options—an investor–state arbitration convention—emerged during the critical juncture, but not the other two options.

The involvement of international officials can take many forms and occur at many stages of institutional development. I follow Johnson in focusing on the actions of officials within existing international organizations with regard to the institutional design of new international bodies.[29] Officials in existing international organizations typically do not have a mandate to design new

[26] Soifer 2012: 1573.
[27] Soifer 2012: 1573.
[28] Capoccia 2016: 90.
[29] Johnson 2014.

organizations, which raises a fundamental question: what enables this type of international involvement? Johnson argues that officials in existing international organizations "often encounter openings for entering the institutional design arena, due to soft spots in states' capabilities and states' laxity in issues other than high politics."[30] These two conditions—low capability and low political salience—can be the source of gaps in state control with regard to a specific issue, which permits international officials a wider remit.

Conditions that Make Gaps in State Control More Likely: Capability and Salience

In general, the greater the capabilities of states with regard to a particular issue, the smaller the scope available for international officials to act in this issue area. A lack of resources exacerbates capability issues: wealthy, established states may find it relatively easy to participate in institutional design, but this is difficult for poorer, less stable states.[31] Jinnah observes that states are more likely to seek input from non-state actors when issues are new or complex: national governments may lack the time or sufficient technical expertise to build independent preferences on complex issues, especially when they have low political salience.[32]

When issues have less political salience, it opens up more room for international officials to play an institutional design role. Salience refers to "the perceived relevance of a problem to a national government, including the visibility of the problem, its perceived urgency, and the level of affectedness of the country."[33] The salience of an issue is not entirely fixed—it can be manipulated through strategic framing. Even in an issue that has the potential for high political salience, decisions can be framed as technical or procedural, lowering its perceived salience to a certain extent. Another way salience might be lowered is if the consequences of the decision can be pushed further into the future. Officials in government usually operate with restricted time horizons, which means that officials "have a strong incentive to pay attention to long-term consequences only if these become politically salient, or when they have little reason to fear short-term electoral retribution."[34]

While national governments usually have greater capabilities and resources than international officials, in practice, the ability and desire of governments to act on a particular issue at a certain moment in time may be compromised, creating an opening for international officials to enter the design process. Investment dispute settlement was a low salience matter for most state officials most of the time in the 1960s: the relevant ministries faced many more

[30] Johnson 2014: 17. [31] Johnson 2014: 48. [32] Jinnah 2010: 6.
[33] Biermann and Siebenhüner 2009: 51. [34] Pierson 1996: 135.

pressing issues where the consequences of their decisions were more immediate. Government officials systematically underestimated, or even ignored altogether, the long-term, low-probability risk of future arbitration cases until their country was subject to a claim itself.[35] Low capabilities and low political salience create gaps in state control and open up space for officials in existing international organizations to become involved in designing new international organizations.

Motivations for International Officials: Advancing Policy Goals and Ensuring Organizational Survival

The existence of gaps in state control does not inevitably draw international officials into design activities, however. What motivates international officials to take on tasks that are likely outside their formal mandate, which may displease states and may not deliver any gain? Scholars identify several motivations; here I focus on two, drawing on Barnett and Coleman.[36] The first is advancing their policy goals and the second is ensuring organizational survival. This first motivation encompasses beliefs an individual holds about their organization's aims and the appropriate means to advance them, beliefs that are shaped by the official's background and expertise.[37] International officials are more likely than other actors to be strongly motivated by certain policy aims: as Johnson notes, international officials "often select themselves into these organizations because of their belief in the mission."[38] Barnett and Finnemore go further, arguing that officials in international organizations "often insist that part of their mission is to spread, inculcate, and enforce global values and norms," and refer to them as "the missionaries of our time."[39] The second motivation, to ensure organizational survival and their own material security, is more straightforward. Vaubel puts the bureaucratic interests of international officials bluntly, arguing they "are interested in the survival and growth of their organization: more staff, a larger budget and increasing competencies."[40] These two motivations have roots in competing approaches—one ideational and one material—but these motivations may intertwine in reality.

With regard to the international officials involved in the creation of investor–state arbitration, I identify specific manifestations of these motivations. Chapter four explores the World Bank's previous experience mediating investment disputes, which I argue strengthened these officials' perceptions

[35] Poulsen and Aisbett 2013.
[36] Barnett and Coleman (2005: 598) also mention autonomy as a third motivation, but I incorporate autonomy elsewhere.
[37] Barnett and Coleman 2005: 598.
[38] Johnson 2014: 57.
[39] Barnett and Finnemore 2004: 33.
[40] Vaubel 2006: 127.

that getting involved with dispute resolution was something the World Bank could, and should, do. There is also a deeper ideational motivation for many of these officials; their personal experiences of expropriation were related to the Second World War (and for one, to the murder of his family in the Holocaust), which may have led them to believe that insurance was insufficient, and only a legal procedure could provide an appropriate sense of justice. With regard to material motivations, by creating ICSID, these officials gained more autonomy as well as prestigious, interesting work, which may have been particularly important to them after Robert McNamara became President of the World Bank and relegated the Legal Department to more mundane tasks then previous presidents.

Resources of International Officials: Information and Reputation

If officials are motivated to act and have an opportunity to do so, what resources can they draw on to advance their policy goals? The most fundamental resources for an international organization are access to staff and budget without having to ask member states for a specific transfer of resources.[41] Many scholars assume that "international organizations with more resources ... are harder for principals [member states] to monitor and sanction."[42] While this is logical, it may not be true in practice, as member states may not invest much time or energy in monitoring smaller international organizations. This is especially likely to be true in instances where officials in an existing international organization create a new, smaller international organization, which is more removed from member state control and not funded directly by national governments but through the general budget of the larger international organization.

International organizations that appear similar with regard to formal measures of their resources may have different actual roles, reputations, and influence. Biermann and Siebenhüner's edited volume compares several secretariats of environmental treaties that are "largely similar in mandate, size, financial means, and principals" yet vary in their roles and influence.[43] Therefore, I do not focus here on operational resources; instead I follow Beach, who articulates two broad types of resources commanded by international officials—comparative informational advantages and reputational advantages, with informational advantages including both expertise and access to privileged information.[44]

41 Bauer and Ege 2016: 1022. 42 Brown 2010: 147.
43 Biermann and Siebenhüner 2009: 4. 44 Beach 2004.

Expertise is a defining trait of many international organizations, and is central to the World Bank's influence. As Barnett and Finnemore observe, "the World Bank is widely recognized to have exercised power over development policies far greater than its budget . . . because of the expertise it houses."[45] Weaver elaborates on the particular expertise of the World Bank: "In the past sixty years, the Bank has accrued a reputation as the premier global development institution with the greatest in-house expertise. The budgetary resources and staff allocation for research alone far exceeds that of any academic institution."[46] This expertise is technical, legal, and highly specialized. Constant involvement with specific issues gives international officials skill at "inventing institutional options."[47] Moravcsik's often-repeated claim that national governments command greater bureaucratic and informational resources than even the largest international agencies[48] may be valid in the context he analyzes, but it is not necessarily valid or relevant in other contexts. Moravcsik's claim applies only to a handful of the 180 governments in the world, at most, and even in those governments, the daily work of officials may not lead them to invent institutional options. International officials engaged with a highly specialized task are more likely to be adept at inventing institutional options, especially when the organizations they work within have a broad, vague mandate, like the World Bank.[49] In their discussion of OECD officials, Marcussen and Trondal find the organization's officials compare favorably with national officials in terms of expertise, and they describe its Secretariat as "a veritable powerhouse of idea generation."[50]

The work of international officials also brings with it access to privileged information, another type of informational advantage. The work of international officials involves both direct channels of communication with government officials and observation of intergovernmental discussions. This proximity generates access to privileged information about interests, disagreements, and contentious topics.[51] Access to privileged information is a strategic resource, which comes with the ability to "discuss with each party the nature and intensity of their preference."[52] Here again, the extended time frame of international officials may amplify their advantages—if an international official works on a specific issue for several years, they may be in the room

[45] Barnett and Finnemore 1999: 709. [46] Weaver 2008: 9.

[47] Young 1989: 281. [48] Moravcsik 1999: 269–70.

[49] This echoes Bauer and Ege's (2016: 1024) conceptualization of bureaucratic autonomy as both "the capacity to develop independent preferences within the bureaucracy" and "the ability to translate these preferences into action."

[50] Marcussen and Trondal 2011: 592. They also note, however, that OECD states seem reluctant to let officials produce provocative ideas, and these officials are often given only basic bureaucratic tasks.

[51] Tallberg (2010: 245) even calls this access to information a "power resource."

[52] Beach 2004: 412.

hundreds of times as state officials discuss this issue. Extended time frames also enable international officials to develop trust and personal relationships with national officials, which can be useful for brokering (discussed in the next section).

Reputational advantages are a related but distinct type of resource. International officials and their organizations can possess a "reputation for the provision of acceptable leadership among governments," which can be based upon "a) the recognition of the utility of the actor's contributions; b) the perceived legitimacy of the actor; and/or c) whether the proposals of the leader find an acceptable mid-point among the different positions in a given debate."[53] Individual officials may have personal reputations, too, for instance, as especially expert or even-handed, and recent research has demonstrated the importance of individual officials within several international economic organizations.[54] A reputation for occupying the middle ground prepares international officials well for brokering.

Strategies of International Officials: Agenda-Setting and Brokering

If international officials have the opportunity, motivation, and resources to get involved in the institutional design of a new organization, what leadership strategies do they use? Across many contexts, scholars identify two strategies: informal agenda-setting and brokering. When it comes to the design of a new international organization, the most prominent way that officials can attempt to set the agenda is through inventing institutional options or putting forward policy proposals to serve as focal points. In addition to generating proposals, Pollack adds that officials must match their proposals "to pressing problems in an environment of uncertainty and imperfect information."[55] Ensuring their policy proposal matches or "fits" its context is vital for international officials: the advancement of their proposals depend on creating a coalition or community of individuals that will be sympathetic to the new idea and possibly advocate for it. Technical ideas are implemented when they fit well within a particular moment.[56] New ideas prevail "not because they are the 'best' ideas in a technical or professional sense but because they meet the social, organizational, and political needs of key actors."[57] Ideas do not inherently fit; they are tailored and framed and made to resonate—and international officials

[53] Beach 2004: 412.
[54] Xu and Weller (2008) draw attention to individual officials at the World Trade Organization secretariat, while Kellow and Carroll (2013) and Marcussen and Trondal (2011) study officials at the OECD.
[55] Pollack 2003: 50. [56] Ikenberry 1992: 293. [57] Woods 2006: 96.

may be particularly qualified to tailor and fit their ideas to the needs of member states.

The second, related strategy that international officials employ to influence the institutional design of a new organization is brokering, defined here as the ability to construct coalitions or work skillfully around disagreements and bring actors together.[58] Officials in existing international organizations are particularly well qualified to engage in brokering: their expertise, proximity, and reputation is useful here. A proposal from an international organization is well placed to become a "common carrier" for multiple interests.[59] Brokering may be particularly useful to get around distributional issues: international officials are well placed to finesse proposals and consciously lessen the perceived distributional consequences of an agreement by removing contentious content or using ambiguous language. These are tasks that state officials could also undertake, but which may be difficult for them in a context of low trust. If international officials engaged in brokering are concerned that perceived distributional consequences may derail their proposal, then it is likely that they attempt to manage the process of negotiation more tightly and insulate it from distributional or wider political disagreements. This is also true of the resulting organization; as the intensity of involvement from international officials in institutional design increases, the resulting organizations tend to be more insulated from state control.[60]

Sympathetic Interlocutors and State Capacity

Under what conditions is agenda-setting and brokering by international officials likely to succeed and have influence? The literature on relations between international organizations, specifically the World Bank, and member states, identifies several conditions under which Bank officials are more likely to have influence.

First, World Bank officials are more likely to have influence when they are able to identify and cultivate appropriate counterparts in national governments.[61] Woods observes, "To succeed the IMF [International Monetary Fund] and World Bank must find willing and able interlocutors in borrowing governments."[62] National officials are more likely to become sympathetic interlocutors for World Bank officials if they share a professional orientation and training.

[58] Brokering is common: Biermann and Siebenhüner (2009), Jinnah (2010; 2014), and Jinnah and Lindsay (2015) all employ it in their studies of international officials.

[59] Schickler (2001) developed the term "common carrier" in the context of US legislation.

[60] Johnson 2014.

[61] This echoes, in reverse, Büthe and Mattli's (2011) claim about national agencies being able to influence international regulations.

[62] Woods 2006: 65.

Chwieroth notes that because of similar training, neoliberal economists in national governments and international economic officials "often share common policy orientations and speak the same language (both professionally and linguistically)."[63] The appropriate counterparts in national government for an arbitration convention are individuals who can speak the language of arbitration: international lawyers. As Collier and Lowe explain, international lawyers share a language and way of viewing the world:

> For all these people international law is kind of lingua franca—a language in which relations between them, and the States and corporations that they represent, can be conducted. Indeed, lawyers commonly find that their view of the world has much more in common with that of lawyers from other countries than it has with the views of politicians in their own countries.[64]

International lawyers have the potential to become willing and able advocates for the idea of investor–state arbitration in their home countries.

Second, World Bank officials are more likely to have influence when government officials perceive themselves to be in need of external technical expertise and perceive the World Bank as a provider of such expertise. This combines two distinct traits: first, a national government's capacity when it comes to the technical task of investment policymaking; and second, that government's perception of the World Bank. The World Bank's relationship with a particular state varies by government and across time (as staff and priorities in both the World Bank and the government change), but some generalizations can be made. There is a difference between governments that perceive themselves primarily as shareholders with regard to the World Bank and governments that perceive themselves primarily as borrowers—a distinction which has a rough parallel in investment protection between those governments that perceive their interests primarily as exporters of investment and those that perceive their interests as importers. Governments that perceive themselves as borrowers are less likely to view the World Bank as an agent they control, and more likely to perceive it as an authority to be obeyed or as their teacher—especially if they are newly independent or poorer.[65] Larger borrowers or politically important borrowers may deal differently with Bank officials than smaller borrowers; the Indian government may interact more assertively than the Nepalese government, for instance. Additionally, individuals, such as the World Bank country directors who serve as intermediaries between governments and the Bank, also affect the World Bank's relationship with national governments.[66]

When the agenda-setting and brokering of World Bank officials is successful, we should see governments adopt the Bank's language and reasoning.

[63] Chwieroth 2007.
[64] Collier and Lowe 1999: 3.
[65] Finnemore 1993.
[66] Weller and Xu 2010.

Applied to the ICSID Convention, we should see them repeat the Bank's reasoning during the consultative conferences and then ratify in accordance with this new reasoning. All else equal, I expect states with more experience of foreign investment to be less likely to adopt new ideas about how to attract foreign investment disseminated by the World Bank. These states have stronger pre-existing ideas about foreign investment and less need of external advice about how to attract it.

A few summarizing observations conclude this section on critical junctures and the emergence of one institutional framework. There is one overarching argument: international officials can determine the outcome of a critical juncture. They can do this only if certain conditions are met: if there are gaps in state control and if international officials have adequate resources and motivation. I argue these conditions were met in the 1960s, and therefore argue that international officials used agenda-setting and brokering to bring the ICSID Convention into existence. The success of these officials' brokering in any given government depends on the extent of that country's past experience with foreign investment and the nature of their relationship to the World Bank.

GRADUAL INSTITUTIONAL DEVELOPMENT

When the idea of investor–state arbitration was embodied in an institutional framework (the ICSID Convention), it set future developments moving along a particular set of tracks.[67] The ensuing process of gradual institutional development then proceeded broadly along these tracks, eventually leading to contemporary ISDS. While I argue this process was path-dependent, I reject the "versions of a path-dependent argument that paint a deterministic picture of institutional 'lock in'" and instead grapple with actual mechanisms that drive change and continuity, sometimes at the same time, in a long-term, contested process of institutional development.[68]

In this section, I focus on three mechanisms that have particular relevance for the rise of investor–state arbitration: feedback effects, layering, and conversion. I argue that positive feedback effects drove the development of a new constituency. This occurred over several decades, slowly and endogenously leading this constituency to develop a preference for investor–state arbitration.

[67] Keohane (2017: 326) references Max Weber's remark that "ideas act like switchmen sending action along different tracks" to describe path dependence.

[68] This echoes Thelen (2004: 31), who adopts "an alternative perspective that underscores the contested nature of institutional development and, in so doing, recovers the political dynamics that drive institutional genesis, reproduction and change" after rejecting the deterministic versions of path dependency.

During the same decades, investor–state arbitration clauses were layered into investment treaties, contracts, and domestic laws, over time supplanting other means of dispute resolution. Meanwhile, conversion was also occurring, as national officials put the institution of investor–state arbitration to new purposes over time. Using these three mechanisms of gradual change alongside one another can enhance our understanding of institutional change.[69] Applying multiple mechanisms provides better insight into how institutional structures can be reproduced while simultaneously entailing novel purposes and meanings in world politics.[70]

One characteristic that all three of these mechanisms share is that they occur outside the spotlight of formal deliberations. Processes like layering and conversion are "generally difficult for all but the most attentive political actors to anticipate, monitor, and influence. These features advantage organized interests with long time horizons and the resources to play the long game."[71] Taking these processes seriously means confronting "fundamental questions about who has the power to shape outcomes over the long term."[72] This question is revisited toward the end of this section.

Positive Feedback: When New Policies Create a New Politics

When actors receive positive feedback, it encourages them to take further steps in the same direction: "in the presence of positive feedback, the probability of further steps along the same path increases with each move down that path."[73] In a process propelled by positive feedback, events that occur early in the sequence often have stronger causal impact than subsequent events.[74] Even if an institution or technology is not necessarily the most efficient one in the long run, an early advantage may generate positive feedback that secures it; a well-known example from the world of technology is the puzzling endurance of the "QWERTY" keyboard.[75]

Three potential sources of positive feedback are especially relevant for increasing the stability of international institutions: set-up effects, interaction effects, and cognitive effects.[76] Set-up effects refer to the sunk costs of creating

[69] Thelen (2004) uses these three mechanisms in her explanation and so have many subsequent scholars. Within international political economy, Rixen (2011) uses all three to explain the persistence and transformation of double tax treaties.

[70] Fioretos 2011: 389.

[71] Hacker, Pierson, and Thelen (2015: 181) make these points in the context of their discussion of drift and conversion, but I believe these insights extend to all three mechanisms I discuss.

[72] Hacker, Pierson, and Thelen 2015: 182.

[73] Pierson 2004: 21.

[74] Fioretos, Falleti, and Sheingate 2016: 11.

[75] Pierson 2004: 23.

[76] Zürn 2016: 205–15.

an institution; as Zürn notes, "from the very moment when an institution is set up, it normally has established some mechanisms that lead to additional support and protection of the institution."[77] Additional support can come, for instance, from creating a secretariat. Veto points are an additional hurdle; when governments need unanimity to revise a treaty or institution, states are "often stuck with policies that are recognized as inefficient."[78] Interaction effects occur when actors knit together various institutions, and these interactions create additional self-reinforcing mechanisms.[79] "Configurations of complementary organizations and institutions" can emerge which strengthen all the institutions involved.[80] The third potential source of feedback is cognitive: as actors gain knowledge about how a particular institution works and become accustomed to its operation and how it structures the opportunities they face, they adapt their expectations.

Here I focus on positive feedback processes, which reinforce the stability of an institution, while recognizing that feedback processes can also be "negative" and undermine stability. Institutions can simultaneously generate self-reinforcing and self-undermining feedback, and even a single process, which on the one hand entrenches an institution, can also contain seeds of transformative change.[81] For instance, a positive feedback process may lead international organizations to exercise more and more authority, and this exercise of authority may eventually lead to increased contestation and mobilization.[82]

The central feedback process here is the creation of a constituency. This process is often thought not to operate in international relations, but in their study of international regulatory politics, Farrell and Newman focus on this mechanism, which they define as the ability of new institutions or institutional reforms to "create client groups that then have a strong incentive to push for their maintenance."[83] The literature in other fields of political science brings forth many studies that demonstrate the potential for policies, once enacted, to create a new politics through the creation of new constituencies. Skocpol shows how laws governing pensions encouraged previously dispersed individuals to form political organizations, which led to feedback effects that encouraged these groups to lobby over time for further concessions.[84] Campbell shows that the creation of Social Security in the US significantly expanded political participation among the elderly, especially those who were most

[77] Zürn 2016: 205. Keohane (2017) makes the same point. [78] Zürn 2016: 206.

[79] Jinnah (2010) uses "overlap management" to describe interactions between different institutions or treaties and argues that international secretariats are likely to be active and influential in these areas. Interaction effects relate to the concept of regime complexes, which is also associated with empowering non-state actors, such as secretariats (Raustiala and Victor 2004; Alter and Meunier 2009).

[80] Pierson 2004: 27. [81] Hanrieder and Zürn 2017: 95.

[82] Zürn 2016: 209. [83] Farrell and Newman 2010: 618.

[84] Skocpol 1992.

reliant on the program.[85] Mettler shows that the GI Bill in the US led veterans who took advantage of it to participate in civic and political life more than non-participating veterans.[86] As international institutions increasingly touch individual lives or individual firms, these types of constituency-building feedback processes are likely to operate more.

As new constituencies grow, these actors are likely to develop stronger preferences. For historical institutionalists, institutions do not just channel preferences: they can also shape preferences. As Farrell and Newman observe, "preferences are not the result of exogenous economic factors, but rather of previous trajectories of institutional change and group formation."[87] Current state preferences depend on which interest groups have "succeeded in becoming embedded in the relevant regulatory decision making structures."[88] Institutions vary widely in the extent to which they give rise to "politically efficacious support coalitions."[89] Some institutions or policies, for instance, cash assistance for the poor, gives rise to "an extremely weak, fragmented, and politically demobilized constituency."[90] Investor–state arbitration, on the other hand, gives rise to a strong, sophisticated, and politically mobilized constituency.

Positive feedback may operate in many ways with regard to the rise of investor–state arbitration, but here I focus the development of a constituency, which I argue developed in response to the existence of the ICSID Convention and investor–state arbitration. Over time, this group developed a preference for access to investor–state arbitration.[91] I include law firms, investors (especially in-house counsel) and related interest groups in this constituency. Before and alongside the development of this group, I argue that set-up effects, interaction effects, and cognitive effects were also occurring, all of which served to reinforce the stability of investor–state arbitration and further its development. The commitments that are most important for developing investor–state arbitration may not be actual foreign investments; they are more likely made by law firms that have spent decades building specialized investment treaty practices, by ministries that have spent time negotiating thousands of investment treaties, and by thousands of young law students that have specialized in investment arbitration in hopes of building a lucrative career. For law firms in particular, building specialized investment treaty practices has led to positive feedback in the form of more cases, revenue, and prestige. These feedback effects have over time created a constituency with

[85] Campbell 2003. [86] Mettler 2005.

[87] Farrell and Newman 2010: 619. [88] Farrell and Newman 2010: 620.

[89] Hacker 2004: 247. Patashnik (2008) and Patashnik and Zelizer (2013) articulate reasons why some policies or institutions have not generated increasing returns.

[90] Hacker 2004: 247.

[91] One reason it took so long for this constituency to develop is that World Bank legal officials, who were accustomed to interacting with government officials, were not accustomed to contacting investors and struggled to do so. See Chapter six.

a strong preference for access to arbitration, and a constituency and cognitive effects that make a reversal increasingly difficult over time. These constituencies, and often governments too, develop vested interests in existing designs.[92]

Layering

If investor–state arbitration were being organized anew, it is unlikely that institutional designers would agree to create a network with thousands of treaties, contracts, and domestic laws generating thousands of different formulations of consent clauses to several different arbitration organizations or ad hoc arbitration. This is true of many complex, decentralized institutions: if they were designed *de novo*, they would not look the way they do today.

Institutions are rarely created afresh; instead, they are "multi-layered historical composites."[93] Schickler argues that institutions commonly take the form of multilayered historical composites because they are created through layering. That is, they "typically develop through an accumulation of innovations that are inspired by competing motives."[94] When layering occurs, new institutional components are added incrementally, without dismantling what already exists. These small additions can come from different actors at different times, which means that institutions often embody contradictory (or at least multiple) purposes. Schickler observes, "the layering of successive innovations results in institutions that appear more haphazard than the product of some overarching master plan."[95] Fioretos applies this to international institutions, observing that layering may "contribute to more fragmentation in the international system" and in particular, fragmentation in the responsibilities and work of international organizations.[96]

Layering can be a politically attractive process for officials because it reduces the likelihood of scrutiny and potential opposition from actors who might oppose major reforms if those were implemented instead.[97] The logic of layering is similar to incrementalism or political change by small steps.[98] Incrementalism is not timid leadership: it may provide a more sophisticated, and ultimately more successful path to a long-term goal.[99] A layering strategy is likely to emerge under certain conditions, in particular when it is relatively difficult to dismantle existing institutions or veto players stand in the way.

92 Fioretos 2011: 387.
93 Schickler 2001:17.
94 Schickler 2001: 15. He developed the concept in the context of the US Congress, but it has been applied widely.
95 Schickler 2001: 14. The haphazardness of contemporary ISDS has led to persuasive depictions of it using chaos theory (Pauwelyn 2014), but these depictions overlook the institution's centralized origins and deny the officials within the ICSID Secretariat their key role.
96 Fioretos 2011: 390.
97 Fioretos 2011: 390.
98 Lindblom 1979: 517.
99 Lindblom 1959: 86.

Layering processes are distinct from other forms of incremental change because over time, layering transforms the original institution. In layering, "the introduction of new elements set[s] in motion dynamics through which they, over time, actively crowd out or supplant by default the old system."[100] Institutional transformation that occurs through layering can be designed to proceed incrementally without rupture or fanfare, and to introduce changes "as if their purpose were only to fix or complement the system."[101] Although layering may have multiple applications with regard to the rise of investor–state arbitration, I apply the concept of layering to theorize one particular aspect. I argue that investor–state arbitration clauses were layered into investment treaties. These clauses could be added into investment treaties without removing any content, alongside existing state–state dispute settlement clauses.

Furthermore, I argue that a particular set of actors was instrumental in starting the layering process. The international officials who helped craft the ICSID Convention had even stronger motivation and even more resources when it came to generating a caseload for their new organization. Therefore, I argue that they continued using agenda-setting and brokering in order to elicit state consent to arbitration. It was state officials and negotiators that actually added investor–state arbitration clauses to their treaties, contracts, or laws—but their initial decision to do so and early actions, I argue, were spurred by international officials. This argument echoes the dynamics that Posner identifies in the spread of European stock markets. As he observes, "the accumulation of quotidian bureaucratic action over extended periods of time produces independent effects."[102] Although he does not use the term layering, the logic he identifies at work is the same: "what appears to be abrupt change is actually the culmination of small steps against which no one felt compelled to mobilize."[103]

In conclusion, I argue that investor–state arbitration clauses were layered into investment treaties. Initially these clauses were subtle, unobtrusive additions, but over time they came to supplant the existing institution of state–state dispute resolution entirely.

Conversion

The purposes that institutions are called to meet can change dramatically over time. The concept of conversion calls attention to the process by which actors put an institution to a new purpose.[104] Conversion is "the transformation of

[100] Streeck and Thelen 2005: 24. [101] Palier 2005: 131.
[102] Posner 2005: 21. [103] Posner 2005: 7–8.
[104] Thelen (2004) developed the concept and applied it first to the German vocational training program.

an already-existing institution or policy through its authoritative redirection, reinterpretation, or reappropriation."[105] The institutional form remains stable while the institution is put to new purposes. Formal institutions "do not fully determine the uses to which they may be put," Streeck and Thelen observe, and this "is one important reason why major changes in institutional practice may be observed together with strong continuity in institutional structures."[106] This mixture of stability and change make conversion strategies politically expedient: conversion allows institutional innovators to emphasize continuity, which can help them enlist supporters or neutralize potential opponents of change.[107]

Conversion underlines the reality that international institutions, even at the moment of their creation, rarely have one specific, unambiguous purpose. Vagueness and ambiguous language are common, useful tools when it comes to forging international agreements.[108] Hacker observes that "instead of single-use tools, institutions are usually versatile multitaskers" and this versatility "is itself a crucial variable shaping the strategies of actors who wish to change them."[109] When an institution has a single, clear purpose, it makes conversion less likely to occur. Most institutions, however, allow actors working within their constraints to pursue multiple ends—many institutions are sites of contestation between actors with different interests. Conversion "feeds off rule ambiguity."[110] When institutional purposes are ambiguous or multiple, the potential for conversion is greater.

Conversion provides a way to help understand "how institutions created for one set of purposes come, in time, to be turned to wholly new ends. In this sense, the idea provides a framework for a more tractable approach to the issue of 'unintended consequences'."[111] This potential for repurposing raises the question: who determines the uses to which an institution is put? This question takes on a special importance when new procedural rights are given to individuals and a transnational system supplants an interstate one.[112] As states lose their gatekeeping function, new legal actors are empowered, as the "loss of state control, whether voluntarily or unwittingly surrendered, creates a range of opportunities for courts and their constituencies to set the agenda."[113] In their

[105] Hacker, Pierson, and Thelen 2015: 185. [106] Streeck and Thelen 2005: 17.

[107] Hacker, Pierson, and Thelen 2015: 186.

[108] Linos and Pegram (2016: 591) observe that "to reach agreement, international negotiators can make controversial provisions vague and allow them to admit multiple interpretations," referencing the precision dimension of legalization articulated by Abbott et al. (2000).

[109] Hacker (2004: 246) made this observation in the context of domestic US institutions, but it applies to international institutions too.

[110] Hacker, Pierson, and Thelen 2015: 181. [111] Thelen 2004: 36.

[112] Roberts (2010) argues that arbitral tribunals have not taken sufficient account of the dual roles of governments as both respondents and treaty partners in investor–state arbitration, thereby undervaluing their subsequent agreements and practice.

[113] Keohane, Moravcsik, and Slaughter 2000: 458.

study of the Economic Community of West African States Court, Alter, Helfer, and McAllister demonstrate how the addition of private litigant access "led to the Court's 'conversion' or 'redeployment,' a change that allowed new actors to redirect the institution toward new goals, functions, and purposes."[114] Alter, Helfer, and McAllister argue that it is relatively common for international courts to be repurposed or redeployed over time, citing the European Court of Justice, the East African Court of Justice, and the Tribunal of the Southern African Development Community as additional examples. For the Economic Community of West African States Court, they say it is "ironic" that "an international court established to promote regional integration now adjudicates cases involving high-profile human rights violations while remaining largely unavailable to traders and other economic actors in the region."[115]

International courts are typically repurposed through cases, of course, and investor–state arbitration shares all of the traits, notably private litigant access, that enable repurposing according to Alter, Helfer, and McAllister.[116] There has likely been conversion that occurs through the investor–state arbitration caseload. Yet the focus of this book is not the caseload, but the creation of the investor–state arbitration architecture. Therefore, I apply conversion to the actions of government officials when they negotiated or drafted the instruments providing their consent to ISDS. This is a harder test for the concept of conversion, as government officials should have a broadly similar purpose in mind for investor–state arbitration. In fact, the chapter in which conversion is examined uses a least likely case: the American investment treaty program. The American program is widely perceived as the most consistent (in terms of treaty text) and the most closely managed (by a team of world-class international investment lawyers, who usually have long tenures in post)—this strong tradition of continuity makes it likely that the purpose these officials ascribe to investor–state arbitration has stayed the same. On the other hand, if the purposes that this small group of American officials ascribes to investor–state arbitration when it appears in American investment treaties has changed over time, then conversion is likely to operate elsewhere with regard to investor–state arbitration too.

A few observations conclude this section on gradual institutional change. Previous decisions may dramatically reduce the room for maneuver available to actors like governments or international organizations. This holds across many contexts. Pierson observes that member states in the European Union "do not inherit a blank slate that they can remake at will when their policy preferences shift or unintended consequences become visible"; instead, "the

114 Alter, Helfer, and McAllister 2013: 770.
115 Alter, Helfer, and McAllister 2013: 740.
116 Alter, Helfer, and McAllister (2013: 740) identify direct access for private parties, the absence of specific substantive standards, and non-exhaustion of domestic remedies.

dead weight of previous institutional and policy decisions" seriously limits the abilities of governments to make reforms or change course.[117] Actors seeking to reform the investment treaty regime today face 3000 treaties' worth of dead weight as well as formidable opponents. Yet these opponents—the constituency that today articulates a preference for access to arbitration—did not exist to prior to ISDS; it grew over time through positive feedback processes generated by the existence of investor–state arbitration. The preference for investor–state arbitration is endogenous.

While this constituency was developing, other gradual institutional changes were also occurring. Investor–state clauses were layered into treaties alongside traditional state–state clauses, gradually supplanting state–state dispute resolution. Conversion was also occurring, as different actors put investor–state arbitration toward new purposes, or as new external challenges arose. Conversion helps us understand how institutions can have unintended consequences. These modes of gradual institutional change provide ways to help understand why and how institutions can persist even when they generate unintended consequences that are detrimental to states.[118]

COMPARING MY EXPLANATION WITH OTHER EXPLANATIONS

The introduction chapter summarized the conventional account of investor–state arbitration: this account is a condensed version of what has been, to date, the most influential political science scholarship. This conventional account is not the only possible alternative to my explanation. There are many ways that research questions about investor–state arbitration have been framed, and what different explanations can contribute depends on how researchers focus their attention. This section categorizes existing lines of argument to explain the rise of investor–state arbitration into three international relations traditions: choice-based institutionalism, realism, and constructivism. The conventional account draws primarily on choice-based institutionalism, and draws a little on realism. In order to emphasize the distinctiveness of historical institutionalist ideas, I heighten the contrast between my explanation and existing ones—but this is not to deny that pluralist approaches drawing from multiple traditions can provide a fruitful path for theorizing.[119]

[117] Pierson 1996: 146–7.

[118] Rixen (2011) uses the same tools of layering and conversion to explain the persistence of double tax treaties, despite generating an unintended consequence (under-taxation) that is clearly detrimental to states.

[119] As noted by Hall 2010; Jupille, Mattli, and Snidal 2013; and Keohane 2017.

Conventional explanations for investor–state arbitration emerge primarily from choice-based institutionalism, also known as rational choice institutionalism.[120] Several distinct explanations emerge from choice-based institutionalism, which I discuss as a spectrum, beginning with those that have the strongest assumptions of full rationality and efficient institutional design, moving toward explanations where those assumptions are loosened. Starting with assumptions that governments are fully rational and institutional design is efficient leads to an explanation that governments negotiate dispute resolution clauses when, and only when, these clauses help them to overcome cooperation problems. Koremenos puts forward this argument in its fullest form, and she finds support for this argument in her data on the continent of international law, which includes the dispute resolution provisions of investment treaties.[121] Guzman's early theorizing about why poor countries signed investment treaties as well as Elkins, Guzman, and Simmons' testing of his argument elaborate a similar vision: developing countries were engaged in a rational competition for capital, and provided access to arbitration in order to increase the credibility of their commitments and thereby overcome a cooperation problem.[122] A body of research refined this vision: for instance, Haftel found that ratified commitments were more credible than merely signed commitments, while Büthe and Milner found that more investment is induced by agreements with stronger mechanisms for credible commitment.[123] While substantial research along these lines continues, this research program encountered a serious challenge as evidence accumulated that investment treaties did not lead to additional investment.[124] The core premise of choice-based approaches to investor–state arbitration is that governments agreed in order to receive additional investment: if there is no additional investment, then why do governments bother?

Poulsen answers this question and advances the choice-based literature by loosening the assumption of rationality and allowing for cognitive biases. He argues that officials often systematically underestimated the costs and overestimated the benefits of signing investment treaties that provide access to investor–state arbitration.[125] Officials created large networks of investment treaties for their governments without undertaking formal cost–benefit analyses and without seeking out available information; instead they relied on a series of heuristics and reasoning shortcuts. It was not until the first claim hit

[120] Keohane (2017) prefers choice-based institutionalism to other labels and this section follows his usage.

[121] Koremenos 2016.

[122] Guzman 1998; Elkins, Guzman, and Simmons 2006.

[123] Haftel 2010; Büthe and Milner 2014.

[124] Aisbett (2009) provides the most sophisticated analysis out of the large body of literature looking for a relationship between treaties and investment. Minhas (2016) examines many of the premises of investor–state arbitration with sophisticated methods.

[125] Poulsen 2015.

that officials in some governments took the consequences of signing these treaties seriously—and Poulsen and Aisbett show that governments tend to stop signing investment treaties after they have been hit with their first claim.[126] Choice-based approaches, whether they operate with a strong rationality assumption or assume bounded rationality, have thus far focused primarily on the behavior of officials in governments seeking to attract capital, but scholars are starting to focus on the extent to which governments have learned from previous experiences, including in arbitration.[127]

Applied to the rise of investor–state arbitration as framed in this book, choice-based institutionalism emphasizes that actors believed ad hoc arbitration was the best institutional design to help them to overcome cooperation problems. As a flexible institution, states and other actors could adapt it to many circumstances, and this perspective expects that they have, learning and updating their use of investor–state arbitration over time so that it continues to suit their interests. The primary anomaly that choice-based approaches struggle to explain is institutional persistence. Why does investor–state arbitration persist? It is not at all clear that this form of cooperation has made all actors, or even most actors, better off, yet it endures.

Realist approaches to understanding the rise of investor–state arbitration portray the institution as the creation of powerful states. Here again, there are several distinct explanations that emphasize, in various ways, the importance of power. Allee and Peinhardt find that the presence of access to arbitration in a bilateral treaty is determined by the degree of power asymmetry between the bargaining states.[128] There is a liberal undercurrent in this work that powerful states have an *ex ante* preference for arbitration because a domestic constituency lobbies for it, echoing Maurer's scholarship that the US government has historically gotten involved in investment disputes because they were doing the bidding of powerful investors.[129] These ideas also appear in Wellhausen's work showing that the nationality of investors matters when it comes to investment protection and dispute resolution.[130] Allee and Peinhardt, Maurer, and Wellhausen all emphasize powerful states, while in other accounts, power is central but exercised by actors other than powerful states. Simmons' later work emphasizes that governments provide access to investor–state arbitration only in "hard times," which suggests a larger role for power than her previous scholarship on investment treaties, including coercive influence exerted by international organizations after economic crises, when governments are in positions of supplication.[131] Gwynn argues that structural power,

[126] Poulsen and Aisbett 2013.

[127] Broude, Haftel, and Thompson 2017; Haftel and Thompson forthcoming; Peinhardt and Wellhausen 2016; Manger and Peinhardt forthcoming; Alschner forthcoming.

[128] Allee and Peinhardt 2014. [129] Maurer 2013.

[130] Wellhausen 2015. [131] Simmons 2014.

especially the structural power exercised by international financial organizations, is important to understand the spread of bilateral treaties and investor–state arbitration.[132] Power increasingly appears in recent scholarship on investor–state arbitration, including studies that look at whose model text is reflected in final treaties.[133]

Applied to the rise of investor–state arbitration as framed here, realist approaches emphasize that powerful actors have an interest in investment protection, and investor–state arbitration serves this interest. Weaker actors have constrained choices. The main anomaly that power-based accounts struggle to explain is: why this institutional form? It is not necessarily clear why powerful investors or powerful states would have an interest in investor–state arbitration over other possible institutions, like a substantive code with a court.

Constructivist approaches to the rise of investor–state arbitration emphasize the influence of ideas and norms. Governments provided their consent to investor–state arbitration in these accounts because they were convinced that it was the appropriate way to resolve investment disputes. Jandhyala, Henisz, and Mansfield argue that in the 1990s, governments ratified investment treaties with investor–state arbitration because they perceived them as best practice.[134] This accounts for the "South–South" investment treaty phenomenon, which choice-based approaches cannot explain, since in many of these instances, there was no realistic hope of bilateral investment flows. Other studies have focused on the community of arbitrators. Dezalay and Garth's seminal study of the invisible college of arbitrators touched off a wave of scholarship exploring the demographic, behavioral, and ideological traits of arbitrators.[135] Hale systematically compares the power of ideational factors with material factors to explain the growth of commercial arbitration and finds networks of practitioners to be important carriers of the idea of arbitration.[136] Many of the networks he identifies are relevant for investor–state arbitration as well.

Applied to the rise of investor–state arbitration as framed here, constructivist approaches emphasize that many actors, including government officials, came to view this method of resolving disputes as the most appropriate. The relevant international officials could be seen as norm entrepreneurs, and the spread of investor–state arbitration as an idea that diffused. As more and more actors were socialized into a belief that investor–state arbitration was the appropriate way to resolve investment disputes, an epistemic community for the idea emerged. The main aspect of investor–state arbitration that

[132] Gwynn 2016. [133] Berge and Stiansen 2016; Allee and Lugg 2016.
[134] Jandhyala, Henisz, and Mansfield 2011.
[135] Dezalay and Garth 1996; Waibel and Wu 2012; Puig 2014(b); Franck et al. 2017; Langford and Behn forthcoming.
[136] Hale 2015.

sociological institutionalist accounts struggle to explain is the central role of instrumental behavior. Although investor–state arbitration was at times, for certain audiences, associated with values like development or "depoliticization," these associations were typically an afterthought: the main argument to states was always that providing this additional right to foreigners is a trade-off that will get you more investment. This is a logic of consequences. While it is likely that many lawyers who worked to spread the idea of investor–state arbitration did believe in the power of law to resolve disputes peacefully, focusing on norms overlooks the material incentives that also drove these lawyers and have long been central to the rise of investor–state arbitration.

CONCLUSION

This chapter provides a new explanation for the rise of investor–state arbitration, building from historical institutionalism. The explanation has two phases: first, the critical juncture in which one institutional framework emerged, and second, the process of gradual institutional development triggered by the emergence of that initial institutional framework. In the first phase, the main argument is that the intensity of involvement by international officials can be decisive. Under certain conditions, namely when gaps in state control exist and international officials have sufficient resources and motivation, these international officials may be able to set the agenda by "inventing" institutional options and then brokering these new institutions into existence. This, I argue, is what a small group of World Bank officials did to create the ICSID Convention.

When the ICSID Convention came into force it created a dedicated Secretariat and set future developments on a particular path. The Secretariat had an interest in ICSID's survival and Secretariat officials believed in the idea of investor–state arbitration, which led them to encourage states to provide access to arbitration in their investment treaties. Investor–state arbitration was layered into treaties without fanfare. It was only after treaties with investor–state arbitration existed that a constituency began to develop. The positive feedback this constituency of law firms and investors received in the form of revenue and prestige stabilized investor–state arbitration and led these actors to develop a preference for it. While this constituency was developing, the institution of investor–state arbitration was being put to new purposes. Institutions do not determine the purposes to which they may be put, and identifying and analyzing various modes of gradual institutional change help to explain how unintended consequences emerge and why institutions persist even when they generate unintended consequences.

Part I

Creating the Convention

2

Gunboats and Diplomacy

Antecedents of the ICSID Convention

The ideas and legal traditions brought together in the ICSID Convention have old roots. This brief chapter introduces earlier developments that constrained or enabled officials during the critical juncture of the 1960s. While the history of investment dispute settlement is an important topic for scholarship in its own right,[1] the purpose of this chapter is not to provide new historical analysis. Rather, it sets the stage for the 1950s and 1960s by introducing a few important antecedents. This chapter sets out these antecedents in three sections.

The first section introduces contentious cornerstones of eighteenth- and nineteenth-century investment dispute resolution: separate courts and law for foreigners, diplomatic protection with force, and the existence of an international minimum standard of treatment. These cornerstones generated antagonism between capital-exporters and capital-importers and are the main reasons why this area of law "has always been one of acute controversy."[2]

The second section of the chapter draws out more hopeful developments for international cooperation in investment. Efforts to replace the use of force with arbitration and attempts to reframe foreign investment as a tool for development instead of a tool of imperialism struggled in the early twentieth century. After 1945, these efforts gained traction because they fit with the post-war context and with two broader post-war trends: a general drive for international institutions, and decolonization.

The third section discusses decolonization and its discontents, illustrating the backdrop against which the ICSID Convention was framed in the 1960s. Decolonization brought with it high expectations, but the leaders of many new states found their political independence tempered by a lack of economic independence. Inherited economic arrangements and concession contracts

[1] Scholarship revisiting many of these topics, often with new historical evidence, has emerged in recent years (Chernykh forthcoming; Hale 2015; Miles 2013; Montt 2009; Pinchis-Paulsen 2014, forthcoming; Poulsen 2015; Schill(a) 2009; Waibel 2011; Yackee 2008).

[2] Brownlie 1979: 522.

made nation-building goals seem unreachable. Some leaders began to take back the commanding heights of their economies through nationalization. To investors, these acts were unconscionable property seizures. While some concession contracts were renegotiated with relative ease, such as the Saudi Aramco agreement of 1950, other renegotiations became hostile, such as the Abadan incident of 1951. The chapter concludes with a discussion of Abadan, which illustrates how gunboats, diplomacy, and new multilateral institutions like the UN and World Bank could all operate in the same investment dispute.

CONTENTIOUS CORNERSTONES OF INVESTMENT DISPUTE RESOLUTION

Separate Courts and Law for Foreigners

Investment disputes have long been resolved outside local courts. During the eighteenth and nineteenth centuries, only a handful of countries exported capital, and these capital-exporting governments used a range of means—from colonization to spheres of influence to treaties to diplomatic pressure—in order to protect their capital overseas.[3] Between 1870 and 1913, six European countries accounted for almost 90 percent of global foreign investment, and England alone for 42 percent.[4] It is this small group of capital-exporting states that Oscar Schachter had in mind when he observed: "As a historical fact, the great body of customary international law was made by remarkably few states."[5] Nowhere is that more true than in investment law, where these six states, with the later addition of the United States, had outsize influence.

It was the rules and practices developed in the "informal empire," when investment was secured through treaty and not direct control, which gave rise to international investment law.[6] In areas of direct control, like colonies, authorities applied metropolitan (for instance, British) law and enforcement was direct, whether the court sat in Cape Town, Singapore, or London. In areas of indirect control, treaties and legal innovation were required. Treaties

[3] Platt (1968a: 306) observed that the British government "was compelled on occasion simply to apply diplomatic pressure, at others to colonize, and at others still to reach an international compromise whereby underdeveloped nations were divided into spheres of interest or influence."

[4] Belgium, England, France, Germany, the Netherlands, and Switzerland. Maddison 1995: 65.

[5] Schachter 1996: 536.

[6] Miles 2013. Anghie (2004: 253) argues all international legal discourse has been shaped by imposing "universal standards" that essentially furthered European/Western interests, but this is perhaps most explicitly true in the case of international investment law.

protecting investment first appeared between European states[7] and were then exported outside Europe alongside trading firms like the Dutch East India Company.[8] Miles argues that extending these treaties beyond Europe altered their character: "although initially concluded on equal terms, these agreements were often the first stepping stone to establishing a more intrusive presence within non-European nations."[9] These "unequal treaties" usually established direct consular control within a host state. Within these areas, foreign nationals and their property were not subject to local laws, but remained within the jurisdiction of their home state—an effective way to ensure the security of property, but one which engendered resentment from host states.[10]

Diplomatic Protection and the Legality of Armed Intervention

Law, force, and politics were bound together in the settlement of investment disputes in the eighteenth and nineteenth centuries. Growing competition among imperial powers and an increasing use of direct investment fueled a rise in the use of force during the late nineteenth century, primarily in Latin America.[11] Sometimes force was used as a signal to other capital-exporters, even if no property had yet been damaged. In 1915, for instance, "marines landed in Haiti and subdued political uprisings which threatened the expropriations of European and American properties and the loss of American lives, but this action was taken not so much to protect American investments per se as to prevent a threatened military encroachment by Europeans."[12] Armed intervention could be based on flimsy pretexts and have serious political consequences. For example, the Swiss-French bank of J. B. Jecker and Company lent 75 million francs to the Mexican government, of which Mexico received only 3.7 million francs. Non-payment of 100 percent of the loan and its interest was a justification for armed intervention by the French government, which led to regime change.[13]

International law was advanced in the service of both armed invasion and sovereignty. On the side of armed intervention, officials from capital-exporting states argued that the doctrine of diplomatic protection extended

[7] Sornarajah 2004: 180; Miles 2013: 24. [8] Lipson 1985: 38; Miles 2013: 21.
[9] Miles 2013: 25. [10] Lipson 1985:14; Miles 2013: 26–7.
[11] Miles 2013: 29. Competition was primarily between Germany, the UK, and the US in Latin America. Between 1897 and 1914, US corporations made nearly one billion dollars in direct investments in Latin America (Lipson 1985: 58). British investors had hundreds of millions of pounds in Latin America, a figure that soared and crashed several times over the 1800s, due to reckless speculation and government mismanagement (Lipson 1985: 51).
[12] Oliver 1975: 348. [13] Shea 1955: 14.

to cover disputes concerning the overseas property of their nationals.[14] Diplomatic protection was a long-established doctrine that an injury done to a foreigner was an injury to their state, enabling the home state to take action to remedy the injury.[15] This doctrine was then converted into a system of property protection.[16] For instance, the British government, hegemon of the nineteenth century, asserted that it always had the right to intervene in disputes regarding its citizens' overseas property, but chose not to in most instances.[17] Capital-exporting states asserted an international minimum standard of treatment for their investors. These governments took the position that national treatment did not provide sufficient protection for foreign investors and international legal obligations "were not to be determined by reference to the domestic laws of individual states."[18] Failure to conform to the minimum standard of treatment created a reason for taking action against the violating state.

On the side of sovereignty, officials and jurists from capital-importing states argued for equality: equality among nations and equality between foreigners and nationals.[19] Venezuelan jurist Andrés Bello—a strong supporter of property rights—outlined a vision later picked up by Carlos Calvo and many others to help weaker countries combat abusive diplomatic protection.[20] The two forms of equality lay at the heart of what would eventually be known as the Calvo Doctrine. The doctrine emphasizes, first, that equality among nations is not a concept reserved solely for Europe; all sovereign states, being free and independent, enjoy the right to freedom from interference.[21] Second, foreigners are not entitled to rights and privileges greater than those accorded to nationals.[22] This principle of national treatment commanded widespread support.[23] For instance, the arbitrator in *Rosa Gelbtrunk v Salvador* held:

> A citizen or subject of one nation who, in the pursuit of commercial enterprise, carries on trade within the territory and under the protection of the sovereignty of a nation other than his own, is to be considered as having cast in his lot with the subjects or citizens of the state in which he resides and carries on business. Whilst on the one hand he enjoys the protection of that state, so far as the police regulations and other advantages are concerned, on the other hand he becomes liable to the political vicissitudes of the country... in the same manner as the subjects or the citizens of that state.[24]

[14] Brownlie (1979: 521) notes a sharp increase in legal writing "from the point of view of investor states."
[15] Sornarajah 2004: 18. See also Miles 2013: 47.
[16] Sornarajah 2004: 146.
[17] Miles 2013: 29.
[18] Miles 2013: 49.
[19] Montt 2009: 38–9.
[20] Montt 2009: 40–5.
[21] Shea 1955: 18.
[22] Shea 1955: 19.
[23] Brownlie (1979: 523–4) finds support from jurists in Europe and Latin America, arbitral awards, and seventeen states.
[24] *Rosa Gelbtrunk and the "Salvador Commercial Company" v Salvador* (1902).

During these years, arbitration worked alongside armed intervention and other forms of diplomatic protection. Arbitration did not necessarily replace gunboat diplomacy: gunboats were used, as needed, to bring countries to arbitration. Historically, arrangements for arbitration were made after a dispute arose, not in the initial contract or treaty.[25] Diplomatic protection, force, and arbitration all played prominent roles in dispute resolution.[26] This interplay, as well as other issues raised thus far—separate courts and law for foreigners, and the assertion of a minimum standard of treatment—can be seen in events in Venezuela around the turn of the twentieth century.

Illustrating Investment Dispute Settlement in the Early Twentieth Century: Venezuela

Civil war broke out in Venezuela in 1899. The war "crippled that national industry and paralyzed all commercial enterprise with the exterior" and led Venezuela to default on debts of roughly 26 million pounds.[27] The size of the default was not exceptional, and it followed many previous cycles of lending and default, the result of decades of irresponsible lending and unsteady government. At the time, European powers had substantial economic interests and quasi-colonial outposts in Venezuela. The situation was one of informal empire, with tensions running high because the US stood poised to replace the European states as the dominant external power.[28] In this charged political situation, Venezuela defaulted on its loans. After acrimonious correspondence, the UK, Germany, and Italy bombarded a number of Venezuelan ports, sank three Venezuelan warships, and took over customs houses.[29] Faced with this blockade, Venezuela agreed to arbitration.

A protocol was signed between the blockading powers and Venezuela in February 1903 that set up ten arbitral commissions and referred part of the dispute to the PCA in The Hague. The primary legal question the PCA was called upon to decide was whether "unilateral enforcement by military intervention entitled the intervening powers to preferential payment of their claims under international law."[30] The UK, Germany, and Italy requested preferential

[25] Pauwelyn (2014: 31) terms this "retrospective consent," and notes that the frequency of prospective consent is a central way in which contemporary investor–state arbitration differs from past arrangements. Prospective or advance consent is the subject of Chapter six. Vandevelde (2010: 26 and 31) notes that friendship, navigation, and commerce treaties "typically did not include any kind of arbitration clause or method of resolving treaty-related disputes through the use of binding, third-party procedures."

[26] Platt (1968b: 330) counted at least forty examples of "coercion and the landing of [British] armed forces" in Latin America between 1820 and 1914. Between 1840 and 1940, there were also at least sixty arbitrations in the form of mixed claims commissions (Brownlie 1979: 521).

[27] Hood 1983: 177. [28] Hood 1983: 138. [29] Hood 1983: 186.

[30] Waibel 2011: 30–4.

treatment, since they had born the cost of the armed intervention. Throughout the proceedings of the mixed claims commissions, it was never in dispute that Venezuela would be liable to pay compensation.[31] In an immediate sense, the settlement of the Venezuelan default was a triumph for the right of armed intervention. Yet the legal arguments made in response to the action in Venezuela, combined with geopolitical developments, would one day curtail the right of armed intervention.

To conclude the first section, these contentious issues—in particular, whether or not foreigners require separate courts and law—were unresolved and relevant for officials in the 1960s; they limited what could emerge from the critical juncture. The issue of equality is an enduring controversy, and appears often in the chapters that follow: far from being resolved, the question of whether foreigners need separate courts and law lies at the heart of contemporary debates over ISDS in Europe and the US.[32]

HOPEFUL STEPS FOR INTERNATIONAL COOPERATION IN INVESTMENT

Restricting the Use of Force

In response to events in Venezuela, Luis Drago, the Argentine foreign minister, argued that "the public debt of an American State cannot occasion armed intervention, nor the actual occupation of the territory of American nations by a European power."[33] Drago framed his argument for a US audience, intending the Drago Doctrine to be a corollary to the Monroe Doctrine.[34] Drago wrote an article explaining his logic in the inaugural issue of *The American Journal of International Law*.[35] After an initially lukewarm reaction, the US government eventually took up the logic of Drago's argument, and US President Theodore Roosevelt made it the centerpiece of his 1904 State of the Union Address. His statement came to be known as the Roosevelt Corollary to the Monroe Doctrine. In principle, the Corollary was the Drago Doctrine: it prohibited European intervention in the Americas to coerce payment of debts. The Corollary, however, reserved the right *for the US* to use military

[31] Noted in Miles 2013: 66–8.

[32] Wälde (1996: 446) observed that the Calvo Doctrine has long been the dominant maxim of Western countries when they are respondents. Elaborated in Chapters three, five, seven, and eight.

[33] Drago's argument is quoted in Hershey 1907: 30.

[34] Hershey 1907: 28–31. Drago even quoted Alexander Hamilton and the Eleventh Amendment to the US Constitution, making it clear he sought to appeal to an American audience.

[35] Drago 1907: 692.

action; therefore, in practice it became associated with an increase in the use of force by the US, even serving as justification for US interventions in Cuba, Nicaragua, Haiti, and the Dominican Republic.[36] Wary of the Roosevelt Corollary, Latin American officials continued to pursue the idea of non-intervention in international law.

A few years later, in 1907, the Porter or Drago–Porter Convention stated that military intervention to coerce payment of debts was prohibited, as a general principle of international law.[37] Yet the Convention "left a loophole through which a fleet of warships could sail" because states could still use force if a debtor state refused to reply to an offer of arbitration or failed to enforce the arbitration award.[38] It was a partial, yet significant step toward outlawing the use of force.[39] The principle of substituting peaceful dispute settlement for the use of force would be picked up later, as politics permitted—notably with the UN Charter in 1945. Waibel makes clear the connection between the two: "Article 2 (4) of the UN Charter generalized the principle of the Drago-Porter Convention by outlawing the use of force in international law."[40] The gradual, decades-long effort toward outlawing the use of force dovetailed with the development of permanent institutions for arbitration.

Permanent Institutions for Arbitration

The First World War and the interwar period saw property seizures that were without precedent in both their scale and their nature. For instance, in 1919, the Soviet government repudiated its foreign debt and began to nationalize all property within its territory.[41] Incidents like this could not be settled with gunboats, even if the political will and capacity to do so had existed. In the interwar era, some disputes were dealt with through intergovernmental

[36] The 1933 Good Neighbor policy of the Franklin Roosevelt Administration officially put an end to armed intervention to collect debts.

[37] At the time, it was known as the Porter Convention, after General Horace Porter, the head of the US delegation. It is now referred to as the Drago–Porter Convention. The Convention was negotiated during the Second Hague Conference on International Law (Van Genugten and Scharf 2007).

[38] Shea 1955: 15. In other words, the Drago–Porter Convention provides a suspension of diplomatic pressure, as long as arbitration is progressing. Notably, the ICSID Convention adopts the same approach—they both provide a suspension, and not a removal, of diplomatic pressure.

[39] Waibel 2011: 38.

[40] Waibel 2011: 38.

[41] Jones (2005: 27) notes that around two-thirds of all French and Belgian foreign investment was in Russia/the Union of Soviet Socialist Republics (USSR) at the time of the nationalizations. France and Belgium were not in a position to use force to compel the USSR to pay. The Soviet government took a creative position on compensation (Lipson 1985: 67) and Waibel (2011: 39) notes that when the Soviet Union collapsed, the US was still negotiating a final settlement of the 1917 repudiation.

negotiations, while others relied on relatively new legal institutions. A body of practice began to emerge from the Permanent Court of International Justice (PCIJ), created in 1922, as well as from the PCA, created in 1899.[42] The structure of the PCA and, later, the PCIJ, insofar as they provided permanent dispute resolution machinery untethered to any particular set of rules, would influence the framers of ICSID.[43] States adapted their treaty practice to incorporate these new institutions. Friendship, commerce, and navigation treaties began to specify that the disputes would be submitted to the PCIJ.[44]

During the 1920s and 1930s, several international conferences were held to develop substantive international law on investment protection, usually ending in disagreement. After the League of Nations' First Conference for the Codification of International Law in 1930, Manley Hudson, the American technical representative, summed up discussions on investment: "A sharp divergence of views on the fundamental aspects of the subject was evident from the start, and but slight progress was made toward reconciling the divergence."[45] The crux of the debates was equality: delegates from seventeen of the forty-two states represented at the conference believed that foreigners should not enjoy better treatment in a country than its own nationals.[46] At the Seventh International Conference of American States, held in Montevideo in 1933, governments adopted a Convention that reiterated the national treatment standard, stating that "foreigners may not claim rights other or more extensive than those of the nationals."[47]

The idea of individual investors having standing against states was also discussed in the interwar era. The ICC began working on a draft convention in the 1920s which provided for ICC arbitration.[48] The ICC's efforts helped lead to the adoption of the New York Convention in 1958, which provides recognition and enforcement of foreign arbitral awards.[49] The International Law

[42] Some, like the Case Concerning the Factory at Chorzow, became cornerstones of investment law, as claimants and respondents under BIT arbitrations decades later relied upon PCIJ jurisprudence (Vandevelde 2010: 35).

[43] Broches ([1966] 1995: 172) wrote: "The provisions on jurisdiction in the Preliminary Draft of the Convention which was discussed at the regional consultative meetings were inspired in part by the practice of the International Court of Justice."

[44] Vandevelde 2010: 25.

[45] Hudson 1930: 459. The "Harvard Draft," described in Borchard (1929: 133–239) was the basis of the discussion.

[46] Vandevelde 2010: 36.

[47] Article 9 of the "Montevideo Convention on the Rights and Duties of States," signed December 26, 1933.

[48] Article 14 "should contain detailed provisions for the composition and working of the International Court of Arbitration to which all disputes and differences are to be referred under Article 13. The details are, however, left to be worked out by the negotiating governments" (ICC 1949: 278). See also Vandevelde 2010: 53.

[49] Convention on the Recognition and Enforcement of Foreign Arbitral Awards, 330 UNTS 38; 7 International Legal Materials (ILM) 1046. For more on the New York Convention, see Van Den Berg 1981 and Hale 2015.

Association (ILA) put forward two draft statutes on investment dispute settlement in 1948, both of which gave investors standing against states.[50] One proposed investor–state arbitration, while the other outlined a Foreign Investments Court.[51] These ILA drafts share many features with the ICSID Convention.[52]

Reframing Foreign Investment

During the interwar years, new thinking about foreign direct investment (FDI) emerged that would influence post-war policymaking. This new approach attempted to remove the imperialist associations from foreign investment and recast it as a tool to facilitate development. For instance, while testifying to a Senate subcommittee in 1940, an American Assistant Secretary of State condemned past foreign investment and argued that the purpose of foreign investment should not be profit for private firms, but rather development. He argued:

> The past movements of capital have been regarded as, frankly, imperialist... We are still liquidating many of the 19th century messes which were occasioned by the somewhat violent and not too enlightened moves of capital. As nearly as one can see it, the object would seem to be capital movements which are worked out not merely because some concessionaire wishes to make a profit but following the more careful plans of the various governments involved with a view to the development of the country.[53]

This official was a member of an influential group convened by the Council on Foreign Relations that developed plans for the post-war era, some of which became templates for State Department policy.[54]

[50] Article 3. ILA 1948: 259. One important difference between the ILA draft and ICSID's eventual shape was this, in the ILA draft: "access to the tribunal presupposes the exhaustion of local remedies except where other rules of international law or an agreement between the parties provides otherwise." Article 4b. ILA 1948: 260.

[51] The Court was to have fifteen members, elected for nine years each (Article X). No member of the Court was to engage in any other occupation of a professional nature, or act as agent, counsel, or advocate in any case (Articles XIII and XIV). Costs were to have been borne by the parties proportionally in their percentages of contributions to the costs of the United Nations (Article XXV). ILA 1948: 269–70.

[52] Like ICSID, the proposal suggests arbitral tribunals consisting of three arbitrators: two selected by the parties, and the third by the President of the ICJ if the parties cannot agree (Article 4). ILA 1948: 260. Like ICSID, deliberations continue even in the absence of one of the parties (Article 25). ILA 1948: 264.

[53] Oliver (1975: 96–7) quotes testimony from Adolf Berle.

[54] Shoup and Minter 2004: 119 and 122. Jacob Viner and Alvin Hansen led the Study Group on Economic and Financial Problems, which sent the State Department nearly one hundred reports and sixty-six discussion digests, several of which dealt with international investment.

One idea backed by this Council of Foreign Relations group was an international investment organization, which would help to facilitate pro-development investment. The idea of arbitration appeared in these proposals. For instance, one 1942 memo argued that a multilateral agency could "police international investment by private capital, so as to provide judicial or arbitral facilities for settlements of disputes between creditor and lender, and to remove the danger of the use by creditor countries of their claims as a basis for illegitimate political or military or economic demands."[55] In 1943, the State Department sent the Treasury a proposal for an International Investment Agency that drew heavily on this proposal.[56] In 1945, a quasi-governmental publication describing the proposed agency argued that it would "implement the public character of investment and minimize its former capacity for waste, injustice, and international friction."[57] Arbitration was repackaged with this new emphasis on public investment and development.

The Havana Charter, agreed in 1948, reflected the new thinking on investment. The Charter's text stated that "international investment, both public and private, can be of great value in promoting economic development and reconstruction, and consequent social progress," but clarified that member states have the right "to take any appropriate safeguards necessary to ensure that foreign investment is not used as a basis for interference in its internal affairs or national policies."[58] The Havana Charter was agreed, but never came into force—only the General Agreement on Trade and Tariffs, one part of the Havana Charter framework, began to operate on a provisional basis. The US failed to ratify the Charter, in part because US business organizations objected to the investment provisions.[59] In Havana, there had been "a general unwillingness to give guarantees as to its [foreign investments'] security, and, in some cases, a feeling that such capital in itself was suspect, and a likely tool of foreign exploitation."[60] The provisions on investment, unlike many provisions on trade, were not carried forward in any multilateral architecture. The visions of Keynesian-inspired post-war planners, which provided the intellectual and institutional foundations for post-war trade and monetary policy, were not enshrined in any multilateral institutions for investment.

[55] Oliver (1975: 360) cites a 1942 memo "Problems of International Long-Term Investment, by Jacob Viner." Viner drew on Eugene Staley's ideas, as articulated in his book *Raw Materials in Peace and War*. In writing it, Staley drew on his experience as the rapporteur of a study group that included Alvin Hansen, Jacob Viner, and other Council of Foreign Relations members, that was convened by the American Coordinating Committee for International Studies.

[56] This "Draft of Proposed International Investment Agency" by John Parke Young did not play a role at Bretton Woods. Harry Dexter White's proposal (which emerged within the Treasury) would become the main American proposal at Bretton Woods. Oliver 1975.

[57] Soule, Efron, and Hess 1945: 325–6.

[58] Article 12. Article 93 specifies arbitration to settle disputes (Havana Charter 1948).

[59] Toye and Toye 2004: 41.

[60] Toye 2003: 288.

DECOLONIZATION AND ITS DISCONTENTS

The reality of foreign investment was slower to change than the rhetoric of multilateral planners would suggest. Political independence was not accompanied by economic independence for many of the states that emerged from colonial domination in the 1950s and 1960s. Colonial-era concession contracts remained in force, and FDI relations continued largely as before.

Leaders in many newly independent states found themselves constrained by inherited economic arrangements. As James Crawford put it, "When, after a long process, independence was achieved... the independence that was granted turned out to be less than it seemed."[61] Leaders faced urgent challenges, often including core nation-building tasks like creating health systems, education systems, militaries, and civil services. Their ability to address these challenges was limited by existing foreign investments. Brownlie characterized the situation as one of "partial independence":

> Many of the poorer states have accepted foreign investment at the expense of economic, and therefore political, independence. It is all very well to say that nationalization is possible—providing prompt and adequate compensation is paid. In reality this renders any major economic or social programme impossible, since few states can produce the capital value of a large proportion of their economies promptly. It is common for the poorer economies to be subjected to foreign ownership to a great extent, and the analogy of private law ownership clashes sharply with the desire of states to govern their own economies.[62]

To many leaders, foreign investment still seemed antithetical to development. To them, foreign investment was not an instrument in the service of national development: it was a tool for continued control by external powers. Continuing foreign ownership of key industries was interpreted as cover for political interference.

Concession contracts, which usually confer the sole right to exploit natural resources or license agreements for transport or telephone services, were an area of particular friction.[63] Newly independent governments often inherited concession agreements that were profoundly asymmetrical. For instance, the 1933 concession contract underlying the Abadan Refinery—the largest oil refinery in the world for decades—specified that the company would pay no tax to Iran, the host government, for *thirty years*.[64] Instead, the company paid tax, around 15 million pounds annually—a substantial sum in the 1930s and 1940s—to the British government.[65]

[61] Crawford 2004: xii. [62] Brownlie 1979: 537. [63] Brownlie 1979: 547.

[64] Article 11 of the 1933 Concession Agreement between the Iranian government and the Anglo-Iranian Oil Company (AIOC), quoted in Schwarzenberger (1969: 75).

[65] Abdelrehim (2010: 111) shows that 15 million pounds was paid in 1947, and that other years were similar.

In some instances, capital-exporting governments were willing to renegotiate asymmetrical contracts relatively amicably. For instance, in 1938, when the Mexican government asserted national ownership of subsoil rights, the American government did not dispatch gunboats or force Mexico to arbitration—instead, they opened negotiations and after compensation was paid, recognized Mexico's ownership of the oil fields.[66] Similarly, in 1950, when the King of Saudi Arabia threatened to nationalize the Saudi oil fields, the then-US-owned company Aramco agreed to share profits 50/50 in the Saudi Arabia–Aramco arbitration, one of the "great oil arbitrations" emerging from post-war concession contract renegotiations.[67] The appeal of communism and other geopolitical developments factored into the US government's willingness to renegotiate and reach agreement under more equal terms during these years.[68]

Other attempts to renegotiate post-war concession contracts ended less amicably; despite the new multilateral institutions, the era of gunboat diplomacy was not over yet. Following the example of the Saudi King, Iranian Prime Minister Mohammad Mossadegh nationalized the Abadan Refinery in May 1951, seeking more equal arrangements. In addition to the substantial tax revenue that Abadan provided for the British post-war economic recovery, the British government was also the company's primary owner and the refinery was the chief source of petroleum for the UK.[69] In other words, the British government could not afford to lose Abadan.

The British government pursued every option to reverse the nationalization. They prepared plans to invade Abadan within days of the nationalization. For the next three years, Iranian troops patrolled the perimeter of the closed refinery, while British gunboats circled nearby.[70] Company–state negotiations and then state–state negotiations were attempted. The British government also appealed to the President of the International Court of Justice (ICJ) for arbitration even before direct negotiations broke down.[71] The ICJ was not receptive, and ultimately held that the relevant contract was "nothing but a concessionary contract between a government and a foreign corporation, [and the] United Kingdom Government is not a party to the contract."[72] Before the

[66] US President Roosevelt, no friend of the oil industry, was sympathetic to Mexican President Cardenas, and in 1938–42 (the period of the dispute), the US government had other priorities. Maurer (2011) provides an excellent study of the dispute, including Secretary of State Cordell Hull's actions.

[67] Higgins 1994: 141. She cites: *Petroleum Development Ltd v Sheikh of Abu Dhabi*; *Saudi Arabia v Aramco*; *Sapphire International Petroleum Ltd v NIOC*; *BP v Libyan Arab Republic*; *Texaco v Libyan Arab Republic*; *Liamco v Libyan Arab Republic*; and *Kuwait v Aminoil*.

[68] For instance, Schwarzenberger (1969: 57) explains that the actions of OECD states toward Indonesia must be viewed within the context of a sustained effort to remove Indonesia from the Chinese sphere of influence.

[69] Schwarzenberger 1969: 66. [70] Schwarzenberger 1969: 68–9.

[71] Elm 1992: 174–81. [72] Ford 1954: 124–53 and 164–212.

ICJ could hear the case, the British government appealed to the United Nations Security Council. The Security Council adjourned without acting.[73] Mossadegh, who held a doctorate in international law from the University of Neuchâtel, travelled to New York and made a compelling presentation. Public sympathy for his cause was high in America: he was *Time's* Man of the Year in 1951, the year Abadan was nationalized, and called the "Gandhi of Iran" by many American officials.[74] The British appeal to international institutions backfired.

The British government was still determined to get the refinery back: next they asked the US government and the World Bank to mediate the dispute.[75] Eventually, the US discontinued their negotiations in favor of the World Bank's mediation.[76] Getting involved was outside the World Bank's usual mandate; it was Aron Broches, then-Assistant General Counsel, who wrote the memo arguing that the Bank could act.[77] Within six months, however, the Bank's first attempt at mediation had failed, which some in the Bank partly attributed to the fact that Mossadegh could withdraw Iran's consent to mediate at any point.[78] Recalcitrance from both sides meant that a year after the nationalization, in March 1952, Abadan remained dormant, and the British government (and other AIOC investors) remained outraged. The dispute was ultimately resolved after a coup d'état sponsored by British and American intelligence services removed Mossadegh from power in August 1953.[79] The final Abadan settlement was largely a negotiation between American and British oil companies, with AIOC (renamed British Petroleum) retaining a 40 percent stake in Abadan.[80] Within a year of the

[73] Ford 1954: 124–6. [74] Elm 1992: 340. January 7 1952 edition of *Time*.

[75] By October 1951, the US government's work led to joint proposals ("Memorandum of Conversation," October 23 1951, US TPL). The UK and Iran's common interest in restarting the refinery made the mediation look simple to some Bank staff, particularly Vice President Robert Garner. Prud'homme 1985: 2.

[76] "Steering Group on the Preparations for the Talks between the President and Prime Minister Churchill." January 23 1952. US TPL. World Bank Vice President Garner had earlier met with AIOC representatives and received encouragement from Anthony Eden, UK Foreign Secretary, Dean Acheson, US Secretary of State, and John Snyder, US Secretary of the Treasury. Garner 1961: 66.

[77] Graves 1973: 600. The Bank's decision to act may have been affected by the fact that a high proportion of the Bank's small staff were former UK colonial administrators, including William Iliff, the loan director at the Bank (a position junior only to the Vice President and President), who came to the Bank after a long stint as financial counsellor of the British Embassy in Tehran (Iliff 1961: 1).

[78] Broches 1984 (April): 28–9.

[79] Notably, the first meetings between British and American representatives "for the purpose of discussing joint war and staybehind plans in Iran" were not held until after the World Bank's mediation failed (Wilber 1954: 1).

[80] Schwarzenberger (1969: 66–71) reports AIOC/British Petroleum was paid £25 million in compensation from the Iranian government and £214 million by the consortium of companies who took up the remaining 60 percent.

coup, Abadan was operating again and the stock of AIOC/BP had tripled.[81] After the coup, one of Mossadegh's former advisers asked: "If they were genuinely interested in our independence, was it not fairer to get compensation from us as they did in Mexico, and give us the freedom to run our oil industry?"[82]

The Abadan incident prompted serious reflection. How should complex, politically charged disputes between investors and host states be resolved? For some at the World Bank, the failed Abadan mediation exposed a gap in the international architecture: the world needed some kind of machinery for resolving disputes between host states and investors.[83] Within a decade of Abadan, the World Bank proposed such machinery. The same man who had argued that the World Bank could mediate in the Abadan dispute, Aron Broches, wrote the proposal. Yet ICSID's emergence was by no means inevitable: Abadan also influenced other, more ambitious proposals, which are discussed in Chapter three.

CONCLUSION

This chapter introduces three broad antecedents of the ICSID Convention. The antagonisms emerging from the long history of investment dispute settlement remained relevant in the 1960s. Historical memories about separate courts and separate law for foreigners were politically salient and limited what was possible in the critical juncture discussed in Chapter three. The hopeful developments discussed in the second section, by contrast, provided positive precedents and opened up possibilities for officials in the critical juncture. As Chapter four illustrates, the proposal for ICSID was presented as a continuation of efforts to replace the use of force with arbitration and to reframe foreign investment as a tool for development.

Generally, the post-war era was conducive for creating new international institutions. Investment, however, was still difficult terrain for institutional creation in the 1960s, in part because of tensions relating to decolonization. In spite of efforts to frame investment as a useful tool for development, the reality of foreign investment in newly independent states often seemed disconnected from this rhetoric. Unwinding colonial economic arrangements proved to be a

[81] "In October, 1951, Anglo-Iranian shares stood at £5. Now, on 1st November, 1954, after ratification of the present agreement, they stand at £18, an all-time record." Hansard, November 1 1954 Commons Sitting: Persian Oil Agreement.

[82] Hassan Sadr, writing on August 23 1953, quoted in Elm 1992: 327.

[83] Iliff 1961: 44.

complicated, drawn-out process in many cases, and one that often provoked suspicion on both sides. Disputes like Abadan demonstrated that governments which were historically capital-exporters, such as the British government, were not always ready to renegotiate. These tensions shaped the cooperation which could emerge, both constraining and enabling proposals for new international architecture to settle investment disputes in the 1960s.

3

Intergovernmental Bargaining

"The Lowest Common Denominator Was Not yet Low Enough"

This chapter examines intergovernmental bargaining on investment protection during the 1960s. Capital-exporting governments discussed three multilateral options for investment protection: a substantive code, an insurance organization, and a convention on investor–state arbitration. Why did only one of these options come into force during the 1960s?

This chapter begins to illuminate the argument set out in the theory chapter, namely that it is neither the intensity of interest from investors nor the bargaining efforts of governments that make the difference. A multilateral arbitration convention emerged in the 1960s while the other two proposals did not because the World Bank provided active support for arbitration while refusing to play an equivalent agenda-setting or brokering role for the other two proposals. The World Bank's strategy and advocacy for arbitration is the subject of the next chapter.

This focus of this chapter is the two paths not taken: the code and the insurance. The chapter takes seriously the central expectation of conventional accounts, that investor demand drove the government actions that created investment protection structures. The chapter's empirical content is drawn from an extensive search of the places likeliest to contain traces of investor lobbying: the archives of the four capital-exporting countries most involved with the code and insurance proposals. The analysis that follows is based on letters to officials, internal memos, telegrams, and briefing notes related to investment protection issues in the Federal Republic of Germany, Switzerland, the UK, and the US.

There is the most evidence of lobbying for investment insurance. While there is investor involvement with the code, and certainly more for a code than for arbitration, this involvement did not usually take the form of lobbying as theorized by conventional explanations. There was no groundswell or process of mobilization by firms that owned property, such as factories, in foreign countries and were concerned about seizure. In fact, there is strikingly little evidence of this kind of lobbying. Investors were far more likely to be aware of any of these three investment protection initiatives in corporatist states like Switzerland or Germany, where they heard about these initiatives from their governments in the course of top-down, government–industry group consultations. In general, American and British investors were far less informed than Swiss and German investors.

A few individuals with personal experience of expropriation dominate the surviving records, having spearheaded investor involvement in their own countries and transnationally. In the case of Hermann Josef Abs, by far the most important of these individuals, his involvement was more a personal crusade to right past wrongs committed against Germany than it was conventional lobbying. Abs was a towering figure in German finance who had played an active role in expropriating Jewish property and lived through large-scale, uncompensated expropriations of German-owned property, which he viewed as new wrongs piled on top of past wrongs. It matters that the most influential postwar convention on investment protection begins with him and emerges in the Federal Republic: the ideas, their framing, and their resonance are inextricably linked with the Second World War and the German twentieth-century experience. Every German investor and official working in the 1950s had witnessed livelihoods and lives torn asunder by expropriations. In this context, calls for a "Magna Carta for Investment Protection," as Abs called his Draft Convention, do not sound overblown. They resonate.

The relationship between exceptional individuals like Abs and their governments contradicts conventional explanations. Conventional explanations expect investors to lobby so that their governments take up their views and give voice to them internationally. In contrast, these exceptional individuals were used by their governments as trial balloons.[1] Abs and Hartley Shawcross, his British counterpart, each had the stature to command an international audience and to give this audience the impression that they were informal advisers to their governments. Their governments did not endorse their ideas but rather monitored Abs and Shawcross as they made proposals internationally; if they were received poorly, the governments would distance themselves and note that there were no official ties. Abs and Shawcross were held at a distance, but often a "benevolent distance," by their governments. Yet Abs, Shawcross, and their wider transnational coalition did not see their preferred proposal—a multilateral convention backed by an international court and arbitration—enacted during the 1960s.

Political and economic realities prevented OECD governments from agreeing on the OECD Draft Convention on the Protection of Foreign Property—an

[1] The trial balloon conceptualization was Yannick Stiller's idea and I thank him for it.

intergovernmental, modified version of the Abs–Shawcross Draft, which was itself a modified version of the Abs Draft.[2] The US government was opposed to the Draft Convention initially, as were many of the capital-importing OECD member states. Bargaining over the Draft Convention grew so rancorous by 1966 that it was uncertain if the OECD Council could pass even a non-binding resolution expressing support for the principles in the Draft. As the Austrian representative remarked, "the lowest common denominator was not yet low enough."[3]

Intergovernmental bargaining for a multilateral code failed in the 1960s. Governments would use the lessons they had learned during the lingering death of the OECD Draft in order to negotiate bilateral treaties, but the idea for a court or for arbitration was not moved forward by governments. It was picked up by World Bank officials, who had a new strategy to reframe the idea of investor–state arbitration (discussed in Chapter four).

The chapter proceeds with four sections on the OECD Draft, followed by a fifth section on insurance. The OECD Draft and its predecessors are examined at length because they included individual standing in arbitration. The first section briefly shows that officials perceived themselves as choosing among a code, insurance, and arbitration. The second contextualizes the emergence of Hermann Abs' Draft Convention and details why the postwar German context matters for the Abs Draft's content and resonance. The third section evaluates the "suspicious apathy" of governments toward the OECD Draft. The fourth considers officials' efforts to kill the OECD Draft softly, without damaging customary international law on investment protection. The fifth section discusses proposals for a multilateral insurance agency and why one did not emerge in the 1960s.

A CRITICAL JUNCTURE WITH THREE OPTIONS

Throughout the 1960s, officials in capital-exporting governments saw themselves facing three options for multilateral investment protection: a substantive code; an investment insurance organization; and a convention on investor–state arbitration. Existing scholarship often separates these three institutional choices, but viewing them together brings us closer to how officials saw the situation.

These three options form a strong counterfactual because they were not only historically available; they were actual, formal, intergovernmental proposals. Officials in capital-exporting governments also discussed bilateral treaties or a

[2] Schwarzenberger (1969: 153) used the phrase "toned-down" version.

[3] Telegram from AmEmbassy Paris to SecState WashDC, February 17, 1967 "Draft Convention Protection Foreign Property." US 595219 Box 13.

pan-European initiative on investment protection occasionally, but the main proposals discussed in multilateral settings were the code, the insurance, and the arbitration. Officials discussed all three proposals in the same fora, primarily the OECD Development Assistance Committee (DAC), but also during World Bank annual meetings, bilateral meetings, and in other places.

Officials explicitly compared these proposals. In June 1969, British Treasury officials heading to the Annual Meetings of the International Monetary Fund and World Bank were instructed as follows: "We support the ICSID, have strong reservations about the IBRD draft Agreement for an International Investment Insurance Agency and regard the potentially useful OECD draft Convention for the Protection of Foreign Property as a dead duck."[4] The relevant files in the Swiss archives are called simply "multilateral investment protection" and the papers inside discuss the code, insurance, and arbitration.[5] A memo in the briefing pack for US officials headed to the OECD Ministerial meeting in November 1966 explains: "Encouraging assistance from the private sector... is the basis for our interest in the OECD Draft Convention on the protection of private property, the proposed Multilateral Investment Guarantee Corporation and the recently established World Bank Center for the settlement of investment disputes."[6]

Most officials believed that these three proposals were complementary and might all come into existence. Officials at the World Bank, to get slightly ahead of the story, also saw three options. Asked about the origins of ICSID, Aron Broches responded, "it follows from what I said earlier about the third approach. It's not the code, it's not the insurance, it's the mechanism for settlement of disputes."[7] In 1961, Broches gave a speech in which he described the three approaches, and their merits and shortcomings.[8] Broches and the World Bank began to back arbitration heavily and provide little support to the other two proposals. For instance, in that 1961 speech, Broches describes the OECD Convention and insurance proposal negatively, as infeasible, then makes only positive remarks about the proposal for an arbitration convention.[9] The World Bank's strategy and advocacy for ICSID is discussed at length in Chapter four. Table 3.1 compares the trajectories of these three proposals between 1954 and 1967.

4 IMF/IBRD. Twenty-Second Annual Meeting, Settlement of Investment Disputes: Investment Insurance and Protection, Brief by the Treasury. UK FCO 48/145.

5 CH C.41.124.5.2.

6 "Encouraging Assistance from Private Sector," drafted by Peter F Geithner for the OECD Ministerial Meeting, Paris, November 24–5, 1966. US 595219 Box 4.

7 Broches 1984 (May): 35.

8 Broches, Aron. "Problems of Private Foreign Investment," Third Annual Institute on Corporate Counsel, devoted to Foreign Operations of American Enterprises, December 8, 1961. WB Folder 1651418.

9 Broches, Aron. "Problems of Private Foreign Investment," Third Annual Institute on Corporate Counsel, devoted to Foreign Operations of American Enterprises, December 8, 1961. WB Folder 1651418.

Table 3.1. Timeline of the Critical Juncture: Three Multilateral Options for Investment Protection in the 1950s–60s

	1954	1956	1958	1960	1962	1964 1966
Code	Abs American compensation mission	Abs Draft launched	Abs–Shawcross Committee Germans and British afraid to ask World Bank to take over Abs–Shawcross	OECD DAC produces "OECD Draft"	Consultation with least developed countries on Draft	OECD Resolution passed World Bank refuses American request to take over OECD Draft
		German BIT Drafting		Ongoing BIT negotiations based on European countries models		
Insurance	(1948) World Bank plan for multilateral insurance		Van Eeghen Draft recommended by ICC Council of Europe proposal on insurance European Industrial Fed endorses insurance	OECD DAC asks World Bank to study multilateral insurance	World Bank's "pessimistic" Report OECD Group of Experts: insurance is technically viable, draft clauses for new IO	US takes lead of group supporting insurance at OECD OECD sends outline of multilateral insurance organization to World Bank
				ICC and other investor groups come out strongly in favor, with reports comparing proposals and surveys showing investor interest		
Arbitration	Broches drafts Abadan memo	New York Convention deliberated	American Bar Association Committee (Broches, Lauterpacht, Delaume, etc.) completes proto-ICSID Draft "Appropriate hint" for World Bank to create ICSID inserted into Bloch Report (UN) at Broches' request	Discussion on ICSID within Bank's Board Broches submits memo outlining ICSID idea Broches has private conversations with US State Dept & Treasury, secures American support	ICSID Roadshow (Consultative Conferences in Addis Ababa, Bangkok, Geneva, and Santiago)	ICSID Convention comes into force "No de Tokio" protest during WB Annual Meeting; invitations to ICSID Drafting Committee already written

A "MAGNA CARTA" FOR INTERNATIONAL INVESTMENT

A central intuition of conventional explanations is that particular proposals for international institutions are adopted because they approach an optimal institutional design, given the cooperation problem to be overcome. In contrast to conventional explanations, historical institutionalist arguments emphasize that ideas or proposals emerge in a particular place and time, and rather than being optimal, reflect the milieu in which they were formed. The actors that promulgate and discuss these ideas also reflect their environment, including in ways that may predispose them to certain ideas, even though these ideas may be far from optimal, or prevent them from taking seriously other ideas that provide better technical solutions.

The most influential proposals for a multilateral investment code emerged from the Federal Republic of Germany in the 1950s, and this is not a coincidence. Ideas have influence when they resonate with their context, and the idea of a new, multilateral agreement on investment protection resonated in postwar Germany. Every German investor or official working in the 1950s had lived through large-scale expropriations undertaken by the Reich government, hundreds of postwar restitution trials, and American, British, and Soviet expropriations of German-owned property during and after the Second World War. These officials also lived with the threat of invasion from the German Democratic Republic, a socialist state on German soil, and saw the sanctity of private property as fundamental to distinguishing the two Germanys.

Proposals for investment protection would have looked different if they had emerged elsewhere or at a different time. American industry groups were not particularly interested in creating international law and an international court or arbitration—they were relatively satisfied with the American investment insurance program and other American government interventions to protect property. This disparity in preference intensity between American and German industry groups could have been because German investors could not rely on their government, with its neutered overseas presence, to intervene in disputes. While their greater reliance on international law may have contributed to the relative enthusiasm of German industry groups for a multilateral code, the far more important force driving efforts toward a multilateral code was personal experience. The importance of personal experience, and the broader German experience during and after the Second World War, comes through in a brief look at Hermann Josef Abs and the draft investment code that bears his name.

Hermann Josef Abs and His Draft Convention

The man driving efforts for investment protection in the 1950s in the Federal Republic was no ordinary, representative investor. Hermann Josef Abs was arguably the most experienced man in the world with regard to expropriation, with unparalleled personal experience as expropriator and as expropriatee. He was the central figure in Deutsche Bank's expropriation of Jewish property during the Second World War.[10] He was a key player in many restitution proceedings in German courts the 1950s, playing multiple roles.[11] He was Germany's lead negotiator in the postwar debt negotiations concluded with the 1953 London Agreements,[12] reprising his role on the Reich's debt negotiating team during the 1930s (which found creative ways to partially default or delay payment on Germany's debt after the First World War).[13] Hermann Abs was head of foreign operations at Deutsche Bank from 1937 to 1945, led the development bank responsible for allocating Marshall Plan aid to Germany (*Kreditanstalt für Wiederaufbau*) from 1948 to 1952, then helped reconsolidate Deutsche Bank, led it as Chairman from 1957 to 1967, and was still involved with Deutsche Bank at the time of his death in 1994. Abs is an extraordinarily complex figure and his many ambiguities will not be dealt with here. The purpose of this section is to show that his work to promote investment protection in the 1960s was not ordinary lobbying: it was a crusade emerging from his personal experiences of expropriation before, during, and after the war.

In the 1950s, when Abs gave speeches promoting his draft investment convention, he referenced the expropriations that had occurred during the war. In a December 1956 speech nominally about the Suez Canal seizure, for instance, Abs argued:

[10] In the leading history of these events, Harold James' book *The Deutsche Bank and the Nazi Economic War against the Jews: The Expropriation of Jewish-Owned Property*, Abs is mentioned more than any other individual. The book ends with an extended discussion of Abs' responsibility (2001: 217). Abs is the only individual that the five eminent historians of the Deutsche Bank-funded "Historical Commission of the Deutsche Bank" project identify by name in their joint introduction to James' book. They note: "we have vigorously debated the person and role of Hermann Josef Abs, and each of us has and will interpret that complex and important individual in a slightly different way" (James 2001: vii).

[11] James (2001: 217) notes: "The mixed involvements of Deutsche Bank's leading banker did not become substantially less tangled when it came to managing restitution after 1945, where again Abs took part in negotiations in many different guises, as the representative of quite diverse interests (sometimes those of new owners, sometimes those of the victims of Nazism, as well as the interests of Deutsche Bank at a time when that institution had ceased to exist)."

[12] Gall 2005: 164.

[13] Abs was the representative for Delbruck Schickler and Co, the bank he worked for before joining Deutsche Bank, to the German Debt Standstill Agreements. Gall 2005: 34.

> A further point which must not be overlooked in an assessment of the causes of the progressive disintegration of international law is that the West itself, by its interferences with duly acquired rights of its own and foreign nationals, has afforded the pretext for similar measures in the rising countries in particular. I do not hesitate to admit that the former German Reich played a large part in such practices. I have in mind the stoppage of the external debt service during the pre-war years, and the interferences with the rights of others by methods of exchange control or on racial and political grounds.[14]

Abs does not mention that he was involved with the implementation of both policies. Instead he notes, obliquely, that the UK and US governments also committed expropriation during the Second World War: "Not less harmful was the policy, stemming from the waging of total war, of expropriating and liquidating for the satisfaction of inter-governmental claims the duly acquired private property of 'enemy' nationals."[15] Abs furthermore notes that to seize the Suez Canal, the Egyptian government simply copied verbatim the British legislation on trading with the enemy that had been used to expropriate German property during the war.[16]

Abs' references to actions during the National Socialist period without any admission of personal responsibility display remarkable audacity given how uncertain his survival was in the immediate postwar period. In April 1945, the Deutsche Bank board (*Vorstand*) debated who to send to Hamburg to negotiate: ultimately they selected Abs, meaning that the alternate choice, Karl-Ernst Sippell, remained in Berlin, where he was shot by Soviet troops the next month.[17] Abs was then considered for prosecution in the Nuremberg trials: he was interrogated by the American prosecution team from September 1945 onward[18] and imprisoned from January to April 1946, awaiting trial.[19] Ultimately, Abs was not prosecuted: the British view that clemency for top bankers was acceptable given the need for a fast German economic recovery won out over the American wish to prosecute the top bankers, in addition to breaking up the big banks.[20] Abs' personal relationships with key British officials may have additionally insulated him.[21] In the end, only one banker,

[14] Text of a Speech by Hermann J. Abs. "The Protection of Duly Acquired Rights in International Dealings as a European Duty: Reflections on the Development of the Suez Crisis." UK T 236/5429.

[15] Text of a Speech by Hermann J. Abs. "The Protection of Duly Acquired Rights in International Dealings as a European Duty: Reflections on the Development of the Suez Crisis." UK T 236/5429.

[16] Text of a Speech by Hermann J. Abs. "The Protection of Duly Acquired Rights in International Dealings as a European Duty: Reflections on the Development of the Suez Crisis." UK T 236/5429.

[17] Abs 1991. [18] Gall 2005: 128. [19] Gall 2005: 128. [20] Gall 2005: 128.

[21] Gall (2005: 128) suggests Charles Gunston of the Bank of England was particularly important. It is possible that the British lead prosecutor at Nuremberg, Hartley Shawcross, also played a role, but his memoirs claim that he met Abs only in the 1950s, and I have not been able to verify earlier meetings.

Karl Rasche of the Dresdner Bank, was tried at Nuremberg; he was convicted on "spoliation" charges.[22] The American chief prosecutor wrote: "Rasche had participated actively, through his position and activities in the Dresdner Bank, not only in the confiscation of Czech banks and industries but also in 'the Reich's indefensible program of Aryanization' in Czechoslovakia and Holland."[23] If Karl Rasche could be found guilty of these charges, it is plausible that Abs would have been found guilty too, if he had been tried.[24]

Today there is extensive evidence of Abs' active participation in "aryanization" (*arisierung*) within Germany and in Austria, Czechoslovakia, the Netherlands, and south-eastern Europe.[25] One of the Germans who had worked for the American prosecution at Nuremberg, Eberhard Czichon, wrote a book condemning Abs for his wartime actions, which led Abs to sue him in 1970 and have the book's distribution halted.[26] In the trial, Abs did not contest his involvement in "aryanization," but argued that his motive had been to hold non-Aryan property until the political climate permitted returning it, and records show he never lost the trust of some Jewish clients, even as he organized the sale of their assets at prices that would later be ruled too low.[27] The moral responsibility of Hermann Abs remains a controversial topic among historians today, but that is not what is at issue here—the relevance here is that Hermann Abs drew on his experience with these and other expropriations to build his argument for a new "Magna Carta" for property rights. Drawing connections between Abs' experience and the Abs Draft helps illuminate the realities of early calls for investment protection that have been obfuscated over time (including realities papered over in the 1950s and 1960s to increase the political palatability of investment protection, as elaborated in Chapters four and five).

One important debate clarified by looking at Abs is indirect expropriation. There is a persistent belief that investment treaties (and arbitration) were constructed to handle direct expropriations only. This is false. The Abs Draft included indirect expropriation explicitly. When put in context, it seems obvious that it would include indirect expropriation—almost all the

[22] Taylor 1949: 82. [23] Taylor 1949: 202.

[24] Rasche was a Nazi Party member, unlike Abs, which may have made him an easier target (even though the American prosecution did not take party membership into account formally), but the extent of his involvement in "aryanization" was not greater than Abs'. Abs also could have been tried in the IG Farben case at Nuremberg, as he sat on the supervisory board (*Aufsichtsat*) of IG Farben from 1937 to 1945.

[25] James (2001) describes Abs' personal involvement in all of these places.

[26] Czichon was a citizen of the German Democratic Republic and political tensions within a divided Germany may have affected the trial in several ways (Gall 2005: 399–404). After Abs' death, Czichon (1995) published an updated version.

[27] Abs secured a statement supporting this line of defense from William Petschek (James 2001: 104), whose family's business Abs had sold as the Petschek family was persecuted (James 2001: 100–4).

expropriations that Abs participated in or experienced during the 1930s and 1940s were technically complex. The typical pattern an "aryanization" expropriation took was for a Jewish-owned firm to be charged with large amounts of taxes owed or with violations of exchange rate policy.[28] These charges, plus potential or actual persecution of the owners, would lead the owners to sell. Deutsche Bank, Dresdner Bank, and other banks would compete to find "aryan" buyers and suitable financing.[29] This experience of excessive taxation, foreign exchange control laws, and other regulations being used as weapons of expropriation were carried forward into the 1950s, while the Abs Draft was crafted. For instance, in a 1956 speech, Ludwig Erhard, the long-serving Minister of Economics (*Bundesminister für Wirtschaft*), included excessive taxation and inflation as forms of expropriation:

> Without any doubt, one will come to the conclusion that the state has assumed private means via excessive taxation… [and] there are other forms of expropriation or of the violation of property, which have found their way into modern economic history; [including] different forms of inflation.[30]

Erhard was addressing the first meeting of the Society to Advance the Protection of Foreign Investments (*Gesellschaft zur Förderung des Schutzes von Auslandsinvestitionen e.V.*). Erhard's comments, which may seem extreme to readers accustomed to orderly economic circumstances, would have had a different resonance for his audience of West German bankers in the 1950s. Historical context and personal experience help explain why Erhard would include inflation as expropriation: as hyperinflation ravaged the German economy in the 1920s, Erhard was completing his doctorate in economics in Frankfurt.

Another important misconception corrected by looking at Abs is geographical application. Evidence examined in later chapters suggests many officials in capital-exporting governments in Europe and America believed they would not be respondents at ICSID, which suggests how influential the World Bank repackaging of investor–state arbitration (as something primarily for use in developing countries) was, since many of the examples of expropriation in the Abs Draft are European or American. In fact, Abs' motivation was likely related to the lack of compensation for German property seized after the Second World War by Soviet governments in Central and Eastern Europe, and during the war by the US and the UK. The commentary on the Abs Draft

[28] In Austria, where "aryanization" was pursued quickly, a special "aryanization tax" was levied, and Jewish owners received barely any compensation (James 2001: 137).

[29] James 2001: 113.

[30] Speech by the Minister for Economics, Professor Dr. Ludwig Erhard, March 27 1956, subject: "anläßlich der Gründungsversammlung der Gesellschaft zur Förderung des Schutzes von Auslandsinvestitionen e.V. (on the occasion of the founding of the Society to Advance the Protection of Foreign Investments)." DE B 102/130141.

draws a large number of its examples from Czechoslovakia, Yugoslavia, and Poland, and notes that the American, British, and Swiss governments all concluded dispute settlement treaties after the Soviet seizure of property in those countries, but that German investors received no compensation.[31] Some of these expropriations may have had a personal relevance for Abs, since his deal-making had followed the advance of the German army.[32] In a 1956 speech, Abs described the Second World War as "a war which has not restored the old moral and legal order in the world, but has unfortunately piled new wrongs on top of the old ones."[33] Piling new wrongs on top of the old ones hints at how Abs felt about American expropriations.

Lingering resentment about the American expropriation of German-owned property during the Second World War matters because it affected cooperation on the OECD Draft between the German and American governments. German officials delayed sharing the Abs Draft with the Americans because they believed it would be perceived by the Americans as a strategy to receive compensation for the expropriated German property.[34]

Abs led the delegation to receive compensation for seized German property in the US in 1954. A series of letters between German officials preceding Abs' appointment provides insight into the relationship between Abs and the German government. German officials agreed that Abs was "the best informed subject expert," inside or outside government, to lead the negotiations.[35] His stature meant the Americans would have to take the negotiations more seriously (the State Department had refused to appoint a high-ranking official and delayed repeatedly), and if the negotiations went poorly (as seemed likely, given the American government's dismissive attitude) then blame could be shifted to Abs and off the ministry or government.[36] There was one problem: German officials were wary because Abs had been the "target of attacks in the United States."[37] The German Ambassador to America asked an American

[31] Proposed International Convention for the Protection of Foreign Investors. UK T 236/5429.

[32] For instance, James (2001: 131) notes that a few days after the German government annexed Austria, Deutsche Bank sent Hermann Abs as head of a small delegation to negotiate bank takeovers.

[33] Text of a Speech by Hermann J. Abs. "The Protection of Duly Acquired Rights in International Dealings as a European Duty: Reflections on the Development of the Suez Crisis." UK T 236/5429.

[34] For instance, a German official "fears that then US might understand official support for the initiative as an attempt of Germany to regain nationalized foreign investments." Internal memo, December 1957, subject: "Maßnahmen zum Schutz von privaten Auslandsinvestitionen (Measures to Protect Private Foreign Investment)." DE B102/130141.

[35] Letter from Ministerialdirektor Dr. Berger to Botschafter Dr. Heinz Krekeler, December 30, 1954. IFZ ED 135/45.

[36] Letter from Heinz L. Krekeler to Herr Ministerialdirektor Dr. Löns, December 17, 1954. IFZ ED 135/45.

[37] Letter from Heinz L. Krekeler to Herr Ministerialdirektor Dr. Löns, December 17, 1954. IFZ ED 135/45.

public relations consultant to assess the likelihood of a serious negative reaction related to Abs' wartime activities. The public relations official and the German Ambassador both believed a negative reaction was likely and that it was "ill advised" to appoint Abs. A Senator had "blasted" Abs as a "known Nazi" on the floor of the US Senate, and an American Ambassador had said "there is no question but that he worked hand in glove with Nazi officials."[38] That Senator lost re-election, however, and the Ambassador was deemed unlikely to make future comments along those lines. What concerned the German Ambassador most was that a nationally syndicated columnist, Drew Pearson, had previously "exposed him [Abs] as a former trusted tool of Nazi banking circles" and the Ambassador deemed the columnist likely to amplify his attacks if Abs were appointed.[39] The German Ambassador insinuated that the columnist worked with "dossiers"[40]—which today we know the Federal Bureau of Investigation and other American agencies did hold on Abs.[41] Over the Ambassador's concerns, officials in Bonn appointed Abs to lead the compensation mission.

Abs' efforts to get compensation from the US government and to promote his Draft *were* perceived to be related—for instance, a 1957 letter to a German-speaking Jewish American who was active lobbying the American government in the 1950s discusses both on the same page.[42] Even in 1967, over twenty years after the end of the war, the German government still thought a main reason for American opposition to the OECD Draft Convention was because they would then be liable for German-owned property seized in America during the war. An American internal telegram reports:

> [German government] lawyer confided that within German government hypothesis has been developed that reason behind US unwillingness to present draft convention for legislative ratification is that US administration still contains personalities who were active in "violation" against principles of Draft Convention in World War II period regarding German property in US.[43]

Despite the "attacks" discussed above, Hermann Abs was widely admired in the US in the 1950s and 1960s. Information about the intensity of his involvement in expropriations appears not to have been widely available until the late 1990s. A 1967 newsletter from the "Association of Jewish Refugees in

[38] Memo from L. Roy Blumenthal to Ambassador Heinz L. Krekeler, subject: "Herman [*sic*] Abs." November 18, 1954. IFZ ED 135/45.

[39] Letter from Heinz L. Krekeler to Herr Ministerialdirektor Dr. Löns, December 17, 1954. IFZ ED 135/45.

[40] Letter from Heinz L. Krekeler to Herr Ministerialdirektor Dr. Löns, December 17, 1954. IFZ ED 135/45.

[41] Abs, Hermann J. 56532. US FBI 65, 105, Box 167.

[42] Letter to Bruno Weils, author unknown (likely Fritz Moses), July 13, 1957. AVL Box 2 (3/9).

[43] Telegram from AmEmbassy Paris to SecState WashDC, January 10, 1967. US 595219 Box 13.

Great Britain" contains an article that describes Abs only as a "star" of postwar banking.[44] While certain parts of the American government had lots of information on Abs' past, this information appears not to have travelled to other departments. In 1967, *Time* introduced Abs as follows:

> In ten years as chief of the Deutsche Bank, West Germany's largest, Hermann Josef Abs became the most distinguished figure in German finance. Only last year, no less an authority than David Rockefeller, President of the US's globe-spanning Chase Manhattan Bank, called him "the leading banker in the world." Suave, witty and self-assured, Abs was more than a banker: a confidant and consultant to monarchs and politicians, he became an unofficial ambassador to the world's financial centers and the undisputed *éminence grise* of German business.[45]

Before moving on, it must be noted that the protagonist of later chapters—Aron Broches—may have known more than most of his Washington-based contemporaries about Hermann Abs' wartime activities. Broches was Dutch, but left Amsterdam in 1938. He was the only member of his family to leave and the rest—his mother, father, brother, sister, niece, and brother-in-law—were all killed during the Holocaust.[46] His parents had owned a successful cigarette manufacturing firm, Broches Sigarets, which was expropriated during the German occupation.[47] Aron Broches went back to Amsterdam in 1945, and "in the next few years he was able to rebuild the factory that had been closed, all the machinery stolen by the Nazis."[48] Someone, perhaps Aron Broches, filed a claim for compensation regarding the family's possessions, including for "valuables surrendered to the Lippmann-Rosenthal looting bank."[49] Deutsche Bank was not directly a part of the Lippmann-Rosenthal arrangement, but Deutsche Bank's management had made the arrangement possible and had "made a substantial contribution by making securities available."[50] It has not been possible to ascertain what information Aron Broches accessed about German banks during those years, but it is plausible—especially given Broches' legal and financial expertise and Hermann Abs' prominence in Deutsche Bank decisions in the occupied Netherlands[51]—that Broches had access to information about Abs' wartime activities. This connection is picked up in later chapters as one possible reason why Broches did not build stronger relations with Abs or his society while promoting ICSID, a rare instance of Broches declining to foster relations with an interested audience.

[44] Reissner 1967: 6. [45] *Time* 1967. [46] Joods Monument 2017.
[47] Alexandra Broches quoted in Parra 2016.
[48] Alexandra Broches quoted Parra 2016. [49] Joods Monument 2017.
[50] James 2001: 175.
[51] For instance, the sale of Adler and Oppenheimer, a Jewish Dutch bank, was closely managed by Abs (James 2001: 92–8).

"Benevolent Distance": The Relationship between Abs and the German Government

Throughout the 1950s, Abs was an informal adviser to Chancellor Konrad Adenauer,[52] which, in addition to his position as the head of the German development bank and his role renegotiating German national debt, gave him a rare ability to influence policy in the Federal Republic. Yet the Ministry of the Economy (*Bundesministerium für Wirtschaft*) was not merely a conduit for Abs' ideas about investment protection. On the one hand, Abs was powerful (and not afraid to write to the Chancellor directly[53]), so officials could not do anything to openly dismiss him, but on the other hand, they needed to distance themselves. These officials were concerned with rebuilding Germany's image abroad after the war and in the context of a divided Germany. The views of individual officials varied, but in general, the economic diplomacy of the early Federal Republic was characterized by caution and studied avoidance of any assertiveness that would be perceived as aggression. For instance, while drafting Germany's first investment treaty, these officials refused to use a particular word because the English translation would likely be "exploitation of capital," which could trigger the wrong sentiments.[54] Abs was not this careful.

Ministry of Economy officials subtly used Abs as a trial balloon to see how the world reacted to his ideas. Many officials may have agreed with Abs' ideas in principle but thought they were neither viable nor beneficial for West Germany's image. The German government did not sponsor the Abs Draft; they were careful to merely suggest it, as a private document, to the Organisation for European Economic Co-operation (OEEC)—the OECD's predecessor—for study. Additionally, German officials were instructed to adopt a posture of "benevolent distance" toward the Draft:

> The German delegates were briefed... that the draft convention of Herrn Abs constitutes only a private work, which has not yet been analyzed officially by the departments; the German delegates have been told to adopt an attitude of benevolent distance when it is further deliberated in the OEEC bodies.[55]

[52] Between 1949 and 1963, Abs made more than a hundred visits to the Chancellor's office. He was "asked for advice concerning all important policies related to the economy and finance" (Gall 2005: 156–7).

[53] Abs wrote to Adenauer on March 13, 1958 to inform him about the OECD Convention and offer his advice; Adenauer's Chief of Staff responded on April 11, 1958. Schutz privater Auslandsinvestitionen und des privaten Eigentums im Ausland (Protection of Private Foreign Investment and Private Property Abroad). DE B102/130141.

[54] In a government meeting discussing the BIT draft, an official did not like the term "die Funktionen von Kapitalanlagen" and proposes "die zweckgemäße Ausnutzung von Kapitalanlagen," which is rejected because of the English translation. Aufzeichnung über die Hausbesprechung (Record of the Internal Discussion), March 11, 1959. DE B102/27082.

[55] Minutes of a meeting with Dr. Krebs, March 20, 1958, subject: "Entwurf einer internationalen Konvention zum gegenseitigen Schutz privater Vermögensrechte im Ausland (Draft International Convention on the Protection of Private Investment Abroad)." DE B102/130141.

That same year, 1958, British officials recognized this distinction between a hesitant German government and an enthusiastic Hermann Abs, noting that, "German Government spokesmen, while expressing sympathy with the objects of the Abs Convention, have not committed themselves to supporting it."[56] Even the conduct of Ludwig Erhard, the Minister for Economy mentioned earlier, exemplifies this benevolent distance approach: Erhard may in principle have supported the Abs Draft, but he let Abs know it was not his top priority. When Abs wrote to Erhard inviting him to attend a talk by Hartley Shawcross about the Promotion of Private Investments in Foreign Countries,[57] Erhard wrote back that he was pleased to be invited and was interested in the topic, but had no time to participate.[58]

Another issue that exemplifies the "benevolent distance" approach is the settlement of investment disputes. Abs believed that legal machinery was crucial. In a 1957 speech, Abs presented a convoluted version of the argument that there is no right without a remedy. He observed that:

> numerous bilateral treaties of commerce and friendship, particularly those entered into by the US, contain clauses that try to safeguard the rights and interests of the citizens of the contracting parties and assure fair treatment of foreign capital. In practice these clauses often do not work. The main reason is, again, that no effective machinery exists for their implementation.[59]

The Abs Draft provides both states and individuals with standing[60] in front of an international court for questions of law,[61] and an arbitration tribunal for compensation questions or lesser disputes.[62] Abs also promoted serious enforcement measures, including refusing new private or public loans.[63] He was against investment insurance as a means of resolving disputes,[64] and

[56] Confidential memo, "IMF/IBRD—Thirteenth Annual Meeting: Protection of Foreign Investors, October 1, 1958." UK T 236/5430–1.

[57] Letter from Hermann J. Abs to Herrn Professor Dr. Ludwig Erhard, October 28, 1959. DE B102/130141.

[58] Letter from Dr. Ludwig Erhard to Herrn Hermann J. Abs, December 7, 1959. DE B102/130141.

[59] Abs 1957: 75.

[60] Article IX (2), International Convention for the Mutual Protection of Private Property in Foreign Countries 1957. UK T 236/5429.

[61] Article X (1), International Convention for the Mutual Protection of Private Property in Foreign Countries 1957. UK T 236/5429.

[62] Article X (2), International Convention for the Mutual Protection of Private Property in Foreign Countries 1957. UK T 236/5429.

[63] Abs 1957: 77.

[64] "It does not serve the purpose for governments of capital-exporting countries to offer state guarantees against political risks abroad" (Abs 1957: 76).

found bilateral treaties to be insufficient protection.[65] As some readers will know, the system of investment protection that German officials produced in 1959 (when Abs was at the height of his influence) was bilateral treaties backed by insurance. German officials did not disregard Abs' ideas, but they saw investor–state arbitration as impossible to create. They also believed arbitration was compatible with insurance, as elaborated below in the section on insurance.

German officials told Abs they could not accommodate his wish for individuals to have standing against a foreign state in front of an arbitration tribunal. In February 1959, a senior German official met Abs' deputy, Paul Krebs, and his notes on Article 8 of the draft BIT ("access to the International Court of Justice or an ad hoc arbitration tribunal") are unambiguous. He noted that, "Dr. Krebs deemed it to be essential that this access is not only open for states, but also particularly for private persons in the event of opinion disputes about the interpretation or application of the treaty under international law."[66] A month later, in his formal minutes about the BIT blueprint, the same official wrote: "The wish of Dr. Krebs to enable private individuals to appeal to arbitration judges cannot be satisfied."[67] From this official's notes, the reason why the German government could not implement Krebs' wish was that individuals did not have standing before the ICJ. These German officials were among the most expert in the world, but without the ICSID Convention, they did not see how to add individual standing to their investment treaties. This is strong evidence that without the ICSID Convention and the ICSID Secretariat, investor–state arbitration would not have been added to investment treaties. Despite the efforts of Krebs and Abs to get individuals standing in the German model BIT, the final draft is identical to the first draft: state–state arbitration at the ICJ. This episode exemplifies the chapter's argument: investor involvement is not what determined the type of investment protection that emerged. Investor–state arbitration did not emerge because Abs (or investors generally) wanted it to; it emerged because Broches (or the World Bank generally) found a way to make it possible.

[65] "Bilateral intergovernmental treaties, too, do not suffice to create an effective protection of foreign investments" (Abs 1957: 76).

[66] Entwurf einer Mustervereinbarung über Kapitalanlagen vom 2.2.1959 (Draft model on investments of February 2, 1959); Stellungnahme von Bankdirektor Dr. Krebs zu dem Entwurf einer Mustervereinbarung (Statement by Bank Director Dr. Krebs on the Draft Model Agreement). DE B102/27082.

[67] Aufzeichnung über die Hausbesprechung (Record of the Internal Discussion), March 11, 1959. DE B102/27082.

Transnational Investor Coordination: Abs, Shawcross, and the APPI

The urbane and cosmopolitan Abs was at the center of an international network of bankers and investors. Abs and his society were part of a network of investment protection organizations collectively known as the Association for the Promotion and Protection of Private Foreign Investments (or APPI, its French acronym). I have not been able to access membership records, but available evidence suggests that the APPI had a small, elite membership, mainly in Switzerland and Germany.[68] Its two main parts appear to be Abs' Society and the Geneva branch, which was headed by an American lawyer living in Geneva, Michael Brandon.[69] The APPI sent out bulletins that informed members of developments related to the protection of investment.[70] APPI members were well-informed and there are instances in which this elite network did serve as a conduit for information between governments. For example, an American official's letter to a German official somehow made it to Abs' deputy, who then passed it through APPI links to the President of Credit Suisse, who gave it a Swiss official, where it circulated through the Swiss government.[71] Apart from a rare appearance like this, however, the APPI is not mentioned much, and almost never appears in US or UK archives.

What, or rather, *who* does appear in the British archives is a figure as singular, cultured, and commanding as Abs—Hartley Shawcross, an acquaintance of Abs and his equal in stature and experience. Although the APPI network was concentrated in Germany and Switzerland, that was no problem for Shawcross, who spoke fluent German (his father was a scholar of Goethe and Schiller).[72] Shawcross was exceptionally distinguished: he was best known for his stirring five-hour opening speech at Nuremberg, where he was lead British prosecutor, but he had also been the Attorney General of the UK,

[68] My main source of information about the APPI was a file on their activities in the Swiss archives. CH C.41.124.5.3.

[69] Brandon (1960: 125–9) provides a contemporary summary of how the Abs–Shawcross drafting intersected with similar initiatives in the Council of Europe and other public and private organizations. He notes that by 1959, the idea of an individual having standing had been put forward forcefully in a Council of Europe report on an investment statute and guarantee fund for African development, and in a report from a British Parliamentary Group's Commission on a World Investment Convention.

[70] APPI American Bulletin, Report No. 45, Recent Events of Interest (July, August, September 1963). CH C.41.124.5.2.

[71] Series of letters between April 14, 1964 and April 27, 1964. CH C.41.124.5.2.

[72] For instance, Shawcross gave a lecture to Abs' Society in Cologne, December 7, 1959, subject: "Die Förderung internationaler Investitionen (The Promotion of International Investments)." Published in: Vortragsreihe des Deutschen Industrieinstituts (Series of lectures of the German Institute for Industry) Nr. 10, pg 1–4, March 8, 1960.

principal British delegate to the United Nations, and President of the Board of Trade. He served as a Member of Parliament from 1945 to 1958 and was made a life peer as Lord Shawcross in 1959. Like Abs, Shawcross had extensive international contacts as well as access to the highest levels of government domestically.

Shawcross also had experience with expropriation: he had acted in several of the postwar oil arbitrations, including as counsel for AIOC/BP in the Abadan Refinery case discussed in Chapter two.[73] During the discussion of the Shawcross Draft, British officials referred to him as "counsel for Shell," where he served as director until 1972.[74] Like Abs, the frustrations Shawcross had experienced previously shaped his advocacy. In the AIOC or Abadan case, the ICJ decided it did not have jurisdiction. Shawcross was displeased with this decision, and ensured it would not happen again in his draft, published just five years after the Abadan proceedings. The first page in the Shawcross Draft booklet has a section entitled "Judicial settlement: its prime importance."[75] Yet the judicial settlement to which Shawcross refers is not investor–state arbitration, it is the ICJ. Article 6 on the settlement of disputes is a straightforward state–state clause: "Any dispute between the Parties as to the application or interpretation of the Convention, not satisfactorily adjusted by diplomacy, shall be submitted to the International Court of Justice, unless the Parties agree to settlement by some other specific means."[76] The Shawcross Draft does not include investor–state arbitration.

Shawcross prepared his draft as a more feasible alternative to the Abs Convention. He knew that British officials "regard[ed] the Abs Convention as unnegotiable as it stands."[77] After promulgating his draft, Shawcross wrote to a British official that he was "hoping to persuade Herr Abs to substitute this draft for his much more elaborate one which I agree is hardly negotiable."[78] British officials did prefer the Shawcross Draft, noting, for instance, that "unlike the German draft Convention, it recognizes that the situation is changed in time of war."[79] Yet in the UK, the idea of a multilateral draft did not have the same resonance as in Germany. In fact, the idea was dead on arrival: the British government was grappling with a serious balance of payments problem, which meant the government could not uphold several of the standards in the Shawcross or Abs Drafts (discussed in the next paragraph), and was

[73] Elm 1992: 267.

[74] Convention on Foreign Investments (Lawyers' Draft) (undated, likely June 1958). UK T 236/5436.

[75] Draft Convention on Foreign Investments, March 1958. UK T 236/5436.

[76] Article 6, Draft Convention on Foreign Investments, March 1958. UK T 236/5436.

[77] Letter from Leslie Rowan to Cavendish-Bentinck, February 26, 1958. UK T 236/5436.

[78] Letter from Hartley Shawcross to Leslie Rowan, March 31, 1958. UK T 236/5436.

[79] Letter from L. Pliatsky to Mr. Grant, April 14, 1958. UK T 236/5436.

unwilling to take any action that might facilitate outward investment. After listing these and other realities, a British official wrote to Shawcross that "these facts, taken together, appear to constitute an insuperable obstacle to accession by the United Kingdom to any multilateral convention on the lines of the Shawcross draft."[80]

The British government found arbitration to be a non-starter.

> The central question seems to me a simple one: are we prepared to agree to compulsory arbitration in advance in respect of any dispute about property in its widest sense owned by foreigners? The answer, I submit, is "No." As long as this stands, there is not much point in discussing drafts.[81]

The reason for this strong opposition is because the British government was thinking of itself as a respondent: since a multilateral convention at the OECD was proposed, they used Germany as the hypothetical other country in their examples. For instance, "Sir Hartley Shawcross, as Counsel for Shell, is interested in the protection of UK-controlled subsidiaries abroad... The corollary, of course, is that foreign-controlled subsidiaries in the UK would be similarly covered and disputes arising could be referred to international arbitration. This is not acceptable to the Treasury."[82] These comments echo Wälde's observation (mentioned in footnote 32 in Chapter two) that the Calvo Doctrine has long been the maxim of capital-exporting countries when they think of themselves as respondents.

Shawcross, despite his prior experience in government, was held at a distance by British officials; publicly this was similar to the benevolent distance that the German government accorded Abs. Mirroring the German government's treatment of the Abs Draft, the British government refused to endorse or officially support the Shawcross Draft. Instead, the Treasury was instructed to "prepare a reply to Sir Hartley, mentioning some of the points of detail which had been discussed, but nevertheless wishing him well in his efforts, without undertaking or implying that H.M. Government would take the lead in sponsoring the Draft Convention."[83] Behind the scenes, British officials were wary of Shawcross. When he overplayed his hand, claiming support from the World Bank when British officials knew better, an official wrote, likely in jest, that "perhaps wishful thinking has tended to exaggerate their idea of the Bank's intentions."[84] When he touted the support his Draft received from

[80] Letter from Sir Gilbert Laithwaite to Sir Hartley Shawcross (undated, likely June 1958). UK T 236/5436.

[81] Note from A. T. K. Grant, April 15 1958. UK T 236/5436.

[82] Convention on Foreign Investments (Lawyers' Draft) (undated, likely June 1958). UK T 236/5436.

[83] Note of a Discussion in the Treasury on May 1, 1958, "Protection of Foreign Investments: Draft Convention prepared by Sir Hartley Shawcross and a group of lawyers." UK T 236/5436.

[84] Response from Peter Reilly to Hester Boothroyd, August 4, 1961. UK T 312/251.

developing countries and asked the British government to make it a Commonwealth initiative, British officials refused to provide any public support and noted that the only developing country supporter of his draft was a former student of his, who had become the Prime Minister of Malaysia.[85] Their wariness was likely exacerbated by his reputation at the time: Shawcross was initially a Labour politician, but in the 1950s had begun to express disapproval of Labour policies, and was considered a turncoat, known by the derisive nickname "Sir Shortly Floorcross" in anticipation of his switch to the Conservative side of the House of Commons. However warily, British officials still acted on requests from Shawcross after he was raised to the House of Lords, at one point even noting: "If we do nothing, Lord Shawcross will very likely write to the Chancellor."[86]

The Shawcross Draft was passed to the OEEC to be merged with the Abs Draft, despite neither of these drafts having official support from their governments. The British government was clear-eyed about the absence of support. In a 1959 briefing note, the main British official handling investment protection wrote: "The Chancellor should be aware, however, that so far no Government of an OEEC country has declared positive for these proposals... [and] the US and Canada have expressed definite opposition."[87] These drafts did not have widespread backing from investors either; while the Abs–Shawcross Draft that emerged in 1960 was primarily the result of private initiative, it was an elite, small network still largely centered around Abs. The Abs–Shawcross Draft had not been driven by a groundswell of support from actual investors. It had been driven by a few exceptional individuals with personal experience of expropriation.

"SUSPICIOUS APATHY": GOVERNMENTS AND THE OECD DRAFT

The Abs–Shawcross Draft officially became an intergovernmental Draft Convention on the Protection of Foreign Property when it was presented to the OECD Council in November 1962.[88] The OECD Draft contained an Annex that outlined an Arbitral Tribunal which gave a national of one party the

[85] Letters between Shawcross, Laithwaite, and Pliatzsky, June 1958. UK T236/5436.

[86] Letter from Hester Boothroyd to Mrs. Hedley-Miller, on the International Bank and Arbitration, November 7, 1961. UK T 312/251.

[87] Notes by L. Pliatzsky "World Investment Convention—brief for the Chancellor," July 23, 1959. UK T 236/5436.

[88] Background Paper for the OECD Ministerial Meeting, Paris, December 2–3, 1964. US 595219 Box 2.

standing to bring a claim directly against a state party.[89] On the surface, it looked like investor–state arbitration attached to a multilateral code would soon be a legal reality.

Initial American and British Opposition

Underneath the veneer of progress, the prospects for the OECD Draft to succeed were never good. Initially, the Draft was imperiled by strong American opposition and British concerns. Both of these countries would change their positions and conditionally support the draft after 1965, but their initial skepticism weakened the Draft's prospects.

American support was considered a *sine qua non* for the Convention's success.[90] Early American opposition was unequivocal, as this 1961 position paper prepared for US officials makes clear:

> [D]uring the second half of 1960 the United States found it necessary to state our unwillingness to adhere to an investment convention of the nature planned. Our objections were based on the fact that a convention limited to the OECD Members would be meaningless; thus, the proposed convention would have significance only if presented to LDC's for acceptance. Drafting such a convention without non-Member LDC participation would be tantamount to handling LDC's a fait accompli and imply an element of coercion.[91]

This stance likely reflected, on the one hand, the progressive tendencies of the Kennedy-era State Department and, on the other, the strategic imperative of cultivating friendly relations with LDCs in the context of the Cold War. Teaming up with former colonizers on an instrument that would be perceived as a tool to protect colonial-era property arrangements was not an effective way to compete for allies against the "anti-Imperialist" Soviet Union—a reality likely not lost on the US government.[92]

The British government took a more ambiguous public position at the OECD, but internal documents suggest that their support was fragile, at best. Due to their balance of payments difficulties during these years, the British government could not participate in any endeavor that they believed

[89] For analysis of the draft's dispute resolution provisions, see Schwarzenberger (1969: 123–34).

[90] "They (France, Germany, and the UK) all agree that adherence by the US is a *sine qua non* to the success of the Convention." Background Paper for the OECD Ministerial Meeting, Paris, December 2–3, 1964. US 595219 Box 2.

[91] Position Paper for the OECD Ministerial Meeting, Paris, November 16–17, 1961, Convention on Protection of Foreign Property. US 595219 Box 2.

[92] The American government's response to the Suez Canal crisis shows the government was wary of aligning itself with former colonizers. So too, does the American government's initial conduct with regard to the Abadan nationalization discussed in Chapter two.

might facilitate outward investment; in addition, their exchange control policies meant they could not comply with or support free transfer provisions.[93] The Treasury also noted they could not necessarily adhere to establishment clauses: "at present the United Kingdom reserves and exercises the right to frustrate certain kinds of investment by non-residents."[94] There was a further difficulty—potential future nationalizations by the British government. One memo described "our somewhat exceptional position as a major capital-exporting country in which further measures of nationalization are a real possibility although the types of acquisitions in question are by no means confined to cases of nationalization in the usual sense."[95] Finally, the British government had grave concerns about their ability to participate in "provisions for the reference to international arbitration of disputes over compensation paid on… foreign-owned rights or property."[96]

Other governments were aware of American and British opposition to the OECD Draft. A Swiss official drafted a report in 1962 that discussed, in precise and accurate detail, British opposition to the OECD Draft as well as the Greek, Turkish, and American opposition.[97] Greece and Turkey's opposition stemmed from their recent history as importers of capital from other OECD countries. Like the Swiss, German officials had doubted for years that the US would participate in a multilateral convention, with skepticism expressed as early as December 1957.[98] By February 1961, American opposition was so well-known that a German official used it almost rhetorically in a letter on investment insurance written to Abs' deputy: "You know yourself the American position towards the idea of a Magna Carta."[99]

In spite of American opposition and British hesitance, in 1962, OECD governments began to consult developing countries about the possibility of

[93] "The United Kingdom itself would in all likelihood find difficulty in two particular respects in subscribing to even the less ambitious of the various draft conventions… First, there would be the difficulty of accepting provisions at variance with our Exchange Control policy." Anglo-German Economic Committee, Sixth Session, London, July 1958, Protection of Foreign Investors. UK T 236/5436.

[94] Appendix: Protection of Foreign Investments, Exchange Control Aspects of the Swiss and German Draft Conventions, July 1958. UK T 236/5436.

[95] Anglo-German Economic Committee, Sixth Session, London, July 1958, Protection of Foreign Investors. UK T 236/5436.

[96] Anglo-German Economic Committee, Sixth Session, London, July 1958, Protection of Foreign Investors. UK T 236/5436.

[97] Protection of Investments in International Law, by Dr. E. Diez, Head of the Legal Service of the Swiss Foreign Office (US government translation of a lecture delivered in German before the Swiss Society of International Law, Berne, November 24, 1962). CH C.41.124.5.2.

[98] Internal memo, December 1957, subject: Maßnahmen zum Schutz von privaten Auslandsinvestitionen (Measures for the Protection of Private Foreign Investment). DE B102/130141.

[99] Letter from Harry Gorn to Herrn Dr. Paul Krebs, February 23, 1961. DE B102/47640.

their adherence to the Draft. An American briefing note observes, "despite [the Europeans'] desire to get the Convention moving, they are coming to recognize that the participation of a representative group of LDC's is not only desirable but necessary."[100]

Consultations with Developing Countries

After the 1962 Draft was declassified, the largest capital-exporting OECD countries (France, Germany, the UK, and the US) then consulted developing countries about it. In the summer of 1964, "the Secretary-General of the OECD asked representatives of France, Germany, the UK and the US to meet with him to discuss the results of the soundings these governments had taken."[101]

The US notes that responses to their request "were scanty—those countries which did respond were largely noncommittal."[102] The other three governments had received more responses but "the results still did not indicate positive support of the draft Convention but rather showed a lack of interest on the part of these countries."[103] British briefing notes, which featured more acerbic wit, described this lack of interest as "suspicious apathy": "the draft has conspicuously failed. Soundings taken by H.M. Government of Commonwealth countries in 1963 and 1964 revealed a general reaction of suspicious apathy, which is evidently shared in other developing countries."[104]

The initial records from the British and German consultations were sent to the Swiss government by a banker. Table 3.2 below lists the reactions of developing country governments to the OECD Convention in 1963, according to the British and German governments.[105]

As some of the lines in the table suggest, by 1963, bilateral treaties were already supplanting the OECD Draft. This development would gather momentum and eventually prove fatal to the Draft itself.

[100] Background Paper for the OECD Ministerial Meeting, Paris, December 2–3, 1964. US 595219 Box 2.

[101] Background Paper on the Draft Convention on Protection of Foreign Property (prepared November 23, 1964). US 595219 Box 2.

[102] Background Paper on the Draft Convention on Protection of Foreign Property (prepared November 23, 1964). US 595219 Box 2.

[103] Background Paper on the Draft Convention on Protection of Foreign Property (prepared November 23, 1964) US 595219 Box 2.

[104] IMF/IBRD. Twenty-Second Annual Meeting, Settlement of Investment Disputes: Investment Insurance and Protection, Brief by the Treasury. UK FCO 48/145.

[105] Letter from Robert Dunant to E. Diez, July 8, 1963. CH C.41.124.5.2.

Table 3.2. OECD Convention—Reactions of Developing Countries (as of July 1963)[106]

Country	British Report	German Report
Argentina	At present adverse	Slightly more positive
Australia	Non-committal but believed might ultimately be in favor	Not collected
Bolivia	Might accede once the US is in support	Positive response not to be expected
Brazil	At present negative	Same (as British)
Ceylon	At present negative	Not collected
Chile	Uncertain	Uncertain, but more favorable than the British suggest
Congo	Uncertain though negotiable	Both statements more or less concurring
Gabon	Likely to be in favor	Less favorable
Ghana	In principle interested in the Convention	Substantially the same (as British)
Guinea	Averse to the multilateral approach but ready to conclude bilateral treaties on similar terms	Same (as British)
Honduras	Might, if appropriately influenced, take a favorable attitude	Essentially the same (as British)
India	Equivocal. Likely to support principles of the Convention but finding Constitutional difficulties regarding arbitration provision. Likely to prefer bilateral agreements to the OECD Convention	No prospects for a multilateral agreement. (Indians were avoiding us)
Jamaica	Favorable	Same (as British)
Lebanon	At present unlikely to find a need to accede in view of adequate constitutional provisions	Same (as British)
Liberia	In principle preferring the bilateral approach, but attitude might change in favor of OECD Convention if appropriate influence is exerted	Same (as British)
Libya	Equivocal	Same (as British)
Madagascar	Likely to be favorable	Essentially the same (as British)
Malaya	Likely to be favorable	Same (as British)
Morocco	Believed would be favorable if Convention were concluded outside OECD	Essentially the same (as British)

(*continued*)

[106] Information from the Haager Freundeskreis (Hague Circle of Friends), "OECD Konvention—Reaktionen von Entwicklungsländern gemäß englischer und deutscherseits eingeholter Informationen (OECD Convention—Reactions of Developing Countries According to English and German Information)," included in Letter from Robert Dunant to E. Diez, July 8 1963. CH C.41.124.5.2.

Table 3.2. Continued

Country	British Report	German Report
New Zealand	Favorable	Not collected
Nicaragua	Likely to be favorable	Same (as British)
Nigeria	Not unfavorable. Appropriate influence might produce a positive attitude	Same (as British)
Pakistan	Probably favorable	Same (as British)
Peru	Negative	Same (as British)
Philippines	Probably favorable	Same (as British)
Rhodesia	In favor	For political reasons, no reaction is expected
Somalia	Likely to be negative	Positive reaction to the substance, but they appear unlikely to participate in an OECD initiative
Sudan	Probably favorable	In principle, opposition from officials and private bodies
Tanganyika	Favorable	Same (as British)
Thailand	Likely to prefer bilateral treaties rather than the OECD Convention	Almost the same (as British)
Venezuela	At present unfavorable, but possibility of change in attitude if appropriate influence is exerted through private efforts	Substantially the same, somewhat less favorable. Referenced the North American–Venezuelan Investment Guarantee Agreement

Germany and Switzerland Prefer Bilateral Treaties

Between 1962 and 1965, support for the OECD Draft from the Swiss and German governments dwindled. Through their experience negotiating BITs, Swiss and German officials learned that BITs were an easier, more strategic means of achieving the standards of investment protection they sought.

Swiss internal documents illustrate this lesson clearly. In a November 1962 speech, the main Swiss official responsible for investment protection was ambivalent as to whether a multilateral or a bilateral approach was better. He observed that Switzerland generally preferred multilateral initiatives, but if enough BITs had been signed then a multilateral solution might become redundant.[107] By March 1963, the government position had changed: Swiss officials all agreed that no action should be taken to promote the Draft, and

[107] Protection of Investments in International Law, by Dr. E. Diez, Head of the Legal Service of the Swiss Foreign Office (US Government translation of a lecture delivered in German before the Swiss Society of International Law, Bern, November 24, 1962). CH C.41.124.5.2.

instead they should intensify their efforts to conclude BITs.[108] In September 1963, the same official wrote that the convention is, on the one hand, the maximum possible for a multinational convention, but, on the other, the minimum possible in BITs.[109] By November 1963, that Swiss official was arguing that the government should not promote the OECD Draft because it would necessarily include compromises, and these compromises would weaken the Swiss bargaining position in BIT negotiations. He observed that the already concluded BITs are better than the multilateral convention, and if Switzerland supports the convention then future negotiating partners would prefer the "minimalistic solutions of the convention."[110] This position held, and was expressed in similar terms in March 1965: Switzerland had "concluded a large number of BITs, which are better than the convention," and therefore the government had "limited" incentives to promote a multilateral approach.[111]

It soon became clear to others within the OECD that bilateral treaties were replacing the Draft. By 1965, American officials at the OECD had learned of the Europeans' diminishing support:

> Although several European OECD members have been anxious to obtain ratification of the Convention, it appears that some of them, particularly Germany, which initiated the Convention, have undergone a change of heart and do not wish to go as far as the present US position. The Germans are concerned that opening the Convention for signature and possible lack of acceptance of it would endanger German bilateral agreements with more than 30 countries.[112]

By 1967, it was clear that bilateral treaties had outpaced the Draft Convention. Bowing to this reality, in 1967 the OECD Secretary General described the Draft Convention as a model for bilateral treaties: he "[s]tressed Draft was only a model; [which] could be modified for use as bilateral treaty."[113] By the late 1960s, it seemed that bilateral treaties were the way forward and that the Draft Convention was, as one British briefing note put it, "dying a harmless though lingering death."[114]

[108] Letter from Micheli to the Swiss Ambassador at the OECD, March 25, 1963. CH C.41.124.5.2.

[109] Internal note from Emanuel Diez, September 23, 1963. CH C 41.124.5.2.

[110] Letter from Micheli to the Swiss Ambassador at the OECD, March 25, 1963. CH C.41.124.5.2.

[111] Letter from E. Diez to the Swiss Ambassador at the OECD, March 1, 1965. CH C41.124.5.2.

[112] Talking Points for the OECD Draft Convention for the Protection of Foreign Property, OECD Ministerial Meeting, November 25–6, 1965. US 595219 Box 3.

[113] Telegram from AmEmbassy Paris to SecState WashDC, February 7, 1967, Subject: Draft Convention Foreign Property. US 595219 Box 13. This supports Schill's argument (2009(a): chapter 4).

[114] IMF/IBRD. Twenty-Second Annual Meeting, Settlement of Investment Disputes: Investment Insurance and Protection, Brief by the Treasury. UK FCO 48/145.

American Business Takes an Interest

The death of the Draft Convention was prolonged by an unexpected development in 1965: American industry groups, which had been inactive until then, got interested. An American memo noted that the US Business and Advisory Committee, an umbrella group for American industry at the OECD, "has recently become more active. It has taken a strong position in favor of the OECD draft Convention on the Protection of Foreign Property."[115] As part of their lobbying efforts, American business figures began passing information from their correspondence with Hermann Abs and his associates to the State Department.[116]

Increased business interest drove a change in American policy.

> US support for the Convention had been conditioned on its utility if subscribed to by a representative group of less-developed countries. This view was challenged by the United States Business and Industry Advisory Committee... [a] compromise has been developed under which the US will support Council acceptance of the Convention in principle...but that ratification by OECD countries will await further efforts to solicit the views of the LDCs vis-à-vis the Convention.[117]

Despite the policy shift, the US government continued to prioritize a "meaningful exchange of views with the developing countries" and was quick to say this exchange of views could "take any of several possible forms and we are not pressing for any particular solution. The important thing is to give the developing countries a chance to state their views and offer constructive amendments or additions."[118]

US support for the Convention had another dimension: toward the late 1960s, American investment in Europe became a sensitive political issue. As one memo in late 1967 put it:

> [T]he US is also aware of and sensitive to the economic, political and psychological problems arising from large-scale investment in Europe. This is particularly the case in...fields...important to countries' security, sovereignty, prestige and industrial development. These considerations are the theme of a recently published French book attracting considerable attention in Europe and abroad—'The American Challenge' (*Le Defi Americain*), by Servan Schreiber.[119]

[115] Background Paper on BIAC (Business and Industry Advisory Committee) for the OECD Ministerial Meeting, Paris, November 25–6, 1965. US 595219 Box 3.

[116] Letter from R. J. Blair to Ulf Siebel, January 31, 1967. (Sent to the Assistant Secretary for Economic Affairs by Emilio Collado, previously a US government official at the time with Esso Europe.) US 595219 Box 13.

[117] Talking Points for the OECD Draft Convention for the Protection of Foreign Property, OECD Ministerial Meeting, Paris, November 25–6, 1965. US 595219 Box 3.

[118] Talking Points for the OECD Draft Convention for the Protection of Foreign Property, OECD Ministerial Meeting, Paris, November 25–6, 1965. US 595219 Box 3.

[119] Talking Points: US Direct Investment in Europe, OECD Ministerial Meeting, Paris, November 30–December 1, 1967. US 595219 Box 4.

The late interest of American industry groups was not enough to turn the tide: although the US government moderated its stance in response to their interest, the Draft was still dying.

KILLING THE OECD DRAFT SOFTLY

Once they realized that the Draft was unlikely to open for ratification or ever emerge as a binding legal document, government officials active in OECD discussions faced a dilemma: how could they end their discussions on this Draft without weakening customary international law regarding investment protection?

Customary International Law Was at Stake

The stakes were high: many officials were concerned that abandoning the Draft would impact understandings of customary international law. In the 1960s, customary international law on investment protection was far from settled.[120] In 1964, the United States Supreme Court noted:

> There are few if any issues in international law today on which opinion seems to be so divided as the limitations on a state's power to expropriate the property of aliens... The disagreement as to relevant international law standards reflects an even more basic divergence between the national interests of capital importing and capital exporting nations.[121]

In this context, finding a way to kill the OECD Draft without weakening investment protection became a priority for officials.

Some officials had anticipated this circumstance. For instance, a 1958 memo from the British Treasury stated: "The United Kingdom have grave doubts whether a worthwhile international convention, (i.e. a multilateral convention between Governments) specifying the protection to be accorded to foreign investors could be negotiated, and think that the process of negotiation might do more harm than good."[122] Along similar lines, a 1963 letter to the Swiss government argued that if the Draft failed, it would degrade investment protection because it could be concluded that the draft did not codify existing norms of international law.[123]

[120] Lowenfeld (2003: 125) observes that the law governing investment was unsettled in 1964. Investment protection was also the subject of a number of resolutions at the General Assembly.

[121] *Banco Nacional de Cuba v. Sabbatino* (US Supreme Court): 428–30. The US Supreme Court refused to get involved with the expropriations of American investors in Cuba.

[122] Confidential memo, IMF/IBRD—Thirteenth Annual Meeting: Protection of Foreign Investors, October 1, 1958. UK T 236/5430–1.

[123] Letter from Dr. Thomas Faist to the Political Department, March 28, 1963. CH C.41.124.5.2.

In terms of the way forward, American officials argued that "the issue is whether to 'approve the Convention in principle' in the Council . . . or whether to sign and ratify the Convention."[124] The difference between these two choices mattered: one would have created binding law, the other would not. Swiss officials saw the decision the same way.[125] A decision was taken in 1966 to pursue a non-binding resolution expressing support for the principles in the Draft Convention—yet even agreeing a non-binding resolution provoked serious discord within the OECD, as the next section shows.

Disagreements over a Resolution

The support of Canada, Denmark, Greece, Norway, Portugal, Spain, Sweden, and Turkey for a resolution was considered uncertain by American officials.[126] Notably, these governments were all historically importers of capital. The exporter–importer divide within the OECD was explicitly referenced in debates. For instance, the representative from Canada explained that the "draft convention created same difficulties for Canada as for some LDC's, since Canada [is a] major capital importer."[127] Most of these governments eventually succumbed to pressure from capital-exporters, and enduring opposition to the resolution was expressed only by Turkey and Spain.

After Turkish officials reported that they would abstain, officials from certain European countries made explicit threats. American officials summarized the events: "France, Switzerland, and Belgian Chairman hit hard at Turkish position. Swiss representative said his country will be watching what position is taken by Turks . . . Chairman and US tried to remove blackmail aspect from any pressure on Turkey."[128] A month later, another telegram back to Washington suggests that the Turkish government was still under pressure to support the Resolution, and shows how important Spanish support was considered:

> UK put matter more bluntly, saying if Turks don't agree, they will be losers. Spanish abstention, however, could cast doubt on value of the draft Convention. UK feels effort must be made to change Spanish position from abstention to

[124] Memo (likely to Mr. Leddy and Mr. Hinton, but recipient unnamed), OECD Convention on Private Property, April 7, 1966. US 595219 Box 5.

[125] Telegram from the Swiss Delegation to the OECD to Diez, May 5, 1966. CH C.41.124.5.2.

[126] Telegrams from January to March 1967. US 595219 Box 5. Not all these governments had expressed opposition. Norway and Sweden had said they could only accept the resolution if there were no abstentions, and some of the others had not yet received instructions from their capitals.

[127] Telegram from AmEmbassy Paris to SecState WashDC, February 7, 1967, Subject: Draft Convention Foreign Property. US 595219 Box 5. The official also noted that Canada's federal system might create problems.

[128] Telegram from AmEmbassy Paris to SecState WashDC, February 17, 1967, Subject: Draft Convention Protection Foreign Property. US 595219 Box 5.

acceptance of Resolution.... If Turks continue maintain abstention under these circumstances, quote blood will be on their own heads unquote.[129]

The Spanish government had two reasons for abstaining: the ongoing Barcelona Traction case,[130] and because it did not think the Resolution would matter for attracting investment.[131] The Spanish Ambassador to the OECD explained to an American official that "the atmosphere is clouded very much by a particular case, which he identified as the Barcelona Traction case and which I gather involves a Belgian investment in Barcelona. He intimated the Spanish experience with this investment had exerted a restraining influence on some Spanish lawyers."[132] Despite repeated envoys to Spanish officials, the Spanish abstained from the Resolution,[133] as did Turkey, and Sweden noted that it might not be in agreement on all details.[134]

The World Bank: Still Not Interested

Amid discussions of how to wind down the OECD Draft, the US government tried again to interest the World Bank—in 1967, the US government made repeated requests to have the World Bank take over the OECD Draft Convention.[135] These interactions are analyzed in later chapters, but to foreshadow that analysis, World Bank officials repeatedly refused to take over the OECD Draft. This occurrence directly contradicts conventional accounts, which suggest that when states (as principals), and particularly the US government, as the largest shareholder and an actor known to wield formal and informal influence over the World Bank, make a request of an international organization (its agent), the agent complies and enacts the request. With regard to investment protection, the World Bank displayed considerable autonomy in refusing the American requests.

[129] Telegram from AmEmbassy Paris to SecState Washington DC, March 17, 1967, subject: Draft Resolution on Draft Convention Protection Foreign Property. US 595219 Box 13.

[130] Memo of conversation with Enrique Puig, April 5, 1967, subject: Recent Spanish Actions Relating to the Invisibles Committee. US 595219 Box 13.

[131] Reporting that the Spanish Ambassador had said, "Spain is a country sufficiently attractive to foreign investors so that the Spanish Government and its citizens prefer to make separate individual deals with investors and feel they have something with which to bargain." Letter from Philip H. Trezise to Frank Taylor, March 17, 1967. US 595219 Box 13.

[132] Letter from Philip H. Trezise to Frank Taylor, March 17, 1967. US 595219 Box 13.

[133] Telegram from the Department of State to the AmEmbassy Paris, July 11, 1967, Subject: Resolution on Protection of Foreign Property. US 595219 Box 13.

[134] OECD Resolution, October 12, 1967. US 595219 Box 13.

[135] For instance, a telegram from Secretary of State Dean Rusk (subject: OECD Draft Convention on the Protection of Foreign Property) in November 1967 states: "Concur with mission view para 1 reftel that it would be useful try again to interest IBRD in Draft Convention... USG Officer together with US Exec. Dir. will discuss possibility informally with George Woods in near future." US 595219 Box 13.

Even more remarkably, ten years earlier, British and German officials discussed the possibility of asking the World Bank to take over the then-Abs Draft. These officials self-censored rather than ask the Bank; they decided not "to undertake the probably vain attempt to convince the management of World Bank and IFC [International Finance Corporation] of the advantages of an international convention about the protection of foreign property."[136] This behavior also directly contradicts conventional accounts: the principals (governments) are not theorized to be afraid to ask their agents (international organizations) to undertake tasks. As further evidence of the autonomy of the World Bank, one way that Abs' deputy tried to lobby the German government to take action on the Abs Draft was by telling a German official that the President of the World Bank (whom the German government knew to be initially unenthusiastic) was now interested.[137]

A Final Plea to the United Nations Conference on Trade and Development (UNCTAD)

A final American proposal for ending the OECD Draft was to introduce it to UNCTAD II, held in 1968.[138] American officials discussed the plan on multiple occasions during the autumn of 1967, before deciding that opening up discussions of the Draft at UNCTAD II would hurt the cause of investment protection.

The plan was for American officials to make an "informal suggestion" to a Dutch former official, Dirk Stikker, that he include the Draft Convention in the report he was drafting on private enterprise for UNCTAD.[139] American officials argued, "this course of action has one possible advantage: the Draft Convention would be part of the basic documentation for the Conference, and therefore probably less susceptible to attack by the LDCs than if it were a developed country initiative."[140] American officials had discussed this approach

136 Report on a Meeting between the German and British Executive Directors on the Issue of Investment Protection, by Prof. Dr. O. Donner, December 16, 1957. DE B102/130141.

137 Minutes from a meeting with Dr. Krebs, March 20, 1958, subject: "Entwurf einer internationalen Konvention zum gegenseitigen Schutz privater Vermögensrechte im Ausland (Draft International Convention on the Protection of Private Property Abroad)." DE B102/130141.

138 UNCTAD I was held in 1964, and it would only later become a permanent organization (UNCTAD 1964).

139 The Stikker Report's formal title is "The Role of Private Enterprise in Investment and Promotion of Exports in Developing Countries." Memo from John Leddy to Mr. Rostow, subject: "UNCTAD and the OECD Draft Convention on the Protection of Foreign Property, 31 July 1967." US 595219 Box 13.

140 Memo from John Leddy to Mr. Rostow, subject: "UNCTAD and the OECD Draft Convention on the Protection of Foreign Property, 31 July 1967." US 595219 Box 13.

with US industry groups, who expressed support.[141] This sort of influence, in which the US government consults with industry and then throws its weight around to influence an international organization, is what we would expect if conventional explanations hold. The problem is that it did not work. Stikker refused to include the Draft Convention in his report: "As for the OECD Property Convention, Stikker said there was no chance at all of getting UNCTAD II to endorse it. He doubted whether the Convention should even be discussed at the Conference."[142] With that, the OECD Convention was allowed to die, although its principles and the idea of an international court or arbitration would live on through the work of other actors.

INSURANCE

The World Bank released its first proposal for a multilateral investment insurance agency in 1948. By 1962, there were more than a dozen detailed proposals circulating. It is extremely puzzling that none of these proposals were realized during the 1960s. Out of the three multilateral options, insurance had the most widespread investor support. It also had support from powerful states: the US government was willing to take the lead in creating a multilateral insurance agency. Conventional accounts cannot explain why insurance did not come into existence during the 1960s. If investor demand and backing from powerful states determine outcomes, it would have been created. Instead, the failed negotiations on insurance in the 1960 illustrate my argument: the intensity of involvement from investors and support from powerful states are not what determined the outcome of the critical juncture. The reason a multilateral insurance agency did not emerge in the early 1960s is because the World Bank discouraged action, and refused to play an agenda-setting and brokering role on insurance, despite repeated requests from powerful states to do so.

Investors Display Strong Interest in a Multilateral Insurance Agency

The proposal for a multilateral insurance institution had strong support from the private sector. Investment insurance proposals were discussed at several

[141] Memo from John Leddy to Mr. Rostow, subject: "UNCTAD and the OECD Draft Convention on the Protection of Foreign Property, 31 July 1967." US 595219 Box 13.

[142] Memo of conversation, subject: "Mr Stikker's report for UNCTAD on the role of private investment in the developing countries, 3 November 1967." US 595219 Box 13.

annual meetings of the ICC during the 1960s. The most prominent proposal was associated with E. H. (Ernst Henri) van Eeghen, a Dutch banker. After the 1960 ICC annual meeting, van Eeghen wrote that "practically everybody agreed to this [the necessity of an international guarantee institution to cover the political risks of private capital]" and claimed a wide base of support, arguing that "the leaders of the Indian, Pakistan, Ceylonese, Thailand, and Japanese delegations fully agreed with my views," as did Hermann Abs' deputy.[143] Van Eeghen energetically canvassed industry groups and key officials in Europe and America afterwards.[144] At the ICC conference in March 1963, the "promotion of private international investments through the adoption of a multilateral investment insurance scheme" was again discussed in a prime slot.[145]

The idea of a multilateral insurance agency was advanced in other investor organizations as well. For instance, in a 1961 conference, the Chairman of the European Industrial Federations, Marcus Wallenberg, also proposed the creation of a new international guarantee fund to cover political risks.[146] The idea of a multilateral insurance agency commanded sustained interest from private industry, and serious resources were devoted to developing and advancing proposals—more than for a code, and certainly far more than for a standalone arbitration convention.

Even Hermann Abs believed that investment insurance was effective at facilitating investment. "When investors do go into such areas ['high-risk' countries] it is often because of state guarantees granted by their own governments,"[147] he argued. The reason he preferred a code and arbitration was that he wanted the risk of expropriation to be shifted onto the shoulders of the countries receiving capital. This shows that Hermann Abs was not interested in promoting investment—he was interested in protecting it. His reasoning again emerges out of the German Second World War experience:

> Through governmental guarantees they relieve traders of a large part of the political and transfer risk. In the post-war years, when it was necessary to reconstruct the European economy and in particular to start exports going, this kind of self-reinsurance was doubtless necessary. Now however that this phase is past, one is bound to feel serious doubt whether that system ought still to be

[143] Letter from E. H. van Eeghen to Ministerialdirektor Dr. von Spindler, December 21, 1960. DE B102/47640.

[144] Letter from Dr. Henckel (recipient unnamed) subject: "Anreise für Kapitalinvestitionen in Entwicklungsländern (Trip regarding capital investment in developing countries)," August 14, 1961. DE B102/47640.

[145] Letter from P. J. Pointet to Emanuel Diez, March 29, 1963. CH C.41.124.5.2.

[146] "Internationaler Garantiefonds? Vorschläge zur internationalen Kreditsicherung auf der Konferenz in San Franzisko (International Guarantee Fund? Proposals for International Loan Guarantee at a Conference in San Francisco)" Handelsblatt, September 14, 1961. DE B102/47640.

[147] Abs 1957: 72.

applied to the same extent as hitherto, and whether the risks ought not by degrees to be put on the shoulders of the receiving countries.[148]

This is a revealing observation: Abs believed that insurance worked—that is, it facilitated investment which assisted with reconstruction and development—but he did not believe that it should be extended to facilitate investment in newly independent countries. Instead, with regard to developing countries, Abs suggested that insurance gave governments an incentive to seize property without facing consequences—a false argument.[149] One reason he made this argument was so that he could argue investment insurance should be tied to a multilateral code.[150] In 1961, the APPI came out with a report that argued that if insurance was made conditional on a country ratifying a multilateral convention, then "far from providing an incentive for bad conduct, the establishment of an organ of this kind [a multilateral insurance agency] could not but favor widespread adherence by the countries to the code of good conduct and their observance of its rules."[151] The rules of conduct they recommend, unsurprisingly, closely resemble the Abs Draft.[152]

Abs had put forward a similar line of argument during the drafting of the German model BIT three years earlier, in 1958. His deputy wrote to an official and argued that countries should be eligible for investment insurance only after ratifying both a bilateral treaty with Germany and the Abs Draft, which Abs believed would soon be adopted by the OEEC.[153] Abs' deputy argued that in order to be eligible for investment guarantees, a country must agree to be subject to dispute settlement by either the ICJ or an arbitration tribunal in the treaty.[154] Abs viewed insurance, arbitration, and a code as complements—all weapons in the armory for investment protection.[155] As the next section shows, he was not alone in this view.

[148] Text of a Speech by Hermann J. Abs, "The Protection of Duly Acquired Rights in International Dealings as a European Duty: Reflections on the Development of the Suez Crisis." UK T 236/5429.

[149] Insurance programs, like the one that emerged decades later at the World Bank, are backed by subrogation and recovery from host countries: governments do make amends.

[150] Letter from Dr. Paul Krebs to Herrn Ministerialdirektor Dr. Hans Henckel, subject: "Plan zur Errichtung eines Internationalen Garantiefonds für Auslandsinvestitionen (Plan for the Establishment of an International Guarantee Fund for Foreign Investments)." February 9, 1961. DE B102/47640.

[151] Report of the Working Committee of the APPI on the Establishment of an International Guarantee Fund. Paris, September 13, 1961. DE B102/47640.

[152] Minutes of the "Vorbereitung der Jahresversammlung von Weltbank, IDA und IFC (Preparation of the World Bank's Annual Meeting, IDA, and IFC)." Bonn, September 11, 1961. DE B102/47640.

[153] Letter from Dr. Paul Krebs to Herrn Ministerialdirigent Dr. Henckel, December 15, 1958. DE B102/27082.

[154] Letter from Dr. Paul Krebs to Herrn Ministerialdirigent Dr. Henckel, December 15, 1958. DE B102/27082.

[155] O'Keefe (1980: 292) observed that advance consent to arbitration becomes "another weapon in the armory for protection of foreign investment."

Why Multilateral Insurance, Investor–State Arbitration, and a Code Are All Complements

Since the late 1960s, investor–state arbitration has been celebrated as a move away from politics: Aron Broches recommended ICSID arbitration because it could help "to remove investment disputes from the intergovernmental political sphere."[156] One of Broches' successors as ICSID Secretary General, Ibrahim Shihata, described ICSID as a forum that "attempts in particular to 'depoliticize' the settlement of investment disputes."[157] Depoliticization has both a specific legal meaning in the ICSID Convention[158] and often a wider, looser connotation of replacing a political process with a legal one.[159] The "depoliticization" language that emerged with the drafting of the ICSID Convention at times blurs into a more general belief that arbitration has replaced other means of dispute settlement. This belief is incorrect.

Investor–state arbitration does not replace other modes of dispute resolution, it works alongside them. German and Swiss officials publicly discussed arbitration and insurance as complementary. In April 1958, German officials noted that providing investors with access to arbitration would ease the burden on the diplomatic service. At the same time, these officials argued that in certain instances, the full weight of the German government might be needed in order to get compensation.[160] A newspaper article on the new German model BIT, written in June 1959, trumpets that insurance guarantees put the full weight of the German government behind the investor, observing that the treaty's "most striking feature is that the partner country recognizes the federal government as the legal successor of the investors in disputes. Hence, in a situation of guarantee, the government can punch its entire political and moral weight in order to enforce the claims of the Federal

[156] Broches [1963] 1995:163. That said, Parra (2012: 16–18) does not give depoliticization a prominent role in his institutional history of ICSID.

[157] Shihata (1986: 4) described ICSID as "a forum for conflict resolution in a framework which carefully balances the interests and requirements of all the parties involved, and attempts in particular to 'depoliticize' the settlement of investment disputes." Puig (2013: 550–3) argues that ICSID's connection with depoliticization became stronger during Shihata's tenure as Secretary General.

[158] Article 27 of the ICSID Convention provides a limited suspension of diplomatic protection. Paparinskis (2010: 271) elaborates the limits of depoliticization for all actors and challenges the usefulness of depoliticization in contemporary discussions.

[159] For instance, Schreuer et al. (2009: 416) observe that under the ICSID Convention, "[t]he dispute settlement process is depoliticized and subjected to objective legal criteria."

[160] Übersicht über die wichtigsten Grundsätze in dem Entwurf einer Internationalen Konvention zum gegenseitigen Schutz privater Vermögensrechte im Ausland (Overview of the main principles in the draft International Convention on the Mutual Protection of Private Property Abroad.) April 25, 1958. DE B102/130141.

Republic."[161] The article then observes that these efforts go hand in hand with individual standing in the Abs Draft, and that government officials believe these two plans complement each other harmoniously.[162] Similarly, within the German government, proposals for a multilateral insurance institution were envisioned as a complement to the substantive multilateral code.[163]

Subsequent experience proves these German officials correct: home government involvement, investment insurance, and arbitration have been used in several of the same disputes. For instance, three of the earliest ICSID cases, filed against Jamaica, were filed amid ongoing negotiations between the Jamaican government and the companies, mediated by the US government. The US government's political risk insurance agency had written 500 million dollars of guarantees for these corporations. In the middle of this, the firms filed a claim at ICSID, according to internal US government documents, only as a way to improve their bargaining position in the ongoing negotiations, not with the intention of resolving the dispute on the legal field. The interplay between different modes of dispute resolution will be picked up and elaborated on in later chapters—the insight here is that arbitration was not considered a replacement for other modes of dispute settlement in the early 1960s before ICSID emerged; it was considered a complement to them.

Governments Support a Multilateral Insurance Agency

The German government supported proposals for a multilateral insurance agency. As early as 1960, serious interagency discussions were held about the viability of van Eeghen's plan for a multilateral insurance agency at the World Bank.[164] After examining van Eeghen's proposal, the relevant German officials thought it was "in every regard supportable."[165] The Netherlands, Belgium, and Switzerland also supported a multilateral insurance agency strongly: "as small industrialized countries, with sizeable investments but little influence in

[161] "Verträge zum Schutz von Auslandsanlagen (Contracts for the Protection of Foreign Investment)" Handelsblatt, Nr 78, June 2, 1959. DE B102/27082.

[162] "Verträge zum Schutz von Auslandsanlagen (Contracts for the Protection of Foreign Investment)" Handelsblatt, Nr 78, June 2, 1959. DE B102/27082.

[163] Letter from E. H. van Eeghen to Ministerialdirektor Dr. von Spindler, December 21, 1960. DE B102/47640.

[164] Invitation from the Minister of the Economy, September 8 1960, subject: "Internationale Garantierung von Kapitalanlagen in Entwicklungsländern (International Guarantees for Investment in Developing Countries)." DE B102/47640.

[165] Letter from Dr. Beelitz to Herr Professor Donner, January 1, 1961, subject: "Internationales Garantieinstitut zur Abdeckung von politischen Risiken für Kapitalanlagen in Entwicklungsländern (International Guarantee Institution to Cover Political Risks for Investments in Developing Countries)." DE B102/47640.

most LDC's, [they] are pressing for [the] establishment of a multilateral investment guarantee system."[166]

Crucially, the US government supported proposals for a multilateral insurance agency, in stark contrast to its initial stance on a multilateral code.[167] After a 1964 OECD meeting, Swiss officials noted that "the group who wants to draft a system: Belgium, Netherlands, Italy, Denmark, the EEC [European Economic Community] Commission, and the US. Sensationally, the US delegate took the lead of this group and promoted the idea vocally and promised that the US would participate even though they have a national system in place."[168] There was no opposition within the OECD—France and the UK were "unenthusiastic, but have not come out in flat opposition."[169] Their concerns were that multilateral insurance would cause their investors to demand a national system (France) or that insurance was too effective at stimulating investment (the UK). After a meeting, one Swiss official noted, "Only France was against the idea and that was because French industry would demand a national system and the French government cannot afford one since their investment is mostly in Africa, which is subject to African Nationalism."[170] The British government stated their position on insurance clearly: "While we do not oppose the scheme, we do not see ourselves as founder members of it, because we cannot in balance of payments terms afford the stimulus to investment that this scheme would provide."[171] The same memo, to preview a line of argument developed further in Chapter four, made it clear that the UK government supported ICSID because it would not stimulate outward foreign investment.[172] Broches understood these British views in the 1960s well; he later remembered that "the British were not in favor [of insurance] because they said, 'We don't really want to encourage capital export'."[173]

OECD member states believed that the technical challenges to creating a multilateral insurance agency could be surmounted. In February 1963, the OECD DAC convened a group of experts to investigate the technical and legal

[166] Background Paper: Multilateral Investment Guarantees, OECD Ministerial Meeting, Paris, November 19–20, 1963. US 595219 Box 2.

[167] Background Paper, OECD Ministerial Meeting, Paris, December 2–3, 1964, topic: "Multilateral Investment Guarantee System." US 595219 Box 2.

[168] Letter from Montandon to the Trade Section of Economic Department, April 30, 1964. CH C.41.124.5.2.

[169] Background Paper: Multilateral Investment Guarantees, OECD Ministerial Meeting, Paris, 19–20 November 1963. US 595219 Box 2.

[170] Letter from Montandon to the Trade Section of Economic Department, April 30, 1964. CH C.41.124.5.2.

[171] IMF/IBRD. Twenty-Second Annual Meeting, Settlement of Investment Disputes: Investment Insurance and Protection, Brief by the Treasury. UK FCO 48/145.

[172] IMF/IBRD. Twenty-Second Annual Meeting, Settlement of Investment Disputes: Investment Insurance and Protection, Brief by the Treasury. UK FCO 48/145.

[173] Broches 1990: 15.

issues of insurance schemes. The Americans summarized the report issued by this group a few months later with a clear statement: "the experts believe that a multilateral investment guarantee scheme would not pose any insurmountable technical or legal difficulties."[174] Then, in April 1964, the US government stated it would support a multilateral system with other DAC members; following that, the OECD prepared the "key clauses of a convention which would set out the basis for a multilateral guaranty system."[175] Swiss notes from these discussions echo the Americans' positive perceptions: Swiss officials noted that the Secretary General of the OECD had commissioned a study that showed the idea was technically viable.[176] The same Swiss official then wrote to several individuals outside the government letting them know that the expert study on the viability of a multilateral insurance scheme was positive.[177] In September 1965, the Swiss government listed minor shortcomings—all relatively technical issues—to be discussed (and presumably quickly overcome) during the drafting of a multilateral investment guarantee.[178]

In June 1965, the OECD Council formally sent the World Bank a "Report on the Establishment of a Multilateral Investment Guarantee Corporation" which "outlined the principal features of a multilateral investment insurance scheme, likely to receive the widest measure of support."[179] The OECD member states delegated the subsequent task of creating a multilateral insurance agency to the World Bank. The US government, the World Bank's main shareholder and main principal, was clear: "Our position is one of general support for the concept of a multilateral investment guaranty institution within the IBRD [International Bank for Reconstruction and Development] family embodying generally the principles of the OECD proposal."[180] The proposal had resolved the key distributional hurdle; capital-exporting states had agreed in principle to a "loss-sharing formula not based on subscribed capital but on the extent of use of the multilateral investment insurance facility by a member country's nationals."[181]

[174] Background Paper: Multilateral Investment Guarantees, OECD Ministerial Meeting, Paris, November 19–20, 1963. US 595219 Box 2.

[175] Background Paper: Multilateral Investment Guarantees, OECD Ministerial Meeting, Paris, November 19–20, 1963. US 595219 Box 2.

[176] Letter from Montandon to the Trade Section of Economic Department, April 30, 1964. CH C.41.124.5.2.

[177] Letter from Montandon to several recipients, July 29, 1964. CH C.41.124.5.2.

[178] Letter from Swiss Delegation to the OECD to Diez, April 9, 1965. CH C.41.124.5.2.

[179] Background Paper on the Multilateral Investment Insurance Proposal and IBRD Arbitration Convention, OECD Ministerial Meeting Paris, November 24–5, 1966. US 595219 Box 3.

[180] Background Paper on the Multilateral Investment Insurance Proposal and IBRD Arbitration Convention, OECD Ministerial Meeting Paris, November 24–5, 1966. US 595219 Box 3.

[181] Background Paper on the Multilateral Investment Insurance Proposal and IBRD Arbitration Convention, OECD Ministerial Meeting Paris, November 24–5, 1966. US 595219 Box 3.

At this point, the proposal for multilateral investment insurance seemed like a surefire success. The US government had strong-armed the World Bank into creating the IFC and the International Development Association (IDA) in the previous decade, and was still in a commanding position with regard to the World Bank. The OECD's technical experts believed the details could be worked out. OECD governments had agreed to a loss-sharing formula. So why did multilateral investment insurance not come into force?

The answer is that the World Bank chose not to play an agenda-setting or brokering role. OECD governments delegated the actual setting up of an agency to the World Bank. The World Bank subtly discouraged and delayed action. World Bank officials did not formally disobey their member states; they produced the required reports. What these officials did not do is play the active agenda-setting and brokering role that they played for ICSID. The resources devoted to developing the idea of ICSID overshadowed the resources devoted to developing the idea of insurance. This is despite the fact that no government ever formally requested the Bank to work on the idea of ICSID, and OECD governments—perhaps the World Bank's most powerful collective principal—formally requested the Bank to develop the idea of a multilateral insurance agency on repeated occasions.

The World Bank's Inaction and Subtle Discouragement of Insurance

OECD states requested the World Bank to develop investment insurance proposals throughout the 1960s. In July 1960, as the result of an American initiative, the World Bank was tasked with undertaking "a study of the feasibility of an investment guarantee program."[182] The study was issued in March 1962, and, while it did not formally take a position, its "pessimistic" tone surprised governments.[183] Swiss officials, for instance, were surprised that the Bank's study found that a multilateral guarantee system would "not trigger many new investments" and would not contribute to an improvement of the investment climate, as this ran counter to the widely shared, mainstream view.[184]

[182] Position Paper on the Convention on Protection of Foreign Property, OECD Ministerial Meeting, Paris, November 16–17, 1961. US 595219 Box 2. Same reported in the German archives, Letter from Dr. Henckel (recipient unnamed) subject: "Anreise für Kapitalinvestitionen in Entwicklungsländern (Trip regarding capital investment in developing countries)," August 14, 1961. DE B102/47640.

[183] Bemerkungen zum Bericht der Weltbank über die multilaterale Investitionsgarantie (Summary of the World Bank Report about a multilateral risk guarantee for investments). CH C41.124.5.2.

[184] Bemerkungen zum Bericht der Weltbank über die multilaterale Investitionsgarantie (Summary of the World Bank Report about a multilateral risk guarantee for investments). CH C41.124.5.2.

The World Bank report's pessimistic tone was additionally peculiar because the ICC, which had collaborated with the World Bank in preparing and sending out the survey underlying the report, came to the opposite conclusion. In their report issued the same year as the World Bank's report, the ICC "came out strongly in support of the creation of a multilateral insurance scheme."[185] While it is puzzling that the World Bank and the ICC came to opposite conclusions based on the same data, this result did not surprise German officials. Germany's official at the World Bank wrote in February 1961 (over a year before the report was completed) that his impression was that the relevant World Bank officials were opposed to the idea of investment insurance. A German official summarized a meeting in which the German Executive Director expressed a positive view of insurance, his Dutch counterpart expressed a very supportive view, and then two attending World Bank officials expressed a series of doubts about insurance's viability.[186] By May 1961, still almost a year before the report was finished, the German Executive Director wrote back to Bonn with an unequivocal prediction about the report's contents: "The World Bank staff intends to draw up an opinion... [F]rom various remarks made by staff members, I have the impression that this opinion will not be positive."[187] One of the main staff members that the German Executive Director heard from was Aron Broches, who was heavily involved with the insurance report, along with two other senior officials.[188] Broches' reasons for being pessimistic about insurance are discussed in Chapter four, because he believed that arbitration could be framed in a way to overcome the problems he perceived with insurance. In fact, the problems he perceived with the World Bank becoming involved in insurance directly impacted the way he framed ICSID.

The core insight here is that although the distributional conflicts over who pays for investment insurance were serious, non-World Bank documents from this era give a sense that a technical solution could likely have been found. An American summary of a World Bank meeting from 1965 notes that, "in the Bank's informal meetings outright opposition [to insurance] was expressed on behalf of only one member, a capital-importing country."[189] That certainly represents less opposition than was expressed toward the idea of ICSID. Yet just one year later—coincidentally the year in which the World Bank was

[185] Nwogugu 1965: 87, quoting ICC Doc No 111/114, 4:5:62.

[186] Letter from Harry Gorn, Alternate Executive Director to Herrn Dr. Paul Krebs, February 23, 1961. DE B102/47640.

[187] Letter from Prof. Dr. O. Donner to Dr. vom Hofe, subject: "Garantierung von Kapitalanlagen auf multilateraler Grundlage (Guaranteeing Investments on a Multilateral Basis)," May 4, 1961. DE B102/47640.

[188] Broches 1984 (May): 28.

[189] Background Paper on Multilateral Investment Guarantees and IBRD Arbitration Convention, OECD Ministerial Meeting, Paris, November 25–6, 1965. US 595219 Box 3.

tasked with consulting developing countries about an insurance agency—the US government's assessment of the OECD insurance proposal's feasibility had changed dramatically: the "establishment of a multilateral investment guaranty institution along the lines of the OECD proposal is not to be anticipated in the near future because of the length and complexity of the OECD proposal, the lack of agreement on a number of issues, as well as the unenthusiastic response from the developing countries."[190] The opposition from developing countries to insurance was opposition to the specified level of burden-sharing—a technical detail that can be adjusted. This was not the same as the unyielding, principled opposition that many capital-importing countries initially expressed toward the idea of arbitration. Even in 1969, American officials were still discussing how the burden-sharing could be tweaked: burden-sharing was seen as tough but not impossible to negotiate.[191] For capital-importing countries, any form of burden-sharing that was being considered in an insurance scheme was a more advantageous proposition than arbitration. As later chapters will explain, arbitration places the entire burden on the capital-importing state.

Some experts from capital-importing states may have realized this on their own, but some probably did not. The World Bank officials who framed and massaged the idea of investor–state arbitration in order to make it politically palatable and to emphasize its benefits for development did not do the same framing and massaging for insurance. The case for insurance is much stronger, *ceteris paribus*, and easier to make to a capital-importing government—so if World Bank officials had done even half the work to support, develop, and advance proposals for insurance as they had for ICSID then it is likely that insurance could have come into effect. During the 1960s, however, they did not.

CONCLUSION

The path that emerged from the critical juncture was not determined by the intensity of lobbying from private investors. Private investors, to the extent they were involved with investment protection during the 1960s, expressed more enthusiasm for the idea of a code or insurance than for arbitration. Yet by and large, there was little lobbying, and almost none of the bottom-up

[190] Background Paper on the Multilateral Investment Insurance Proposal and IBRD Arbitration Convention, OECD Ministerial Meeting Paris, November 24–5, 1966. US 595219 Box 3.

[191] Meeting between the Assistant Secretary of Economic Affairs and business community representatives, subject: Multilateral Investment Guarantees (undated, likely April 28, 1969). US 595219 Box 13.

variety expected by conventional accounts. Investor lobbying for, or involvement with, any of these three proposals was relatively limited. Furthermore, where investors were involved, their involvement almost never resembled the theorized lobbying, which would have emerged from individual direct investors whose day-to-day business is affected by a particular policy or institution. The individuals who led investor involvement did so because of personal experience with expropriation. Investors in the US and UK were largely uninformed. Investors in corporatist states were better informed, because their governments wrote to them and arranged meetings to hear their opinions on the draft and insurance. In short, investor involvement affected the arrangements for investment protection that eventually emerged, but did not directly determine them.

The most important investor involvement with regard to calls for individuals to be given permanent standing in a multilateral investment court or arbitration took hold in the Federal Republic of Germany in the 1950s. While proposals for individual standing existed before then and in other places, the idea had a new, powerful resonance in the Federal Republic during these years. The proposals that emerged were tied to their framers' personal experience with expropriation; these proposals would not have emerged or would have different content if they had emerged elsewhere or at a different time.

Finally, the chapter focuses on expert officials within the governments of capital-exporting states, which makes clear that these officials, except for British officials, preferred insurance. If the World Bank and the US had developed insurance proposals, however, British officials would likely have gone along with them; they believed their balance of payments problem was temporary and did not want to be excluded from new initiatives. Insurance had distributional consequences and technical details that needed to be resolved immediately, but documents from several governments suggest that these could have been worked out. With backing from the World Bank, it is likely that a multilateral insurance agency could have emerged, and potentially a multilateral code of some kind. What explains why neither of these proposals, considered viable by well-informed officials at the time, were realized is in large part because the World Bank refused to play an agenda-setting or brokering role for either proposal during the 1960s.

4

Supranational Agenda-Setting

The World Bank's "Modest Proposal"

This chapter evaluates World Bank officials' motivations, resources, and strategy for creating the ICSID Convention. It probes why the World Bank became involved in investment protection and why the involvement of World Bank officials led to this particular "modest proposal."[1]

The first section elaborates on the World Bank's access to privileged information about multilateral insurance and a code. World Bank officials had such extensive access to these proposals and proximity to key officials that Bank officials were able to forecast why these proposals would fail, and may even have facilitated their failure by refusing states' requests to take over both proposals. That the World Bank was able to set the agenda (away from a multilateral code or insurance agency and toward arbitration) and broker an arbitration convention into existence does not mean that the World Bank was in any way fooling its member state governments. On the contrary, World Bank officials had a clear sense of the group of government officials that could stop its plans, and always made sure to act within parameters that they believed this group of officials would find acceptable. The second section discusses who was in this group of officials and what information the Bank had about their views on foreign investment. These government officials were well-informed strategic actors with special expertise on protecting and promoting foreign investment. They had a clear-eyed understanding of ICSID as a lowest common denominator solution that they supported due to a lack of better alternatives.

The third section delves into why the early World Bank was an improbable organization to create legal machinery related to investment protection. During the 1960s, the Bank was a small lending body, not the large development

[1] George Woods, President of the World Bank, often praised ICSID as "a modest proposal"—presumably not intending to echo Jonathan Swift's essay of the same name. Broches ([1963] 1995: 163) also used "modest" to describe the proposal for ICSID.

organization it would later become. At the time, the Bank operated by taking conservative steps within the political constraints set by its largest shareholder, the US government. Yet the World Bank had strong institutional reasons to become involved with investment protection—its Articles of Agreement task it with promoting private investment. This mandate gave World Bank officials a clear policy goal and strong motivation. In trying to fulfil this mandate, Bank officials developed unparalleled expertise, access to privileged information, and a reputation for reliable, competent leadership.

The fourth section of the chapter discusses the World Bank's experience mediating investment disputes before drafting the proposal for ICSID. This experience gave Bank officials expertise and access to privileged information. It also positioned the World Bank as a broker—an actor able to find acceptable mid-points between capital-importing and capital-exporting states with regard to investment disputes.

The final section of the chapter evaluates how World Bank officials introduced their proposal to states. These officials were so concerned that distributional disagreements would derail the proposal that they designed an entirely new, regional, consultative "roadshow" procedure in order to make it nearly impossible for states to derail the drafting. The Bank invited states to send experts-designate, not formal representatives, and structured the participation of these experts within a consultative and regional framework, with Bank officials having final say over any changes. Bank officials also engaged in extensive behind-the-scenes brokering.

ACCESS TO PRIVILEGED INFORMATION: THE BANK'S INVOLVEMENT IN CONCURRENT PROPOSALS FOR INVESTMENT PROTECTION

The Bank's management had exceptional access to information about the proposals for investment insurance and a substantive code discussed Chapter three. Bank officials refused to take these initiatives over, but studied them to draw lessons about how best to ensure ICSID would succeed.

The Bank's senior management was well-informed about the Abs Draft and watched as it was turned into the Abs-Shawcross Draft and then into the OECD Draft Convention. In 1957, when Hermann Abs released his draft, several high-ranking officials of the World Bank—including President Eugene Black—were in the audience.[2] World Bank officials were not there solely to

[2] This draft was launched at the International Industrial Development Conference, October 14–18, 1957, in San Francisco, which had as its main theme "the preferred means of stimulating the flow of private capital to the less developed areas of the world" (Miller 1959: 372).

hear Abs, but they did have a close relationship with him. In 1959, Abs launched a daring operation in support of the Bank's first European bond issue. In that year, the Bundesbank adopted a restrictive monetary policy, which caused bond prices to fall. If the World Bank bonds had been allowed to fall beneath their issue price, it would have damaged the Bank's standing. Abs decided that Deutsche Bank—alone among the German banks involved—would buy all the bonds necessary to keep the market price above the issue price. Deutsche Bank eventually bought over 66 percent of the bond issue, sustaining large losses in the process but earning Abs tremendous goodwill with the Bank's management.[3] When Hermann Abs spoke, the Bank listened—particularly since the Bank viewed bond markets as its primary audience, as subsequent sections show.

The World Bank had close institutional ties with the OECD DAC, the organizational home for most investment protection discussions and had access to relevant OECD documents.[4] World Bank officials also had informal channels of communication with important individuals working on the OECD Draft; for instance, Broches had informal contact with John Blair, assistant to Lord Shawcross, through a Committee of the American Bar Association.[5] The Bank's senior management recognized that the OECD Draft Convention was unlikely to succeed early in the process. In 1961, Broches made a public speech observing that the US government was opposed to the proposal, dooming it.[6] The Bank acted as though the OECD proposal had failed long before it actually did. Broches told the World Bank Executive Directors in 1962 that: "If [the OECD Convention was] adopted and adhered to by a substantial number of capital-exporting and capital-importing countries" then ICSID was unnecessary.[7] Yet Broches and the Bank's Executive Directors clearly did not think ICSID would be unnecessary, because they dedicated substantial resources to advancing the proposal while the OECD Draft Convention was still under consideration.

As mentioned in Chapter three, the World Bank's management was repeatedly asked to take over the OECD Draft Convention. The OECD Secretary General as well as the US government made this request, and World Bank officials always refused. Internal briefing notes for the US representative to the

[3] Kopper 1997: 456.

[4] For instance, Broches (1984 May: 30) later recalled, "a draft was discussed in OECD. I was interested, so I read the papers."

[5] Letter from John Blair to Hester Boothroyd, November 13, 1961. UK T 312/251.

[6] Broches gave a speech at Fordham in 1961 in which he observed: "Whatever the merits of these arguments pro and con, it is a fact that to date no decisive progress has been made in OECD with the convention, in large part, although certainly not entirely, due to the unenthusiastic attitude of the United States." Broches, Aron. "Problems of Private Foreign Investment," Third Annual Institute on Corporate Counsel, devoted to Foreign Operations of American Enterprises, December 8, 1961. WB Folder 1651418.

[7] Point 3, Memorandum of Meeting, April 10, 1962, quoted in ICSID 1970: 13.

OECD describe one exchange: "The Secretary General of the OECD discussed the Convention with officials of the IBRD . . . It was made clear in these discussions that the Bank would be unwilling to negotiate on the Convention with the developing countries."[8] As discussed in Chapter three, the US government wanted the Bank to take over the OECD Draft, and Broches recalled that around UNCTAD I in 1964, it was decided that the Bank "should be asked to look at the OECD package."[9] Broches recalled that the OECD "handed the whole file over to us" and asked "whether we would be prepared to take over the code." He continued:

> I was the spokesman for the Bank. I said that we wouldn't do it, because the code was a one-sided document limited to the protection of foreign property and the obligations of the host countries. If we were to take it over, we would have to look at the other side, namely the obligations of investors. The developing countries would still feel that the Bank presented a proposal cooked up by their adversaries, and the industrialized countries would accuse us of watering down a wonderful document. We were liable to end up having everybody mad at us, or, possibly even worse, coming out with a meaningless document. So, we definitely said no to that.[10]

This quote illustrates several important points. First, it demonstrates how Broches perceived his autonomy: he was not merely doing the bidding of states. When he thought that states were trying to delegate a bad idea to him, he said no to their requests on behalf of the Bank. At the same time, this quotation shows how attuned he was to the views of states and how careful he was to act as a trusted broker and avoid "having everybody mad at us." It also gives his frank assessment of the OECD Draft and shows how seriously he took the distributional conflict between capital-exporters and capital-importers. Broches followed the OECD Draft closely, learned lessons from its initial drafting, and used those lessons to improve the chances of success for the ICSID Convention.

The World Bank was also asked to create a multilateral insurance agency, but demurred and discouraged this initiative, as Chapter three mentioned. In 1990, after Broches' successor as General Counsel, Ibrahim Shihata, created a multilateral insurance agency at the Bank, Broches discussed why he was "discouraged" about insurance and why he had told Shihata "you might as well forget about it" when Shihata asked him about the chances of creating an investment insurance program.[11] Broches cited the hardening of the American position toward loss sharing (which made insurance more difficult to negotiate from the mid-1970s), but focused on Latin American opposition to

[8] Talking Points, OECD Draft Convention for the Protection of Foreign Property, OECD Ministerial Meeting, Paris, November 25–6, 1965. US 595219 Box 3.

[9] The US government discussed this recommendation before UNCTAD I and UNCTAD II.

[10] Broches 1984 (May): 30.

[11] Broches 1990: 18.

insurance.[12] He said: "there was a very angry opponent of most of the elements [of insurance], for instance, arbitration. They didn't like it—it was the Latin Americans, in the first place."[13] This is a curious statement; while it is correct that all Latin American governments maintained a principled opposition to arbitration during the 1960s, investment insurance does not require arbitration, and in fact, many Latin American governments signed investment insurance agreements with the US government and others in the 1960s.[14] Latin American opposition cannot explain why an investment insurance agency was not created at the Bank in the 1960s.

A more plausible explanation for why insurance was not created is that World Bank staff failed to play an agenda-setting or brokering role for insurance. The actions of the World Bank staff can be interpreted as a subtle campaign to discourage action on insurance, which began with the "pessimistic" report on insurance that came out in March 1962. Broches, a lead author of that report, later explained its conclusions. His explanation is quoted at length because his views were very different to those held by most governments and investors:

> We went through these various schemes, but the real question we were asked, more important than the merits or demerits of the various ideas, was whether investment insurance as such had merit, and whether the Bank could be involved in it. The answer to the first question was, frankly, we don't know. It might be. It's awfully hard to say. If investors are looking for oil or minerals they may not have much choice of where to go and investment insurance might not be crucial to their decision. On the other hand, if it's a question of industrial investment, or of marketing, there's much more choice, and then the investment climate will make a greater difference and investment insurance may encourage such investment. But there's no statistical way of proving the value of investment insurance.[15]

This argument is interesting for two reasons. First, most others in Broches' milieu drew the conclusion that insurance worked—as mentioned in Chapter three, the ICC report using the same data came to the conclusion that insurance was effective at facilitating investment. Investment insurance was widely believed to be effective, and the German and American insurance programs were high-visibility successes. For instance, in a meeting between American industry representatives and officials, an investor "pointed out that [the US Agency for International Development] AID had written a great deal

[12] Broches 1990: 18.

[13] Broches (1990: 15) said this in the context of expressing his frustration that no one ended the insurance discussion, despite expressing opposition to the idea.

[14] For instance, Argentina and Brazil, arguably the most outspoken opponents of investor-state arbitration, signed Investment Guarantee Agreement agreements with the US in 1959 (updated in 1963) and 1965, respectively.

[15] Broches 1984 (May): 28.

of insurance under its own program and suggested that this was a key to the present level of investment funds flowing to the LDCs."[16] The US investment insurance program was widely considered to operate well and be effective at facilitating investment. Second, Broches' argument that the value of investment insurance must be proven was the opposite of the approach he took to arbitration. During the drafting of ICSID, Broches eschewed attempts to quantify or otherwise measure the value of arbitration. He repeated claims that access to arbitration improved the investment climate, without any empirical evidence, as elaborated in Chapter five.

From his speeches and interviews, the main reason that Broches demurred on insurance appears to be that the World Bank would have a conflict of interest. He believed that the Bank might find its relationship with borrowing countries unduly complicated by insurance, and the Bank might find its lending power a bargaining weapon in the settlement of claims. He framed the conflict of interest clearly:

> We expressed reservations as to a possible role of the Bank. I was the one who felt most strongly that the Bank's shouldn't be put in a position where it was an insurer and a lender. I mean, an insurer of money invested by others and a lender to that country, which might disturb its relations with both. Therefore, there should be a clear separation between the two functions.[17]

This conflict of interest is not avoided with the proposal for ICSID. In fact, the Bank's status as creditor was integral to the success of ICSID: it is precisely why many capital-exporting governments thought ICSID would be effective, as the next section shows. British officials even questioned the appropriateness of locating an arbitration center within the World Bank in 1961, noting that "it is doubtful whether the world's biggest international lender should also be the biggest arbitrator of disputes."[18]

A more immediate reason why Broches was discouraged about insurance was that it required funds to set up. Broches was keenly aware of the disagreements about burden-sharing and more generally about who would bear the costs of insurance.[19] Here the proposal for ICSID does have a short-term advantage: unlike insurance schemes, which require the "who pays" question to be answered up front, arbitration pushes this question into the future, allowing officials to ignore it and sparing them the domestic battle of having to carve out a new budget in order to ratify. This makes it easier for officials

[16] Meeting between the Assistant Secretary of Economic Affairs and business community representatives, subject: Multilateral Investment Guarantees (undated, likely April 28, 1969). US 595219 Box 13.

[17] Broches 1984 (May): 30.

[18] Letter from Hester Boothroyd to Mrs. Hedley-Miller, on the International Bank and Arbitration, November 7, 1961. UK T 312/251.

[19] Broches 1984 (May): 33.

to ratify an arbitration convention, which has no costs up front, than an insurance convention, which has visible costs. Broches and other officials were well aware of this reality, which Broches expressed with characteristic lucidity: ICSID "wouldn't require money."[20]

This logic, while perceptive as regards the ease with which initiatives could be agreed, at the same time fails to anticipate the way arbitration distributes costs. For capital-importing countries, any form of burden-sharing in an insurance scheme is more advantageous than arbitration. Arbitration usually places the entire burden on the capital-importing state. Furthermore, investor–state arbitration developed into a system where host governments—albeit inconsistently and after long legal battles—insure foreign investors against a wider set of risks than home government insurance programs or private insurance programs. This development is not necessarily one that the framers of ICSID could have anticipated, but it happened quickly: the firms that filed some of the first ICSID cases did so knowing that the government's actions were not confiscatory enough to trigger the political risk insurance that had been written by their government.[21] Broches was the Secretary General who registered these cases.

A final reason why Broches preferred investment arbitration to insurance likely stems from his training as a lawyer and life experience. As someone who had written a doctorate in international law at the University of Amsterdam in the 1930s, Broches was steeped in the interstate peacebuilding lineage of arbitration. He likely aspired to bring an elegant legal process to complex investment disputes. He also likely believed that legal processes could provide a sense of finality and justice that insurance could not match: some of the investment disputes that Broches had been involved with—notably the expropriation of his parents' firm (followed by their murder in the Holocaust) and the Abadan dispute—were not disputes that insurance could have resolved completely.

In conclusion, World Bank officials considered the proposal for ICSID feasible: it was not the most effective solution to the problem of investment protection, but equally, there were few obstacles to creating it. The World Bank, due to its successful mediation experience and its position as a creditor but also as a postwar development organization, was well-positioned to create it. Broches summed up this line of thinking:

> Well, since we were under general pressure to do something in the field of encouragement of foreign investment, I thought dispute settlement was the least controversial approach, and also something that wouldn't require a large organization. It wouldn't require money, and I thought it was something that the Bank ought to take up.[22]

[20] Broches 1984 (May): 36.

[21] Elaborated in Chapter seven.

[22] Broches 1984 (May): 36.

Bank officials took up the proposal not because states asked them to, but because they believed, on the basis of their access to information and expertise, that it was the best way forward.

THE WORLD BANK'S AUDIENCE: GOVERNMENT OFFICIALS

Since this chapter creates an impression that the World Bank could do anything it wanted, it is worth clarifying that the World Bank had an audience that could stop it, knew who was in this audience, and was careful not to take any actions to trigger censure. Chapter five will focus on the responses of government officials to the actual proposal for ICSID, which they were given relatively late, after a complete draft existed within the Bank. Most of the materials discussed in that chapter were written to assuage the concerns of capital-importing countries, whose ratification was considered most in doubt. While capital-importing governments were an important audience, they were not the first audience the Bank needed to satisfy.

The first audience, and the audience that could stop the World Bank, was made of officials from capital-exporting governments. These officials came from governments with the capacity to monitor the World Bank's actions, and envisioned their role as shareholders of the Bank. These governments also met regularly in the OECD DAC, which made them, at times, akin to a collective principal for the World Bank. That said, these officials knew that their governments, despite being capital exporting, had different objectives with regard to foreign investment. Tensions between capital-exporters tend to be erased from the history of investment law, leaving a binary capital-exporter versus capital-importer picture, but actually, tensions *between* capital-exporters probably mattered more in determining the outcome of the 1960s critical juncture. Describing discussions at the DAC, where the most in-depth discussions of investment protection issues occurred during the 1960s, provides a sense of how these expert officials viewed foreign investment and how they perceived ICSID.

Officials in the DAC discussed and commissioned research on several policies and institutional innovations to address the lack of investment flows to poor countries. These officials knew a great deal about what worked to facilitate private investment to poor countries, and thus knew enough to know that the main purpose of arbitration was to *protect* investment. Investment protection is related to investment promotion, insofar as investors may be less willing to invest if they perceive themselves to have no remedy for disputes, but this mechanism is indirect and inconsequential for most investors. When governments were serious about *facilitating* investment flows, they discussed initiatives like the "fiscal incentives in capital exporting countries to stimulate private investment in less-developed countries" brought up by the OECD Secretary General in 1963.[23] In 1965, the US representative to the OECD listed a number of actions capital-exporting could take to facilitate outward flows: designing tax concessions for governments to invest overseas; designing aid programs to help create opportunities for private investment; bearing part of the risk by providing insurance; and providing investors with better information about investment opportunities.[24] There was no shortage of actions that governments could take to facilitate investment.

Officials at the DAC were accustomed to measuring the impact of actions taken to facilitate investment. The DAC invested serious resources in measurement and officials involved understood how difficult it was to measure investment flows.[25] A DAC expert group even wrote a report on "Problems of Measuring Capital Flows to Less-Developed Countries" which was derestricted in 1968.[26] This expertise matters because it makes clear that when these officials heard the claim that access to arbitration would facilitate investment (but that no attempt would be made to measure this effect), they likely perceived this claim as a politically useful piece of public rhetoric, not a statement that reflected expert understanding. In other words, they knew better. They were unlikely to believe that access to arbitration would lead to a measurable increase in investment—British officials, for instance, were clear that they supported ICSID because it would *not* lead to investment.[27]

Officials at the DAC also viewed private foreign investment as one type of financial flow that could be channeled to poor countries, and one that typically came to the fore when other, preferable forms of finance had dried up. Simmons observes that BITs took off in the 1980s and 1990s, as debt financing became less available.[28] This pattern is observable in earlier decades too: in a meeting of top American officials in 1968, for instance, one commented that "the outlook for public development assistance was not very good and that we would have to be looking more and more to private development funds to take up the slack in the developing countries."[29] The distinction between public

[23] "Private Capital" in the Report by the Secretary General to the Ministerial Council of OECD, November 19–20, 1963. US 595219 Box 2.

[24] Notes for Deane Hinton speech, OECD Ministerial Meeting, Paris, November 25–6, 1965. US 595219 Box 3.

[25] Memo from Anthony M. Solomon to Mr. Rostow, subject: UNCTAD II—Restrictive Business Practices and Foreign Private Investment. DAC-9, 1968. US 595219 Box 11.

[26] Recent Activities and Events in the Field of Private Enterprise. DAC-9, 1968. US 595219 Box 11.

[27] IMF/IBRD. Twenty-Second Annual Meeting, Settlement of Investment Disputes: Investment Insurance and Protection, Brief by the Treasury. UK FCO 48/145.

[28] Simmons 2014.

[29] Meeting in Mr. Rostow's office, May 1, 1968. DAC-9, 1968. US 595219 Box 11.

development assistance and private funds was important for officials in the DAC at the time. Public investment, a term for loans from a development bank or similar types of finance, was generally oriented toward national development goals and typically reinforced the government's authority insofar as it had some say over how this money could be used. In contrast, private investment might not contribute toward national development goals, and governments might not have any say over how the money was used.

Officials involved with the DAC did not believe that private foreign investment contributed automatically to development. Development is at the core of the DAC's mandate and measuring development impact is fundamental to fulfilling this mandate. Officials involved with the DAC in the 1960s were more likely to believe that the extent to which private investment contributed to development was an empirical question, with an answer that varied on a case-by-case basis. The minutes of a 1961 meeting show that the DAC asked to be informed of capital flows from all sources to individual "underdeveloped" countries, and that the participants concluded that "there was a need to study the impact which these capital flows were having or were likely to have, and to consider, together with other international bodies, their relation to the development objectives of the underdeveloped regions or countries."[30] Thinking about how to achieve development objectives was serious and sophisticated in the 1960s. In 1965, Arthur Watson, Chairman of IBM, finalized a report for the US government on how private corporations could contribute to development objectives, which gave concrete recommendations on what types of financing led to actual development impact. Watson had spent time on the ground in Asia and Latin America and had a sustained interest in building local economies, but he was no left-leaning idealist: he was the President of the ICC in 1967 and 1968 and a strong advocate for free trade, someone who believed that business should play a role in development. The Watson Report did not see the OECD Convention or access to arbitration as initiatives designed to facilitate development. The Watson Report recommended the creation of a balanced code "under international sponsorship": it recommended that the US government "be prepared to accept a reasonable statement of the obligations of investors, to accompany a statement of the obligations of host countries."[31]

Some officials involved with the DAC were concerned about the political sensitivity of private foreign investment. To varying degrees, officials were wary of foreign investment's associations with imperialism. For instance, when some State Department officials considered asking Turkey to reconsider

[30] Minutes of the 7th Meeting of the OECD Council, Paris, November 16–17, 1961. US 595219 Box 2.

[31] Report of the Advisory Committee on Private Enterprise in Foreign Aid, Arthur K. Watson, Chairman, July 1965. US 595219 Box 13.

its opposition to the OECD Draft, an official from the American Embassy in Ankara wrote back that it was "advisable to refrain" from this because it would "raise past ghosts of concessions and international controls which came to dominate the Turkish commercial scene under the late Ottomans."[32] Decolonization was still ongoing in the 1960s, and private foreign investment was inseparable from sensitive political questions about political and economic independence. Private investment was still perceived as cover for political interference by many capital-importing governments, and some officials in capital-exporting governments were sympathetic to this fear. In a 1968 meeting, one American official observed that "there was a limit, on political grounds, on the amount of private assistance [foreign direct investment] a country could absorb. He cited some examples from his experience in Latin America in particular of the problems created by foreign investment, and cautioned against undue reliance on this type of financing."[33] The fear of private foreign investment as cover for political interference was not limited to Latin America—similar tensions were apparent between the American government and European governments (especially the French) in the late 1960s and early 1970s.[34]

In conclusion, the World Bank's first audience was expert officials with a sophisticated understanding of foreign investment. This audience provided constraints on the World Bank's scope for action, and the Bank was careful to operate within the parameters that its officials perceived these government officials set. These officials, in turn, understood the World Bank's approach and while they did not support it strongly, found it unobjectionable. These officials saw the ICSID Convention as likely ineffective but harmless; they understood that claims about improving the investment climate or "depoliticizing" investment disputes were to some extent political window-dressing that helped make the idea of arbitration more palatable to capital importers. For instance, in an internal meeting to discuss Swiss accession to the ICSID Convention, one official noted that he believed the draft excluded all controversial propositions to ensure that as many states as possible would adhere to it.[35] A year earlier, another Swiss official observed "we support ratification only due to a lack of better alternatives."[36] The question is: after refusing to

[32] Letter from Edwin Martin to John Howison, July 24, 1967. US 595219 Box 13.

[33] Meeting in Mr. Rostow's office, May 1, 1968. DAC-9, 1968. US 595219 Box 11.

[34] Tensions discussed in "Talking Points: US Direct Investment in Europe" for the OECD Ministerial Meeting, Paris, November 30–December 1, 1967. US 595219 Box 4.

[35] Graf's comments in the Minutes of the Commission for Foreign Affairs of the National Council meeting (Ständerätliche Kommission für auswärtige Angelegenheiten) January 23, 1968. CH C.41.124.5.1.

[36] Letter from the Vice Director for Trade to the Head of the Legal Service of the Political Division, July 17, 1967. CH C.41.124.5.1.

lead on a code or insurance, why did World Bank officials decide to get involved with investment arbitration?

THE WORLD BANK: AN UNLIKELY HOME FOR INVESTMENT PROTECTION ISSUES

Investor protection divided the World Bank's member states, and typically the World Bank was hesitant to wade into controversial issues during this era. All organizations created at the Bank before ICSID came about through US initiative; bucking this trend, it was Bank officials, not the US, who proposed the ICSID Convention.[37] In order to understand the institutional drivers behind ICSID's creation, it is necessary to flesh out the place of private investment in the Articles of Agreement of the IBRD (now the World Bank). The Articles create a Bank whose relationship with private investors was fundamental to its success. Three characteristics of the Articles contextualize the emergence of ICSID within the Bank: the Bank has to borrow in order to lend; encouraging private investment is a core purpose of the Bank; and the Articles have always been interpreted expansively. These three characteristics gave Bank officials the motivation, resources, and reputation to propose the ICSID Convention.

Motivation and Reputation: The Bank Must Borrow in Order to Lend

The Bank was structured in such a way that it had to fundraise from private capital markets. The Bank's paid-in capital was relatively small: in 1948, its ability to lend was dwarfed by the US Export-Import Bank and the Marshall Plan. In addition, the early Bank faced widespread skepticism and had no reputation or institutional credibility. In the 1950s, the Bank's first order of business was to prove its creditworthiness. Its creditworthiness was judged not by member governments, but by the bond markets, which meant by investment banks in New York (and later in Europe and elsewhere). The Bank did not earn a triple-A credit rating until 1959, after thirteen years of operation.[38] During these years, and for some time afterward, the Bank's management did not take its eyes off that triple-A credit rating. All decisions were influenced by it.

[37] Just a few years after the ICSID Convention came into force, Broches ([1972] 1995: 192) observed: "The Convention came about as the result of an initiative taken by the World Bank."

[38] Kapur, Lewis, and Webb 1997: 1169.

The Bank's need to demonstrate to bond markets that it was a disciplined lender influenced the Bank's early policies on default and expropriation. The Bank established a strict policy that a government must settle any defaulted debt before receiving a loan from the World Bank.[39] Broches recalled a default on Greek public debt "which had caused the Bank to refuse to lend to Greece for almost twenty years."[40] The Bank established an equally strict policy for expropriation: "the normal practice is to inform governments who are involved in such disputes that the Bank or IDA will not assist them unless and until they make appropriate efforts to reach a fair and equitable settlement."[41] In other words, the Bank did not lend if a state had outstanding claims against it. Expropriation without adequate compensation arguably prevented Bank loans that otherwise would have been made to Algeria (after 1964), Indonesia (throughout the Sukarno regime), Iraq (the mid-1960s), the United Arab Republic (most of the 1960s), and the Democratic Republic of the Congo (1961–9).[42]

The Bank's stance on defaulted debt loomed over its relations with Latin American states. Even if the defaulted debts long pre-dated the existence of the Bank, there was no lending until the debts were settled. This policy led the Bank to become involved in settlements between states and bondholders. In an extreme example, Luis Machado, a Latin American Executive Director of the Bank, mediated the settlement of a Guatemalan debt from 1829. The Bank arranged for the Guatemalan government to pay investors—mostly speculators, since the original bondholders were long dead—for loans issued 137 years earlier.[43] This policy did not endear the Bank to its borrowers, but it did impress the Bank's primary audience: bond markets, particularly in the US and Germany. Since the Bank had to borrow to lend, its early policies needed to please its lenders—bond markets—even if that meant displeasing its borrowers.

Motivation and Resources: The Bank is Charged with Encouraging Private Investment

Encouraging private investment is prominent in the IBRD's Articles of Agreement.[44] The encouragement of private investment was taken up eagerly, but the Bank's staff soon found that they lacked "adequate tools" to do much.[45]

[39] Mason and Asher 1973: 337.
[40] Broches 1985: 9–10.
[41] Mason and Asher 1973: 338, quoting the IBRD Policies and Operations Manual of June 1969.
[42] Mason and Asher 1973: 338.
[43] Mason and Asher 1973: 337.
[44] Article I (ii) of the IBRD Articles of Agreement. Interestingly, lending does not figure prominently in the Articles.
[45] Haralz 1997: 815. This enthusiasm, like the Bank's unflinching posture on debt default, was likely reinforced by the prior careers of many staff (notably the American senior management) in the private sector.

Therefore, during the early years, Bank staff created tools with which they could encourage private investment. The most notable was the IFC.[46]

The Bank's experience with the IFC influenced the creation of ICSID. When the IFC was proposed at the Bank's Annual Meeting in 1952, the majority of bankers and businessmen in attendance opposed the proposal, observing, "the problem for private investment in developing countries was not the lack of capital but the absence of an appropriate investment climate."[47] The IFC was created despite these objections, likely because it had support from the US government. It was only after an unsatisfying first decade that the IFC began to concern itself with "investment conditions rather than with individual investments."[48] By the early 1960s, the IFC and the Bank began to focus on the "climate" for foreign private investment.[49]

The investment climate was approached from the perspective of foreign investors. The Bank's staff recognized the importance of mobilizing domestic savings for growth, but believed that development required foreign investment. It was assumed that poor countries needed foreign capital:

> The perception at the time was that private foreign investment was not significantly recovering after the war and that developing countries were thus being deprived of much needed capital, and, even more important, of the technical and managerial knowledge that ordinarily went with direct foreign investment.[50]

The Bank's staff was searching for ways to funnel private capital to poor countries.

Despite the centrality of private investment in the Articles, the Bank was not set up to solicit ideas from companies about FDI. Nor did the early management, even those with backgrounds in the private sector, have much experience with foreign *direct* investment. The private sector backgrounds of the management were concentrated in investment banks or other firms that were one step removed from direct investment. They had managed balance sheets, not factories. The staff was also very small at this time, which prevented sustained engagement on the ground. Bank officials interacted with government officials, not investors, as Kapur, Lewis, and Webb observe:

> Despite the World Bank's ideological leaning in the 1950s, it did little active fraternizing with foreign private profit-seeking firms trying to trade with or invest in developing countries, other than in mining—and the protocol was that the Bank was to relate to indigenous developing country firms only through their governments.[51]

[46] Mason and Asher 1973: 335. [47] Haralz 1997: 810.
[48] Haralz (1997: 821) quoting a 1961 letter to IFC President Garner.
[49] Mason and Asher 1973: 336. The IFC did continue to make individual equity investments.
[50] Haralz 1997: 815. The observation was made about the founding of the IFC, but is equally valid for the creation of ICSID.
[51] Kapur, Lewis, and Webb 1997: 1171.

Despite the emphasis on encouraging foreign investment, the Bank was an interstate organization. The management reported to Executive Directors, who spoke for states, and the Bank's clients were states.

The Bank's early efforts to encourage private investment—including by setting up the IFC—resulted in two realizations that shaped the creation of ICSID. First, improving the investment climate of borrowing states was a priority. Second, new organizations could be created in-house. The IFC's creation provided a precedent that guided the creation of ICSID. Many of the individuals who shaped the IFC would reprise their roles to create ICSID.

Resources: The Articles of Agreement are Interpreted Expansively

The IBRD Articles of Agreement were not constraining for the early Bank. Commenting on the Articles during the creation of IDA, President Eugene Black said, "we can do what we want."[52] Black may have stretched the truth a little, but not much. Many of the men shaping the World Bank's role in the 1950s considered the individuals at Bretton Woods their peers. These men saw the Articles as provisions that had been cobbled together in a hurry amid the uncertainty of the Second World War. Broches, who attended Bretton Woods as part of the Dutch delegation, said: "The Articles weren't very artistically drawn, even though there were a number of lawyers around. It would have been handled quite differently if there had been more time."[53] The primary focus of most delegates to Bretton Woods had been the creation of the International Monetary Fund: the World Bank (then the IBRD) was an afterthought.[54] Additionally, much of the deliberation about the World Bank focused on the reconstruction of Europe—a business the Bank quickly left after the Marshall Plan was announced. As the Bank repositioned itself, the staff grew comfortable with activities that went beyond what was explicitly set out in the Articles.

Broches and others adopted a three-pronged test to see if the Bank could get involved in an activity. As he put it:

> it has been the view of successive General Counsel—including myself—that, to put it in extreme terms, everything that's not prohibited is permitted [1], as long as it serves the purpose of the institution [2], and as long as it is not inconsistent with anything else in the Articles [3].[55]

[52] Kapur, Lewis, and Webb (1997: 159) note that the full quote is: "We can do what we want. The charter of IDA gives the management and staff the right to do almost anything."

[53] Broches 1984 (May): 4. [54] Helleiner 2014. [55] Broches 1984 (May): 4.

Broches applied this three-pronged test to justify the Bank's involvement in the Abadan dispute, discussed in Chapter two. Broches did not personally support the mediation (he later called the "scheme" a "hare-brained plan"), but still argued in his memo to the Executive Directors that it was something the Bank could do.[56] Broches also applied this test to the creation of new organizations within the World Bank Group. As he saw it:

> What the [Executive] Directors were doing was to add something to the existing instruments for promoting economic development. In the case of IFC, it was to give emphasis to the private sector. In the case of IDA it was to give emphasis to those countries whose absorptive capacity was greater than their credit-worthiness. In the case of ICSID, to get slightly ahead of the story, it was to create a set of instruments which might help attract foreign investment to the countries that needed it, thereby once again assisting the task of the Bank.[57]

Overall, throughout its first decades the World Bank's management sought ways to leverage the Bank's resources to encourage private investment. The management was open to creating new types of organizations and had a sufficient mandate to do so.

THE BANK SEARCHES FOR A MIDDLE WAY THROUGH INVESTMENT DISPUTES, 1950–60

The Bank's emphasis on promoting private investment and its inability to lend in the context of an outstanding default or expropriation led it to become involved in investment dispute mediation in the 1950s—mediations were viewed as a way to restore investor confidence and restart investment flows. This experience gave the Bank's management a special type of expertise and a reputation as a broker, an actor able to find a middle ground between opposed sides.

Expertise and Reputation: The Bank as Skilled Mediator and Dispute Resolution Broker

The Bank's involvement in the Abadan dispute, discussed in Chapter two, was not a success, and the Bank's management did not view it as an endeavor worth repeating. However, the dispute made the Bank's management aware of the lack of machinery for resolving disputes between investors and states.

[56] Broches 1984 (April): 28–9.

[57] Broches 1984 (May): 2.

Nationalizations were a growing global trend, and given the Bank's policy of refusing to lend to states with outstanding expropriation claims against them, these nationalizations concerned the Bank's management. In a 1961 interview, the Bank's most senior Vice President, William Iliff, explained the Bank's position:

> The Bank has really been quite concerned about the question of the lack of machinery for resolving disputes between governments and private interests, and we have been called in on several—for example, Suez for one. Just at the moment we have another one on our plate, where the Colombian government has officially approached us . . . Now, we get into this thing I think as much for this reason as any other, that there isn't any appropriate machinery today, either in the field of conciliation or in the field of arbitration that can settle these disputes.[58]

In the absence of dedicated international machinery, the Bank[59] became involved in several mediations in the 1950s. "Black's Bank" was remarkably good at dispute resolution and successfully forged several settlements. The largest was between India and Pakistan over the Indus River system. This was a state–state dispute, unlike the others, which were disputes between states and foreign investors. The Indus mediation is important as regards the creation of ICSID because it was a large, visible success: it established the Bank as a mediator. Hundreds of millions of people were affected by the dispute, and the issue was technically complex and politically charged. The Bank had considerable leverage in this mediation because both India and Pakistan were borrowers, and the Bank provided funds for post-settlement engineering works. The mediation took almost a decade but ended in public success with the signing of the Indus Water Treaty in 1960.[60] Importantly, this mediation (unlike Abadan) was closely managed by President Black and Vice President Iliff, both skillful diplomats with personalities conducive to effective mediation.[61]

The Indus settlement was important, but it did not directly inspire the creation of ICSID. The inspiration for ICSID came from two smaller mediations managed by Black: the Suez Canal Company and the City of Tokyo compensation cases.[62] These cases involved states, as one party, and investors

[58] Iliff 1961: 43–5.

[59] In some of these mediations, President Eugene Black agreed to act "in his personal capacity." This changed little about the conduct of the mediation. As Iliff (1961: 64) put it: "the President was acting in his personal capacity . . . if you go in for that sort of fiction."

[60] Graves 1973: 610. Parra (2015) also discusses these mediations.

[61] Broches (1990: 12) succinctly observed, "Black is a charming person."

[62] Years later, Broches was asked if the Abadan dispute was "a forerunner that rang the bells and started you thinking about ICSID." He replied, "No, no. The forerunners for that were rather Black's conciliation role in connection with the City of Tokyo bonds, and the Bank's mediation between the Suez Canal Company and Egypt." Broches 1984 (April): 30.

seeking compensation, as the other. In the Suez Canal Company case, President Black arranged for the Egyptian government to compensate the company after the expropriation of equipment.[63] This settlement "helped Egypt to international financial respectability" and "opened the way for the Bank to lend the Suez Canal authority $56.6 million."[64] Black's efforts were similarly successful in settling a long-running dispute between French bondholders and the City of Tokyo.[65] These successes were attributable to Black himself, whose personal involvement lent gravitas to the negotiations, and the Bank's involvement being interpreted as a promise that settlement would pave the way to financial respectability and better access to capital for the defaulting party.

The Bank's—and Black's personal—success in these mediations helps us understand why he supported the idea of institutionalizing dispute resolution at the Bank. From the outside, investment dispute resolution was divisive and therefore an odd issue for President Black, whose tenure at the Bank was marked by conservatism and consensus-building, to take up. When informed of the proposal for ICSID, one British official wrote that the British Executive Director at the Bank "felt, as I did, that this was all rather a strange idea on the Bank's part, but he said that it was a personal baby of Mr. Black's own, and that he was very keen on it."[66] It is easy to see why Black was keen on it—he had a string of mediation successes behind him which had generated goodwill and positive media coverage for the Bank while enabling it to fulfil its core mandate better. The reputation of conservatism and consensus-building that he had cultivated for himself and the Bank made him uniquely qualified to create investment dispute resolution architecture.

The Bank's status as a creditor was central to its success mediating disputes in the 1950s. For many capital-exporting governments, the Bank's status as creditor was what underpinned the proposal for ICSID too. "The real reason why we expect the parties to accept the Centre's arbitration decision," wrote a British official in a confidential telegram back to London, "is the authority and lending power of the Bank."[67] The authority and lending power of the Bank was expected to generate two outcomes. First, capital-importing countries would be more likely to participate in arbitration under the auspices of the World Bank than other organizations, like the PCA or ICC. The British government believed that existing arbitration organizations were not well-regarded by capital-importing countries, especially newly independent ones:

[63] Iliff 1961: 30–45. [64] Mason and Asher 1973: 642.
[65] Waibel (2011: 83–4) summarizes the dispute.
[66] Note from Stuart Milner-Barry, February 1, 1962, "Arbitration Centre." UK T 312/251.
[67] Telegram from Foreign Office to Washington, December 12, 1962. UK T 312: 545 (1962–3).

"The Foreign Office were doubtful whether the PCA, established on European initiative, could be suitably 'dressed up' to be more acceptable to the new independent countries."[68] After describing the ICC's "extensive arbitration machinery which is widely used by Western countries," a British memo observes: "We appreciate that the ICC would have less appeal to developing countries and therefore favour the International Bank's initiative."[69] The World Bank was a postwar institution that cultivated good relationships with newly independent countries, viewing them as customers. Capital-exporting governments understood the importance of this: "we recognize that an arbitration centre under IBRD auspices is likely to be more widely used especially by newly independent countries in Africa and Asia. Most under developed countries respect the Bank and would not wish to prejudice their chances of future loans by refusing to avail themselves of its arbitration facilities."[70]

Second, capital-exporting governments expected capital-importing countries to ratify the Convention and abide by any arbitration decisions because to do otherwise would lock them out of access to international finance. This reasoning was made clear in internal discussions: "we think that the main force behind the new centre . . . will be the very considerable prestige of the International Bank and the fact that to flout an agreement to resort to the new centre for arbitration or conciliation would be very damaging to the credit-worthiness of the party concerned."[71] Officials from capital-exporting countries were careful not to discuss this reasoning openly, fearing that would destroy any chance of capital-importing countries joining the proposed center. Even some officials in capital-exporting governments questioned the wisdom of locating ICSID within the Bank, because doing so might make countries skeptical of the Bank: "If, as is likely, most of the judgments favoured the lender rather than the borrower, this might make the IBRD less popular among under developed countries."[72] This was a minority view, however—in general, the Bank's experience brokering settlements and its commanding reputation as a creditor was perceived to qualify it well to propose a new arbitration organization.

[68] Briefing for H.M. Ambassador in Washington, result of a meeting held at the Treasury, January 5, 1962 "Settlement of Disputes between Governments and Private Parties." UK T 312/251.

[69] Draft Telegram to Washington: IBRD Arbitration (undated, likely December 1962, written by Hester Boothroyd). UK T 312: 545 (1962–3).

[70] Briefing for H.M. Ambassador in Washington, result of a meeting held at the Treasury, January 5, 1962, "Settlement of Disputes between Governments and Private Parties." UK T 312/251.

[71] Draft Telegram to Washington: IBRD Arbitration (undated, likely December 1962, written by Hester Boothroyd). UK T 312: 545 (1962–3).

[72] Letter from Hester Boothroyd to Mrs. Hedley-Miller, November 7, 1961. UK T 312/251.

THE BANK'S STRATEGY FOR CREATING DISPUTE RESOLUTION MACHINERY

The previous sections demonstrated the Bank's motivation for promoting private investment, its experience with investment dispute resolution, and the privileged information it had about other proposals. In this context, the Bank's management approved a minimalist proposal for dispute resolution machinery. The Bank's management designed a strategy to shepherd the proposal into force that relied upon consultation and small steps to build support for the proposal. This section traces the Bank's strategy in creating ICSID. The focus here is on the Bank's strategy; the next chapter analyzes states' responses.

The Initial Proposal—and the Brokering that Preceded It

Addressing the Board of Governors during the 1961 Annual Meeting, Bank President Eugene Black recalled that the Bank had been asked to mediate disputes several times before, and then gently introduced the idea of ICSID:

> Our experience has confirmed my belief that a very useful contribution could be made by some sort of special forum for the conciliation or arbitration of these disputes. The results of an inquiry made by the Secretary-General of the United Nations show that this belief is widely shared. The fact that governments and private interests have turned to the Bank to provide this assistance indicates the lack of any other specific machinery for conciliation and arbitration which is regarded as adequate by investors and governments alike. I therefore intend to explore with other institutions, and with member governments, whether something might not be done to promote the establishment of machinery of this kind.[73]

Black's address to the Board of Governors illustrates two traits that defined how World Bank officials used agenda-setting and brokering to shepherd the ICSID Convention into existence. First, the tone is humble and deferential.[74] There is nothing prescriptive; he places the Bank in a studious posture, emphasizing that it would survey the problem in cooperation with other organizations. He only hints at the possibility that after much consideration, the Bank might act. Black's hesitant approach may have been disingenuous. A draft Convention had already been written (although not circulated) and

[73] Address by Eugene Black to the Annual Meeting of the Board of Governors, September 19, 1961, quoted in ICSID 1970: 3.

[74] These two traits were characteristic of Black, who cultivated good relations with the Bank's Board. Black's successor George Woods adopted a similarly sensitive approach in the case of ICSID, unlike his approach to other issues.

Broches had set out detailed plans for ICSID in an internal memo four months before Black spoke—and the organization that eventually came into being is, in its main features, identical to the one laid out in the memo.[75]

The second defining trait is that the World Bank had engaged in serious brokering. The deferential framing of Black's speech belies the amount of brokering that had gone on behind the scenes. In his speech, Black observes that "the results of an inquiry made by the Secretary-General of the United Nations" suggests support for the World Bank becoming involved with investment arbitration.[76] The reason this UN inquiry, called the Bloch Report, expressed support for this involvement is because Broches asked Bloch to insert support for the idea into his report. A letter written to a British official in June 1961, three months before Black's speech, says: "Broches has discussed with Bloch the interaction between ECOSOC [the United Nations Economic and Social Council] and the proposed World Bank scheme. The latter was quite happy about the proposed launching of the World Bank scheme and thought that he could give it an appropriate degree of support."[77] Broches had asked for the report to "make an appropriate hint in the direction of the World Bank."[78]

Since the passages on investor–state arbitration in the Bloch Report reflect conversations between Broches and Bloch, they can be viewed as indicators of Broches' thinking in 1960—ostensibly before the Bank even began to consider the idea of a formal arbitration convention. The report provides several pages of astute analysis, observing that: (i) limiting the agreement to arbitration would be more practical or politically feasible than the OECD Drafts;[79] (ii) feasibility would be bolstered by building on existing instruments, such as US investment guarantee agreements, that provide for arbitration of disputes "without formulating the governing rules of law";[80] and (iii) creating a new arbitral body "not identified with a commercial approach might be more readily acceptable to the governments of some capital-receiving countries."[81] Contemporary observers, such as Brandon, agreed with the report, observing that the "establishment [of an arbitral system] could in some circumstances be facilitated from the political standpoint if it were considered separately [from

[75] SecM 61–192, August 28 1961, quoted in ICSID 1970: 13.

[76] Progress Report by the Secretary General, United Nations Economic and Social Council, February 26, 1960 (E/3325): 76–81. See also Parra 2016: 155.

[77] Letter from J. Blair to Hester Boothroyd, Treasury, June 28, 1961. UK T 312/251.

[78] Letter from J. Blair to Hester Boothroyd, Treasury, June 28, 1961. UK T 312/251.

[79] Progress Report by the Secretary General, United Nations Economic and Social Council, February 26, 1960 (E/3325): 79.

[80] Progress Report by the Secretary General, United Nations Economic and Social Council, February 26, 1960 (E/3325): 79.

[81] Progress Report by the Secretary General, United Nations Economic and Social Council, February 26, 1960 (E/3325): 81.

a multilateral investment treaty]."[82] Brandon also agreed with the Bloch Report that the conclusion of a separate arbitration agreement would not hinder the conclusion of substantive agreements, and in fact might facilitate their conclusion. As the Bloch Report notes: "If such an agency were able to achieve a wide practice and prestige, it might in time become the natural fulcrum for the conclusion of bilateral, and possible multilateral, agreements between governments on foreign private investments."[83] For those monitoring developments closely, then, the image of a standalone arbitration convention as the central node connecting a vast array of bilateral and multilateral agreements was clear as early as 1960. It is worth emphasizing this point: international officials laid out a vision for investment governance that would be realized fully over the next six decades. More remarkably, the realization of this vision looked so chaotic that law professors in 2014 claimed the development of investment governance could only be understood using chaos theory.[84]

A year later, in 1961, British officials received word that Broches had "discussed the idea [of Black proposing ICSID] with US State Dept and US Treasury who both seemed in favour."[85] When the relevant official from the British Embassy in Washington was sent to investigate, he was charmed by Broches ("the able and very friendly General Counsel of the Bank"), who gently convinced him that the Bank should be tasked with setting up arbitration facilities. This is what informal agenda-setting looks like when it is subtle, suggestive, and effective. The official wrote back to London:

> Whatever is decided the Bank would hope not to be frozen out. They would like to be consulted because, so it seemed to Mr. Broches, they could probably play a more useful role in this connection than the United Nations where discussions tend to become acrimonious. It might, therefore, be useful for the initiative to be passed to the Bank.[86]

Broches asked for a mandate in a subtle, diplomatic way. This mode of transmission—Broches having conversations with British officials in Washington, which were then described to the relevant officials in the Foreign Office and Treasury back in London—was central to reversing the British position towards ICSID. British officials were initially skeptical and opposed, but over time, and after Broches and his staff provided detailed responses to their concerns, they dropped their opposition. All of this happened years before the consultative conferences.

[82] Brandon 1960: 125.

[83] Progress Report by the Secretary General, United Nations Economic and Social Council, February 26, 1960 (E/3325): 81.

[84] Pauwelyn 2014.

[85] Letter from Hester Boothroyd to Mr. Milner-Barry, July 12, 1961. UK T 312/251.

[86] Letter from Peter Reilly to Hester Boothroyd, August 4, 1961. UK T 312/251.

Broches' conversation with the British embassy official demonstrates another aspect of brokering—embodying the middle ground can require distancing oneself from all sides. Broches was likely aware that Lord Shawcross's unyielding advocacy for investment protection and connections with Shell had led some officials within the British government to be wary of Shawcross, so he distanced himself from Shawcross in conversations with British officials and downplayed the information about his plans for ICSID that Shawcross gave to British officials. After a conversation with Broches, a British official wrote: "Lord Shawcross's ideas about the Bank's views have probably reached him via his connection with Shell. Shell have been pushing the idea of international conciliation and arbitration for some time and have been talking with the Bank staff. Perhaps wishful thinking has tended to exaggerate their idea of the Bank's intentions."[87] Yet the reality was likely more complicated than "wishful thinking" would suggest—Shawcross's assistant, John Blair, had excellent information about the proposal for ICSID. Blair was involved, alongside Broches, in the formulation of a 1961 Draft Convention that is a precursor to ICSID. Then he sent this 1961 Draft, in confidence, to the British government.[88]

The 1961 "Draft Convention on the Conciliation and Arbitration of International Investment Disputes" was produced by a tiny committee organized under the auspices of the American Bar Association. The committee was Broches, Georges Delaume of the World Bank, Elihu Lauterpacht, Clifford Hynning, George Haight, L. Sandberg, and Shawcross's assistant Blair.[89] There is a connection between the composition of this committee and the Abadan dispute, which was concluded merely six years earlier. Lauterpacht drafted the articles for dispute resolution in the Consortium Agreement that ended the Abadan dispute, ideas which he then expanded into a memo for the Shawcross Draft, which later became the appendix for the Abs–Shawcross Draft.[90] Blair, Haight, and possibly Sandberg were counsel for Shell. Hynning and Haight were prominent American lawyers who were central to the US ratification of the New York Convention.[91]

This Draft Convention was not an official World Bank document, but it is unmistakably an early version of the ICSID Convention. This Draft also

[87] Letter from Peter Reilly to Hester Boothroyd, August 4, 1961. UK T 312/251.

[88] Letter from John Blair to Hester Boothroyd, November 13, 1961. UK T 312/251.

[89] Letter from John Blair to Hester Boothroyd, November 13, 1961. UK T 312/251.

[90] Lauterpacht (2008: 8) and Chernykh (forthcoming). This is where individual standing in investment and individual standing in human rights connect. Hersch Lauterpacht developed the idea of individual standing against a state in his writings on the European Court of Human Rights, which his son transposed to the investment context after the ICJ decided it had no jurisdiction in the Abadan (AIOC) case. Individual standing was rare but not unprecedented: individuals had standing at the Central American Court of Justice and a few other bodies.

[91] Hale 2015: 217–21. Haight was head of the US section of the ICC and general counsel for Royal Dutch Shell's US affiliate.

includes source notes that show provisions were, for instance, "adapted from Statute for the International Court of Justice, Articles 4, 9, 16 & 21"; "adapted from Article VII of the Articles of Agreement of the International Bank for Reconstruction and Development"; "adapted from International Chamber of Commerce, Rules on Conciliation and Arbitration (1955)"; or "adapted from the Final Draft (1958) of the Model Rules of Arbitral Procedure of the International Law Commission."[92] The source notes show provision-by-provision how public and private international law were blended to craft this Draft. This Draft also includes a provision that jurisdiction could come from an investment treaty—showing that as early as 1961, the connection between investment treaties and investor–state arbitration was clear.[93] The finished American Bar Association Draft Convention is dated October 20, 1961, but work on it must have begun earlier, especially as this Draft cites an earlier "Delaume Draft," which would have emerged within the Legal Department of the Bank.[94] This Draft remained confidential, and has not been mentioned in any publication.[95]

The first official proposal for ICSID was Broches' August 1961 memorandum.[96] The memo plays to capital-importing states more than the 1961 ABA Draft: for instance, while the ABA Draft states that arbitration takes the place of local remedies, Broches' memo suggests "the establishment of such machinery" need not interfere with a requirement to exhaust local remedies, which he terms a "customary principle of international law."[97] The double-consent formulation was already present, and being used to pre-empt the concerns of capital-importing states: the memo promises that ICSID would have no compulsory jurisdiction, and would operate only by specific state consent.[98] Separating the consents in time and instrument allowed difficult issues, including substantive standards, to be pushed into the future. Pushing debates over substance into the future was important not only to secure agreement from capital-importing states, but also to secure agreement among OECD states, which had not been (and have not since been) able to agree binding substantive standards among themselves. In his response to Broches' memo, the American Executive Director recognized the absence of substance as a

[92] American Bar Association, Section of International & Comparative Law, Convention on the Conciliation and Arbitration of International Investment Disputes, October 20, 1961. Included in the Letter from John Blair to Hester Boothroyd, November 13, 1961. UK T 312/251.

[93] Article III (1) 3. American Bar Association, Section of International & Comparative Law, Convention on the Conciliation and Arbitration of International Investment Disputes, October 20, 1961. Included in the Letter from John Blair to Hester Boothroyd, November 13, 1961. UK T 312/251.

[94] Named after Georges Delaume, the World Bank Legal Department official.

[95] Schreuer et al. (2009) and Parra (2017) do not mention this Draft.

[96] SecM 61–192, quoted in ICSID 1970: 1.

[97] SecM 61–192, quoted in ICSID 1970: 2.

[98] Point 4, SecM 61–192, quoted in ICSID 1970: 2.

virtue that enabled the US to support ICSID: "Since the Bank's proposal did not attempt to establish some such substantive rules of law, his Government did not look at it with the same reservations as they had for a multilateral investment code."[99]

In conclusion, the proposal for ICSID emerged essentially complete from the Bank's Legal Department. The idea was then explained to the Bank's President, then to the Bank's main shareholders (a handful of capital-exporters), and then to the Bank's member states generally. Broches recalled how George Woods (who replaced Eugene Black as Bank President in 1963) introduced the idea of ICSID to officials over lunch, as a way of building support for the idea.[100] This was brokering in action: Woods had lunch with the Executive Directors "in order of importance," which was an opportunity to get to know them and for Broches (who attended in case Woods needed to be corrected on the substance of ICSID) to get to know their countries' views on the proposal.[101] This is not the path that ideas are expected to travel in conventional approaches: ICSID, unlike earlier arms of the World Bank, was not an idea delegated by a powerful state to its agent. The ICSID Convention started with World Bank officials and then travelled to states.

Introducing the Idea to States: the Strategy Behind the Roadshow and the Committee

The proposal for ICSID travelled to states in a literal sense. After preparing a Draft and holding initial meetings with the Executive Directors, the World Bank's Legal Department took "the show on the road" and convened a series of consultative conferences in different regions of the world to introduce governments to the idea. Then, after further meetings with the Executive Directors and a vote in the Board of Governors, the Bank held a three week-long Legal Committee in Washington DC. After this, the Legal Department submitted a finished Convention to the Executive Directors, who opened the Convention for ratification by states.

The World Bank invented a new procedure in order to create ICSID. The Bank decided against following its past procedure of drafting new organizational charters fully internally (as it had done with the IFC and IDA), but also decided against holding a diplomatic conference to which states would send representatives.[102] On the one hand, if the Convention were drafted internally,

[99] Point 17, SecM 62–68, quoted in ICSID 1970: 13.
[100] Broches 1984 (May): 36. [101] Broches 1984 (May): 36.
[102] Parra (2017: 26, more generally 25–7; 48–9; 59–61) discusses this decision, noting "[t]he Bank might instead have taken the more usual approach of having the texts of such treaties drawn up at international conferences convened for the purpose."

it might not be considered representative or legitimate enough to garner wide support, while on the other hand, if a full diplomatic conference were held, several officials appear to have believed that the proposal for ICSID would fail. Therefore, a solution was created that mimicked the representativeness of a diplomatic conference, yet with operating procedures that meant only the World Bank had the power to change the document.

Comparing ICSID's drafting against the drafting of the IFC and IDA Articles shows the extent to which ICSID's creation was a *sui generis* process. The Articles for the IFC and IDA were drafted internally by the Bank, discussed by the Executive Directors, and then submitted to states for ratification.[103] These Articles emerged fully formed from within the Bank and then states could decide whether to join or not. Broches remembered the drafting of the IFC Articles: "There was no diplomatic conference, and the treaty was drafted and opened for signature and acceptance not by the plenary organ of the Bank, the Board of Governors, but by an executive organ, the Executive Directors, then seventeen in number."[104] The distinction between the Executive Directors and the Board of Governors is important. On the Board of Governors, each member state has one seat and one vote. Thus, as the Bank's membership grew rapidly in the late 1950s, the number of seats on the Board of Governors grew from fifty-eight in 1959 to 102 in 1964. In contrast, the number of Executive Director seats did not change to reflect this growth. Executive Directorships are allocated using a formula that relies primarily on shares of Bank capital owned.[105] The largest shareholders each appoint a Director. Smaller shareholders share an Executive Director: sometimes one Director represents twenty-one states.[106] The largest shareholders also tend to be capital-exporting states. The Bank's smallest shareholders tend to be the poorest, smallest states; their representation on the Executive Directors is least direct, and their awareness of what happens during Executive Director meetings tends to be weakest.

The main voices in the debate during the crafting of the IFC and IDA Articles were those of the capital-exporting states.[107] This was seen as appropriate because the IFC and IDA were funding mechanisms, at their core

[103] As Broches (1990: 7) put it, "one of the interesting things [about] the World Bank is that all the affiliate institutions would draft [were drafted]—not at international conferences but in the Board of Directors of 20 to 22 people."

[104] Broches [1959] 1995: 29.

[105] Each member receives votes consisting of share votes (one vote for each share of the Bank's capital stock held by the member) plus basic votes (calculated so that the sum of all basic votes is equal to 5.55 percent of the sum of basic votes and share votes for all members) (World Bank 2014).

[106] In 2012, two Executive Directors—representing twenty-one countries each—represented Africa (World Bank, Corporate Secretariat 2014).

[107] It should be noted that the proposal for IDA emerged from the Board of Governors. Yet IDA was very much an American proposal—put forward by the US Treasury Secretary at the

agreements among rich countries about what arrangements they would use to channel capital to poor countries.[108] ICSID, in contrast, was a legal mechanism. The main voices in its drafting could not be those of Executive Directors from capital-exporting states—these Directors represented exactly the wrong constituency. The proposal's success rested upon the perceptions of capital-importing states. Capital-importing states had a voice in UN organs by 1964, and expected the same from the World Bank. President Woods went out of his way to make "a supportive speech" to the first UNCTAD.[109] He announced that the Bank was beginning agriculture loans, and loans for education were to be expected—these were signs that the Bank was aligning its focus more with borrowers' priorities and less with the bond markets.[110] Woods' overture was warmly received.[111] It was not window-dressing either: the Bank saw UNCTAD as a forum for its borrowers and listened to it—at least on a few issues.[112] For ICSID to have any legitimacy, Woods and other top officials knew the representativeness of ICSID's drafting needed to match—at least outwardly—the representativeness of the UNCTAD proceedings.

While matching the representativeness of the UNCTAD meetings, capital-exporters and the World Bank sought to avoid a full diplomatic conference, seemingly out of a fear that the proposal would fail. As the British Executive Director put it: "While he was not against intergovernmental conferences per se . . . the outcome would, in his opinion, be very much in doubt."[113] The idea of a diplomatic conference to negotiate the ICSID Convention was proposed repeatedly during the consultative conferences and subsequently discussed in meetings of the Executive Directors.[114] It was rejected by the World Bank's management, with Woods arguing that a diplomatic conference would "unnecessarily delay and impede progress."[115] After returning from the Santiago consultative conference, an American official was reported informing the Executive Directors: "From his experience as an expert at the Santiago meeting, he thought it extremely doubtful that a multilateral diplomatic conference could deal effectively with a Convention of such scope and complexity."[116]

Annual Meeting in 1958—and key discussions did not extend beyond the Bank's main shareholders.

[108] In the case of the IFC, it was funding for private enterprises; in the case of IDA, it was concessionary loans or grants.

[109] Kapur, Lewis, Webb 1997: 16.

[110] Mason and Asher 1973: 570.

[111] After this address, Raul Prebisch described Woods as the Bank's Pope John XXIII, who had proved an unexpected revolutionary, stressing human rights and appealing to richer nations to help the poor. Noted in Kapur, Lewis, Webb 1997: 176–7.

[112] Oliver 1995: 108.

[113] ICSID 1970: 587.

[114] For instance, one delegate "felt . . . that an instrument of such significance ought to be discussed in a wider forum than that offered by a regional meeting" (ICSID 1970: 543).

[115] SID/64-3, quoted in ICSID 1970: 556. Parra (2017: 59) also notes this quote and discusses the ensuing meeting of the Executive Directors (2017: 59–61).

[116] ICSID 1970: 590.

This concern about effectiveness was likely a euphemism: at the Santiago meeting he had witnessed principled, unyielding opposition to the idea of investor–state arbitration, and that opposition might make a multilateral conference ineffective. The Bank's strategy was to keep meetings consultative: first in consultative regional conferences and subsequently in a committee of experts.

The Consultative Roadshow

Between December 1963 and May 1964, the Bank's Legal Department, with help from the UN, convened four conferences in different regions of the world. As Broches explained:

> We hit on the idea of taking the show on the road to get comments from member countries, because we didn't get them through the Directors... I have to take credit for the idea of having four regional consultative meetings in the four capitals of the UN: Geneva, Santiago, Bangkok, and Addis Ababa. The Bank paid for up to two experts for one week—travel and subsistence... [these] representatives of countries were not really representing these countries, they were experts-designate.[117]

The four conferences were attended by experts from eighty-six countries. These experts-designate came from a mix of backgrounds: some were private lawyers, while others were professors, cabinet members, or elder statesmen who had attended Bretton Woods.[118] A typical representative was a legal counsel from a finance ministry or a central bank.[119] The defining trait these experts-designate shared was legal training. The Bank asked member states to prioritize expertise, even if that meant sending individuals who were not in government. States duly sent lawyers expert in procedure, not the individuals responsible for foreign investment policymaking. This group of lawyers was exactly the group the Bank wanted, as they could provide expert feedback and a semblance of representativeness, but in a cordial setting where participants

[117] Broches 1984 (May): 38.

[118] For instance, this is how attendance at the Santiago conference was summarized for the Bank's board: "Most of the delegates were lawyers, some of them of great distinction, like Mr [Guillermo] Sevilla Sacasa of Nicaragua [Ambassador to the US 1943–1979, second in succession to the President] and Mr Alfonso Espinoza of Venezuela [former Finance Minister, former President of the Central Bank, lawyer and economist by training] both veterans of Bretton Woods. Mr Roberto Ramirez, President of the Central Bank of Honduras and an old friend of the Bank, represented his country." ICSID 1970: 365.

[119] For example, Australia sent: "Principal Legal Officer, Attorney General's Department." Israel sent: "Legal Adviser, Ministry of Finance" and "Senior Economist, Bank of Israel." Malaysia sent: "Principal Assistant Secretary, The Treasury" and "Senior Federal Counsel, Attorney's General Office." Pakistan sent: "Joint Secretary, Ministry of Law." ICSID 1970: 459.

saw themselves as moving the discussion on investment protection "above" politics and into the realm of law.

World Bank officials carefully structured these conferences in a format that was designed to give an impression of representativeness, but without being deliberative. It was always the Bank's decision whether or not to incorporate any feedback. As Broches remembered: "There was no voting at these meetings. In addition to comments, suggestions were advanced, and some compromises were reached but all in the framework of consultations."[120] The experts-designate were not representing their governments. No expert-designate spoke on behalf of their government, even those experts-designate that were employed by the governments that sent them. They were expressing quasi-personal views in a closed, consultative forum.

The Bank structured the conferences to diffuse any disagreements that might impede the proposal. The regional structure kept resistance to the Convention fragmented and enabled the Bank to present responses to the Convention along regional lines. Latin America was characterized as intransigent in its opposition, while other capital-importing regions were presented as receptive.[121] This misrepresented the actual responses from both Latin American and other capital-importing states, as Chapter five details.

The Bank went to great lengths to avoid opposition uniting. The Bank chose not to circulate summary records from the earlier consultative conferences at later consultative conferences.[122] When asked during the later conferences about how states in other regions had responded, Broches gave vague or selective indications.[123] The Bank was concerned that different strands of resistance would unite and the Convention would not be agreed. As chair, Broches said that the Bank did not circulate summaries in order to conserve resources.[124] Yet the Bank was prepared to pay for over one hundred experts to attend the regional consultative conferences, and then to pay for over one hundred experts to fly to Washington from national capitals for the drafting committee, which required three weeks of per diems for each expert. Given the considerable funds invested in the creation of ICSID, it is extremely unlikely that the reason for not circulating summaries was a financial or resource constraint.

[120] Broches 1984 (May): 37. [121] For instance, Szasz 1970: 256.

[122] Although never stated explicitly, it is clear in the records that the delegates, even at the final consultative conference, had not been sent any summaries or comments from previous consultative conferences. This can be clearly inferred from a comment Broches made as chair (ICSID 1970: 547).

[123] For example, when asked a question in the Bangkok consultative conference, Broches answered: "In Africa, no delegate had dissented from the view that it would be advantageous to remove disputes from the intergovernmental sphere. On the contrary, they had expressed a preference for the approach embodied in the Convention" (ICSID 1970: 541).

[124] ICSID 1970: 475. Broches was responding to a request for copies of statements made earlier at the same conference.

The roadshow served two purposes for the World Bank. First, in a practical sense, the Bank's management needed more feedback, particularly from legal experts with an interest in procedural matters.[125] Second, and more important, was that in a political sense, the Bank's management needed to familiarize governments with the proposal, as familiarity was likely to build support and lessen skepticism about it. The experts-designate also provided Broches and his team at the Bank with valuable information: an assessment of how likely their countries were to join such an institution, if one were created. As Woods said, it was "a method of gauging the reactions and opinions of those countries which had formed at least a preliminary opinion on the proposal."[126] This was one of the most important functions of these experts. The way Broches spoke about it years later demonstrates the centrality of this function:

> The consultative meetings gave an enormous amount of useful information. After these four meetings, I wrote a report to the Board—and I didn't do all these things alone, I had two or three people working with me—in which I said that on the basis of these reports of the consultative meetings, I was satisfied that it would be possible to work out something that would command wide support.[127]

The Bank used the consultative conferences to check that both capital-importing and capital-exporting states were sufficiently receptive to move forward with the proposal.

The consultative conferences also spread the idea of ICSID. The Bank explained the idea to legal experts, who could then spread it in each of their countries. This was particularly important in newly independent countries with capacity-constrained ministries. Many experts asked the Bank to teach or disseminate information about investment agreements and dispute resolution. For instance, the expert-designate from China (Taiwan) referred to a proposal from Lebanon that the Bank "provide expert legal guidance in the drafting of investment agreements" and then asked if the Bank "would also consider sponsoring seminars or training courses at which legal experts could be trained in those subjects."[128] The records from the consultative conferences show representatives becoming acquainted with the idea of ICSID, and in some cases taking up its logic.

On the basis of the consultative conferences, the Bank's management believed that there would be enough support for the proposal to succeed,

[125] Creating ICSID posed legal questions, but the Executive Directors and the people in government they consulted, were not lawyers. Broches (1984 May: 37) said: "Executive Directors report to Ministries of Finance, and while the purpose of the exercise was developmental, the technique was not only legal, but procedural. It was particularly difficult for people who are not lawyers, or who are lawyers but not interested in procedural matters."

[126] SID/64-3, quoted in ICSID 1970: 554.

[127] Broches 1984 (May): 37–8. [128] ICSID 1970: 544.

even though some countries would resist.[129] In other words, the Bank's management expected that a show of opposition would occur when the idea was put to a vote at the Board of Governors, but also believed, correctly, that this show of opposition would not be sufficient to stop the proposal.

The "No de Tokio" and the Legal Committee

At the 1964 Annual Meeting of the World Bank, President Woods asked the Board of Governors to pass a resolution asking the Executive Directors to prepare a Convention on the Settlement of Investment Disputes. President Woods first discussed investment insurance, and then introduced the proposal for ICSID as "another approach [to facilitating foreign investment], which we have actively sponsored."[130] He asked the Board of Governors to pass a resolution that requested the Executive Directors of the Bank "to formulate a convention" and explained that a committee of experts designated by interested governments would be assembled to help the Executive Directors "keep in mind the desirability of arriving at a text which could be accepted by the largest possible number of governments."[131] President Woods then urged the unanimous support for the resolution.

The resolution did not get unanimous approval. Instead, the proposal triggered the "No de Tokio" protest. The Chilean Governor, Felix Ruiz, also Vice President of the Banco Central de Chile, acted as a spokesman for a group of twenty-one states, primarily but not exclusively Latin American, which opposed the proposal. After stating that the legal systems of all Latin Americans "prohibit confiscation and discrimination" and require that expropriation be accompanied by compensation, Ruiz focused on equality:

> The new system that has been suggested would give the foreign investor, by virtue of the fact that he is a foreigner, the right to sue a sovereign state outside its national territory, dispensing with the courts of law. This provision . . . would confer a privilege on the foreign investor, placing the nationals of the country concerned in a position of inferiority.[132]

The vote on this resolution was the only moment, apart from ratification, when officials could formally express their governments' views on the proposal for ICSID. If there had been global deliberations or more information sharing, would more states have joined the Chilean statement? Possibly, as will be seen in Chapter five. As it happened though, resistance was fragmented along regional lines—and then written off as the product of Latin America's particular history with investment protection. The Board of Governors approved

[129] Broches 1984 (May): 39.
[130] ICSID 1970: 605.
[131] World Bank 1964: 34.
[132] ICSID 1970: 606.

the Bank's resolution for the Executive Directors to draft a Convention, with assistance from a committee of legal experts.

The Legal Committee met for three weeks in November–December 1964. Broches opened the committee by closing off the possibility of debate on the idea of investor–state arbitration, telling the experts-designate: "The present meeting was no longer concerned with the question of the desirability of creating machinery for facilitating the settlement of investment disputes since that question had already been decided in the affirmative."[133] During the Legal Committee, as during the consultative conferences, the formal power to change the document remained with the Chair (Broches) and the Bank. When experts-designate encountered an issue on which they disagreed, they would decide if they considered it important. If representatives felt the issue was not particularly essential, they would resolve it then and there with a show of hands. If the issue was felt to be important, it was removed from the discussion and reported to the Executive Directors. Broches, who chaired the committee, later termed it a "voting/non-voting system," and noted that it "was pretty innovative" and "worked pretty well."[134] The system got things done. The drafting committee and remaining steps were handled efficiently: by December 11, 1964, Broches submitted a Revised Draft of the ICSID Convention to the Executive Directors, then in a series of meetings from February to March 1965, the Executive Directors discussed the Convention before approving a final version of the Convention on March 18, 1965.[135]

The puzzling aspect of the Legal Committee is that it was unnecessary. The World Bank Executive Directors could have formulated the Convention without the assistance or advice of the Legal Committee. If they sought legal advice, the Executive Directors could have mailed the Draft Convention to a few ministries or eminent lawyers or professors. Why did President Woods—not known for profligacy or consensus-building—take the unprecedented step of announcing that the Bank would pay for every member country to send a legal expert for three weeks of drafting?[136] In a note to the Executive Directors, he wrote:

> I have considered whether it would be possible to limit in some way the size of the Committee... However, there appears to be no practicable formula which would guarantee a balanced composition of a committee with limited membership, since very few of the Executive Directors representing more than one country represent

[133] ICSID 1970: 674. [134] Broches 1984 (May): 38–9.

[135] Parra (2017: 81–5) describes these meetings in detail.

[136] All 102 member states of the Bank were invited to send experts, but experts from only sixty-one actually took part (Parra 2012: 75). For perspective, the drafting committee lasted the same length of time as the entire 1944 Bretton Woods conference, and more than double the number of states were invited.

> homogeneous groups. I have therefore concluded that we should give every member the right to send a representative to serve on the Committee.[137]

Woods indicates, obliquely, that the Legal Committee was an exercise in consensus-building and representation. These two aims were crucial given the international political landscape of 1964, and were likely the main reasons why the Legal Committee was held. There are also related reasons why the Bank decided to fund a Legal Committee.

ICSID's Articles were a chance for Broches and his team to leave a stronger framework for ICSID than the one bequeathed to the Bank by Bretton Woods. The formal authority for interpreting the World Bank's Articles rests with the Board of Governors, but in practice interpretation rests with the Legal Department, of which Broches was the head. In any international organization, a great deal of interpretation takes place informally, within the organization.[138] Typically, lawyers use preparatory papers or records from drafting conferences to substantiate interpretations. Yet no official papers existed from Bretton Woods.[139] Those working in the Bank's Legal Department bemoaned the lack of *travaux préparatoires* from Bretton Woods. As Broches put it:

> The technical organization of the [1944 Bretton Woods] conference was very poor. There were no proper records of the proceedings. There were documents but there were no minutes, which might have explained why a particular provision was adopted or changed. The Fund did have some minutes about some meetings which may still exist. Some draft minutes are said to have been destroyed because there were such gaps they were regarded as more harmful than helpful. On the Bank there's nothing except documents.[140]

The lack of minutes was inconvenient for the legal departments of the IMF and the World Bank, but not a serious problem, since the authority to interpret their Articles is held within those institutions. For ICSID, however, the power to interpret the Convention would rest with tribunals. The individuals on these tribunals would come from diverse backgrounds and would operate outside the Bank's institutional culture and without board oversight. The proposed Convention did not limit their interpretive powers. The framers of ICSID therefore believed it was imperative to leave these tribunals with thorough *travaux préparatoires*.

137 Point 2, R 64–105, quoted in ICSID 1970: 604.

138 Chayes and Chayes 1995: 201.

139 In recent years, papers from the US delegation have been published by a think tank and been used by researchers as *travaux préparatoires*. These papers, however, are not a formal institutional record, have never been stored at the Bank, and were never used in a formal capacity by Broches or others.

140 Broches 1984 (April): 2.

ICSID needed a strong framework of procedure so that awards rendered under its auspices would be perceived as legitimate. The Bank's earlier mediations of investment disputes followed no formal procedure: they were ad hoc, personality-driven affairs. ICSID was the Bank's first foray into creating legal mechanisms, and was led by the Legal Department: the relevant officials were keen to ensure that the Convention had excellent procedural credentials. After the Convention was agreed, the Bank spent two years formulating precise regulations and rules of procedure for ICSID.[141] In 1965/66, the Bank hired Paul Szasz, on his way to becoming one of the world's foremost experts on procedure in public international law, to work exclusively on the regulations and rules of procedure.[142] The Convention is sent to states in a packet: the Convention itself (twenty-eight pages), the accompanying Report of the Executive Directors (sixteen pages), and the Regulations and Rules of Procedure (sixty-nine pages). Each of these documents sets out what ICSID is and what it is not. Collectively, they reflect the intent of Broches and others to leave a stronger framework than the World Bank's Articles.

A final reason why the Bank's management took the extraordinary step of forming a Legal Committee was because it would provide a chance for individuals from many states—particularly officials from poor, postcolonial states—to learn about ICSID. Educating officials was tied to representation and consensus-building: it was through explaining the logic of investor–state arbitration and the purported benefits (put bluntly, more investment and no espousal) that consensus could be built. A close reading of the Bank's internal documents show that education was important, even though it was rarely stated explicitly. In large part because the Legal Committee was an additional opportunity for education, Woods believed that it was important to invite all World Bank member states, especially those "who have had reservations or who, for whatever reason, do not now envisage joining any convention which may emerge."[143]

The World Bank's strategy to create ICSID was summarized in a November 1963 article in *The Washington Post*. Under a section titled "Low-Key Approach," the article stated: "Extended and enthusiastic public discussion of the mechanism has been deliberately avoided. The low-key approach is designed to reassure developing nations which might otherwise fear that the

[141] The Rules of Procedure clarify certain issues that were intentionally left ambiguous in the Convention itself. Broches recognized that small controversies could be pushed forward and dealt with in the Rules of Procedure, after state officials had finished discussing (and ratifying) the Convention. I am grateful to an official at the ICSID Secretariat for this insight.

[142] Szasz subsequently joined the office of Legal Counsel at the United Nations. He was later instrumental in drafting the constitutions of Bosnia, Namibia, and the International Fund for Agricultural Development, in addition to many other notable contributions to international law. See Szasz 1988; Brown Weiss 2002.

[143] George Woods' opening speech to the Drafting Convention, quoted in ICSID 1970: 673.

capital-exporting countries are trying to put something over on them."[144] The World Bank pursued this careful strategy throughout the drafting of the ICSID Convention: "enthusiastic public discussion" was avoided, steps were taken to prevent open disagreements, and all discussions were structured as consultations.

CONCLUSION

This chapter sets out the context in which the World Bank proposed ICSID and analyzes the Bank's motivation, resources, and strategy in doing so. The first section elaborates on the World Bank's access to privileged information about multilateral insurance and a code. World Bank officials then set the agenda, away from a multilateral code or insurance agency and toward arbitration. World Bank officials set the agenda with a clear sense of their audience; they knew the group of government officials that could stop their plans. The second section discusses who was in this group of officials.

The third section delves into why the early World Bank was an improbable organization to create legal machinery related to investment protection. Yet the Bank's Articles of Agreement task it with promoting private investment, and in fulfilling this mandate, Bank officials developed unparalleled expertise, access to privileged information, and a reputation for competent leadership. The fourth section of the chapter discusses the World Bank's experience mediating investment disputes before drafting the proposal for ICSID. This experience positioned the World Bank as a broker—an actor able to find acceptable midpoints between capital-importing and capital-exporting states when it came to investment disputes.

The final section of the chapter evaluates how the World Bank officials introduced their proposal to states. The creation of ICSID was almost entirely Bank-led, and had a profoundly interstate and legal character. Investors were largely absent. Bank officials were so concerned that distributional disagreements would derail the proposal that they designed an entirely new procedure in order to make it nearly impossible for states to derail the drafting. The Bank invited states to send experts-designate, not formal representatives, and structured the participation of these experts within a consultative framework, with Bank officials having final say over any changes. Bank officials also engaged in extensive behind-the-scenes brokering.

[144] Bernard Nossiter, "Foreign Fund Safeguard Program Taking Shape," *Washington Post*, November 30, 1963. Tellingly, Nossiter described ICSID as "a new World Bank plan to protect overseas investment."

Contemporary observers recognized the Bank's skillful brokering. In 1969, Schwarzenberger wrote:

> The crucial question is the extent to which the draftsmen of the Convention considered it prudent to commit the governments of capital-importing states, without unduly rousing their susceptibilities as sovereign and equal members of the United Nations. They have come as near as is possible to the point of squaring this particular circle. With remarkable ingenuity, they have couched the minimum of legal commitments in a form which leaves everything on the level of optional undertakings, but attains as much as, in the present political climate, is likely to be attained for the protection of foreign investments through conciliation and arbitration.[145]

Schwarzenberger was impressed with the Bank's strategy. The analysis in this chapter demonstrates that World Bank officials had strong motivation, unparalleled resources, and a clear strategy for creating the ICSID Convention. These ingredients bode well for success, but did not make it inevitable. Ratification was still necessary, and ratification is a political decision. How would state officials react to the World Bank's proposal? Would the Bank's strategy be effective? Chapter five takes up the question of the extent to which the Bank's dissemination of ICSID was successful.

[145] Schwarzenberger 1969: 142.

5

Intergovernmental Discussion and Ratification of ICSID

Chapter four demonstrated that the World Bank had the motivation and resources to propose and disseminate the idea of ICSID. Yet this did not make success inevitable—despite the World Bank's brokering, in 1964, it still seemed improbable that the ICSID Convention would secure enough ratifications to be useful. The World Bank could insulate the early stages of the process from politicking, but a sizeable number of capital-importing governments would need to ratify the ICSID Convention in order for it to become meaningful—and ratification is ultimately a political decision, usually requiring approval from a national legislature.

For capital-importing countries, there was not a strong positive case to be made for the benefits of ratification: there was no evidence to support the claim that additional investment would flow to states that ratified. The Bank's argument was usually that ratification would improve the investment climate, a different and more ambiguous claim. Possible costs of ratifying the Convention were raised during the drafting, but there was ambiguity here too. While experts-designate raised many issues that look prescient given today's world of arbitration, like public policy concerns, these issues were often viewed differently then or dismissed without extensive discussion. Although officials who saw their countries as likely respondents generally raised the most prescient concerns, the double-consent formulation made it easy for officials to underestimate the likelihood that their countries would face arbitration cases. Since ratifying the ICSID Convention would not actually give investors the ability to bring claims, concerns had to be voiced in hypothetical and general terms—which made them seem more distant and meant they could be dismissed more easily.

The drafting of the ICSID Convention was not a traditional interstate negotiation process. The Convention was drafted by the World Bank's Executive Directors, which in practice meant the Legal Department. Broches, head of the Legal Department, later explained: "I worked on the Convention. I was also the principal draftsman and negotiator of that treaty. It took a fair amount of my time."[1] The way that the World Bank structured ICSID's drafting is important for understanding why certain topics were or were not discussed in the drafting process. For instance, one reason why the central premise of ICSID—that ratifying the Convention would improve the investment climate—was not interrogated more was because Broches opened the Legal Committee by closing off the possibility of deliberations.[2] The individuals in the Legal Committee were experts providing advice to the World Bank, not representatives of their governments.[3] There were no actual intergovernmental negotiations at any point in the drafting of the ICSID Convention.

The consultative conferences and Legal Committee helped the Bank improve their draft and helped them get a better sense of which countries could agree to investor–state arbitration. The conferences and committee were also a chance to disseminate the idea of investor–state arbitration. If the Bank's strategy for dissemination was successful, we would expect governments to adopt the Bank's language and reasoning, and then ratify in accordance with this new reasoning. To what extent was the Bank's initial dissemination successful? To anticipate the chapter's findings, the answer is mixed. A sizeable minority of state experts-designate did adopt the Bank's framing, and their states did join after the Convention opened for ratification. Most experts from capital-importing states, however, were skeptical. In particular, several experts questioned if ratifying ICSID could have an impact on inward investment flows, and disputed whether access to arbitration was something that mattered to foreign investors.

The first section of the chapter establishes that all parties believed that the success of the ICSID Convention depended on ratification by capital-importing countries. The second section examines what state officials made of the argument that ratifying the ICSID Convention would improve the investment climate. The third section identifies concerns raised by states but not fully addressed during the consultative roadshow and Legal Committee. The fourth turns to state behavior, and describes the initial pattern of ratifications. When the ICSID Convention opened for ratification, the initial uptake by states was sufficient to bring the organization into existence in 1966. ICSID's initial membership was diverse, but far from universal. Many states remained outside the organization in 1970, and important states are still outside the organization today. The fifth section investigates the domestic political process behind ratification in the US—a state whose ratification could not be taken for granted.

[1] Broches (1985: 7–8) was answering a general question about who administers ICSID cases; he started by explaining his involvement in the creation of ICSID.

[2] ICSID 1970: 674. As mentioned in Chapter four.

[3] As mentioned in Chapter four, these individuals were "expert-designates" not "representatives" because they were attending as private citizens and some were not employed by the governments that sent them.

SUCCESS DEPENDS ON RATIFICATION BY CAPITAL-IMPORTING STATES

The success of the ICSID Convention depended on its ratification by capital-importing states. When he first saw the proposal, the relevant official from the British Treasury said, "we should see how the newly emergent and under-developed countries reacted to them."[4] At the consultative conference in Geneva, the expert sent by Germany "stressed the willingness of the developing countries to participate in the scheme was a decisive factor in its success."[5] The expert from France expressed the same sentiment more diplomatically, emphasizing that the Convention "was important only in so far as it attracted ratifications from a sufficient number of countries, capital-importing and capital-exporting alike."[6]

The focus was states where property rights were considered least secure. These were mainly former colonies, as one confidential British memo put it: "what we are perhaps mainly concerned with is the likely reaction of politicians in the more difficult newly independent countries (by definition the less difficult under-developeds are less of a problem)."[7] This focus remained unstated because of the political and intellectual milieu in 1964. Concurrently with the consultative conferences, Raul Prebisch, the persuasive voice of dependency theory, was preparing for the first UNCTAD by travelling to many capitals—both developed and developing—to strengthen the solidarity of developing countries and build support for his plans regarding the forthcoming conference.[8] In this context, a new organization's legitimacy was inversely related to the amount of leadership shown by former colonial powers in creating it. This position was expressed in a private memo to the US Secretary of State. In the memo, an adviser briefed the Secretary on US support for ICSID:

> The United States has at all times indicated its support for the Convention, but has deliberately not led the way, since the thought has been that this Convention, unlike the OECD Convention, should not have the appearance of being prepared by the capital exporting countries for signature by the capital importing countries.[9]

[4] Briefing for H.M. Ambassador in Washington, result of a meeting held at the Treasury, January 5, 1962, "Settlement of Disputes between Governments and Private Parties." UK T 312/251.

[5] ICSID 1970: 374.

[6] ICSID 1970: 373.

[7] Parenthesis in the original. Letter from Martin Reid to Hester Boothroyd, January 30, 1963. UK T 312: 545 (1962–3).

[8] Toye and Toye 2004: 192, and, more generally, 191–4 and 204–5. Prebisch's proposals earned favorable publicity around the world (Toye and Toye 2004: 200).

[9] Memo from Leonard Meeker for the Secretary of State, concerning "Circular 175 Authority for Signature of World Bank Convention on Settlement of Investment Disputes: Action Memorandum," undated but likely March 1965. US LA: Bill S.3498.

This type of language was reserved for internal discussions. US experts-designate avoided saying anything like this publicly.

Attendees from capital-exporting countries had an easier time supporting the proposal because they did not expect their governments to be respondents. Officials were careful to ensure that this understanding was rarely publicly acknowledged, since it would have reinforced perceptions of the Convention as a one-sided document. Years later, Georges Delaume, a French official in the World Bank Legal Department who translated the Convention into French, recalled: "Politically, the Europeans were not for [ICSID]—except as potential users taking advantage of the institution to protect their investors against developing countries. So it was all biased."[10]

The understanding that capital-exporters were not expecting to be respondents is clear in internal documents from these governments. In the run-up to ratification in the United States, a State Department official wrote a letter to the head of the Securities and Exchange Commission, who was concerned that foreigners could use ICSID to challenge US financial regulations. The letter from the State Department official affirms that the Convention would only apply in one direction:

> The support of the United States for the Convention is primarily designed to establish another mechanism for peaceful settlement of investment disputes between investors and the less developed countries... Also, from the nature of the Convention, *there appears to be little likelihood that claims against the United States by private investors would be suggested for decision under the Convention.* The legal and administrative remedies already available to the private investor in the United States are broad and effective.[11]

This understanding was shared by other capital-exporting governments. While ten years earlier when discussing the Abs Draft, the British government had considered itself a respondent (and thus not supported the Draft), with the World Bank's framing, they no longer saw themselves as a respondent. British officials attending their first meeting at ICSID were briefed that: "One of our main concerns... has been to ensure that there is no bias in favour of governments, as opposed to private parties to disputes, since the British interest will relate almost entirely to the latter."[12] As mentioned in earlier chapters, only a handful of governments—six or seven European governments who had been colonizers in the recent past, and the United States—perceived their interests during the drafting of the ICSID Convention as those of capital-exporters.

[10] Delaume 2004: 52.

[11] Letter from MacArthur to Harris, dated March 27, 1965. Emphasis mine. US LA: Bill S.3498.

[12] Letter from W. S. Ryrie to J. M. Stevens, January 1967, "International Centre for Settlement of Investment Disputes." UK FCO 48/145.

States that were "developed" capital-importers provide a different perspective. This category included many European countries, as well as Australia, Canada, Japan, New Zealand, and others in the 1960s. The Geneva consultative conference, which was attended by European states and South Africa, was split nearly evenly between capital-exporting and capital-importing states. Ireland, Spain, Portugal, Greece—all OECD members—were some of the investment-importing states represented at the Geneva conference.[13] Germany had even signed a BIT with Greece in 1961.[14] The comments of their officials at the consultative conferences demonstrate that these "developed" capital-importers perceived themselves as potential respondents, and had concerns. Many of these states were slow to ratify, but they were not the focus of the effort.

The Connection between ICSID and Bilateral Investment Treaties

The drafting of the ICSID Convention occurred after the start of the BIT movement, and both shared an initial focus on newly independent states. Officials in several European capital-exporting governments were aware of both developments. The connection between BITs and ICSID was clear to these officials before, during, and after the drafting of the ICSID Convention.

In 1961, the UK government responded to a UN questionnaire by observing: "The negotiation of a world-wide network of bilateral treaties with provision for arbitration of investment disputes is inevitably a slow and difficult process and this suggests the desirability of a multilateral approach."[15] In 1962, during the first discussion of the World Bank's memo on ICSID, a German official outlined the possibility of using the proposed Centre to enforce investment treaties. Although Germany's new investment treaties did not include investor–state arbitration, as Chapter three discussed, German officials understood the relationship between treaties and arbitration well.[16] The official said: "Questions of jurisdiction, procedure, and applicable law might be dealt with in bilateral agreements between interested countries... Germany had conducted a number of so-called promotion treaties with different countries, and... the

[13] These states were OECD members, but also still World Bank clients. These states could be considered "developing states," depending on how one distinguishes developing from developed states.

[14] Germany–Greece BIT, 1961.

[15] Extract from UK Reply to UN Questionnaire April 1961. UK T 312/251.

[16] For instance, in 1959 discussions on the German model BIT, officials debated Hermann Abs' proposals for a BIT provision providing individuals with standing in arbitration, February 16, and March 11, 1959, Aufzeichnung über die Hausbesprechung (Record of the Internal Discussion). DE B102/27082.

Bank's proposal might be a valuable supplement."[17] During the Geneva consultative conference, the French expert-designate made an extended comment on the Convention's "relation to bilateral agreements" with suggestions on how to avoid inconsistent decisions or multiple dispute resolution options.[18]

It matters that officials from several countries understood that bilateral treaties could provide the second consent to ICSID, in part because it corrects a prevalent misunderstanding that investment treaty arbitration was unforeseen by experts-designate: for instance, in a 2017 lecture, Thomas asserts that the "key assumption" of Broches and others was that "the future caseload [was] expected to be contractual disputes."[19] This is not correct. From the beginning, all available evidence suggests that Broches envisioned a system with treaty-based consent, domestic law-based consent, and contract-based consent. Broches rejected a suggestion to limit the jurisdiction of ICSID to disputes "arising out of contractual transactions."[20] One reason why the connection between investor–state arbitration and treaties was not widely discussed is out of fear of "unduly rousing" the suspicions of capital-importing states and deterring them from ratifying.[21] The lack of discussion means that the connection was not widely understood: an article published in an American law journal in 1968 does not mention treaty consent in its list of methods by which consent to ICSID can be granted.[22] The limited circulation of information about treaty-based consent helps explain how the misconception took hold, and why some observers may have been taken by surprise in the late 1980s when the first treaty claim was filed.[23] Yet there is an important

[17] Point 6, SecM 62–68, quoted in ICSID 1970:13.

[18] ICSID 1970: 434–5. Parra (2017: 56) calls this observation "interesting in light of later developments."

[19] Thomas (2017: thirty-seventh minute) bases his assertion on a comment from Broches (ICSID 1970: 495), but fails to account for the fact that Broches was arguing against the Indian expert-designate, who was suggesting additional requirements for jurisdiction. Broches first repeated the request of the Indian expert, "to be eligible for settlement under the auspices of the Center, the dispute should, in addition [to other jurisdictional requirements], arise out of some contractual relationship between the investor and host state." Then, as part of his argument against this requirement, Broches said "90 to 95 percent of the disputes which parties might want to bring before the Center" would likely arise out of situations with previous agreements, as prelude to his point that ICSID should be available even for situations in which the investor and state have no previous agreement. Given Broches' consistent recommendations for investor–state clauses to be inserted into domestic laws and treaties, and his repeated statements that treaties created a large potential caseload, it seems prudent to view his response to the Indian expert-designate (who seemed to frustrate him) more as a persuasive lawyer looking to make a point, and less as his prediction for ICSID's future caseload.

[20] Exchange in the Santiago conference (ICSID 1970: 321); Parra (2017: 51) mentions it.

[21] The language of rousing suspicions is from Schwarzenberger (1969: 142).

[22] "Comments: New Approach" 1968: 266.

[23] Pauwelyn (2014: 26–8) calls the first investment treaty case a "silent revolution." Articles like Jan Paulsson's (1995: 232) "Arbitration Without Privity" and others did much to create a sense of discovery and make investment treaty arbitration better known, especially among law firms, but the treaty architecture was already largely in place.

difference between a small group of experts understanding the connection and no one understanding the connection: Broches and other well-informed officials active in the drafting of ICSID understood treaty-based consent.

Capital-importing governments, especially in Latin America, also looked beyond ratification and were apprehensive about a link to BITs or a similar type of document that would provide broad consent to ICSID in advance. In a confidential summary of the first discussion of the idea for ICSID among the Executive Directors, it was noted that "the other two Latin American Directors did not speak [and Latin American Executive Director Luis] Machado told me afterwards that while some of his countries *were frightened of advance obligations*, they might be ready to make use of a centre in particular cases."[24]

Advance obligations or advance consent was the real battleground in the eyes of well-prepared officials from both capital-exporting and capital-importing governments. The lessons of the Abadan dispute—which many British officials and World Bank officials thought would have ended differently if Iran had provided advance consent—still loomed large for some officials. In a conversation with Broches about the ICSID Convention, British officials observed that consent to ICSID would fix the "weakness of the Agreement to arbitration in Anglo-Iranian concession with Iran," which was that the concession contract had no advance consent.[25] After their conversation with Broches, British officials observed that:

> The question hinges on whether, in the absence of a convention, the unwilling party (usually the State concerned) would go to arbitration. The "real reason" namely reliance on the "authority and lending power" of the Bank, means reliance on the power of the Bank to withhold loans. This is an argument we could not use in open debate. It is precisely what the under-developed countries are frightened of.[26]

The value of the ICSID Convention to these British officials was that it might induce capital-importing states to provide access to arbitration, ideally in advance, when outside of an initiative by the World Bank, they would be unlikely to provide this access. The special relationship between the World Bank and its borrowers appeared in other ways too: one official wrote that ICC arbitration used between Western governments would not be appropriate for less-developed countries, but "it is hoped that a similar situation might develop under which contracts and concessions etc. would provide for IBRD arbitration, with no further ado."[27] The provision of advance consent was

[24] Eager [Telegram] from Washington to the Foreign Office, subject: the Bank Board meeting, March 13, 1962. UK T 312/251. Emphasis mine.

[25] Letter from Peter Reilly to Mr. Pliatsky, December 6, 1962. UK T 312: 545 (1962–3).

[26] Letter from Peter Reilly to Mr. Pliatsky, December 6, 1962. UK T 312: 545 (1962–3).

[27] Letter from Hester Boothroyd to Mr. Mitchell, subject: IBRD and Arbitration, February 6, 1962. UK T 312/251.

perceived by many officials as key, even though the double-consent formulation obscured this and took any battles over binding consent out of the spotlight during deliberations on the ICSID Convention.

Capital-Exporters Let the World Bank Lead

During intergovernmental deliberations on the ICSID Convention, capital-exporting governments largely let World Bank officials be the chief advocates for the Convention. Given the political climate in 1964, this was a strategic decision: overt backing from the US for an initiative of this type would not have encouraged ratification by newly independent countries. This setup at first glance seems like evidence that the World Bank was doing the bidding of its largest shareholder, the US government. However, the US interest in the ICSID Convention was not strong. As a World Bank official later remembered: "we managed to put together this convention, which was a good idea. But there was such a resistance or no interest really from the Europeans or Americans, not much from the government."[28] The US government was in favor of ICSID, *ceteris paribus*, but did not consider it an idea worth fighting for—US officials would offer support if the World Bank got the initiative off the ground, but would not intervene if it ran into headwinds.

This position is best illustrated by the circumspect behavior of US government officials during the consultative conference they attended in Santiago. This consultative conference was dominated by Latin American states opposed to the idea of ICSID. The head of the US delegation was then-General Counsel of the Treasury Gaspard D'Andelot Belin, an elegant and progressive Kennedy appointee.[29] In the opening session, the Argentine expert-designate asserted his country's opposition to the Convention, and noted that Argentina refused "to curtail its jurisdiction and felt that to detract from national sovereignty was not an acceptable method for improving the investment climate."[30] Speaking immediately after that pronouncement, Belin gently offered US support to the Convention, conditional on its acceptance by capital-importing states. He said: "If a sufficient number of countries proved interested in working out some arrangements on the basis of the draft, then the United States would support it. He stressed the voluntary nature of the arrangements proposed in the draft, which should appeal to many countries."[31] The US delegation remained quiet while experts-designate

[28] Delaume 2004: 25.

[29] Belin was accompanied by the Acting Assistant General Counsel of the Treasury, and the Assistant Legal Adviser for Economic Affairs at the State Department, Andreas Lowenfeld, who would go on to become a notable figure in investment arbitration.

[30] ICSID 1970: 308. [31] ICSID 1970: 308.

from other states pummeled the idea. Meanwhile, Broches, chairing the conference on behalf of the World Bank, actively defended the Convention. He engaged in longer interventions and fairly combative exchanges with experts-designate to correct what he perceived as misrepresentations of the Convention in Santiago.[32]

Officials from other capital-exporting states also took a backseat to the Bank. Broches overruled or ignored the wishes of capital-exporting states when he believed they were wrong. The Dutch expert-designate requested the Bank share how the experts at the earlier African consultative conference had responded to the idea of the Convention:

> It would appear necessary for the Meeting to have some further information of the reactions of those attending the Regional Consultative Meeting in Africa regarding whether it would be wise to institute procedures under for the settlement of investment disputes under the auspices of the Bank... It was extremely important to know the views of the African experts regarding the desirability of a link between the proposed Center and the Bank.[33]

As mentioned in Chapter four, the World Bank chose not to share minutes from the earlier regional consultative conferences with the later ones, despite requests to do so. The Dutch expert-designate ultimately chose to drop the request and to support Broches' strategy. Capital-exporting states supported the proposal for ICSID, but looked to the Bank to convince capital-importing states of the idea.

THE PROMISED BENEFIT: AN IMPROVED INVESTMENT CLIMATE

The Convention was presented to capital-importing states as a tool that would improve their investment climate. Broches opened each consultative conference with a speech introducing the ICSID Convention and conveyed the proposal made to capital-importing states. In line with the rhetoric of postwar planners, who aimed to remove the imperialist connotations of foreign investment and reframe it as a tool for development, Broches explained that:

> In the past, international investment might justifiably have been of interest chiefly to the capital-exporting nations and their citizens. Today it was universally recognized as a factor of crucial importance in the economic development of the less developed parts of the world and had become one of the major features of the partnership between the richer and poorer nations.[34]

[32] ICSID 1970: 307–10. [33] ICSID 1970: 375. [34] ICSID 1970: 302.

Broches then observed: "Unfortunately, private capital was not moving in sufficient volume to areas in need of capital, one of the most serious impediments to its flow being the fear of investors that their investment would be exposed to political risks."[35] In other words, lack of trust in local institutions prevented capital from flowing where it could be most productive. In this view, investment protection was a contemporary development problem, which the World Bank could assist states in solving by creating a new policy tool. This was how Broches offered the World Bank's assistance: "The Bank had therefore been led to wonder whether, in view of its reputation for integrity and its position of impartiality, it could not help in removing that obstacle to international private investment."[36] The lack of appropriate dispute resolution machinery was an impediment to the flow of investment: ICSID would remove this obstacle, which would improve the investment climate.

There is an important and underappreciated nuance in the words Broches chose. He usually spoke of improving the investment climate. While his words may have left a lingering impression of additional foreign investment, he rarely made direct claims that access to ICSID arbitration would result in additional inward investment.[37] Improving the investment climate is not the same as facilitating new investment. The World Bank cannot promise new private foreign investment, but improving the investment climate is something the Bank can do. In fact, improving the investment climate has long been central to the work of the World Bank, and it was through the concept of "investment climate" that Broches tied the creation of ICSID to other World Bank efforts. Broches' speech to the consultative conferences conveys how he packaged ICSID within the broader efforts of the Bank.

> The World Bank's initiative in promoting an international agreement in a field which might not be regarded as falling directly within its sphere of activity was not unusual in view of the nature of the Bank, which was not merely a financing mechanism but, above all, a development institution . . . much of its energy and resources were devoted to technical assistance and advice directed toward the promotion of conditions conducive to rapid economic growth, and the creation of a favorable investment climate in the broadest sense of the term.[38]

The vagueness of the term investment climate was valuable: while it likely had an intuitive meaning for most participants, these officials probably did not conceive of it as something easily measured. In 1961 during a speech given in his private capacity, Broches offered something like a definition: "I want to talk about investment climate in a somewhat narrower context: governmental

[35] (ICSID 1970: 302). [36] ICSID 1970: 302.

[37] The Report of the Executive Directors (which Broches drafted), however, does contain direct claims, for instance: "the broad objective of the Convention is to encourage a larger flow of private international investment." Section III (13) of the Report of the Executive Directors.

[38] ICSID 1970: 301–2.

attitudes and actions friendly or unfriendly to private foreign enterprise and the likelihood of effective protection of legal rights."[39] Increasing "the likelihood of effective protection of legal rights" is not the same as facilitating investment.[40] Broches, with his sophisticated understanding of these issues, must have known this, yet must have believed that he did not have the luxury of making the more limited claim. Imagine how different reactions would have been if he had opened the consultative conferences by promising "more effective legal protections for foreign investors" rather than "more investment and development for your country." The claim had to be "more investment" in order to justify ICSID's creation at the Bank and in order to convince states to ratify. The Report of the Executive Directors, sent to governments with the Convention, states: "adherence to the Convention by a country would... stimulate a larger flow of private international investment into its territories."[41]

The World Bank did not provide any empirical evidence that joining ICSID could facilitate investment. Some delegates assumed the Bank had done econometric impact assessments.[42] It had not: no econometric work had been commissioned, no survey work had been commissioned, and available records from the World Bank do not turn up any evidence that Broches contemplated a way of measuring impact, apart from the number of advance consents. This is interesting when contrasted with Broches' words in 1962 about the importance of measurement for investment insurance:

> The proposals for establishment of a multilateral program proceed from the premise that insurance against the non-commercial risks of private overseas investment is an effective technique for stimulating that investment. Presumably, before creating new international machinery, expending the very substantial effort involved in establishing an international program, and undertaking the financial and other obligations which would attach to participation in the program, governments would wish to be satisfied as to the validity of that premise.[43]

Here again, it matters that insurance requires money up front, while arbitration does not: if governments are asked to pay for something, they are more

[39] Broches, Aron, "Problems of Private Foreign Investment," Third Annual Institute on Corporate Counsel, devoted to Foreign Operations of American Enterprises, December 8, 1961. WB Folder 1651418.

[40] ICSID has always been separate from efforts to improve local judicial systems or the "Rule of Law"—these projects started only in the 1990s at the World Bank and pursued a different agenda (Carothers 2006).

[41] Section III (9) of the Report of the Executive Directors.

[42] See the expert-designate from Ecuador's comment (ICSID 1970: 310). The official record does not show Bank officials correcting this misperception when it was voiced in the African or the Latin American consultative conference.

[43] Broches, Aron, "International Investment Guarantees: Possibilities and Problems." Address to the American Society of International Law, April 27, 1962. WB Folder 1651418.

likely to seek evidence that it works. It is easier to eschew the question of effectiveness if governments are not required to put up money or deal with distributional questions before they ratify. Broches' writing on insurance demonstrate that he had nuanced views on what facilitated investment: Broches spoke about "the variety of considerations which influence investment decisions" and observed that

> the degree to which the political risk (in the broad sense of the term) is going to be a deterrent to an investor depends not only on the investor's estimate of the likelihood that the risk will materialize, but, among other factors, also on the freedom of choice which the investor has to go or not go abroad.[44]

From internal documents of capital-exporting governments, it is possible to discern what these governments, which presumably had contact with their large firms, thought about the likelihood that the ICSID Convention could facilitate additional investment flows. The British government was clear that it did not expect ICSID to facilitate any additional investment. In a 1961 questionnaire from the United Nations, a question read: "Is the expansion and institutionalization of the arbitration (or conciliation) of investment disputes likely to add substantially to the security of foreign investments, and thus to encourage the flow of such investments?"[45] The British government responded:

> Increased resort to arbitration for the settlement of investment disputes is highly desirable and should do much to improve investors' confidence in the security of their property overseas. *It will not in itself ensure an increased flow of international capital* since this depends on a number of other factors including the general political climate of the foreign country concerned and the normal pull of economic forces.[46]

In fact, one reason the British government supported the ICSID Convention was because the relevant officials perceived it to be ineffective at facilitating investment flows. As mentioned in previous chapters, the British economy had balance of payment difficulties and the government did not want to encourage any additional outward flows of investment. British officials were clear about how they assessed these proposals:

> [I]nsofar as they protect existing investment, they are welcome, insofar as they stimulate new investment, they are unwelcome. The balance of our interests determines our attitude to each project. In the present case [the ICSID Convention] our view has been that the balance works to our advantage since *we do not*

44 Broches, Aron, "International Investment Guarantees: Possibilities and Problems," Address to the American Society of International Law, April 27, 1962. WB Folder 1651418.
45 Extract from UK Reply to UN Questionnaire April 1961. UK T 312/251.
46 Extract from UK Reply to UN Questionnaire April 1961. UK T 312/251. Emphasis mine.

> *expect the existence of the Centre to give any major stimulus to new investment at a rate in the short term.*[47]

Some capital-importing governments were also skeptical of the ICSID Convention's ability to improve the investment climate. The Jordanian expert-designate questioned the idea that investment was impeded by a lack of machinery for the settlement of disputes:

> [He] believed that foreign investment should be encouraged and protected by the host state, yet there was no compelling reason for establishing institutional facilities for the settlement of disputes concerning them... In his opinion, the main concern of an investor was the political stability of the country in which he sought to invest rather than any lack of adequate machinery for the settlement of disputes.[48]

Similarly, the expert-designate from Thailand questioned whether ICSID could improve the investment climate. The Thai expert-designate "expressed doubt whether the establishment of facilities for voluntary conciliation and arbitration of investment disputes would do much to improve the investment climate."[49] This question struck at the core of the proposition made to capital-importing states: if joining ICSID could not facilitate investment flows, why ratify?

Some investment-importing states struggled to find a convincing answer. The Australian expert-designate, having identified Australia as a primarily capital-importing state, puzzled over the Convention's purpose. He observed that Australia's domestic legal system was fully satisfactory for foreign investors. In his remarks, he pointed out "that in practice the remedies provided in Australia by the local courts had to date proved satisfactory to foreign investors and that the current inflow of foreign capital was at a relatively high level."[50] Many capital-importing states, however, did not have the benefit of extensive experience with foreign investment. These states were reliant on the World Bank for information about investors, and in particular for a sense of how important ICSID was to investors.

A sizeable minority of capital-importing countries adopted the World Bank's framing and announced their support for the Convention. The expert-designate from Nepal spoke Broches' words back to him almost verbatim: "[The proposed] machinery would promote the flow of private capital to the developing countries by allaying investors' fears of expropriation or of the dishonoring of the terms of an agreement by the host state."[51] The delegate

[47] Letter from W. S. Ryrie to J. M. Stevens, January 1967, "International Centre for Settlement of Investment Disputes." UK FCO 48/145. Emphasis mine.

[48] ICSID 1970: 549.

[49] ICSID 1970: 466.

[50] ICSID 1970: 473. This quotation illustrates that the crux of the issue was perceived to be trust in local courts. Australia's courts were trusted by its investors.

[51] ICSID 1970: 469. The expert-designate from Vietnam makes a similar comment on page 547.

from the Philippines was equally unambiguous: "His delegation was in full accord with the underlying principles of the Convention, and his government, as a capital-importing country, welcomed the proposals believing that they would improve and encourage the flow of capital into the country."[52]

Experts-designate from other states noted that ICSID would only address a fragment of a country's investment climate.[53] Others, like the expert-designate from Malaysia, "said that the principles underlying the Convention were acceptable to his government which was doing everything possible to promote foreign investment in the country."[54] These experts-designate seemed unsure how much actual impact the proposed organization would have in practice, but still accepted the premise that investors would pay attention to the ICSID Convention, and thus, that ICSID could affect inflows.

Other states thought that ICSID was unacceptable, even though they sought instruments to encourage inward investment. This is the way most Latin American opposition was voiced during the consultative conferences. Experts-designate emphasized that foreign investment was welcome, but that ICSID was unacceptable. In his welcome to the Santiago conference, the Deputy Secretary of the UN Economic Commission for Latin America (ECLA) noted:

> Foreign private investments could contribute much to the economic development of the Latin American countries... On the other hand, the investment of private capital made necessary a juridical system guaranteeing the legitimate interest of the investor. Hence the importance of finding a formula that could effectively guarantee such interests, while respecting the sovereignty of each country in accordance with the principles of international law and the constitutional rules of the country.[55]

Within this diplomatically worded statement is a clear message that ICSID was not a formula that respected the sovereignty of each country. Latin American opposition was principled, unyielding, and expertly expressed—it emerged from a different interpretation of customary international law, not from a lack of enthusiasm for foreign investment. Yet Latin American opposition was mischaracterized as the result of insufficient desire to attract foreign investment. Toward the end of the Santiago consultative conference, frustrated by the unyielding opposition, Broches framed the decision to join ICSID as a trade-off. He reminded Latin American experts-designate that their states

[52] ICSID 1970: 547. The Philippines representative then participated in the "No de Tokio" protest, suggesting a failure to communicate between the expert-designate and the representative at the World Bank Annual Meeting.

[53] ICSID 1970: 546. Expert-designate from Pakistan speaking.

[54] ICSID 1970: 549.

[55] ICSID 1970: 301. This comment is echoed by experts-designate; for instance, the Peruvian expert-designate on page 311. ECLA would later become ECLAC, when the Caribbean was added to the title. Raul Prebisch was Executive Secretary of ECLA from 1948 to 1962, immediately prior to his work on UNCTAD.

already traded rights—in the form of concession contracts and investment incentives—for additional investment. ICSID was another right they could trade for more investment. In his words:

> He did not expect that delegates would uncritically accept the Bank's views on the suitability of the proposed Convention but he did suggest that in considering the proposed Convention delegates should bear in mind the fundamental question whether their countries wished to attract private investment—and he thought most of them did—and, if so, what price they were prepared to pay by way of special concessions and incentives for investors. Most such incentives involved conferring rights on foreign investors, and for that reason he found it difficult to appreciate criticism of the proposals based on the sole argument that they gave investors "additional rights."[56]

Broches may have found this criticism difficult to appreciate, but there were certainly countries outside Latin America who agreed with it. India was one such state. The Indian expert-designate was unequivocal: the ICSID Convention gave additional rights without countervailing obligations or clear benefits for India. At the Asian consultative conference, months before the Latin American conference, the Indian expert-designate anticipated Broches' question. India was willing to give investors additional rights, but not willing to ratify the ICSID Convention. As he framed it:

> His country wished to attract private capital and to maintain a favorable investment climate, and for that purpose it was prepared to give the foreign investor the necessary safeguards including additional rights. His criticism, however, had been addressed to the fact that *the proposals in their present form gave investors additional rights of unspecified scope.*[57]

The separation of procedure from substantive standard is at the heart of the Indian expert-designate's comments. He noted that states had no way of knowing what they were enabling by ratifying ICSID, since substance would be negotiated separately. The risks outweighed the possibility that ICSID might lead to additional investment.

The diversity of views explored in previous paragraphs shows the premise—that joining ICSID would improve the investment climate and facilitate greater in-flows of capital—was not convincing to many experts-designate. Yet these experts-designate did not attend the consultative conferences or drafting committee to evaluate this argument. They were there to offer technical, legal guidance—and many in the audience may have been predisposed by their legal training to view arbitration favorably. If the drafting participants had consisted primarily of economists, or chief operating officers from multinational firms, the lack of empirical evidence might have created

[56] ICSID 1970: 476. [57] ICSID 1970: 476. Emphasis mine.

difficulties. The assembled legal experts, however, were asked to believe the premise that ICSID could improve the investment climate without empirical evidence. What stood behind that claim was not evidence, but the institutional credibility of the World Bank. This was sufficient for many of the experts, whose primary concern was law. The overwhelming majority of the discussion focused on implications for international law. The next section turns to concerns about the risks of ICSID and the consequences for international law discussed during the consultative conferences.

THE POSSIBLE COSTS: IMPLICATIONS FOR INTERNATIONAL LAW

This section evaluates the success of the Bank's attempt to frame ICSID as an extension of existing practice. Broches asserted that the proposal was compatible with any legal system and with any substantive standards. Yet many in his expert audience were skeptical, and concerned that the Convention would have serious implications for international law.

The Bank's Argument: ICSID Protects States from Espousal

Broches argued that the proposed Convention, despite granting investors standing against states, was not a departure from international law. He set out this argument during his opening speech at each consultative conference. Although ratification equaled formal state recognition that investors could bring a case directly against a host state,[58] he argued that this recognition was in the interest of capital-importing states, because it protected them from espousal. In his words:

> As a corollary of the principle allowing an investor direct and effective access to a foreign state without the intervention of his national state, the Convention introduced an important innovation, namely, that the investor's national state would no longer be able to espouse the claim of its national.[59]

Broches' speech celebrated the Convention's ability to remove investment disputes from the realm of power, and place them in the realm of law.

[58] In Broches' words: "recognition of the principle that a non-state party, an investor, might have direct access in his own name and without requiring the espousal of his cause by his national government, to a state party before an international forum" (ICSID 1970: 303).

[59] ICSID 1970: 303.

In Broches' words, the Convention offered "a means of settling directly, on the legal plane, investment disputes between the state and foreign investor, and would insulate such disputes from the realm of politics and diplomacy."[60] This idealism fit well with the aims of developing states in other international fora, such as UNCTAD. Broches may have overstated the case, however, as ICSID provides a suspension of diplomatic pressure only.[61] States can and do use diplomatic pressure before a case has been registered and after a tribunal hands down a decision.[62]

Did this framing convince the experts-designate? Did they adopt it? As the next paragraphs illustrate, the picture is mixed—some states adopted the Bank's framing, while others remained unconvinced or were troubled by particular aspects. The paragraphs below draw out four areas that were of particular concern for some officials.

Concern One: Equality of Status between Individual Investors and States

Many state experts-designate found the idea of equal standing between investors and states to be unsettling: the idea was criticized at all four consultative conferences. In Geneva, the expert-designate from South Africa phrased his concern diplomatically when he "wondered whether it was in fact a sound principle to elevate the individual to the status of a subject of international law."[63] The Brazilian expert-designate pointedly defined arbitration as an exclusively interstate institution during the Santiago conference.[64] At the Asian conference, the expert-designate from India described how the Convention departed from existing practice, and how this departure would unduly privilege foreign investors.

> [He] shared the doubts expressed by the delegates of Thailand and Ceylon. The basic principles as set out in the Preamble did not, in his opinion, state the problem adequately and failed to bring out the fact that *the Convention involved an important departure in international law*. The Convention aimed at setting up a forum where States and individuals were placed on a par.[65]

Later in this passage the Indian expert-designate applied a principle of legal reasoning, that rights are balanced by obligations. Under the ICSID

[60] ICSID 1970: 303. [61] Paparinskis 2010.

[62] Recent work on investment protection suggests that diplomatic protection never ceased to be the primary method of adjudicating disputes between investors and states—particularly techniques like exchanges of letters or ambassadorial discussions (Gertz 2016).

[63] ICSID 1970: 378. [64] ICSID 1970: 306.

[65] ICSID 1970: 470. Emphasis mine.

Convention, investors were given standing, which was a right, but had no counterbalancing obligations.[66]

Many experts-designate found it unsettling that the ICSID Convention effectively privileged foreign investors over domestic investors, because the facilities created by ICSID would only be available to foreign investors. As the expert-designate from Jordan noted, "the present Convention seemed to... place a foreign investor in a better position than the local investor."[67] Another expert-designate "was not clear... why it was considered necessary to create a forum where a foreign investor was placed in a position vis-à-vis the host state different to that of the national investor."[68] Granting an individual the same standing as a state under international law was not a continuation of existing practice.[69] Many experts-designate were unconvinced by Broches' ambiguous answers about the consequences of raising individuals to the same standing as states under international law. This concern deterred ratification. Few of the states that voiced this concern joined ICSID initially.[70]

Concern Two: Local Remedies

In general, it is logical to expect capital-exporting states to seek direct access to arbitration (without any requirement to exhaust local remedies), while it is logical to expect capital-importing states to want disputes that arise in their territory to go before their national courts, to use local remedies. Requirements to exhaust local remedies arose historically in opposition to international arbitration; local remedies and arbitration were traditionally seen as alternatives. The 1961 ABA Draft, a precursor to the ICSID Convention discussed in Chapter four, reflected this traditional understanding. It had a section on local remedies which stated that "any undertaking by a Contracting State to have recourse to arbitration under this Convention... shall relieve the other party to such dispute of any requirement that local or other remedies should first be exhausted."[71]

Broches, in trying to appeal to capital-importing states, put forward a relatively audacious argument that access to ICSID was consistent with a

66 ICSID 1970: 470. 67 ICSID 1970: 549. 68 ICSID 1970: 471.

69 Although individuals had access to international tribunals prior to ICSID (for instance at the Central American Court of Justice), the practice was not widespread (Puig 2014a: 241).

70 While Brazil, India, and South Africa remain outside ICSID even today, fifty years later, some of the states that voiced this concern did join ICSID as their positions changed with new governments or new economic realities—demonstrating the importance of analysis over time.

71 Article V (2). American Bar Association, Section of International & Comparative Law, Convention on the Conciliation and Arbitration of International Investment Disputes, October 20 1961. Included in the Letter from John Blair to Hester Boothroyd, November 13, 1961. UK T 312/251.

requirement to exhaust local remedies. Broches included this argument in his first memo about ICSID, in 1961:

> Nor need the establishment of such machinery interfere with the customary principle of international law pursuant to which claims cannot be brought before an international tribunal until local remedies (whether administrative or judicial) have been exhausted. This rule would be left intact, although it would, of course, be open to any government to agree that the procedure before the international arbitral tribunal would be in lieu of whatever local procedures or remedies may be available.[72]

Three years later, in his opening speeches to the consultative conferences, Broches again argued that (capital-importing) states could ratify the ICSID Convention and then insist investors exhaust local remedies before bringing a case to ICSID. Broches' explanation conveys the way in which he attempted to bring together competing doctrines to appeal to all states:

> While the Convention implied a recognition that local courts were not necessarily the final forum for the settlement of disputes between a state and a foreign investor, *it did not imply that local remedies could not play a major role.* When parties consented to arbitration, they would be free to stipulate either that local remedies might be pursued in lieu of arbitration, or that local remedies must first be exhausted before the dispute could be submitted for arbitration.[73]

Broches argued that ratifying the ICSID Convention did not necessarily give investors the ability to bypass local remedies. While this is correct, insofar as states can write a requirement to exhaust local remedies into their contracts, treaties, or laws—it requires relatively high ministerial capacity and continuity over time to do so. Another way that Broches suggested arbitration was compatible with local remedies is that governments could make reservations to the Convention specifying that local remedies must be exhausted before a claim can be brought.[74]

Some experts were convinced by Broches' argument that arbitration and local remedies could be complementary. These experts usually came from states with the least experience of investment arbitration. The expert-designate from Nepal is a good example, and his words echo Broches' own: "The investor ought to be required to exhaust all his local remedies before he could avail himself of international conciliation or arbitration facilities such as those provided by the Center."[75] In practice, Nepal did not ratify with a reservation to that effect. In fact, no capital-importing state ever ratified the Convention with a stipulation that local remedies should be exhausted first.[76]

[72] Point 4, SecM 61–192, quoted in ICSID 1970: 13.
[73] ICSID 1970: 303. Emphasis mine.
[74] In the final Convention, these are Article 25 (4) exceptions. [75] ICSID 1970: 543.
[76] Israel is the only state to have made an Article 25 (4) reservation that local remedies must be exhausted. ICSID 8/D.

Furthermore, the Report of the Executive Directors stated, and early tribunals proclaimed, that reservations under the ICSID Convention serve for information purposes only.[77] The ICSID Convention helped create a system which enabled investors to bring claims directly against governments without engaging local remedies—but many governments, especially the most severely capacity-constrained or the least experienced with arbitration, like Nepal, were unable to see this direction of travel and did not take actions to prevent it.

Many experts, especially from larger or more experienced capital-importing states, did not adopt the Bank's view that ICSID was compatible with local remedies. Strong opposition to the Convention centered on this point, with some experts emphasizing that access to arbitration allowed investors to bypass national courts. Many Latin American experts-designate invoked their national constitutions. The Venezuelan expert-designate noted that his constitution "clearly distinguished" interstate agreements from "contracts touching the public interest that the Government, in its administrative capacity, concluded with private persons."[78] The latter was "reserved to the exclusive competence" of domestic courts.[79] Some argued their national constitutions made it impossible for them to privilege foreign investors over domestic ones, which was intrinsic to the structure of ICSID. The Ecuadorian expert-designate put it plainly: "In Ecuador, as in other countries, the Constitution embodied the principle of equality of nationals and foreigners before the law. To make a different jurisdiction available to foreigners would place them in a privileged position."[80] This point was not disputed. Broches responded by noting that states already gave foreigners rights in order to attract investment.

Some Latin American experts-designate, notably those from Brazil and Argentina, argued that their national constitutions prevented their ratification of ICSID.[81] Many experts-designate placed principles like independence and sovereignty at the core of their opposition. As the expert-designate from El Salvador put it:

> There must be an attempt to reconcile the constitutional side of the question with the need to find incentives to development, but that did not mean that in order to obtain such incentives, principles vital to the very existence of the Latin American countries could be abandoned. A way should be sought to reconcile differences, and if necessary to seek other solutions, always bearing in mind the idea of conciliation and arbitration.[82]

This quotation is a good representation of the position of most Latin American states. As currently framed, the ICSID Convention was unacceptable, but their

[77] Parra 2013: 169. See also Parra 2017: 120.
[78] ICSID 1970: 309.
[79] ICSID 1970: 309 (expert-designate from Venezuela).
[80] ICSID 1970: 310.
[81] ICSID 1970: 306 (expert-designate from Brazil).
[82] ICSID 1970: 310.

opposition was phrased in expert legal terms. Their states sought investment from foreigners, and were keen to find peaceful means of dispute resolution, but the means should not bypass national legal systems and violate the principle of equality in their constitutions.

Concern Three: Public Policy Implications

Public policy implications were another area of concern, particularly in the Asian consultative meeting. Broches did not raise issues of public policy in his opening speech. In the Bank's framing, it seemed clear that public policies enacted in good faith would be unaffected by the ICSID Convention. Many experts-designate accepted this framing, but others were concerned that ICSID's jurisdiction could indeed affect domestic policymaking. The expert-designate from India argued that policy that affected all investors equally would not be suitable grounds for ICSID jurisdiction. He argued that "a refusal [of jurisdiction to ICSID] might very well be entirely bona fide as where, for instance, the matter concerned national policy, or again if the matter did not involve discrimination between foreign and national investors."[83] Cases stemming from domestic legislation that was not explicitly discriminatory against a foreign investor were recognized as a possibility before the ICSID Convention came into force. In his remarks, the expert-designate from Venezuela brought together constitutional problems and the pre-eminence of domestic policy.[84]

For the few experts-designate that raised public policy concerns, these concerns were a crosscutting argument that integrated several different reasons not to ratify. In his comments, the expert-designate from Thailand argued that ICSID's jurisdiction entered the terrain of public policy, and consent was an inadequate limit on ICSID's jurisdiction. In his words:

> Among the characteristic features of voluntary jurisdiction which unfortunately appeared also in the provisions of the draft Convention, was the fact that no detailed definition was given of the types of disputes which would come under the jurisdiction of the proposed... Center. The term "dispute of a legal character" given in Article II, Section 1 could give rise to uncertainty, particularly in view of the fact that *a State, in the ordinary course of exercising governmental functions, may have to take various broad measures which could affect the interests of foreign investors, e.g. measures required to protect the health, morals and welfare of the community, as well as the security of the nation.*[85]

This passage anticipates debates that would take shape nearly five decades later which revolve around the question whether investment agreements

[83] ICSID 1970: 470. [84] ICSID 1970: 309.
[85] ICSID 1970: 466. Emphasis mine.

unduly limit states' policy autonomy.[86] Unlike Thailand or India, many experts-designate did not take seriously the idea that ICSID jurisdiction might restrict their policy autonomy. When Broches summarized the Asian consultative conference for the Bank's Executive Directors, he noted the priority given to public policy concerns.[87] Public policy arose again when the German Executive Director of the Bank, echoing earlier comments from the German expert-designate, pushed for a public policy exception in the internal Bank meetings to finalize the Convention.[88] These concerns were acknowledged but not fully addressed by Broches; in Broches' framing, it was difficult to imagine ICSID having an impact on public policy.

Concern Four: Is Consent Enough? Limiting ICSID's Jurisdiction

Consent was at the core of the Bank's appeal to capital-importing states. Some experts found the Bank's argument compelling, and believed the double-consent formulation provided adequate protection against the abuse of ICSID's jurisdiction. At the same time, consent was insufficient to allay the concerns of several state experts-designate who sought more precise limits to ICSID's jurisdiction. For these experts-designate, the "optional character of the draft Convention" was not enough—the lack of precision was a "fundamental weakness."[89] Some state experts-designate believed that consent was an inadequate limit.[90] Despite these objections, Broches remained firm that consent alone was a sufficient limit to the jurisdiction of ICSID. At the end of the Asian conference, he reiterated that "the clearly established consensual nature of the mechanism established by the Convention offered adequate protection."[91]

The ICSID Convention does not define "investment," "investor," "dispute," or other central terms. Contemporary observers, like Schwarzenberger, wryly noted an intentional lack of specificity on several key points in the Convention: Schwarzenberger observed that "none of the operative terms were defined" in the Convention, and that "actually, all of them are sufficiently controversial to

[86] Gallagher 2010; Spears 2010; Kleinheisterkamp 2012; Van Harten 2013; Côté 2014; Mitchell and Sheargold 2015.

[87] ICSID 1970: 540. Broches elided concerns about how access to ICSID could shift bargaining power with concerns about public policy.

[88] Parra (2017: 79 and 81–2) elaborates on these requests.

[89] ICSID 1970: 306 and 470.

[90] ICSID 1970: 465. Parra (2017: 51–3) describes discussions over jurisdiction, noting the attention it received and that many experts from developing countries believed existing limits were unsatisfactory.

[91] ICSID 1970: 540–1.

call for definitions in an interpretive section."[92] Experts-designate also brought up the absence of definitions frequently. At the Geneva conference, for instance, the South African expert-designate wondered whether "the definition given of 'national of another Contracting State' were sufficiently circumscribed."[93] The expert-designate from Portugal, an investment-importing state, made his position clear:

> [He] considered the definition of "investment" inadequate—both from the economic and from the legal angle. In particular he was disturbed by the word "contribution" which he thought was too broad... Actions of the state which expressed its sovereign powers should not properly be the subject of disputes under the Convention... He did not think the Center should question the fiscal, economic, and financial policies of a contracting state.[94]

The non-definition of "investment" in the Convention has become the subject of extensive legal analysis and an area where tribunals have taken different approaches.[95] In an influential recent article, Mortenson argues that some tribunals have begun applying a restrictive definition of investment, which "proceeds from a basic misunderstanding of the process that created Article 25 [which defines ICSID's jurisdiction]."[96] Mortenson argues that "tribunals should treat the definition of 'investment' under the Convention as encompassing any plausibly economic activity or asset"[97] because criteria for the definition of investment "were explicitly considered and rejected during the drafting process."[98] While it is true that criteria for a definition were discussed and then do not appear in the final text, Mortenson's loose terminology to describe the drafting process obscures what actually occurred. First, Mortenson uses the word "negotiations"[99] and treats the individuals discussing the draft as though they were representatives of their governments.[100] This was not a negotiation and attendees were not representing their countries; they attended as legal experts and advanced suggestions to the World Bank in the framework of consultations. Second, Mortenson identifies "two blocs of countries" which he terms "developed" and "developing":[101] he admits that this characterization

[92] Schwarzenberger 1969: 142.

[93] ICSID 1970: 378. Concerns about effective nationality may have been influenced by the Nottebohm case (*Liechtenstein v Guatemala*) at the ICJ, which was decided in 1955.

[94] ICSID 1970: 708.

[95] Schreuer's (2001: 82–344) commentary is the most influential analysis.

[96] Mortenson 2010: 280.

[97] Mortenson 2010: 261.

[98] Mortenson 2010: 260 and 281.

[99] Mortenson 2010: 257, 259, 280, 283, 298, 307.

[100] For instance, of the Legal Committee, Mortenson (2010: 286) says, it was here "that the real give-and-take among signatory nations took place." This is a mischaracterization: the Bank had invited countries that did not intend to become "signatory nations" to send experts; experts were not formally representing their countries; and "real give-and-take" implies more potency than suggestions advanced in a consultation with experts.

[101] Mortenson 2010: 259.

is loose, but it reinforces incorrect stereotypes. Several developed states sought limits. For instance, the expert-designate from Japan, who was broadly in support of the proposal, reported the following views: "Although he sympathized with the view of the Bank's staff that inclusion of a more precise definition of those terms would involve various difficulties and would not necessarily be useful, some further clarification of those terms—and, therefore, of the scope of the proposed scheme—seemed necessary."[102] The Israeli expert-designate concurred, noting that a "more precise definition of some terms in the draft Convention seemed desirable, in particular of the terms 'investment dispute' and 'of a legal character'."[103]

Most importantly, although Mortenson notes that the World Bank, "sponsored, advocated, and substantially drafted the treaty,"[104] he does not make clear the extent to which the World Bank had the final say. In Mortenson's account, a compromise drafted by the British expert-designate, which kept the definition of investment as broad as possible, is the final word on the matter and what contemporary interpreters should use as guidance.[105] Yet British officials themselves did not see it this way. At the next meeting related to ICSID after the Convention came into force, British officials were instructed to ask Broches for additional clarification of the definition of investment. Officials in London wrote to British officials in Washington:

> We have considered whether some clarification of the term "investment" is not needed in the rules of procedure....we wondered if overseas portfolio investors, who were considering taking a dispute to the Centre, might be deterred by doubts as to whether that types of dispute came within its purview, given that certain provisions (e.g. those in Articles 33 (2) (b) and 36 of the provisional Arbitration Rules) clearly refer only to direct investment. Our legal advice on this point is that any definition would be more likely to have a restrictive rather than a liberalizing effect.[106]

The British officials in Washington had a quiet word with Broches and reported back to London:

> Broches was quite clear that the term "investment" was always intended to be interpreted in the widest possible way and he drew attention to Articles 28 and 36 of the Convention... There was no doubt in his mind that portfolio investments would be within the scope of the Convention.[107]

Broches may have believed this, but it is doubtful that this understanding of investment was widespread among those that attended the Drafting Committee.

[102] ICSID 1970: 474. [103] ICSID 1970: 468. [104] Mortenson 2010: 263.
[105] Mortenson 2010: 289–93.
[106] Letter from W.S. Ryrie to J.M. Stevens, January 1967. "International Centre for Settlement of Investment Disputes." UK FCO 48/145.
[107] Memo from J.M. Stevens to W.S. Ryrie, February 15, 1967. UK FCO 48/145.

The experts-designate that had attended the Committee may not have shared an understanding of the limits of ICSID's jurisdiction. The structure of the drafting matters: they did not need to reach a negotiated deal; they merely offered recommendations to the World Bank. Did this consultative structure make experts-designate more willing to recommend vague language than if they had been engaged in deliberative negotiations? It is difficult to assess, but the fact that even the British government—whose officials wrote the Convention text on jurisdiction—believed that clarification was needed, is evidence of lingering uncertainties about the limits of the Convention's jurisdiction. The fact that British officials sought clarification from Broches, in turn, is strong evidence of the commanding role played by Broches and the Bank.

This section and those preceding it have drawn out themes from the responses of state officials to the ICSID proposal. First, the Convention's success depended on ratification by capital-importing states. Second, the World Bank's appeal to capital-importing states relied on the premise that the Convention could improve a state's investment climate. Some states accepted this premise, but many did not—particularly at first. Third, the Bank's strategy involved arguing that the Convention would not have serious implications for international law—it would merely institutionalize an existing practice. This argument was contested at all four consultative conferences. Many implications of the Convention were advanced, including that elevating individuals to equal standing with states was a profound change for international law, and that the Convention's jurisdiction was not bounded.

INITIAL RATIFICATIONS: TO JOIN OR NOT TO JOIN?

Once the ICSID Convention opened for signature and ratification in 1965, did states act in accordance with the views their experts-designate voiced during the consultative meetings? The answer is largely yes. The first wave of ratifications between 1965 and 1970 had three defining characteristics. First, capital-exporting states ratified. Second, many states emerging from British colonialism ratified quickly. Third, there were strong regional trends: Latin American states were uniformly opposed, while most sub-Saharan African states ratified within five years.

Most capital-exporting states ratified ICSID easily and quickly. This matches their supportive statements during the consultative conferences. Domestic deliberations on ratification were easier since their policymakers and domestic legislatures did not imagine themselves as respondents in ICSID cases. Some of these states waited to sign until a quorum of capital-importing states had signed the Convention. For instance, all US action was predicated on the

Convention's acceptance by investment-importing states.[108] Eighteen out of twenty-four OECD member states ratified ICSID before 1971.[109]

The six OECD states that did not join ICSID were capital-importers: Australia, Canada, Ireland, Portugal, Spain, and Turkey. The ratification decision was different for capital-importers that were considered "developed" states. Officials in New Zealand, for instance, noted that although "New Zealand is not a capital exporter or a developing nation she is still in search for capital to develop and diversify her economy. Full contractual membership of the convention can only assist her in that search."[110] Yet ICSID's ability to "assist in that search" was not rated highly; the New Zealand government waited fifteen years to ratify, and when it did, the three reasons given were because ICSID will "promote the international climate for foreign investment generally; New Zealand will acquire additional credit-worthiness to the good reputation which we already have; and New Zealand will stand in better stead at the Bank... [including] her suitability as a potential borrower."[111]

If reputational concerns and the belief that ratifying would improve their likelihood of World Bank loans mattered for New Zealand, then it is likely these concerns mattered even more for poorer countries. Some smaller states were explicitly afraid of negative consequences if they did not sign up. The expert from Bolivia "observed that if the draft Convention were not unanimously rejected, foreign capital might blacklist the countries that did not wish to submit their disputes with investors to international adjudication."[112] States with more experience of inward foreign investment or less difficulty attracting it did not share this fear. Saudi Arabia's expert-designate noted his country was reforming its foreign investment framework and said the consultative conference "had helped considerably to clarify the problems which might arise

[108] In the words of an adviser briefing the Secretary of State on US support for ICSID: "We have not wanted to be the first to sign the Convention. Now, however, Tunisia, Jamaica, Ivory Coast, Nigeria, and Pakistan, as well as the United Kingdom, have signed the Convention, and Japan has formally communicated, to the President of the Bank, its intention to sign. It therefore seems appropriate for the United States now to signify its support for the Convention and to begin the necessary mechanisms for ratification and implementing legislation." Memo from Leonard Meeker for the Secretary of State, subject: "Circular 175 Authority for Signature of World Bank Convention on Settlement of Investment Disputes: Action Memorandum." Undated but likely March 1965. US LA: Bill S.3498. The US signed the ICSID Convention on August 27 1965.

[109] The eighteen OECD states that ratified ICSID before 1971 were: Austria, Belgium, Denmark, Finland, France, Germany, Greece, Iceland, Italy, Japan, Korea, Luxembourg, the Netherlands, Norway, Sweden, Switzerland, the UK, the US. Data from ICSID Secretariat and OECD.

[110] "Ratification of the Convention by New Zealand" Internal Memo, likely August 1972. NZ 241.

[111] "Ratification of the Convention by New Zealand" Internal Memo, likely August 1972. NZ 241.

[112] ICSID 1970: 308.

in connection with such investments."[113] The Convention might be useful, but Saudi Arabia could take it or leave it. As it happened, Saudi Arabia did not join ICSID for fifteen years, after it had become an exporter of large volumes of capital. As if to highlight that it only wanted ICSID to operate when it was an exporter, Saudi Arabia joined with a restriction that ICSID cases could not be brought against it that concerned oil or gas.[114]

World Bank officials, consistent with their active brokering in earlier stages of the process, followed up with countries until they ratified. The British archives reveal a stream of letters and phone calls from Broches, President Woods, and other World Bank officials:

> *January 1966*: I enclose a copy of a memorandum we have received from the President of the World Bank about the ratification of this Convention by the UK[115]
> *May 1966*: As you probably know, Woods called on Sir Denis Rickett at the Treasury on 26 April and gave him a memorandum, of which I enclose a copy, urging early UK ratification.[116]
> *May 1966*: Since that reply [to a letter from Broches about British ratification] was sent Mr. Broches has appeared again and done his own bit of lobbying, and seen the people concerned in the Foreign Office.[117]
> *July 1966*: We have been pressed from time to time by members of the IBRD to ratify as soon as possible.[118]
> *July 1966*: Several enquiries have been received from the IBRD about the timing of ratification by the UK.[119]

The New Zealand archives show a similar stream of reminders, stretching over a ten-year period: "the officers of [ICSID] have been taking an interest,"[120] "the Centre has once again taken an interest,"[121] and "Treasury has been asked by the Secretary-General of ICSID."[122] New Zealand was not a country whose ratification was particularly meaningful, which means that if the ICSID Secretariat put this much effort into New Zealand's ratification, then it is

113 ICSID 1970: 550. 114 ICSID/8-D.
115 Letter from R. E. Radford to Robins, January 19, 1966. UK T 312/1498.
116 Letter from R. E. Radford to the Foreign Office, May 9, 1966. UK T 312/1498.
117 Letter from J. Kelley to Mr. Jenkyns, May 12, 1966. UK T 312/1498.
118 Letter from Mr. Butler to Mr. Ryrie, July 7, 1966. UK T 312/1498.
119 Draft from Mr. Hildyard to Mrs. White, subject: "Legislation in Connection with the IBRD Convention on the Settlement of Investment Disputes (undated, likely July 1966)." UK T 312/1498.
120 Letter from the Secretary of Foreign Affairs to the Secretary to the Treasury, November 30, 1971. NZ 241.
121 Letter from the Secretary for Foreign Affairs to the Secretary for Justice, August 11, 1972. NZ 241.
122 Letter from the Secretary to the Treasury to The Secretary, Justice Department, May 31, 1978. NZ 241.

likely to have put equal or greater effort into other states. It is not unusual for international organizations to send reminders about ratification, but the volume of reminders and their insistence is unusual. The UK ratified in November 1966, with no controversy.[123]

The British decision to ratify was straightforward, but it mattered because of the UK's privileged relationship with its former colonies.[124] The year the ICSID Convention opened for signature, 1965, was the same year that the Commonwealth Secretariat was created. Within five years, almost all state members of the Commonwealth would sign and ratify ICSID. The Commonwealth had thirty states by 1971, not counting the UK. Of these thirty states, twenty-five were members of the World Bank.[125] Of the twenty-five Commonwealth states eligible to join ICSID, nineteen signed and ratified quickly.[126] Archival records suggest that the Commonwealth Relations Office within the British government wrote to relevant officials in these countries urging ratification. For instance, in April 1966, the Office wrote a letter to the High Commission for Pakistan that "expresses hope that the Government of Pakistan will itself ratify the [ICSID] Convention in the near future."[127] Pakistan did ratify a few months later, in November 1966. Many Commonwealth states were still moving toward greater self-rule, and had little experience of FDI.

The six Commonwealth states that did not join ICSID were Australia, Canada, India, New Zealand, South Africa, and Tanzania. Apart from Tanzania, which was on a path to African Socialism under President Julius Nyerere at the time, these states can be distinguished from other Commonwealth states by their comparatively extensive experience with investment.[128] Policymakers in these states did not believe ICSID was necessary. Their relatively high volumes of investment—or relative confidence that they could continue to attract

[123] At the relevant session, this comment was made: "All that I need say after the rapid progress which we have made is to thank the House, on both sides, for their assistance in this matter. The Bill will be of great assistance to international investment. It includes no controversial principles, and we are fortified in the belief that the House will give it a Third Reading." Hansard, November 26, 1966 Arbitration (International Investment Disputes) Bill [Lords].

[124] President Woods and other officials told the British government their ratification was imperative because there would not be any common-law countries represented at the first Administrative Council meeting, and that the meeting would be dominated by newly independent African countries. Letter from R. E. Radford to the Foreign Office, May 9, 1966. UK T 312/1498.

[125] Barbados, Malta, Nauru, Samoa, and Tonga would join the Bank in later years.

[126] With year of signature: Botswana (1970), Cyprus (1966), Ghana (1965), Guyana (1969), Jamaica (1965), Kenya (1966), Lesotho (1968), Malawi (1966), Malaysia (1965), Mauritius (1969), Nigeria (1965), Pakistan (1965), Sierra Leone (1965), Singapore (1968), Sri Lanka (1967), Swaziland (1970), Trinidad and Tobago (1966), Uganda (1966), and Zambia (1970).

[127] Letter from Downing Street to the Office of the High Commissioner for Pakistan, May 5, 1966. UK T 312/1498.

[128] Nyerere's policies included taking a hard line with the World Bank (Aminzade 2013).

investment if they sought it—meant they could afford to be ambivalent. They were not dependent on the World Bank for advice on how to attract investment.

There are strong regional trends as regards ratification. Many African states ratified quickly: the first five ratifications were Ivory Coast, Nigeria, Mauritania, Central African Republic, and Gabon.[129] ICSID membership was proportionally highest in Africa, and particularly in sub-Saharan Africa.[130] When discussing early ratification years later, a World Bank official noted the "outspoken hostility from Latin American countries" and the slow start generally, before observing that "the exception was the African countries, which were willing to accept anything to get investments."[131] Here again, limited available evidence suggests that the Bank played an active role in encouraging these ratifications: "the Bank believes that the energetic canvassing of Executive Directors representing other African countries will soon result in further ratifications."[132] Francophone African countries may also have received encouragement to ratify from their former colonizer. Years later, when an interviewer remarked that "my impression is that initially a number of African countries, former colonial countries or countries in transition, did join ICSID early on," Georges Delaume, a French national who worked at the World Bank, replied, "Yes. They were pushed by the French."[133]

By contrast, only three of the World Bank's twenty-two member states in the Western hemisphere were members: Jamaica, the US, and Trinidad and Tobago. None of these states were Spanish-speaking, and none were on the continent of South America. The uniform rejection of the Convention by Latin American states troubled the Bank's staff. In 1970, Paul Szasz observed that

> perhaps the question most frequently put to those of us in the World Bank who administer the International Centre for Settlement of Investment Disputes is: Is such-or-such Latin American country party to the Convention on the Settlement of Investment Disputes between States and Nationals of Other States? And, on hearing our regretful negative reply...[134]

[129] Of the twenty ratifications required for the Convention to enter into force, fifteen were by African states: Nigeria (1965), Mauritania (1966), Ivory Coast (1966), Central African Republic (1966), Gabon (1966), Uganda (1966), Tunisia (1966), Congo-Brazzaville (1966), Ghana (1966), Sierra Leone (1966), Malawi (1966), Chad (1966), Upper Volta (1966), Malagasy Republic (1966), and Dahomey (1966). The five non-African states were: the US (1966), Iceland (1966), Malaysia (1966), Jamaica (1966), and the Netherlands (1966).

[130] The World Bank had forty African member states in 1971. Of these forty, thirty-one were members of ICSID. Algeria, Egypt, Ethiopia, Libya, Mali, Rwanda, South Africa, Sudan, and Tanzania were the nine African states that were not ICSID members in 1971.

[131] Delaume 2004: 25.

[132] Letter from R. E. Radford to Nicholson, Foreign Office, April 18, 1966. UK T 312/1498.

[133] Delaume 2004: 13.

[134] Szasz 1970: 256.

The Bank pursued ratifications most actively in Latin America. Discussing the opposition to the Convention among Latin American states, Szasz also noted:

> If they did not join the Centre, it was not for lack of persuasion. An early effort was made by Mr Broches, the General Counsel of the World Bank and in practice the Father of the Convention—who later became the first Secretary-General of the Centre. In an address delivered on May 27, 1965 in San Juan, Puerto Rico, to a joint meeting [of a series of bar associations] . . . Mr Broches stated what he felt were the five principal "wrong" arguments that had been advanced in Latin America against the Convention and presented his refutations.[135]

According to Broches, the five "wrong" arguments were: (i) the Convention introduces compulsory arbitration, (ii) submission to international arbitration of investor–state disputes is prohibited by Latin American constitutions, (iii) the Convention violates the constitutional principle of equality of citizens and aliens, (iv) establishing international arbitration facilities is evidence of an unacceptable lack of confidence in the integrity and independence of national courts, and (v) the history of international arbitration in Latin America has been an unfortunate one.[136] Despite the efforts of Broches and the Bank to convince Latin American states to drop their opposition, these states remained uniformly opposed into the 1980s.

CASE STUDY: THE US RATIFICATION OF ICSID

The US government had refused to ratify the Havana Charter and the OECD Draft. Yet the US government ratified the ICSID Convention within a year. Why? There are two central reasons. First, it was possible for the US to ratify because the State Department considered it plausible to tell concerned legislators that the US government would not be a respondent. Second, the US government was able to ratify because the ICSID Convention lacked substance: the US government would not have ratified a treaty that weakened its stance on investment protection, and any substantive treaty arrived at through multilateral negotiations would likely have been weaker than the US government's stance.

In the US, then the world's largest exporter of investment, there was intense political pressure for strong investment protection standards. The two Hickenlooper Amendments were passed in the five years preceding the creation of ICSID. The first Hickenlooper Amendment (1962) required the President to

135 Szasz 1970: 258.

136 Address by A. Broches, General Counsel of the World Bank before the American Bar Association, Section of International and Comparative Law San Juan, Puerto Rico, May 27, 1965. WB Folder 1651419.

suspend aid to any country that expropriated American-owned assets without paying "speedy compensation for such property in convertible foreign exchange, equivalent to the full value thereof."[137] The Hickenlooper Amendments demonstrate that the US government was prepared to take a hard line on expropriation. While some Senators were concerned that the Convention could "perhaps get around our requirement that aid be suspended,"[138] the State Department did not see any conflict between the Hickenlooper Amendment and ICSID. The State Department asked Senator William Fulbright, Chair of the Senate Foreign Relations Committee, to liaise with Bourke Hickenlooper. Fulbright then reported back to Thomas Mann, Undersecretary of State for Economic Affairs.[139] Fulbright wrote on the margins of a private memo to his chief of staff: "Aug 18, I informed Sec Mann that there were no objections... Sen [ator] Hick[enlooper] has feeling convention has no guidelines for compensation and determining value."[140] It was ICSID's lack of substance that earned Hickenlooper's support. With Hickenlooper's assent, the ICSID Convention looked set to be ratified quickly.

Then an obstacle arose: would the ICSID Convention affect US domestic law? The head of the US Securities and Exchange Commission (SEC) and concerned Senators raised this question. The SEC Chairman wanted the US to declare an exception for financial regulation. An extensive exchange of letters between the SEC, the State Department, and Senators' offices ensued, which was ended only by the State Department explaining that it did not envision the US ever being a respondent in a dispute.[141] The same type of question arose later from Senators: would ICSID decisions have the ability to alter provisions of US law? In response to these questions, the State Department again argued that ICSID would have no domestic policy implications in the US, because the US would not be a respondent in ICSID cases. In response to a question from Senator Church, the State Department Legal Adviser observed:

> We should not anticipate arbitral awards given against the United States which would have the effect of altering any provision of US law. The reason I say that is that when a foreign investor invests in this country he most often does it not

[137] The second Hickenlooper Amendment (1964) was included in the next Foreign Assistance Act, in response to anger at the US Supreme Court ruling in *Banco Nacional de Cuba v Sabbatino*.

[138] Senator Aiken speaking, Report on the "Convention on the Settlement of Investment Disputes, 89th Congress, 2d Session, May 11, 1966." US LA Bill S.3498.

[139] Thomas Mann was an authority on Latin America within the US State Department, with a reputation for providing strong support for US business. He set out a policy of supporting regime change to promote the interests of US business, which has been called "the Mann Doctrine" (LaFeber 1993:186).

[140] "Memo from Carl Marcy" August 16, 1965. US LA Bill S.3498.

[141] SEC Letters, including Letter from MacArthur to Harris, dated March 27, 1965. US LA Bill S.3498. The SEC concern is referenced on pages 10–11 of the Report on the "Convention on the Settlement of Investment Disputes, 89th Congress, 2d Session, May 11, 1966." US LA Bill S.3498.

> pursuant to some special contract or agreement... instead, when an investor comes here he does so understanding that the US laws are going to apply to him just as to any other entrepreneur.[142]

When investors came to the US, they accepted that domestic law and domestic courts would govern the investment. One is reminded here of Thomas Wälde's observation that "the Calvo-doctrine, much opposed by Western governments with respect to developing countries, has in fact been—and still is—the dominant maxim of Western countries themselves."[143]

Would ICSID be effective? The Senate Foreign Relations Committee decided the answer was largely no, or at least not immediately. Most of the US expropriation disputes were with states in Latin America.[144] When asked for examples of investment disputes from the last decade that could have been submitted to ICSID, James Meeker, the State Department Legal Adviser, gave an example of Argentine bonds and American-owned property in Brazil that had been expropriated. In response to this example, Fulbright asked, "But have any Latin American countries signed this agreement?" The question was likely rhetorical, and Meeker did not answer it. No Latin American states were expected to join ICSID.

The State Department argued that through use of the ICSID procedure, a new body of substantive law on investment protection would emerge—the State Department expected that ICSID would reshape investment law subtly, through practice and precedent, and gradually redefine customary international law. Meeker's written testimony conveys the expectations of the State Department:

> The World Bank Convention does not lay down any substantive rules regarding investment... and the like. The Bank's judgment, in which we concur, is that any attempt to lay down such rules could not have won the substantial support this convention has found among the less-developed states. However, it is anticipated that decisions through the convention's mechanism will create a significant new body of international law. Thus international law in this area can be expected to grow as the result of this convention.[145]

[142] Report on the "Convention on the Settlement of Investment Disputes, 89th Congress, 2d Session, May 11, 1966." US LA Bill S.3498.

[143] Wälde 1996: 446.

[144] The Hickenlooper Amendments were promulgated in response to seizures in Brazil and Cuba. Hogan (1969: 79) notes: "the Enactment of the Hickenlooper Amendment of 1962 was probably the immediate result of the taking of the Brazilian holdings of the International Telephone and Telegraph Company by the Government of Brazil;" and: "The 1962 Amendment was also the result of the vast number of American holdings which were expropriated by the government of Cuba without compensation."

[145] Appendix: written statement from James Meeker. Report on the "Convention on the Settlement of Investment Disputes, 89th Congress, 2d Session, May 11, 1966." US LA Bill S.3498.

The US government expected ICSID to facilitate a slow evolution in international investment law. How would ICSID facilitate this evolution? The answer is through broad consent to ICSID in other agreements, primarily in individual investment contracts and bilateral treaties. Meeker wrote in his testimony to the Senate Committee on Foreign Relations: "As investment agreements providing for use of the convention's facilities become more common, the total climate for international investment will, we believe, improve substantially."[146] Investment agreements are the mechanism through which the ICSID Convention could reshape international law on investment protection. These agreements would create the substance, as politics permitted, to fill in the structure created by the Convention.

The few letters written to the US government in support of the ICSID Convention argued that it needed to be complemented with substantive agreements. Many US exporters used the ICSID Convention as an opportunity to urge the US government to negotiate substantive rules on investment. One example is a letter from the President of the National Foreign Trade Council (NFTC) to Fulbright, who urged "action by the US government" on the OECD Draft. Later in the same letter, the NFTC urged bilateral treaties: "the NFTC is strongly in favor of the negotiation of additional treaties with individual foreign governments for the protection of private investment."[147] Fulbright only received letters in support of the Convention, and no letters against it.[148] No opposition to ICSID appears in any archive records associated with US ratification of ICSID.

Another reason for the lack of opposition is because the ICSID Convention was couched in soft, pro-development language. Apart from concerns about the US being a respondent, no concerns were raised about the consequences of ICSID. Under-Secretary of the Treasury Barr opened his testimony about ICSID to the Senate Foreign Relations Committee with a statement that was filled with sympathy for the political plight of leaders in former colonies:

> As new nations come into the world, they adopt certain policies for what may be good political reasons. However, sometimes these good political reasons do not jibe with the economic realities that are in the world today. For instance, I think the great multinational corporations have much to offer in the world today, but some small countries are very frightened, perhaps for good reasons. Perhaps the conduct of the corporations in the past has provided the excuse. But regardless of

[146] Appendix: written statement from James Meeker. Report on the "Convention on the Settlement of Investment Disputes, 89th Congress, 2d Session, May 11, 1966." US LA Bill S.3498.

[147] Letter from Norris to Fulbright, dated March 1, 1966. The US was concluding friendship, commerce, and navigation treaties at the time, which included investment provisions. US LA: Bill S.3498.

[148] I reviewed all of Senator William Fulbright's papers related to ICSID at the US National Archives. US LA: Bill S.3498.

> the reason, economic facts show the small nations need this investment; political facts, however, seem to hold it off.[149]

This empathetic tone is maintained throughout his testimony.[150] This tone also characterized the only speech made on the floor of the Senate about ICSID, titled "A New Hope for Developing Nations."[151] The overriding priority was getting capital to the places it was needed most. Cold War security imperatives were not mentioned, nor were past investment disputes.

The ICSID Convention passed easily through the US ratification process for many reasons. First, the Convention was for use in less-developed countries, and would not apply or affect investment disputes in the United States. Second, the Convention lacked substance, so it would not weaken the Hickenlooper Amendments. Despite the absence of substance from the Convention itself, the practice of dispute resolution that it created was expected to reshape international investment law. This understanding was shared by decision-makers in the State Department and by interested investor lobby groups, but does not appear to have been widely shared beyond those groups. When presented to large audiences, the ICSID Convention was couched in pro-development rhetoric. None of this would have been possible without the World Bank's agenda-setting and brokering in support of the ICSID Convention. The World Bank had crafted a multilateral treaty on investment that the US government could ratify. The American government had not led its creation, but equally, no part of the US government found sufficient fault with the treaty to prevent ratification. The World Bank had correctly anticipated what content would be politically possible for its largest shareholder to ratify.

CONCLUSION

This chapter evaluates how states responded to the World Bank's proposal of the ICSID Convention. Despite the Bank's strategy, success would still require capital-importing countries and capital-exporting countries to ratify. That was improbable: previous attempts to create a multilateral organization dedicated to investment failed, and the drafting process could easily become a political battlefield.

The Bank's strategy of using legal expertise to shield the drafting process from politicking was effective. Every legal expert involved in ICSID's drafting

[149] Under Secretary Barr speaking, Report on the "Convention on the Settlement of Investment Disputes, 89th Congress, 2d Session, May 11, 1966." US LA Bill S.3498.

[150] This language is likely the product of both genuine internationalist sentiment and the strategic Cold War imperative of courting allies in "the Third World."

[151] Senator Hartke speaking, Congressional Record—Senate, May 5, 1966.

had lived through the Second World War, the signing of the UN Charter, and decolonization debates: the appeal of peaceful dispute settlement was strong, and the idea of arbitration "fit" this context and this audience well. These experts did not demand econometric evidence that the ICSID Convention could facilitate investment flows; they were sympathetic to the idea of arbitration and were more concerned about legal implications. These experts' concerns tended to cluster around four topics. Many experts questioned the wisdom of granting individuals standing under international law. Some were concerned about the long-term effect of giving investors the ability to bypass local remedies and national justice systems. Experts-designate from Latin America, India, and other states asserted that arbitration was interstate, and that disputes between an investor and a state were a matter for national courts. Some experts-designate suggested the Convention might have public policy implications.

Broches and the Bank attempted to assuage these concerns by emphasizing that two forms of consent would be required to register a dispute at ICSID. Many experts found the double-consent formulation insufficient to allay their concerns. Despite the fact that no advance consent clauses existed in bilateral investment treaties yet, officials from some states—such as Germany, Switzerland, the UK, and the US—had discussed the possibility of their inclusion, while officials from other states, including many in Latin America, were concerned by the possibility of something like investor–state arbitration clauses in investment treaties. They understood that the Convention was just the beginning. The ICSID Convention made it possible to reshape international investment law through bilateral treaties and arbitral jurisprudence, without having acrimonious multilateral debates.

Part II

Eliciting State Consent

6

Layering

How Investor–State Arbitration Was Added to Investment Treaties

After the ICSID Convention came into force in 1966, the architecture for ISDS was only partially complete. The Convention's double-consent formulation means that in order for ICSID to have any cases, states must provide consent to ICSID jurisdiction in another instrument—a domestic law, contract, or treaty. Who elicited this consent from states, and why? This is the second phase of the puzzle examined in this book.

In conventional accounts, investors and capital-exporting states are expected to elicit consent from capital-importing states. Both foreign investors and capital-exporters have excellent reasons to elicit consent: investors benefit from having standing to bring claims directly against states, and capital-exporting governments, in theory, no longer need to entangle themselves in disputes involving their investors.

In contrast to conventional accounts, I argue that the international officials who had shepherded the Convention into existence then began to elicit consent from states, using the same strategies of agenda setting and brokering. These officials still had the same resources at their disposal, and if anything, their motivation to ensure organizational survival intensified after the Convention came into force. Officials within the ICSID Secretariat now had a strategic interest in eliciting advance consent, to ensure their organization survived.[1]

This chapter adjudicates between these two competing explanations, and finds that international officials did play an influential role. In fact, the chapter can be framed as a counterfactual: in the absence of agenda-setting and brokering from ICSID officials, would investor–state clauses have been inserted into investment treaties? It is unlikely that these clauses would have been

[1] In this chapter, "the Secretariat" and "the Centre" are used interchangeably, following usage in ICSID publications from this period.

inserted into treaties when they were, and perhaps ever, without the actions of the ICSID Secretariat. Arbitrations between investors and states on the basis of contracts would exist, but it is doubtful that "investment treaty arbitration" would exist without the Secretariat's actions. The idea of treaty arbitration was made feasible and then promoted by the World Bank (not by the German and Swiss governments, even when they discussed investment treaties in great detail).

The Secretariat's informal agenda-setting took the form of model clauses that showed states how to consent to ICSID arbitration in contracts and in treaties. Then Bank officials disseminated these clauses widely and brokered ISDS clauses into existence in hundreds of contracts and investment treaties. When investor–state arbitration clauses first appeared in treaties, these clauses looked like the ICSID model clauses. The first clauses only mentioned ICSID; it was only after several years that other fora and arbitration rules began appearing. The ICSID Secretariat was the centralized starting point for ISDS clauses in treaties. Until the mid-1980s, investment treaties were centralized enough that the ICSID Secretariat could keep a list of all investment treaties that provided access to arbitration.

Investor–state arbitration clauses were layered into investment treaties, that is, they were inserted alongside existing state–state provisions, without removing any content. As we would expect with layering, state–state dispute resolution is still written into most investment treaties, but its use to resolve investment disputes has become rare. Investor–state arbitration was introduced as an unimportant procedural option, but gradually supplanted state–state arbitration.

Beginning in the early 1980s, the ISDS architecture became more expansive. New procedural options like the United Nations Commission on International Trade Law (UNCITRAL) Rules and ICSID Additional Facility were drafted; arbitral organizations like the PCA and the Arbitration Institute of the Stockholm Chamber of Commerce (SCC) started to compete for ISDS cases; and treaty negotiators invented new permutations of advance consent clauses, including versions that fall somewhere between consent and non-consent, like giving the ICSID Secretary General appointing authority for non-ICSID arbitrations or giving tribunals the right to decide the amount of compensation only. All these incremental actions create an ISDS architecture that is fragmentary, inconsistent, and hard to reform—exactly what is expected when layering operates. Layering can result in institutions that "appear more haphazard than the product of some overarching master plan."[2] The haphazardness of contemporary ISDS, and the interest of investors today, has led scholars and others to assume the system had decentralized origins and was

[2] Schickler 2001: 14.

created through investor demand. Through methods that focus only on the moments of interstate bargaining, these accounts found support. Yet they are incomplete: these accounts miss the centralized origins of ISDS and deny the officials within the ICSID Secretariat their key role.

The Secretariat's dynamism is remarkable given that it had no mandate for activities beyond administering cases: during the Legal Committee, several experts-designate objected to a provision in the Draft on "possible ancillary activities of the Centre, such as the collection and dissemination of information on investment law" and the provision was deleted.[3]

This chapter is organized in three sections. The first sets out the ICSID Secretariat's motivation and resources. The second analyzes the Secretariat's strategies: agenda-setting and brokering. The most important agenda-setting took the form of model clauses, but this was accompanied by what the Secretariat termed its "Information Activities"—efforts to generate awareness of its activities. The Secretariat was most successful in its brokering with governments. The third section turns to the early ISDS clauses in BITs, and evaluates the extent of investor involvement with these clauses compared with ICSID Secretariat involvement with these clauses.

MOTIVATION AND RESOURCES

Motivation

Previous chapters identified two motivations of international officials. The first is the pursuit of policy goals: in the case of international officials, this means the beliefs that officials held about the desirability of investor–state arbitration. Available evidence indicates that many of these officials believed that advance consent prevented disputes from arising, that binding consent to arbitration kept disputes within the realm of law and out of the realm of power, and that the existence of dispute settlement procedures would facilitate greater investment and thus, greater development. Officials' commitments to these beliefs may have grown stronger during the creation of the ICSID Convention, as they elucidated the logic of the Convention and its benefits in front of several audiences. The second motivation, ensuring organizational survival, unequivocally grew stronger after ICSID was created.

One testament to the strength of these officials' motivation is how hard they worked to foster awareness about ICSID, and the extent to which they saw fostering awareness as an important part of their mission. The first Annual

[3] Parra 2017: 69.

Report notes: "With the entry into force of the Convention, an urgent task of the Centre became the distribution of information to acquaint potential parties (both public and private) to proceedings under the Convention."[4] Fostering awareness was not always easy for the small Secretariat. During ICSID's first decade, the Annual Reports had a subheading titled "Information Activities." Under this subheading, the Secretariat reported on its progress in publicizing ICSID. ICSID produced a leaflet: the Second Annual Report notes, "the Centre has issued in three languages and distributed widely a small information leaflet, similar in format to the pamphlets used by other members of the World Bank Group."[5] The Secretariat also built mailing lists.[6] The "Information Activities," later termed "Promotion of the Centre," continued for many years, with mixed results. Limited awareness of the Centre was still a concern in the Centre's Seventh Annual Report, published in 1973. The report noted: "As in the past years, the Centre's activities were directed mainly towards the encouragement of a greater use of the Centre . . . as in the previous years, [it has] continued to distribute information about the functioning of the Centre to governmental agencies, private business firms and other institutions."[7]

The strong motivation of Secretariat officials contrasts with the lack of interest among investors. Between 1960 and 1981, ICSID was mentioned only four times in the *Financial Times*, and once in *The New York Times*.[8] In 1976, Ryans and Baker conducted a survey of the top legal counsel within Fortune 1,000 firms, seeking to determine "practices regarding, and attitudes toward, the provisions of the [ICSID] Convention."[9] The second question in their survey asked, "Are you familiar with the Convention on the Settlement of Investment Disputes?" Only 15 percent of the respondents, of which there were 165 in total, answered that they were familiar with ICSID.[10] Ryans and Baker concluded that: "While the total responses of the 165 participants in the study do provide some interesting insights, they seem to mainly reinforce the dramatic lack of knowledge and understanding of the Convention and ICSID on the part of a group that seemingly should be aware of their features."[11]

[4] ICSID First Annual Report: 4. Parra (2012: 132) also notes this quote, arguing, "In ICSID's initial years, Broches and his staff were preoccupied with the 'urgent task' of disseminating knowledge about the Centre to potential parties to proceedings."

[5] ICSID Second Annual Report: 4.

[6] ICSID Second Annual Report: 4.

[7] ICSID Seventh Annual Report: 3.

[8] My search of archives, including ancillary terms, such as "World Bank investment court." Three out of four references in the *Financial Times* concern the Jamaica bauxite cases, discussed in Chapter seven. While coverage in investor press is an imperfect indicator, it is illustrative to compare those twenty years with the period since 2000, when ICSID has appeared nearly fifty times in the *Financial Times*.

[9] Ryans and Baker 1976: 69.

[10] Ryans and Baker 1976: 70. Eighty-one percent were not familiar and the rest did not report an answer.

[11] Ryans and Baker 1976: 73.

Secretariat officials worked hard to disseminate information that might spark demand, but for two decades their efforts seemed unsuccessful. Georges Delaume, who worked in the Bank's Legal Department from 1956 to 1986, recalled that in its first twenty years, ICSID was "begging for cases [but] cases didn't come."[12] He remembered that ICSID was considered a failure within the Bank: "It didn't succeed at first. It was a total calamity originally. Everybody was actually laughing at it in the Bank. They all said—'ICSID, well, you do nothing!'"[13] In the absence of cases, ICSID officials came up with a new benchmark for success: the number of consents provided by states.

Advance Consent as the Benchmark for ICSID's Success

The Secretariat could not use the number of cases as an indicator of success, because there was not a single case during ICSID's first seven years. Already in 1967, World Bank President George Woods moved away from caseload as a standard of evaluation: "the success of the Centre is not to be judged by the amount of litigation it handles."[14] Subsequently, ICSID and the Bank took a consistent line: advance consent and not the number of disputes defined success. As Broches put it in 1972:

> The test for the success of the Centre was not the number of conciliation or arbitration proceedings that came before it, but rather the willingness of investors and host governments to agree in advance to accept the jurisdiction of the Centre.[15]

Accordingly, the Centre reported the number of new agreements that included advance consent to ICSID. The Third Annual Report notes:

> While no cases have been brought to the Centre, the number of instruments—including investment contracts, bilateral investment treaties and national legislation—containing provisions for the conciliation or arbitration of future disputes pursuant to the Convention is increasing.[16]

The justification for using advance consent as a benchmark was that the presence of advance consent to arbitration encourages settlement. Robert McNamara

[12] Delaume 2004: 13. [13] Delaume 2004: 12.

[14] "Opening Remarks of George D Woods, Chairman, to the First Annual Meeting," September 25, 1967.

[15] "Address by Aron Broches to the Sixth Annual Meeting," September 28, 1972.

[16] ICSID Third Annual Report: 3. Another example is in the Fourth Annual Report of ICSID: 5, or the accompanying Press Release: "While no disputes have yet been submitted to the Centre, provision is made in an increasing number of legal instruments for the submission to the Centre of legal disputes to the Centre."

articulated this in 1970: "I share the widely held belief that the confidence inspired by the mere existence of such an ultimate forum will go a long way to avoiding the very situation for which it was created, by providing an atmosphere favorable to the adjustment, by the parties, of the disputes by means of negotiations."[17] This is a common argument in general arbitration: "knowing that arbitration will occur if a dispute is not settled induces settlement."[18] Broches often emphasized ICSID's deterrent effect:

> If there are no disputes, so much the better. In some cases there are disputes, but they don't come to ICSID, even though there's an agreement to take them to ICSID. Why? Because at the last moment, both sides realized that they may win or may lose, and make a last effort at settlement, which is often successful. Generally, an ironclad commitment to go to a court or to arbitration is a strong incentive to settlement. The preventative value of these institutions is very great.[19]

While Broches spoke of advance consent encouraging both sides to settle, in practice, the provision of advance consent strengthens the bargaining position of investors. Investors can use the threat of an ICSID case to induce a better settlement from states. Advance consent weakens the bargaining position of the state, all else equal. In 1980, O'Keefe observed that for investors and capital-exporting states, access to ICSID becomes "another weapon in the armory for protection of foreign investment."[20] Broches did not see it this way, and advocated advance consent at least in part because he believed that it discouraged home state involvement.

As years passed without cases, the Centre began presenting advance consent as an effective deterrent—ICSID had few cases because advance consent deterred disputes.[21] This allowed Broches to argue that the Centre was useful, even if it never received a request for arbitration. In 1969, he told the Administrative Council: "The Centre serves a useful role through its very existence... But this does not mean the Centre should remain entirely inactive, pending the submission of disputes."[22] The Centre was not inactive, as this chapter demonstrates. It used its resources to actively pursue its goal of advance consents, in domestic laws, contracts, and treaties.

[17] "Opening Remarks of Robert S McNamara, Chairman, to the Fourth Annual Meeting," September 23, 1970.

[18] O'Keefe 1980: 287–8. He also argued ICSID's caseload compared unfavorably with that of similar cases at the ICC, on the basis of the limited information available about the caseloads of both institutions (O'Keefe 1980: 289–90).

[19] Broches 1984 (May): 43.

[20] O'Keefe 1980: 292.

[21] ICSID Tenth Annual Report: 3.

[22] "Address by A. Broches to the Third Annual Meeting," September 29, 1969.

Resources

Why did the ICSID Secretariat struggle to raise awareness about itself? There were several obstacles to an influential Secretariat. First, the language used by Bank officials during ICSID's creation and emergence suggested that the Secretariat would be passive: the organization's mandate was to administer arbitrations and do little else. When ICSID had no cases, it had nothing to administer. Second, many states, even World Bank member states working to attract foreign investment, remained outside the organization. Third, the ICSID Secretariat had few resources. It was tiny—it had four to five staff members and its operating budget in its first year was $32,000.[23] Even in 1966, this was not much money for an autonomous international organization. By comparison, the IDA, another recently created arm of the World Bank, had an administrative budget over $3,350,000 in the same year.[24] The ICSID budget did not grow much either; sixteen years later, the 1982 budget was only $251,000, and the Secretariat still had only four to five staff members.[25]

Monetary amounts are illustrative, but underrepresent the resources that ICSID had at its disposal. Chapter one discussed three types of resources: expertise, access to privileged information, and reputation. In these, ICSID was rich. The officials working on ICSID specialized in investment law, developing unparalleled expertise, and continued to serve as high-ranking officials of the World Bank which provided them with the Bank's access to privileged information and formidable reputation. All ICSID staff are World Bank employees; for the first three decades, lawyers and administrators went back and forth between the World Bank Legal Department and ICSID as needed and the senior officials had dual job titles. For Broches, the Bank and the Centre's resources were interchangeable. The Bank paid ICSID's operating costs during this period.[26] For instance, Broches was paid as the head of the Bank's Legal Department, not as the head of ICSID, yet he spent a considerable amount of time on ICSID work.[27] The arrangement was similar for other members of the Bank's Legal Department; when one of ICSID's two lawyer positions was vacant,

[23] The main salary costs were paid by the World Bank, since Broches and others were employed by the World Bank's Legal Department (Parra 2012: 128, footnote 55).

[24] IDA 1966: appendices F and D.

[25] Proposed Budget of Revenues and Expenditures for Fiscal Year 1982. Administrative Council, 1981 Annual Meeting, Agenda Item 3. UK FCO 69/667.

[26] Revenues from the sale of ICSID publications were credited to the World Bank, but these revenues were "tiny." As Parra (2012: 128, footnote 55) explains: "In accordance with the Memorandum of Administrative Arrangements between ICSID and the World Bank, the expenditures were all covered by annual contributions to the Bank."

[27] Parra 2012: 125–7.

"and when the need otherwise arose, Legal Department lawyers were asked to work temporarily on ICSID matters."[28] This arrangement ensured that any project ICSID took on would be *de facto* a project of the Bank's Legal Department. In addition to resources, the ICSID Secretariat was able to rely on the World Bank's credibility.

As World Bank officials, ICSID staff had privileged access to officials in many governments, especially governments that might look to the World Bank for technical advice and lending. The World Bank had relationships with the governments of newly independent states where property was considered least secure and disputes considered most likely—in other words, governments whose consent to ICSID was most sought after. ICSID officials cultivated informal advisory relationships with officials in newly independent states. The Bank's Legal Department, as mentioned in Chapter four, had "a very broad and deep top" and was accustomed to more diverse work than most legal departments.[29] Additionally, the Legal Department, and particularly its head, Aron Broches, had direct access to governments around the world.

ICSID officials used this privileged access to government officials. Broches' first request was for member states to help spread the word: "I hope that we may count on the governments of Contracting States to draw attention to the existence of the Centre."[30] Broches saw it as his mission to bring more states into the ICSID fold. Broches did not undertake this mission on behalf of investors. He believed ICSID provided a better way of solving disputes—one that would benefit host states—by removing force and fostering confidence among investors. As he put it in his address to the second meeting of the ICSID Administrative Council: "It will take time before the contracting states and other states which have not yet joined the Centre fully realize and exploit the potential benefits... *It is our task to help bring about this realization.*"[31] As General Counsel of the World Bank, Broches had more tools to bring about this realization than almost anyone else.

The Secretary General, widely known as "Ronnie," was personable and forcefully compelling when explaining the logic and benefits of ICSID.[32] Broches

[28] Parra 2012: 127.

[29] Delaume (2004: 17) notes that before McNamara arrived, lawyers had been counsel, and presidents sought their advice, while in the McNamara era, "the role of the lawyer by itself declined. The lawyers became draftsmen, not counsel."

[30] "Opening Remarks of Aron Broches to the First Annual Meeting," September 25, 1967.

[31] "Address by Aron Broches to the Second Annual Meeting," September 30, 1968. Emphasis mine.

[32] The *travaux* provide many examples of Broches' firm leadership and persuasiveness in action. In a randomly selected and generally representative Legal Committee meeting, Broches made thirty-seven of the eighty-nine comments recorded. This count includes a few comments that were administrative statements from the chair, but the majority of the thirty-seven

played an outsize role in promoting the institution. There are two reasons why Broches had time to devote to ICSID while serving as General Counsel of the World Bank. First, Broches was sidelined when Robert McNamara became World Bank President, and was not asked to fulfill many of the General Counsel's typical tasks.[33] McNamara preferred to rely on Lester Nurick, the Bank's Associate General Counsel.[34] Nurick was an American with experience in the US government, like McNamara. Although Broches remained General Counsel throughout McNamara's tenure as President, it was Nurick who acted as the President's lawyer. Although Broches was still involved with the running of the Bank, his workload was lessened by this arrangement. Second, Broches viewed ICSID as his primary legacy. The World Bank's historian during this era, a friend of Broches, referred to ICSID as "his baby."[35] McNamara, in contrast, neglected ICSID. ICSID fit awkwardly with his vision and plans for the Bank, and he disliked being referred to as the Chairman of ICSID.[36] McNamara often failed to attend the one meeting each year that had to do with ICSID. This meeting only lasted one hour, but in many years McNamara could not be bothered to chair it.[37] McNamara's neglect and sidelining of Broches were not detrimental to ICSID's development. If anything, this state of affairs left Broches with time, the Bank's credibility, and the Bank's legal experts at his disposal to promote ICSID. During McNamara's tenure, the Bank grew and shifted focus from large infrastructure projects to pro-poor policies.[38] ICSID was largely unaffected by these developments. It remained a tiny and relatively low-status part of the Bank.

comments explained the logic of particular Articles. OECD states made twelve comments, and forty comments were made by non-OECD states, including detailed amendments put forward by Haiti and Australia. "Summary Proceedings of the Legal Committee Meeting, 30 November," quoted in ICSID 1970: 711.

[33] When asked why the Bank had created ICSID, Georges Delaume (2004: 12) said, partially in jest: "Because Mr. Broches, who was General Counsel at the time, didn't get too well along with McNamara. He decided to create something else where he could maybe one day retire." Note: While ICSID was created before McNamara became President, Delaume's memory of ICSID as an outlet or haven for Broches once McNamara was in power is telling.

[34] Broches 1984 (May): 40–1.

[35] Broches 1984 (May): 45.

[36] As Broches (1984 (May): 45) recalled, "he saw himself as the friend of the poor, and since ICSID had to do with private investment, he did not like to have identified himself as Chairman of the Administrative Council of ICSID."

[37] For instance, the 1972 meeting, discussed below. In an oral history, Asher, the Bank's historian, asked Broches well-informed questions that give away the nature of McNamara's feelings for ICSID. "Asher: You indicated that McNamara's interest was less than intense, and I guess that's understandable." Broches 1984 (May): 45.

[38] The changes in the Bank's focus were also related to broader geopolitical shifts and US political developments, including increased scrutiny from Congress of the Bank's activity. See Gwin 1997: 210.

STRATEGIES: AGENDA-SETTING AND BROKERING

International officials at ICSID continued to use agenda-setting and brokering after the ICSID Convention came into force. Agenda-setting involves inventing institutional options or putting forward policy proposals to serve as constructed focal points. The ICSID Secretariat engaged in agenda-setting related to all three instruments of consent: domestic law, model clauses for contracts, and model clauses for treaties. Secretariat officials, in particular Broches (travelling as General Counsel of the World Bank) did a considerable amount of brokering in person, meeting with government officials around the world to discuss ICSID. The ICSID Annual Reports from the first decade mention dozens of such trips. For instance, in 1968:

> The Secretary-General has continued to address interested groups privately and publicly on the subject of the Convention. In the course of a journey to Australia, Indonesia, the Philippines and Singapore devoted largely to the affairs of the Centre, he had the opportunity of talking to groups of officials in several of these countries.[39]

Or the next year, when the Secretary General "visited several countries in Africa and Europe for conversations with officials about the affairs of the Centre."[40]

Domestic Laws: Advisory Work and the "Investment Laws of the World" Project

Only a few years after ICSID's creation, Broches proposed an ambitious project to catalogue all the investment laws of capital importers. Broches drew on the resources of the wider World Bank Group for "the initiation of a pilot project for the creation, classification, and eventual dissemination of national legislation and international agreements relating to foreign investments. The World Bank, the IFC, and the Centre are well situated for gathering much of this information as part of their routine operations."[41] The investment law project put ICSID in an advisory relationship with states.[42] The Secretariat constructed a role for itself classifying domestic laws on investment and informally advising

[39] ICSID Second Annual Report: 4. [40] ICSID Third Annual Report: 3.

[41] "Address by A. Broches to the Third Annual Meeting," September 29, 1969.

[42] Broches also continually announced that ICSID stood ready to act in an advisory capacity, outside the investment law project. For instance, during his address to the Sixth Annual Meeting, he "mentioned this activity principally to remind contracting states that the Centre stood ready to render this advisory service." "Address by Aron Broches to the Sixth Annual Meeting," September 28, 1973. Note: Later Secretary Generals of ICSID distance the Centre from advisory work.

governments on how to reform them. From this position, ICSID could: (i) encourage ratification; (ii) facilitate advance consents; and (iii) do preparatory work for a potential multilateral agreement.[43]

The investment law project reflected the ambition of ICSID, not its current membership. Eight of these nineteen states included in the initial project were not ICSID member states. The nineteen states had been "selected to represent a variety of legal systems and traditions."[44] In 1970, Broches announced that the project aimed "to encompass all those requiring foreign capital to further their development."[45] The project was not a means of facilitating ratification; of the eight states that were not ICSID members when the project began, only one joined ICSID during the project—the Democratic Republic of Congo.

The investment law project was more successful at eliciting consent in domestic laws. The World Bank advocated for advance consent to be enshrined in domestic laws long before and long after the investment law project—even the Report of the Executive Directors sent to states with the Convention suggests consent in domestic law.[46] The Centre did not believe it appropriate to publish model clauses for legislation but noted that "it stands ready to advise governments on the formulation of appropriate provisions to be included in such instruments."[47] Broches saw advice about legislation as straightforward technical assistance, well within the tradition of the Bank:

> At times the World Bank group is asked to provide technical advice or assistance to its member governments in preparing suitable legislation for the promotion and protection of investments. In relation to these the expertise of the Secretariat will be readily available to help formulate, if the government so desires, appropriate clauses for settlement of disputes.[48]

This quote also illustrates the ease with which Broches switched from being Bank General Counsel to being ICSID's Secretary General. If the Bank were asked for assistance, ICSID would respond, relying on the Bank's legal expertise. ICSID made announcements when domestic laws were promulgated that referred disputes to it.[49] By the end of Broches' tenure in 1981, thirteen domestic laws gave advance consent to ICSID.[50]

[43] The project aimed to create a repository of investment laws and a classification scheme that could have served as preparatory work for a later effort to harmonize substantive standards. "Address by A. Broches to the Fourth Annual Meeting," September 23, 1970.

[44] Afghanistan, Chad, Chile, Democratic Republic of the Congo, Ethiopia, Ghana, Indonesia, Iran, Ivory Coast, Jamaica, Kenya, Malaysia, Mali, Nigeria, the Philippines, Thailand, Tunisia, Turkey, and Uganda. "Address by A. Broches to the Fourth Annual Meeting," September 23, 1970.

[45] ICSID Fifth Annual Report: 5.

[46] ICSID 1970: 1077.

[47] ICSID Fifth Annual Report: 4.

[48] "Address by Aron Broches to the Second Annual Meeting," September 30, 1968.

[49] ICSID Fifth Annual Report: 4 (citing new legislation in Botswana and Ethiopia).

[50] Afghanistan, Benin, Congo (Brazzaville), Egypt, Ghana, Madagascar, Niger, Senegal, Sudan, Sri Lanka, Tunisia, Upper Volta, Zaire. Annex 4 "Provisions Relating to ICSID in National Investment Laws," ICSID Fifteenth Annual Report: 28.

Contracts: Fostering Awareness Among Private Investors

ICSID was created with an expectation that it would be useful for investors, but stimulating interest among actual investors proved difficult. The Secretariat set out to create its own demand, as the Eighth Annual Report notes:

> In addition the Secretariat *has sought to stimulate interest* in the Centre through discussions with governments, government agencies, groups representing investors as well as practicing lawyers. During the year the Secretary-General addressed an information conference organized by the Federation of Belgian Industries.[51]

ICSID officials were excellent at reaching government officials and were good at reaching international lawyers, but they were not well-equipped to reach private investors. One World Bank official later said that ICSID "was not known" because Broches was accustomed to speaking with other public international lawyers and government officials, and was not good at reaching investors.[52] Broches himself would later note that ICSID "has had more attention in legal periodicals than in business periodicals, and that's partly my fault."[53] Talking to lawyers did not stimulate investor demand.[54]

The lack of demand troubled the Secretariat. The Sixth Annual Report noted: "although the Centre was established some five years ago, its existence and the services it can render are not yet sufficiently known to the investing community."[55] New actions were needed to stimulate demand. At this point, Broches, true to his roots as a public international lawyer, went to governments. This time he went to the insurance agencies of capital-exporting governments. The Sixth Annual Report explained the Secretariat's new pathway for reaching investors: "The Secretary-General has been in contact with the authorities of a number of contracting states... as a result of these contacts the investment guarantee institutions of several contracting states are now drawing the attention of investors to the existence of the Centre."[56] ICSID began introducing itself to investors through national investment insurance programs. The Seventh Annual Report noted that by surveying users of the Overseas Private Investment Corporation (OPIC), it was "able to bring the Centre to the attention of many investors who were otherwise unaware of it."[57] OPIC's customers were an ideal audience for ICSID to advertise itself.[58]

[51] ICSID Eighth Annual Report: 3. Emphasis mine.
[52] Delaume 2004: 24.
[53] Broches 1984 (May): 44.
[54] For instance, of the six Broches speeches reported in the First Annual Report (4), four were given to legal organizations.
[55] ICSID Sixth Annual Report.
[56] ICSID Sixth Annual Report.
[57] ICSID Seventh Annual Report.
[58] OPIC (2017) has a strong track record in settling disputes informally, without arbitration, but investors have to pay for OPIC, whereas they do not pay up front for ICSID.

Other capital-exporting insurance agencies promised to help publicize ICSID to their investors. In 1972, the UK representative at the Administrative Council meeting reported that

> the United Kingdom had taken a number of active but modest steps to give further publicity to the Centre's work. The Secretary-General had mentioned the interest of Lloyd's, which was perhaps something that went beyond publicity. But apart from that, in publicizing the new overseas investment insurance scheme, the United Kingdom government had drawn attention to the Centre's facilities.[59]

Secretariat officials, underwhelmed with initial investor interest in ICSID, were getting creative.

If investors (or states negotiating contracts with investors) were interested, the ICSID Secretariat had prepared model clauses that showed investors and states how to provide consent to ICSID. The Secretariat reported demand for technical assistance on consent clauses, since ICSID's jurisdictional requirements are unusual.[60] In early 1968, the Centre released its first set of model clauses, which appeared in a twenty-seven-page document that showed governments and investors how to consent in contracts.[61] The introduction noted that the Convention itself left open many options with respect to the law and the procedure to be applied.[62] This openness was a recipe for jurisdictional challenges. The model clause document approaches the Convention primarily in terms of its requirements, and how to meet them. The introduction states: "a properly drafted consent clause can serve as a check-list or a reminder of the applicable jurisdictional requirements."[63]

The Secretariat suggested providing consent in the original contract: "it is advisable to record an understanding in advance—and this can most conveniently be done as part of the consent agreement."[64] Although the document presents states and investors with many options, including some that exclude particular types of disputes or require additional consent, in general the document pushes toward earlier consent. As mentioned above, key ICSID officials believed that an "ironclad commitment to go to a court or to arbitration" was a strong deterrent to disputes.[65]

[59] ICSID Sixth Annual Meeting: 8. Broches had already noted that Lloyd's was actively promoting provision for recourse to ICSID arbitration of disputes arising out of investments insured by Lloyd's against political risks.

[60] "Many of the specific inquiries addressed to the Centre relate to the formulation of the written consents recording agreements to submit actual or potential disputes to the jurisdiction of the Centre." Second Annual Report: 4.

[61] ICSID Second Annual Report: 4. The primary drafter of the model clauses was Paul Szasz, the same young lawyer who drafted ICSID's Rules of Procedure (Parra 2012: 132, footnote 88).

[62] The Convention "confirms the great freedom accorded to the parties as to the modalities of recording that consent." ICSID/5: 3. Broches and Szasz took care to ensure the clauses in this document could be modified so as to comply with many legal traditions.

[63] ICSID/5: 3. [64] ICSID/5: 3. [65] Broches 1984 (May): 43.

The model clauses were an additional opportunity for the Centre to act in an advisory capacity. When he discussed the model clauses, Broches offered the Centre's advisory services.[66] The model clauses were widely adopted. There was no official count of their adoption, since not all of the investment contracts that used ICSID clauses were furnished to the Centre. Yet enough contracts were furnished to the Centre for Broches to feel the model clause effort had been successful. The ICSID Annual Report for 1971 noted: "The texts furnished to the Centre do yield significant indications of some of the types of transactions in which an ICSID clause was used, more and more of which reflects the language of the model clauses formulated for this purpose by the Secretariat some years ago."[67] The model clauses for contracts were important, but if the Secretariat had stopped with contracts, then it is likely that investor–state arbitration would look different today. The Secretariat's revolutionary innovation was the model clauses it issued for investment treaties. With its interstate pedigree, the ICSID Secretariat was able to promote new clauses in which governments provided individuals with standing in treaties.

Treaties: The Secretariat Writes Model Clauses for BITs

The ICSID Secretariat released a document of model clauses tailored to BITs in 1969, and then disseminated it widely.[68] Before these clauses were released, no BITs included investor–state arbitration clauses.[69] Investor–state arbitration clauses in BITs spread only *after* the Secretariat provided model clauses and advisory help. The Secretariat's advice started the practice of inserting investor–state arbitration into investment treaties. These model clauses are the centralized origin of investment *treaty* arbitration.

The ICSID Secretariat advised governments on how to insert ICSID clauses into their investment treaties. This is how Broches offered the Secretariat's assistance:

> Since foreign investments are increasingly being made with the encouragement and under the protection of investment treaties, it appears that these instruments too could become a vehicle incorporating both governmental consent to the jurisdiction of the Centre and appropriate inducements for investors to submit

[66] "Address by Aron Broches to the Second Annual Meeting," September 30, 1968.

[67] ICSID Fifth Annual Report: 4.

[68] These clauses were later released as Model Clauses Relating to the Convention on the Settlement of Investment Disputes Designed for Use in Bilateral Investment Agreements ICSID/6. They were released in ILM in September 1969, as 8 ILM 1341. They were also announced in the Third Annual Report: 4. Once again, these clauses were drafted by Paul Szasz (Parra 2012: 133).

[69] There was one exception to this, the Netherlands–Indonesia BIT, discussed below in the section "ICSID First Appears in an Investment Treaty."

> on their part. To assist in the formulation of such provisions, the Centre has just issued a set of Model Clauses for Insertion into Bilateral Investment Treaties.[70]

An Annual Report from a few years later notes: "further consultations have taken place between interested governments and the Centre [about BITs]. The set of model clauses prepared for the Centre for use in such treaties may be of assistance to the states concerned."[71]

The Secretariat was instrumental in the early BIT movement. In 1968, McNamara even implied that ICSID was created to facilitate investment treaties: "The Centre, through its very existence, is helping to ease and accelerate the process of negotiating investment agreements and is thus already fulfilling the purpose for which it was so recently established."[72] McNamara saw ICSID as an agent capable of facilitating agreements and influencing BIT provisions—unlike conventional accounts of BITs, which accord ICSID no agency in this regard.[73]

Broches and the ICSID Secretariat appear frequently in government documents from this era that relate to BITs. The following paragraphs provide a sense of how frequently, drawing from one government (the British government) in one year (1981): Broches appears by name several times in relation to investment treaty negotiations. In the government's negotiating brief explaining their model treaty for future negotiators, the Article 8 (investor–state arbitration provisions) description ended with, "It could be useful to mention in negotiation that the wording of this Article has been approved by the Secretary General of ICSID."[74] The British government encouraged their negotiators to leverage the World Bank's reputation in order to encourage capital-importing states to provide access to investor–state arbitration. The negotiating brief also specified: "where an initialed Agreement contains an Article providing for the reference of disputes to ICSID (Article 8), a copy should be sent to the Secretary-General of ICSID for his information."[75] It was not just the negotiating brief, either: even a letter from the Bank of England to the Foreign Office, titled "ICSID Clauses in Investment Agreements," reminded the official to "bear in mind ICSID's interest in information on this subject."[76] British officials reported the results of their investment treaty negotiations back to the Secretariat.

70 "Address by A. Broches to the Third Annual Meeting," September 29, 1969.

71 ICSID Sixth Annual Report: 5.

72 "Opening Remarks of Robert S McNamara, Chairman, to the Second Annual Meeting," September 30, 1968.

73 Poulsen (2015: chapter 3) was the first scholar to treat international organizations, including ICSID, as actors with autonomy and the potential to influence investment treaties.

74 IPPA: General Negotiating Brief, enclosed in a letter from Mike Powles to Edna Baker, May 11, 1981. UK FCO 69/662.

75 Model Investment Promotion and Protection Agreement (May 1981 Version): General Negotiating Brief. UK FCO 69/662.

76 Letter from R. R. Langley to M. W. Powles, September 30, 1981. UK FCO 69/667.

Conversations between Secretariat officials and British officials went even further: a British official in Washington wrote to London that "they [ICSID] are gradually succeeding in awakening an interest in ICSID in many of the Latin and Central American states."[77] In response, he was instructed to "pass on any information which might come your way . . . [about ICSID's discussion with non-members, which would] help us to decide when to approach those countries and how hard to press them [for investor–state arbitration in treaties]."[78] Earlier that year, a British official wrote to his colleague in Washington that: "it was we [the British] who urged the Paraguayans to join ICSID after they had signed an IPPA [an investment promotion and protection agreement] with us earlier this year which contained an article on ICSID arbitration."[79] These references provide a one-year "snapshot" of the relationship between Broches and the British government with regard to investment treaties and arbitration—a relationship that lasted over thirty years. Advance consent was a theme throughout, from the Abadan dispute in the 1950s (in which both Broches and British officials lamented the lack of advance consent), to Broches' encouraging the British government to include investor–state clauses in treaties negotiated in 1970,[80] to efforts in 1981 to share information about changing positions toward arbitration in South America. Broches and the Secretariat had advised states, drafted model clauses, and disseminated them widely: what impact did the ICSID Secretariat's work have on the initial spread of investor–state clauses? The next section takes up that question.

EARLY ISDS CLAUSES IN INVESTMENT TREATIES

Advance consent clauses are the defining feature of modern BITs. Franck, for instance, observes, "the real innovation of BITs was the provision of procedural rights that gave investors a mechanism to enforce the substantive rights directly."[81] Many existing accounts suggest that consent provided in treaties was not anticipated.[82] Even Elihu Lauterpacht, who had participated with Broches and others in the small committee that wrote a 1961 precursor to the ICSID Convention (which explicitly mentioned that jurisdiction could

[77] Letter from Myles A. Wickstead to M. W. Powles, October 22, 1981. UK FCO 69/667.

[78] Letter from M. W. Powles to M. A. Wickstead, November 2, 1981. UK FCO 69/667.

[79] Letter from M. W. Powles to R. W. Wootton, October 14, 1981. UK FCO 69/667.

[80] Poulsen 2015: 60.

[81] Franck 2007: 343. See also 2005; Yackee 2007; Allee and Peinhardt 2010; and Poulsen and Aisbett 2013. This argument recalls a much older legal principle, which Puig (2014a) references in the title of his chapter about ICSID, "No Right Without a Remedy."

[82] For instance, Thomas (2017).

come from a treaty), would later write as though the consent in treaties had been unforeseen.[83] This is a false impression. Broches mentioned that treaties could provide advance consent to ICSID in his first speech to the Administrative Council as Secretary General in 1967.[84] Every government whose internal documents during the drafting of the ICSID Convention were examined for this book—Germany, Switzerland, the UK, and the US—had expert officials who understood the relationship between investment treaties and investor–state arbitration before and during the ICSID Convention's drafting.

The German and Swiss governments understood how investor–state arbitration and investment treaties could fit together, yet they did not insert investor–state clauses into their treaties. As early as 1962, German officials and World Bank officials discussed investor–state arbitration clauses and BITs together, with German officials observing that "the arbitration court would constitute a valuable complement of the bilateral investment treaties."[85] The use of "complement" is important, because at that time (before the "depoliticization" rhetoric that surrounded ICSID) the government thought that investors would use arbitration in some instances and insurance with government subrogation in others, as appropriate. In 1966 consultations between the Swiss government and industry groups, it is clear that industry group representatives understood the connection between the ICSID Convention and BITs.[86] In 1966, the Swiss government even explained to capital-importing governments, such as the Kenyan government, why ICSID and BITs were not redundant, and that they needed to ratify both.[87] The Swiss Embassy did this even though their treaties did not include ICSID clauses at the time: their treaties used investment insurance and interstate mediation to resolve disputes, but the Swiss government wanted investment insurance,

[83] Lauterpacht (2009: x) wrote in the foreword to Schreuer's Commentary: "Consent to jurisdiction under the system was originally foreseen as deriving principally from express references to it in the arbitration clauses of investment contracts. However, the sources of consent have been significantly widened by the development of recourse to ICSID on the basis of legislation and provisions in inter-state bilateral investment treaties as well as by multilateral arrangements such as NAFTA and ECT." 1961 Draft Convention discussed in Chapter four.

[84] Parra (2012: 114) quotes Broches recommending advance consent to ICSID in BITs at the first meeting of the ICSID Administrative Council. Parra does not discuss the ramifications of this advocacy at length.

[85] Besuch von Weltbank-Präsident Black am 17. Januar 1962 (Visit of World Bank President Black, January 17, 1962). DE B102/48464.

[86] Compte rendu de la réunion du 12 octobre 1966 consacrée a un échange de vues sur la Convention pour le règlement des différends relatifs aux investissements entre Etats et ressortissants d'autres Etats. (Minutes of the Meeting held October 12, 1966 to exchange views on the Convention on the Settlement of Investment Disputes between States and Nationals of other states), Bern, October 17, 1966. CH C.41.124.5.1 (64–7).

[87] Letter to the Swiss Ambassador in Nairobi, subject: Investitionsrisikogarantie/Schiedskonvention der Weltbank/Bilateraler Investitionsschutzvertrag (Investment guarantees, World Bank arbitration agreement, bilateral investment protection treaties), December 16, 1966. CH C.41.124.5.1 (64–7).

state–state procedures, and ICSID as options. Unfortunately, neither the German nor Swiss archives provide a singular, clear answer for why they chose not to add ISDS to their treaties until the 1980s.[88] A mix of technical reasons (some officials believed that treaties between states should refer disputes to the ICJ only) and political ones (other officials believed insurance was preferable to ISDS, because the entire weight of the government was behind the investor) kept these governments from inserting ICSID access into their treaties.

ICSID First Appears in an Investment Treaty

The first treaty to include a reference to ICSID was the Netherlands–Indonesia agreement of 1968.[89] The relationship between the two governments was fraught, since the treaty was negotiated following extensive, uncompensated expropriations of Dutch property in Indonesia.[90] Yet both countries had special relationships with ICSID and the World Bank. Broches was Dutch, as mentioned in earlier chapters, maintained relationships within the Dutch government,[91] and made presentations in the Netherlands earlier in 1968 mentioning that investor–state access could be included in BITs.[92] Broches' archival files include a number of speeches in Dutch or made to Dutch-American groups, as well as many Dutch-language newspaper articles about ICSID.[93] The World Bank had a special relationship with Indonesia: in an unprecedented action, McNamara had established a resident office working closely with the government.[94]

[88] Citing a German archival document, Poulsen (2015: 52–3) argues that the German government feared investor–state arbitration could "politicize investment disputes by turning 'every case of expropriation into an international litigation with political relevance'." While correct, in my reading this was not the only reason why German officials did not insert investor–state arbitration into their treaties.

[89] Article 11 of the Indonesia–Netherlands Agreement on Economic Cooperation.

[90] On the expropriation, see Lindblad 2011.

[91] Broches had been a member of the Dutch delegation to Bretton Woods, which likely gave him cachet in the eyes of younger Dutch diplomats. The Dutch delegation to Bretton Woods was noted for its excellent preparation and outsize influence on the negotiations, despite the wartime weakness of the Dutch government-in-exile.

[92] A. Broches, Voordracht Voor de Afdeling Utrecht van de Nederlandse Studentenvereniging voor Internationale Betrekkingen. (Presentation for the Utrecht Department of the Dutch Student Association for International Relations), Utrecht, February 22, 1968. WB Folder 1651420.

[93] "New Way Found to Settle Investment Disputes," Netherlands–American Trade (Luncheon in New York). January 7, 1967. "Hoge functie voor Nederlander bij Wereldbank" (Dutch High Official at the World Bank). *Dagblad v. West Friesland Hoorn*, February 7, 1967. WB Folder 1651419.

[94] Bell 1990: 8–12. The office in Indonesia had nine World Bank staff and exceptionally good relations with the Indonesian government at the time. It was led by Indonesia expert Bernard Bell.

In 1968, the Indonesian government signed and ratified the ICSID Convention.[95] In the same year, Indonesia became one of the participants in ICSID's investment laws project.

The ICSID Secretariat was well-informed about the treaty's development. The agreement was a headline in the 1968 Administrative Council meeting.[96] The reference to ICSID makes this treaty a turning point for international law on investment protection, even though the reference to ICSID might not provide consent to investor–state arbitration. Broches took the view that this clause did not represent consent, but rather an undertaking to give consent when requested by the investor.[97] In any event, the Netherlands changed its practice in 1968 to include a reference to ICSID by default; ten out of their next thirteen treaties included references.[98] The Dutch government also added protocols with ICSID references to two pre-existing treaties, with Côte d'Ivoire and Cameroon.[99] The first Dutch model treaty, drafted in 1979, also included a reference to ICSID arbitration.[100] The Dutch government acted first, but was not alone in adding ICSID references to its treaties; in the late 1960s, European capital exporters began gradually adding ICSID references to their treaties.

ICSID References Slowly Added to European Model Treaties

The spread of bilateral investment treaties can be visualized as a hub and spoke pattern. The hubs were the model treaties of European capital exporters, and the spokes were the actual treaties they negotiated with other governments. References to ICSID, and later to investor–state arbitration at other fora, spread through the same hub and spoke pattern. That is, once a capital-exporting government added a reference to ICSID into one of their treaties, they typically updated their practice and began inserting references to ICSID by default, meaning that it appears in most of their subsequent treaties, just like the Netherlands. The question is: what explains why capital-exporting governments inserted references to ICSID when they did?

I argue that the appearance of references to ICSID in treaties signed by European governments before 1981 can be traced to visits and advocacy from

[95] Indonesia ratified ICSID on September 28, 1968.

[96] ICSID Second Annual Meeting Press Release, September 30, 1968.

[97] Parra (2012:133) notes this, citing Broches [1982] 1995: 447. The clause states: "The contracting parties in the territory of which a national of the other contracting party makes or intends to make an investment, shall assent to any demand on the part of such national and any such national shall comply with any request of the former contracting party, to submit for conciliation or arbitration, to the Center established by the convention of Washington of March 18 1965, any dispute that may arise in connection with the investment."

[98] ICSID Fifteenth Annual Report and UNCTAD (1996).

[99] Dolzer and Stevens 1995: 130, footnote 362.

[100] Schrijver and Prislan 2013: 581.

Broches. A visit or several visits from Broches was not sufficient to trigger the appearance of a reference to ICSID, and Broches made a large number of visits to national capitals that did not result in any such clauses—the argument is that Broches was a persuasive, respected official who met senior government officials and encouraged them to put investor–state clauses on government negotiating agendas. There was no rupture or fanfare when investor–state clauses were added; it was merely an additional dispute resolution option, a technical innovation suggested by the World Bank. This addition was layered into treaties, that is, it was inserted without removing the existing option for state–state dispute resolution. When change proceeds through layering, new elements are introduced quietly, but these new elements set in motion dynamics through which they, over time, supplant the old system.[101] The process of layering these clauses into treaties was led quietly by the Secretariat, especially by Broches himself.

Among other trips, Broches had discussions in Italy and Belgium in 1967 and 1968.[102] In 1969, ICSID access appeared in the Italy–Chad treaty.[103] In 1970, ICSID access appeared in a treaty between Belgium and Indonesia. From a comparison of the treaty and the relevant ICSID model clause, it seems likely that the negotiators had read the ICSID model clauses. The text of the relevant ICSID model clause reads:

> Each Contracting Party hereby agrees to submit any legal dispute arising out of an investment to the jurisdiction of the International Centre for Settlement of Investment Disputes for settlement by arbitration under the Convention on the Settlement of Investment Disputes between States and Nationals of Other States.[104]

The treaty language echoes this structure, while adding some flourishes and a sentence equating consent to ICSID with a renunciation of local remedies.

> Each contracting party hereby irrevocably and anticipatory gives its consent to submit to conciliation and arbitration any disputes relating to a measure contrary to this agreement, pursuant to the convention of Washington of 18th of March 1965, at the initiative of a national or legal person of the other contracting party, who considers himself to have been affected by such a measure. This consent

[101] Palier 2005: 131. Investor–state supplanting state–state arbitration is discussed in Chapter eight.

[102] Telegram from the Swiss Embassy Washington to Bern, October 6, 1966. CH C.41.124.5.1. See also: Address by A. Broches, General Counsel of the World Bank and Secretary General of ICSID to Institut Royal des Relations Internationales, Brussels, Belgium, April 4, 1967. WB Folder 1651420.

[103] Article 7 of the Chad–Italy BIT. For an explanation, see Newcombe and Paradell 2009: 45–6. Remarkably, the treaty does not provide for interstate dispute resolution, which was dominant at the time. The last line in Article 8 suggests disputes over interpretation should be settled through diplomatic channels (Potestà 2011: 753).

[104] ICSID/6: 5.

implies renunciation of the requirement that the internal administrative or judicial resorts should be exhausted.[105]

The same exact wording for the dispute resolution clause appeared in the next two treaties that Belgium negotiated, with South Korea and Egypt.[106] In 1978, the wording changed, but the principle of access to ICSID remained: Belgium's subsequent treaties include "irrevocable consent" to ICSID as a general rule, except the reference to ICSID in the treaty with Romania, which is written differently.[107]

French treaties provide compelling evidence that the initial push for investor–state arbitration clauses came from the ICSID Secretariat and not investors. One of the likeliest places where investor demand would appear is from the ICC to the French government. The Paris headquarters of the ICC had long been the global hub of commercial arbitration and the ICC was one of the largest, best-organized groups in the world lobbying for the interests of international firms and investors. If there had been lobbying by the ICC, then early French treaties would likely have included ICC access. They did not. Instead, World Bank archives show Broches visiting Paris[108] and then the French government reporting back to the ICSID Secretariat that they were including investor–state clauses in their treaties. For instance, in 1972, the French representative at the ICSID Annual Meeting said: "[The French government] participated during the last year in negotiations with other countries on agreements for the protection of private investments abroad... Negotiations underway or already concluded have provided for reference to ICSID—explicit reference to ICSID—in the event of disputes."[109] In 1972 the French government signed treaties with Tunisia and Zaire that included references to ICSID. Then the next year France signed treaties that included references to ICSID with Indonesia and Mauritius, then in 1974 with Egypt, Yugoslavia, then in 1975 with Korea, Malaysia, Morocco, and Singapore. The pattern was established and references to ICSID had become a default part of French treaties.[110] The remarkable reality that early French treaties referred to

[105] Article 10 of Belgium–Indonesia BIT, January 15, 1970.

[106] Article 8 (Belgo-Luxembourg Economic Union–South Korea BIT) and Article 9 (Belgo-Luxembourg Economic Union–Egypt BIT).

[107] As discussed below, Romanian treaties from this period limit arbitration to disputes over the amount of compensation only, and arbitration is only an option after local remedies have been exhausted, and within a two-year time limit. Article 3 (Belgo-Luxembourg Economic Union–Romania BIT).

[108] Discours par Mr. Aron Broches à la Société de Géographie Economique (Speech by Mr. Aron Broches at the Society of Economic Geography), Paris, October 14, 1969. WB Folder 1651420.

[109] Sixth Annual Meeting: 5.

[110] During the ten years from 1972–82, France signed twenty-three treaties, and twenty of these included references to ICSID—the treaties with Malta, Panama, and the Philippines did not include references.

ICSID and not the ICC (despite the ICC's Paris headquarters) suggests that without the advocacy for investor–state arbitration by Broches and the Secretariat, governments might not have inserted these clauses.

The appearance of investor–state arbitration in the United Kingdom's treaties also attests to the influence of the Secretariat, and Broches in particular. Broches had frequent contact with British officials relating to ICSID over several decades, including extensive discussions in the late 1950s and early 1960s about investor–state arbitration, a stream of letters from Broches reminding the British government to ratify the ICSID Convention, and British support for electing Broches as ICSID Secretary General was strong.[111] Given Broches' long-standing relationship and reputation for expertise on investor–state arbitration, it is not surprising that the British negotiating brief for investment treaties tells British negotiators to mention that Broches has approved their investor–state arbitration clause. With regard to Article 8, the investor–state arbitration clause, the guidance for negotiators was:

> This [Article] may well be difficult to negotiate since prospective signatories may wish to reserve to themselves the right to decide in the case of each individual dispute whether they are prepared to have it referred to the Centre for arbitration or conciliation, but we have secured this wording in most of our IPPAs [investment treaties] and should do our best to get it in future Agreements. It could be useful to mention in negotiation that the wording of this Article has been approved by the Secretary General of ICSID.[112]

Showing further the centrality of Broches to the spread of investor–state clauses, the negotiating brief then instructs officials that "where an initialled Agreement contains an Article providing for the reference of disputes to ICSID (Article 8), a copy should be sent to the Secretary-General for his information."[113] In his review of archival materials related to early British investment treaties, Poulsen notes the heavy presence of Broches, observing, for instance, that "Broches had encouraged the United Kingdom to include ICSID clauses into economic cooperation agreements with the Ivory Coast and Congo."[114]

The UK mirrors the patterns of France and others, in that access to investor–state arbitration appears in most but not all of their early investment treaties. A reference to ICSID was included in the British model from the beginning, but, "remarkably, the UK found investor–state arbitration a 'desirable but not essential' element of their model."[115] When negotiating partners

[111] Discussed in Chapters three to five.

[112] Model Investment Promotion and Protection Agreement (April 1981 Version): General Negotiating Brief. UK FCO 69/658.

[113] Model Investment Promotion and Protection Agreement (April 1981 Version): General Negotiating Brief. UK FCO 69/658.

[114] Poulsen 2015: 60.

[115] Poulsen 2015: 60 and 65.

raised concerns, the clause could be left out; one example of this is Thailand, which voiced serious concerns about investor–state arbitration and ensured an investor–state arbitration clause was not in their treaty with the UK.[116]

By 1981, when Broches retired as Secretary General, the Secretariat knew of sixty-seven investment treaties that included references to ICSID. Belgium, France, Italy, the Netherlands, and the UK were including references to ICSID by default, and references appeared in most of the treaties.[117] Germany and Sweden had included references in a small fraction of their treaties.[118] After Romania joined ICSID in 1976, the Romanian government concluded twelve treaties with references to ICSID, although these references were limited to disputes concerning the amount of compensation and gave precedence to local remedies.[119] Four treaties without European participation had been signed that included references to ICSID in 1977 and 1980.[120] In sum, by 1981, the practice of including ICSID references in investment treaties was established. Their early spread had been piecemeal and inconsistent, but Broches had gotten the ball rolling. These initial references to ICSID established a practice that would become standard and be replicated thousands of time in the coming decades.

When Broches retired in 1981, access to ICSID in treaties was already transforming into access to investor–state arbitration more generally. The UNCITRAL Arbitration Rules were released in 1976, and after that, slowly, some governments added a reference to these rules into treaties, alongside or

[116] In line with the opposition that Thailand's expert-designate expressed toward the ICSID Convention at the consultative conferences, ten years earlier. Thailand is an exception to the pattern whereby ministries in many capital-importing countries appeared to forget the concerns their experts-designate had voiced when they began negotiating investment treaties. One reason for Thailand's superior institutional memory may be because they hosted the Asian consultative conference in 1964, which likely created more paper trail for future officials and which may have meant the government spent relatively more time scrutinizing the draft in 1964. Of the three capital-importing governments that hosted a consultative conference (Chile, Ethiopia, and Thailand), only Chile ratified the Convention, and did so only in 1991.

[117] Belgium six out of eight treaties; France seventeen out of twenty; Italy four out of four; Netherlands thirteen out of sixteen; the UK eleven out of fourteen. The first number is drawn from the 1981 ICSID Annual Report, while the second column is drawn from UNCTAD (1996). The figures have been corroborated with the original treaty text wherever possible. Data on early BITs is not perfectly reliable. I have corroborated with Dolzer and Stevens (1995) and other sources where possible, but more complete datasets of BITs may emerge in the future and bring to light treaties not reflected here.

[118] Germany three out of fifty-one; Sweden two out of ten. Same sources as above.

[119] For instance, Article 4 (1) of the Pakistan–Romania BIT states: "If a dispute between an investor and the Contracting Party in the territory of which the investment was made, concerning the amount of compensation, continues to exist after the final award of the national tribunal, each of them is entitled to submit the dispute for conciliation or arbitration, according to the procedure provided by the Convention opened for signature at Washington on March 18, 1965, to the International Centre for settlement of investment disputes."

[120] The 1981 ICSID Annual Report lists: Egypt–Japan (1977); Egypt–Yugoslavia (1977); Korea–Sri Lanka (1980); Singapore–Sri Lanka (1980).

in place of ICSID clauses. In 1979, the ICSID Additional Facility was created, which widened access to ICSID, allowing states that had not ratified the ICSID Convention to refer disputes to ICSID for arbitration. Capital-exporting governments still seemed to prefer ICSID: for instance, when the German government did add investor–state clauses to its treaties, ICSID was the only option to appear.[121] The British government had a preference for ICSID, but if their negotiating partners could not agree to ICSID, they would investigate other arbitral fora:

> If ICSID is clearly not acceptable to a particular country, we should investigate their willingness to submit investment disputes to other international arbitration procedures such as the International Chamber of Commerce or the UNCITRAL Arbitration Rules. But omission of ICSID should only be conceded in the very last resort, or we risk undermining the reputation of the Centre. In any event it is essential to obtain proper arrangements for the impartial settlement of investment disputes.[122]

Hundreds of different permutations of ISDS clauses exist today, but all these clauses in BITs spread outward from one centralized starting point—and the ICSID Secretariat was that starting point. The Secretariat was the only organization in the world to keep a list of all treaties that provided advance consent in the 1960s, 1970s, and 1980s.[123] The Centre, and Broches in particular, recognized that investment treaties could bring an enormous potential caseload to the Centre. As quoted in the introduction, Broches testified to the large potential caseload created by advance consents in investment treaties:

> There are now about sixty treaties between states, generally industrialized and developing, which provide for access to ICSID in case of disputes about violations of the treaties. And *those treaties are investment protection treaties. So, ICSID has an enormous potential clientele.*[124]
>
> As a matter of fact, you can expect that the number of cases will increase, because cases are brought on the basis of advance undertakings in investment agreements.[125]

Broches and the ICSID Secretariat had a better view of the spread of consent to investor–state arbitration in treaties than any other actor during this period. The ICSID Secretariat was central to the early spread of consent clauses in

[121] Based on my analysis of Article 10 (the dispute resolution article) in all available German BITs. This was true until 2008, when the government made changes, likely because they were anticipating a future EU model treaty. Dolzer and Kim 2013.

[122] Model Investment Promotion and Protection Agreement (May 1981 Version): General Negotiating Brief. UK FCO 69/662.

[123] "References to the Centre in national legislation and in bilateral treaties between capital exporting and capital importing states have been increasing steadily. Annex 4 gives an up-to-date list of all such laws and treaties." Thirteenth Annual Report: 5.

[124] Broches 1984 (May): 44–5. Emphasis mine.

[125] Broches 1985: 8.

treaties, and without Broches' agenda-setting and brokering, it is unlikely that these consent clauses would have been inserted into treaties when they were, and perhaps at any point.

Coordination among Capital-Exporters

Depictions of investor–state arbitration in BITs spreading through competition between capital-importing states have been influential, but they miss the centralized starting point of ISDS and the coordination among capital-exporters. Archival documents show that the American, British, French, German, and Swiss governments often coordinated their negotiating positions when negotiating bilateral treaties with capital-importers.

The British government met French, German, and Swiss officials roughly once a year to have "talks, in which we compared notes on progress on the negotiation of bilateral IPPAs" in the 1960s, 1970s, and 1980s.[126] In these meetings, governments compared their treaty provisions and compared the success of strategies they had used negotiating with capital-importing countries. For instance, British officials reported being given "a fairly stern lecture from Dr Burkhardt in the Economic Ministry in Bonn" about not altering the wording of Article 6 of their model treaty, because "the Germans (and the French, and the Belgians, and possibly others) attach the greatest importance to this formula. If we negotiate agreements with weaker wording, they will not thank us."[127] Another time, British and German officials negotiated simultaneously with Bulgaria and coordinated their positions, sharing documents that the Bulgarians had given them and discussing strategy.[128] Similarly, British officials decided they "should await information of FRG [Federal Republic of Germany] progress in their negotiations with China before deciding our own policy towards China."[129]

Capital-exporters occasionally competed with each other. After Zimbabwe became independent, the British raced the Germans and the French to get an agreement first,[130] because the British wanted a high-standard agreement, with "a very full definition of investment."[131] One British official argued it was "essential that we should beat the Germans to the starting line in

[126] Letter from G. M. Gowlland, "Anglo-French Investment Talks: 22 September 1981." UK FCO 69/671. See also UK FCO 69/689 (in which the British government study German investment treaties) and UK FCO 69/740 (British government talks with the Swiss government on investment treaties).

[127] Letter to C. Yarnell from G. M. Gowlland, March 30, 1981. UK FCO 69/658.

[128] Note from M. W. Powles to G. M. Gowlland, March 20, 1981. UK FCO 69/658.

[129] IPPA Whitehall Meeting, January 9, 1981. UK FCO 69/662.

[130] Letter from G. M. Gowlland, "Anglo-French Investment Talks: 22 September 1981." UK FCO 69/671.

[131] IPPA: Whitehall Meeting, April 6, 1981. UK FCO 69/662.

Zimbabwe"[132] and another asked the French to wait, because if they went first it would weaken the UK's bargaining position.[133] More often, they cooperated and offered one another advice. For instance, when French officials complained that Thailand "was being particularly difficult, especially over independent arbitration for disputes," UK officials lamented that they could not offer any advice because "our Agreement with Thailand, signed in 1978, was not very good. There was no provision for referring disputes to ICSID, and, as far as we were aware, Thailand was still not a member of ICSID."[134] Similarly, the French and British compared notes about which Latin American country would be "the first to break ranks" and "renounce the 'Calvo' doctrine."[135]

When the US government began exploring an investment treaty program, one of their first actions was to interview European officials. American officials, like German and Swiss officials before them, believed they could get more through a bilateral strategy. One noted that "the efforts of other countries, especially those of the FRG [Federal Republic of Germany] and Switzerland, have helped to establish a situation where the United States, at no political cost, can institute a [bilateral] program which will help us achieve objectives that cannot be attained in multilateral fora."[136]

When Americans surveyed European officials in the late 1970s, they came away with the impression that treaties were useful for dispute resolution, but not because investment disputes actually ended up at ICSID or were resolved without home government involvement. These treaties were useful because governments could refer to them during dispute resolution negotiations. American officials noted that the Germans considered BITs "useful instruments for protecting investments and peacefully resolving investment disputes within a non-political framework" because

> it is extremely rare for a state openly to break a treaty; rather, they will tend to argue its application in terms of the existing treaty, which becomes a valuable tool for dispute settlement. We are advised that in a number of cases reference to the applicable bilateral has led to the correction of local measures incompatible with the agreement.[137]

[132] IPPA: Whitehall Meeting, April 6, 1981. UK FCO 69/662.

[133] Letter from G. M. Gowlland, "Anglo-French Investment Talks: 22 September 1981." UK FCO 69/671.

[134] Letter from G. M. Gowlland, "Anglo-French Investment Talks: 22 September 1981." UK FCO 69/671.

[135] Letter from G. M. Gowlland, "Anglo-French Investment Talks: 22 September 1981." UK FCO 69/671.

[136] Action Memorandum 7720912 from Herbert J. Hansell and Julius L. Katz to Mr. Cooper, Subject: Negotiation of Bilateral Investment Protection Agreements with Less Developed Countries. August 10, 1977. US 2788553. Box 1.

[137] Action Memorandum 7720912 from Herbert J. Hansell and Julius L. Katz to Mr. Cooper, Subject: Negotiation of Bilateral Investment Protection Agreements with Less Developed Countries. August 10, 1977. US 2788553. Box 1.

German and American officials saw BITs as useful teaching tools, texts they could reference in the event of a dispute. They did not see arbitration as replacing diplomatic protection: governments would still be involved, and arbitration might be a useful supplement to other means of resolution. Nor had ISDS replaced investment insurance. In their bilateral meetings, the UK and France discussed treaties in the morning and insurance in the afternoon,[138] and the US government, even at the start of the Reagan administration, voiced strong support for insurance.[139]

CONCLUSION

This chapter uses archival evidence to demonstrate that the ICSID Secretariat was a dynamic actor during the period 1967–72. The influence of legal organizations is usually judged by the evolution of case law under their auspices, but these indicators systematically underrepresent ICSID's activities during these years. The Secretariat introduced itself to states and investors, informally advised states on domestic legal frameworks, drafted model clauses for contracts and treaties, and promoted the idea of investor–state arbitration around the world.

The Secretariat's dynamism did not yield impressive short-term results. ICSID did not have a single case for many years. Many observers, such as O'Keefe, believed that ICSID had failed to live up to its promise and would end without having much impact. These observers often failed to appreciate that thousands of advance consents to ICSID had been provided—in contracts, treaties, and domestic laws—which put in place the infrastructure for a large caseload.

Many observers missed ICSID's potential because consent was elicited through layering; access to ISDS was added alongside existing provisions, slowly and quietly. Many of these early clauses mirrored the ICSID model clauses closely. In subsequent decades, thousands more of these clauses were inserted into treaties; over time and as different governments translated and revised them, the resemblance to the original ICSID model clauses grew weaker.

[138] Letter from G. M. Gowlland, "Anglo-French Investment Talks: 22 September 1981." UK FCO 69/671.

[139] "OPIC [the US government's insurance arm] can serve as an important factor in reducing an investor's perception of risk when entering a new market by insuring the investor against the noneconomic risks inherent in foreign investment." Statement of Adrian A. Basora, Acting Deputy Assistant Secretary, US Department of State, to the United States Council of the International Chamber of Commerce, New York, March 12, 1981. UK FCO 69/711.

Layering is not sufficient to explain all the decisions explored in this chapter. It does not explain why the governments of thirteen capital-importing states enshrined access to ICSID in their domestic law during these years of high resource prices and the New International Economic Order. To understand this requires taking seriously the resources of World Bank officials, in particular expertise and access. The idea to include ICSID access in domestic law travelled to states through technical assistance or informal advisory work. The World Bank's reputation and brokering was crucial. The Secretariat's actions faded because negotiations have been viewed as moments of interstate bargaining, and investor–state arbitration as the product of investment treaties. With a moving picture, the influence of the ICSID Secretariat becomes clear. Without early advocacy from the ICSID Secretariat, it is unlikely that investor–state arbitration clauses would have appeared in investment treaties when they did.

7

Conversion

America Embraces Investor–State Arbitration

When circumstances change, the reasons for investment treaties change. When the reasons for investment treaties change, the purpose of investor–state arbitration within those treaties and the importance of a country's ratification of the ICSID Convention may also change. This kind of gradual institutional change is conversion: when an existing institution is put to new purposes, without a change in its form. This chapter analyzes the extent to which conversion has occurred in investor–state arbitration with a case study of US government attitudes to investor–state arbitration. Unlike previous chapters, this one is not framed as a counterfactual; instead, it focuses on later stages of a broadly path-dependent process, highlighting that even within processes that generate positive feedback effects and exhibit path dependence, gradual institutional changes, like conversion, still occur.

The American investment treaty program is one of the most consistent and well-managed investment treaty program in the world. The responsible agencies and officials within the American government have world-class technical capacity and legal skill, and substantial resources are dedicated to ensuring the coherence of American treaties. These characteristics of the US treaty program make it an unlikely context in which to observe change—if gradual institutional change can be observed in the American program, it can likely be observed in many programs. To foreshadow the chapter's conclusions, analyzing the American treaty program with a "moving picture" approach makes clear that the purposes American officials ascribe to investment treaties *have* changed in response to shifts in their environment and changes in the challenges they perceive. The purpose of access to arbitration, and even ICSID membership, also changed as a result of wider repurposing.

This chapter examines the American program between 1974, when the first cases involving American investors at ICSID were filed, and 1994, when NAFTA came into force. The chapter has four sections—each focuses on a characteristic of American investment protection typically assumed to be stable, which has in fact changed over time. First, the American government, and in particular the State Department, has not always perceived firms having direct access to ICSID as something that advances American interests. In fact, internal US government documents from the first cases involving American investors demonstrate that investor access to ICSID caused the State Department frustration and endangered US strategic interests. Despite this negative first experience, direct investor access to ICSID would later become a pillar of American investment policy. Second, the American investment treaty program was not intended to facilitate or increase outward investments to partner countries. Yet the rhetoric of government officials has changed over time; in the early 1990s, officials used additional investment aggressively, but before and after this period, took pains to specify that treaties and investor–state arbitration do not necessarily lead to additional investment.

Third, American investment treaties became tools for wider political objectives during the 1980s.[1] The purpose of access to investor–state arbitration changed alongside this broader repurposing. In particular, as BITs were used to promote domestic liberalization, investor–state arbitration became increasingly important as a tool to lock in liberalization and prevent backsliding, or make it punishable under international law. The changing role of investor–state arbitration is examined in short case studies of the US–Poland and US–Argentina negotiations, both of which were important steps on the road to NAFTA. Fourth, as part of this repurposing, when the US negotiated with larger, middle income countries like Argentina, Poland, Russia, and Turkey during the George H.W. Bush administration, ICSID membership became a prerequisite for an investment treaty, but this requirement did not apply to smaller countries the US negotiated with before or after this administration.

This chapter is based on a systematic review of accessible State Department files in the US National Archives relating to all pre-NAFTA investment treaty negotiations. It also draws on USTR files, available from presidential libraries, and on the Hearings of the Senate Foreign Relations Committee and associated archival material. The first section of this chapter includes material from WikiLeaks; these are documents which, given their age and security status, in principle should have been available from the US National Archives.

An overarching finding that emerges from these archive materials and runs through this chapter is that in its first twenty years, the US program was not driven by investors. In fact, American archives show remarkably little interest from investors or industry groups. In the places where investor lobbying is likeliest to appear, there are occasional letters, for instance from a subsidiary of Shell interested in a possible US treaty with Cameroon, but these are blips

[1] Chilton (2016) argues that US investment treaties have political purposes, but differs from the account here, insofar as he does not identify specific political purposes or note changes over time.

in a process that, by and large, had little investor involvement. Preferences for investor–state arbitration are endogenous; they emerge largely after NAFTA, when more investors and law firms became aware of the new rights given to them.

THE DESIRABILITY OF PROVIDING FIRMS WITH ACCESS TO ICSID

Access to investor–state arbitration has been a pillar of the US investment treaty program throughout its first forty years, from 1977 to 2017. However, the desirability of firms having the ability to bring cases directly at ICSID—in other words, of the US government forfeiting its gatekeeping power—has not always been as clear. In fact, the first high-profile ICSID cases, which involved US aluminum companies bringing contract claims against Jamaica, created headaches for the State Department. In theory, one reason to provide firms with direct access to ICSID is that they no longer need to rely on their governments for espousal and their governments no longer need to get involved (and jeopardize other strategic interests). Reality is more complicated. In 1974, US firms with direct access to ICSID posed grave risks to the US government: recalcitrant firms "determined to go down in flames" threatened carefully negotiated settlements with Jamaica and put larger US anti-Communist goals at risk. This section discusses these three ICSID cases in their wider political context and from the perspective of the US government.

In the 1970s, bauxite mining was vital for both the Jamaican and the US economies. Unprocessed bauxite was Jamaica's main export and source of foreign exchange, while the US was "dependent on imports of Caribbean bauxite and alumina (processed bauxite) to meet its consumption needs for primary aluminum."[2] The US government, through OPIC, had provided over $500 million in guarantees to aluminum firms—OPIC's most concentrated exposure to a single industry in a single country.[3] The US government was involved in securing American firms access to this raw material and officials even testified that the volume of insurance had "led it [the US government] into the internal politics of Jamaica."[4] Several arms of the US government had been monitoring Jamaican bauxite mining and the firms involved for years.[5]

[2] Deal 1978: 68.

[3] The Church Subcommittee conducted "a special investigation" of the OPIC guarantees in Jamaica because it "appeared to be excessively large." WikiLeaks cable ID: 1973STATE206992_b from October 19, 1973.

[4] WikiLeaks cable ID: 1973STATE206992_b from October 19, 1973.

[5] Even smaller branches of the US government, like the Internal Revenue Service, were monitoring relations between the Jamaican government and the mining companies (the Internal

In 1972, Michael Manley, a charismatic, youthful leader educated at the London School of Economics, became Prime Minister of Jamaica. Before Manley was elected, the US Ambassador told him to keep bauxite ownership out of his campaign.[6] Possible bauxite nationalization in Jamaica received attention from the highest levels in the US: Secretary of State Henry Kissinger himself sent rush telegrams to Kingston over the Christmas holidays in 1973.[7] The State Department considered it imperative to prevent Manley, one of the most eloquent statesmen of the New International Economic Order, from becoming another Castro.

To fund universal education and other popular initiatives, Manley announced a new 7.5 percent tax on bauxite mining. The new tax contravened "no further tax" clauses in existing contracts between the government of Jamaica and North American mining companies. Manley was aware that the tax would violate the contracts; in a public speech on January 3, 1974 he announced that Jamaica's bauxite contracts had been "abrogated by history."[8] Manley likely chose these words carefully—these were colonial-era contracts, which paid the Jamaican government little relative to firms' profit and, in Manley's mind, denied his government revenue for core state-building tasks like education and healthcare. Yet within two days of this public speech, Manley asked for a secret meeting with the US Ambassador in order to emphasize to the American government (whom he relied upon to communicate with the bauxite companies) that he wished only to renegotiate: he did not seek full nationalization, just to increase revenue from bauxite.[9] To the US Ambassador, he pleaded: "improving revenues from the bauxite industry was not only a matter of simple justice for Jamaica, it was a matter of survival."[10]

Manley's renegotiation plans faced formidable opposition. A handful of American and Canadian firms owned 100 percent of the bauxite mines in Jamaica. The US government, through its embassy in Kingston, became an informal mediator and maintained a neutral stance.[11] In spring 1974, the US Embassy sent dozens of play-by-play summaries of the negotiations between company lawyers and the Jamaican government back to Washington, where the "conclave of CEOs" was meeting.[12] US officials recognized that the Jamaican

Revenue Service suspected the companies of tax evasion through transfer pricing). WikiLeaks cable ID: 1973KINGST03921_b from November 17, 1973.

[6] WikiLeaks cable ID: 1973STATE206992_b from October 19, 1973.

[7] WikiLeaks ID: 1973STATE250610_b from December 27, 1973.

[8] WikiLeaks cable ID: 1974KINGST00069_b from January 7, 1974.

[9] WikiLeaks cable ID: 1974KINGST00054_b from January 5, 1974.

[10] WikiLeaks cable ID: 1974KINGST00069_b from January 7, 1974.

[11] WikiLeaks ID: 1974STATE083254_b from April 24, 1974.

[12] For descriptions of the CEOs meeting in Washington, see: WikiLeaks ID: 1974KINGST01492_b from April 26, 1974. For another description of the "conclave of CEOs" in Washington, see: WikiLeaks ID: 1974KINGST01495_b from April 27, 1974.

government was well-prepared and serious about renegotiation. As negotiations continued, the US Embassy in Kingston seemed more impressed with the Jamaican government than with the American corporations. One cable observed that the corporations

> Had no coherent strategy in mind outside of departing from the status quo as little as possible. In addition, they seem to have made the grave error of underestimating their opponents. For once the Jamaicans had done their homework thoroughly and knew as much about most of the issues as the industry.[13]

The negotiations proceeded relatively smoothly.

It is in this context that three of the firms, Alcoa, Kaiser, and Reynolds, filed claims at ICSID. Negotiations had not broken down. The corporations filed their claims at ICSID to strengthen their bargaining positions in the ongoing negotiations. As Lloyd Cutler, a veteran Washington insider representing the firms, put it, they went to ICSID "since the remedy existed and their obligation to their stockholders compelled them to exhaust all available remedies."[14] Manley and his government interpreted the firms' ICSID claims as an escalation of the conflict, an attempt to "come on tooth and claw."[15] The Jamaican government tried to rescind its advance consent to ICSID by making an Article 25 (4) notification shortly before the cases were registered.[16] That was futile: the tribunals found that the government could not limit its consent through this notification, as that "would very largely, if not wholly, deprive the Convention of any practical value for Contracting States and investors."[17] The cases were eventually discontinued in favor of the settlement reached through negotiations but remained throughout the negotiations as a threat.[18]

The ICSID cases caused disquiet within the US State Department. Throughout the dispute, the State Department worked overtime to avoid the appearance of putting diplomatic pressure on Jamaica, which would have given ammunition to Manley—even going out of their way to ensure an IBRD loan to Jamaica for education was approved while the case was pending.[19]

[13] WikiLeaks ID: 1974KINGST01772_b from May 21, 1974.

[14] WikiLeaks ID: 1974KINGST01706_b from May 15, 1974.

[15] WikiLeaks ID: 1974KINGST01706_b from May 15, 1974.

[16] Jamaica's notification was made on May 8, 1974, and excluded from ICSID jurisdiction any dispute "arising directly out of an investment relating to minerals or other natural resources." ICSID 8/D. Note: Article 25 (4) notifications "serve for purposes of information only." Parra 2013.

[17] Schreuer 2001: 256–7, quoting *Kaiser Bauxite v Jamaica*, Decision on Jurisdiction. See also Schmidt 1976.

[18] Broches acknowledged this, noting that "the Tribunals have received repeated requests by the Claimants for extensions of time on the ground that the parties were engaged in active negotiations." Statement by Mr. A. Broches, Secretary General, at the Tenth Annual Meeting of the Administrative Council, October 7, 1976. NZ 241.

[19] World Bank President McNamara discussed the pending ICSID proceedings while approving the loan. WikiLeaks cable: 1974KINGST02613_b from July 29, 1974. Also, WikiLeaks cable: 1974STATE194229_b from September 4, 1973.

The cables from the US Embassy in Kingston increasingly express frustration with the corporations pursuing ICSID cases, and in particular with Alcoa, the most recalcitrant:

> [Former US Supreme Court Justice Arthur] Goldberg noted that it would be typical of Alcoa to go down in flames, possibly inviting expropriation with consequent OPIC claim, and pursuit of the ICSID suit, rather than accede to Jamaican demands, a course which could cause diplomatic problems for the US Government for a long time to come.[20]
>
> Alcoa's position is, as usual, ambiguous. Apparently they mean to negotiate in good faith when the time comes, but from the strongest position they can possibly develop.[21]
>
> Pittsburgh [Alcoa's headquarters] still "trigger happy" and unwilling to change.[22]

The US Ambassador in Kingston reported that an Alcoa board member "indicated his immediate intention to express his dissatisfaction with the job being done by the American Ambassador to Secretary Kissinger" for not being "sufficiently supportive of Alcoa."[23]

This was an empty threat, since Kissinger was not sympathetic to Alcoa. He cabled an article from *The Washington Post* titled "Alcoa's Second Quarter Profits Soar" to Kingston just as ICSID proceedings were getting underway.[24] Kissinger did not provide commentary, but organized the facts of the article into a suggestive outline:

> [Alcoa's] first half revenues were $1.4 billion, and income was $95.8 million, compared with last year's $1.04 billion in revenues and profits of $51.3 million.
>
> Alcoa said earnings for the first six months [same time period as above] were reduced about $7 million because of Jamaica's unilateral action.[25]

Kissinger's arrangement of these facts suggests frustration with Alcoa for drawing in diplomatic resources and risking backlash, when the financial impact had not exceeded $7 million and the company recorded revenue of over $1 billion and record profits.

Ultimately, the negotiations ended in settlement and relations with Jamaica recovered. Externally, the US government made a point of taking ICSID seriously and chiding the Jamaican government for failing to appear at ICSID.[26] Behind the scenes, however, there was frustration that firms had used their access to

[20] WikiLeaks ID: 1975KINGST02242_b from June 11, 1975.

[21] Implicit in this quote is the sentiment that having jurisdiction at ICSID strengthened Alcoa's bargaining position when negotiating with the Jamaican government, who were presumably eager to avoid an ICSID case. WikiLeaks ID: 1975KINGST02242_b from June 11, 1975.

[22] WikiLeaks ID: 1975KINGST02414_b from June 24, 1975.

[23] WikiLeaks ID: 1975KINGST02414_b from June 24, 1975.

[24] WikiLeaks ID: 1974STATE158129_b from July 22, 1974.

[25] WikiLeaks ID: 1974STATE158129_b from July 22, 1974.

[26] WikiLeaks ID: 1975KINGSTON01369 from April 10, 1975.

ICSID in a way that made the State Department's task more difficult and jeopardized relations with Jamaica.

THE RELATIONSHIP BETWEEN INVESTMENT TREATIES AND ADDITIONAL INVESTMENT

Three years after the Jamaica cases, in 1977, the State Department began exploring whether or not to initiate an investment treaty program. State Department officials interviewed the relevant officials from European capital-exporting governments about their experience with investment treaties and surveyed American officials posted abroad. State Department officials researched and thought carefully before initiating the American treaty program. Therefore, it makes sense to look back and see what these officials were thinking as they drafted and negotiated these treaties—in particular, what they considered the core purposes of investment treaties. There is an extensive scholarly literature on whether or not investment treaties (and in particular American treaties) facilitate investment, which is largely inconclusive. To date, no one has gone back and looked to see what American officials were actually expecting as they drafted and negotiated these treaties. From reviewing accessible files relating to all pre-NAFTA investment treaties, my conclusion is that US officials did not expect investment treaties to facilitate additional investment, with a few exceptions.

The initial purposes of US BITs did not include promoting outward investment. In fact, during the initial discussions and publications, American officials went out of their way to say that the treaties would *not* promote investment. They did so because the Carter administration believed that organized labor would oppose treaties that promoted outward investment.[27] The 1977 internal memo to decide whether or not to initiate a US treaty program does not mention promotion—it lists protection as the purpose of the treaties, and even calls the treaties "Investment Protection Agreements."[28] In the late 1970s, the US government sought "investment neutrality," that is, relatively equal inflows and outflows of investment.[29] It was not an era in which politics permitted starting programs that were believed to encourage

[27] Gudgeon 1986: 112 and Vandevelde 1993a: 162, footnote 17.

[28] Action Memorandum 7720912 from Herbert J. Hansell and Julius L. Katz to Mr. Cooper, Subject: Negotiation of Bilateral Investment Protection Agreements with Less Developed Countries, August 10, 1977. US 2788553 Box 1.

[29] This is an important change from earlier years, when the US government was not concerned with sending more investment abroad than it received.

outflows of investment. Yet BITs were not a problem, because they did not promote investment—they just protected it:

> The bilaterals would not constitute a departure from the investment neutrality we seek. The bilaterals entered into by the Europeans do not require the parties to take specific actions to promote investment. The substantive provisions of the agreements deal with the protection of investment.[30]
>
> Notwithstanding the desires of many developing countries to enhance their investment climate to attract foreign investment, the treaty in no way compromises our general policy towards investment inflows and outflows, since no specific actions are required to promote investment and all substantive provisions are directed at investment protection or dispute settlement.[31]

Protection was the chief purpose in internal discussions; then other purposes were added for a wider audience. One 1977 memo observes,

> in drafting the letter to Congress we should make clear that our purpose in undertaking this [BIT] program is not only to protect the rights of investors (as stressed in the GAO [Government Accountability Office] report), but also other purposes such as establishing rules for dispute settlement to avoid future foreign policy problems and promoting development.[32]

Even as the reasons for BITs were expanded for a wider audience, however, there was no mention of promoting outward investment flows.

To the extent that US officials did discuss facilitating outflows, they, like World Bank officials, used the concept of "investment climate." Improving the investment climate, as discussed in earlier chapters, is not the same as receiving investment. The "climate" is made of regulations and policies, primarily domestic. The onus is on the partner government to change their policies to "improve the climate," which might lead to additional investment if foreign investors notice and respond to the policy changes. This logic is clear in a 1982 telegram, which illustrates the way US officials connected BITs to the investment climate and domestic policies in Zaire:

> Negotiation of an investment treaty would enable us to press for the investment climate which the Zairian [domestic investment] code promises, but which remains to be achieved. . . . Our objectives are improved treatment and better protection of US investors on the spot, as well as promotion of *conditions that might attract new investment.*[33]

[30] Memo from Herbert J. Hansell and Julius L. Katz to Mr. Cooper, August 10, 1977. US 2788553 Box 1.

[31] Memo from Richard T. McCormack to Mr. Wallis, October 19, 1982. US 2788553 Box 1.

[32] Memo from Donald Planty to S/S, August 15, 1977. US 2788553 Box 1.

[33] Telegram from the American Embassy Kinshasa to the Secretary of State, Subject: Possible Negotiation of US/Zaire Investment Treaty, November 1982. US 2788553 Box 2. Emphasis mine.

The phrase this official uses—the "promotion of conditions that might attract investment"—means something very different from the promotion of investment. Promoting "conditions" means asking Zaire to change their domestic policies.

In early internal documents, US officials wrote that they were unsure what impact these treaties would have on investment flows:

> The effect of such agreements on the investment climate is the factor most difficult to predict, and the area where our Embassies overseas could be most helpful. Conceivably, firms that would now only go in with OPIC insurance might be willing to go in without it if their rights were guaranteed in the absence of insurance. But the investment climate is the product of the host regime. A treaty would at least be an earnest of good faith on the part of the host countries.[34]

The last line of this quote contains a striking sentiment, which is repeated in several memos from this period: signing a treaty would "at least be an earnest of good faith" or would "demonstrate a positive attitude toward foreign investment."[35] No stronger claim could be made, since there was no evidence that treaties led to additional investment or domestic legal reform. Like the World Bank before them, American officials at no time considered commissioning econometric studies or surveys to measure the impact of BITs on a partner country's investment climate. Yet officials in the State Department did ask economic attachés and other embassy staff to assess what, if any, impact an investment treaty might have.

US Embassy officials, in my review of their telegrams in State Department files related to all pre-NAFTA investment treaties and failed negotiations, generally expected investment treaties to have an indirect relationship, if any, with new flows of investment. The use of a treaty or a treaty negotiation varied by country—although one common theme is that treaty negotiations were often seen as good opportunities to remind or teach the local government about private property rights.[36] US officials did extensive research into a country's investment context before negotiations began. One product of this research was a clear articulation of other factors that affected investment flows from the US into, say, Cameroon. An excerpt from a document prepared in advance of negotiations with Cameroon demonstrates this:

> The year 1982 was a period of unprecedented US government and private sector interest and activity in Cameroon. In January, Secretary of Commerce Malcolm Baldrige and Secretary of Agriculture John R. Block led a team of American

[34] Memo from Russell O. Prickett to Mr. Trimble and Mr. Boeker, May 13, 1977. US 2788553 Box 1.

[35] Memo from Richard T. McCormack to Mr. Wallis, October 19, 1982. US 2788553 Box 1.

[36] For instance, one telegram emphasizes that "the dialogue in a negotiation" would "advance our investment policy in an effective and lasting way." Telegram from the American Embassy Kinshasa to the Secretary of State, Subject: Possible Negotiation of US/Zaire Investment Treaty, November 1982. US 2788553 Box 2.

> business to Cameroon on a trade and investment mission. In July, the then President of Cameroon, Ahmadou Ahidjo, met with President Reagan, toured the US and met with US businessmen in New York City. In September, US and Cameroonian government officials met and explored the possibility of the two countries entering into a BIT similar to the investment treaty concluded between Egypt and the US. Many major US firms seriously investigated trade and investment opportunities in Cameroon. Several of them were awarded major government tenders. A major US bank and several US engineering and construction firms opened offices in Cameroon in 1982.[37]

The excerpt is quoted at length because it shows how much investment facilitation and investment occurred before the BIT: the trips, winning the tenders, and opening offices in Cameroon preceded the BIT and were independent of it. The American government's aim with the BIT was not to facilitate investment but to protect the investment already in Cameroon and to ensure that the US government had a legal document to use in consultations if there were future disputes with Cameroon.

The documents in previous paragraphs were written for use within the State Department and were not intended for a public audience or for treaty partners. The public rhetoric was different and generally more ambiguous about the relationship with additional investment. That said, the degree to which additional investment was used to frame negotiations differs over time and by negotiation. In the late 1980s and early 1990s, during the Reagan and George H. W. Bush administrations, the US government began using increased US investment aggressively to frame treaty negotiations. In 1990, a top US official told the Senate that the link between a BIT and increased investment was undeniable:

> The treaty will serve as a vital step in attracting US investment—investment that Poland desperately needs to facilitate its transition to a market economy. We have already received many calls from US companies asking about the treaty, and the linkage between the treaty and increased US investment is undeniable.[38]

The circumstances of the Polish negotiations were different to previous circumstances. The US government did have a strong interest in facilitating flows to Poland, and, perhaps, given the transition and upheaval in Poland, firms really were waiting for the BIT before they invested. Yet, as the case study of the US–Poland treaty later in this chapter illustrates, US investment was headed into Poland regardless of the treaty: there were enormous profits to be made. For the US government, the treaty was a tool to lock in liberalization

[37] Duane E. Sams, "The Legal Aspects of Doing Business in Cameroon." US 2788553 Box 2.

[38] Secretary McAllister, speaking in the Hearing before the Committee on Foreign Relations of the United States Senate, September 18, 1990. US Treaty Doc 101–18.

reforms and private property norms in the event that the unknown Solidarity government took power.

The promise of additional investment provides leverage in a negotiation: if BITs increase investment, then they are worth tough commitments. It is difficult to assess how often US negotiators used this framing, explicitly or implicitly, because the kind of conversations where it might have been used appear less fully in archival documents than internal discussions.

During the Clinton era, official documents tried to distance the US government from the claim that treaties facilitated investment. In his 1995 letter submitting the BIT with Georgia to the President, the US Trade Representative wrote: "It is US policy, however, to advise potential treaty partners during BIT negotiations that conclusion of such a treaty does not necessarily result in immediate increases in private US investment flows."[39] The same text appears in the letter of transmittal with most treaties during the Clinton era. References to additional investment are rare in official documentation surrounding recent investment treaties. The Committee on Foreign Relations' report on the most recent BIT, signed with Rwanda in 2008, exemplifies this trend. The first section, titled "Purpose," does not mention investment flows, promotion, or facilitation. The first sentence reads: "the Rwanda BIT is intended to provide protections for investors that underscore the shared commitment of the United States and Rwanda to open investment and trade policies."[40]

In conclusion, the US position on the relationship between BITs and increased investment changed over time. While this assumed relationship may have played an important role in some negotiations, for most American officials most of the time, there was little or no relationship between investment treaties and additional investment.

USING INVESTMENT TREATIES TO REWARD AND LOCK IN DOMESTIC LIBERALIZATION

Rewarding and locking in domestic reforms in other countries has become an important motivation for US investment treaties. The US government selects countries for BITs on the basis of previous liberalization reforms, and aims to reward and reinforce these reforms with international law. This purpose was not articulated clearly at the creation of the program, but has become a central tenet of how negotiating partners are selected and why the US government

[39] Letter of Submittal from Warren Christopher, Department of State, to William J. Clinton, President of the United States, dated June 22, 1995. US Treaty Doc 104–13.

[40] Report of the Committee on Foreign Relations, Investment Treaty with Rwanda. US Treaty Doc 110–23.

negotiates treaties. The Senate Foreign Relations Committee Report for the most recent investment treaty expresses this clearly: "The Executive Branch chose to negotiate a BIT with Rwanda, in part, based on its strong economic reform program, which has helped to rebuild the Rwandan economy since the 1994 genocide."[41] The BIT was a reward for, and reinforcement of, the Rwandan government's earlier reforms.

To understand how American investment treaties have been used to lock in liberalization, treaties must be viewed in their domestic political context. This section provides short case studies of two investment treaty negotiations: US–Poland and US–Argentina. These case studies highlight the role of ICSID membership and access to arbitration in these negotiations. The Polish and Argentine governments were both unwilling to join ICSID. In Poland, US officials decided that other concessions were more important than ICSID membership, and rewrote the treaty text to include the key enforcement provisions from the ICSID Convention. In Argentina, US officials doubled down and insisted that the Argentine government join ICSID, recognizing the symbolic importance of an Argentine reversal on arbitration. When investment treaties were reconceptualized as tools to lock in liberalization reforms, access to arbitration (and ICSID membership itself) was reconceptualized as a means of making any backpedaling from liberalization reforms punishable under international law.

The US–Poland BIT Negotiations

Poland signed a US BIT in 1990, a time when the Polish government was in a position of supplication to the US and the Bretton Woods institutions. Yet Poland did not join ICSID in 1990, and has not joined ICSID since. Why?

This section probes the US–Poland negotiations, with two conclusions. First, although ICSID membership was a priority for US negotiators, they were willing to sacrifice it for intellectual property concessions and other gains. Second, what the US really desired was direct access to arbitration with the enforcement benefits of the ICSID Convention. US negotiators found a way to put what they desired—the enforcement benefits of ICSID—right into the text of the US–Poland bilateral treaty. This legal innovation made it unnecessary for Poland to join ICSID.

This case study proceeds in three subsections. The first provides context, the second articulates why a BIT with Poland mattered to the US administration,

[41] Section VI. Article A, Report of the Committee on Foreign Relations, Investment Treaty with Rwanda. US Treaty Doc 110–23.

and the third looks at how US negotiators compensated for Poland not being a member of ICSID.

The Polish Domestic Political Context and Relationship with the US

In June 1989, President Bush went to Poland to address the Sejm, the lower house of the country's parliament, and announce a large aid package to assist in the Polish transition to a market economy and democracy. Behind closed doors, Bush and his advisers were concerned about Solidarity—a worker's party with no experience in government—gaining power. At the time, General Jaruzelski, a Communist, was still in power as President, but with dwindling support. The US administration sought structures that could be put in place to tie Solidarity's hands in the future, while strengthening the hand of pro-market reformers in Poland. At the same time, the US administration did not want to be seen dictating terms to Poland. In order to shift blame for his unpopular domestic reforms onto Western governments and organizations, Jaruzelski sought external pressure, saying to Bush, "in this period in which Poland needs severe austerity, pressure is needed from the outside to adopt the reforms."[42] For several reasons, Bush hesitated to put direct pro-reform pressure on Poland. Bush framed American support for Polish reforms this way: "We want you to succeed. We want to help you, and to do what is right... but I do not want to complicate your efforts through US zest."[43]

US officials were racing against the clock: the opportunity for hands-tying was *before* Solidarity came to power. Table 7.1 below places the BIT negotiations in their context: from Solidarity leader Lech Walesa convening strikes to becoming President took less than two years, yet the BIT was in place before he took office.

President Bush himself signed this BIT with the Polish Prime Minister—an unprecedented move and an indicator of the urgency that the US accorded this treaty.[44] Support for the US–Poland BIT was so strong within the US government that there was debate over whether a hearing in the Senate Foreign Relations Committee was even necessary.[45]

[42] Memcon between President Bush and Wojciech Jaruzelski, July 10, 1989, Belwedere Palace. US BPL.

[43] Memcon between President Bush and Krzysztof Skubiszewski, September 25, 1989. US BPL.

[44] Confirmed with President Bush's Daily Schedule. BITs were usually signed by the USTR or an Ambassador.

[45] In his comments, Jesse Helms, the ranking minority member of the Senate Foreign Relations Committee, makes a point that, "Every bill should be given a hearing, however brief it may be... at a minimum, we will be making a record here." Hearing before the Committee on Foreign Relations of the United States Senate, September 18, 1990. US Treaty Doc 101–18.

Table 7.1. Timeline of Polish Political Transition, with US BIT Dates Included

Date	Event
December 1988	After large strikes, the governing Communist Party approaches Solidarity for talks.
February 6–April 15, 1989	Roundtable talks restructure the Polish government and Solidarity is declared a legal organization.
July 10, 1989	President Bush visits Poland. He addresses the Sejm, announces aid package.
July 19, 1989	Elections. Solidarity sweeps all the seats for which it is eligible (the Communist Party had been guaranteed 65% of the lower house). Controversially, the Communist leader Jaruzelski is elected President.
December 1989	Radical "Balcerowicz" Reform Program announced.
March 21, 1990	US BIT with Poland signed.
October 28, 1990	US Senate approves BIT.
December 9, 1990	Lech Walesa, Solidarity leader, becomes President.

Reasons the US Administration Sought a BIT with Poland

For the US administration, a BIT was an ideal instrument for reinforcing domestic reforms because Polish reformers could use the BIT as an embodiment of additional capital flows, and offset unpopular policies by arguing they were necessary for the BIT.[46] The treaty pushed liberalization even further than the Polish domestic reform program,[47] which is remarkable given the radical nature of the domestic reforms, such as the immediate convertibility of the *zloty* and the immediate elimination of price controls and subsidies.[48] The US BIT cemented many of these reforms with international law and constrained the ability of future Polish governments to reconsider the reforms.

There were two additional reasons the US government wanted the Polish BIT, however. First, the administration wanted to use Poland as a "lead country" for reforms in the former Soviet bloc. Senator Sarbanes, ranking member of the Committee on Foreign Relations, said that putting "the Polish treaty in place" would "give [the USTR] an opportunity to use it sort of as a lead country in Eastern Europe."[49] The idea of using this agreement as regional precedent was elaborated by a US negotiator:

[46] I use the term "reformers" because this is the language US negotiators used at the time.

[47] For instance, on the transferability of *zloty* profits, from 15 percent transferable to 100 percent transferable by 1995. Hearing before the Committee on Foreign Relations of the United States Senate, September 18, 1990. US Treaty Doc 101–18.

[48] Poland's "shock therapy" program has been well studied; Murrell (1993) provides a contemporary critique. Jeffrey Sachs and David Lipton were influential in developing these ideas with Solidarity leadership; their advice was radically different from the World Bank mission, which suggested a five-year period for achieving convertibility of the *zloty* (Johnson and Kowalska 1994: 194–5).

[49] Hearing before the Committee on Foreign Relations of the United States Senate, September 18, 1990. US Treaty Doc 101–18.

> *The Treaty serves as a key precedent in the region.* We are currently negotiating with Czechoslovakia and Yugoslavia, as well as with the Soviet Union. We will begin negotiations shortly with Hungary and Bulgaria on investment treaties. We have strongly advanced the message to these countries that they will be competing with each other for foreign investment and that Poland is a model.[50]

The strategy was to set high standards with Poland and then extend these standards across the region. Notably, the Polish BIT contains many clauses not in the model of the time, some of which are mentioned below; negotiators innovated during the drafting of the Polish BIT.

Second, and arguably most important, the US–Poland treaty included intellectual property provisions, a first for a BIT. These provisions did not just bring Poland up to current global practice; they raised the global standard for intellectual property protection. An American negotiator testified: "[T]he treaty reflects Poland's 'stretching to join the West' by its acceptance of broader investor access to international arbitration and by *its willingness to adopt intellectual property standards which are now among the highest in the world*."[51] If the agreement came into force, American negotiators could use this agreement as a precedent in multilateral negotiations on intellectual property, then underway.[52] Intellectual property rights were the real battleground of the negotiations and American negotiators were willing to make concessions in other areas in order to secure the intellectual property provisions.[53] The State Department secured the intellectual property provisions by implying that they would lead to additional investment: "we made the pitch to them that, by protecting intellectual property rights, they will attract more investment than they otherwise would. So, we made the case to them that it was in their interest."[54] Poland's concessions on intellectual property were so serious that the treaty almost never came into force. The Polish legislative branch resisted implementing the required intellectual property legislation for four years, until the multilateral negotiations were

[50] Hearing before the Committee on Foreign Relations of the United States Senate, September 18, 1990. US Treaty Doc 101–18. Emphasis mine.

[51] Hearing before the Committee on Foreign Relations of the United States Senate, September 18, 1990. US Treaty Doc 101–18.

[52] Negotiations on intellectual property were underway in the Uruguay Round. US negotiators were aggressively pursuing intellectual property protection in multiple fora, including through Section 301 reports and bilateral negotiations, with the ultimate strategic aim being high multilateral standards (Correa 2000: 4–12).

[53] Braithwaite and Drahos (2000: 78–80) argue that maximizing intellectual property privileges had become the top priority of US trade policy at this time, due to the effective mobilization of US pharmaceutical corporations, particularly Pfizer.

[54] Hearing before the Committee on Foreign Relations of the United States Senate, September 18, 1990. US Treaty Doc 101–18.

ending. The US government refused to put the BIT into effect until Poland had passed the legislation.[55]

US Negotiators Find a Way around Poland's Non-Membership in ICSID

American officials were concerned that requiring Polish ratification of ICSID might endanger the entire BIT, a risk that these officials were not willing to take. Yet the enforcement provisions of the ICSID Convention had become a crucial part of the US program. So the technical challenge facing US negotiators was to provide US investors with the protections of the ICSID Convention, but without requiring Polish ratification of ICSID. They took clauses on enforcement from the ICSID Convention and put them into the text of the BIT itself, including clauses on automatic enforcement, final and binding awards, obligation to comply, and enforcement in its territory. Vandevelde pointed out these developments in 1993: "US BIT negotiators sought to ensure that investors who selected an arbitral mechanism not subject to the ICSID Convention would have a final, enforceable award. They did this by incorporating counterparts to the ICSID clauses into BIT provisions."[56] These ICSID-inspired enforcement clauses were not in the text of the model at the time. The negotiators were innovating in response to external events. Subsequently, these clauses have become a part of US practice—they were added to the model treaty in 1992 and were included in NAFTA.[57]

The US–Argentina BIT Negotiations

Access to arbitration was the crux of the US–Argentina BIT negotiations. Unlike in Poland, Argentina ratifying the ICSID Convention was a requirement for the BIT to come into force. Argentina joined ICSID on October 19, 1994, the day before the US BIT came into force. Yet ratifying ICSID was not enough. US officials also refined the treaty text, removing any ambiguity from the state's consent to arbitration and making other changes that would then be carried forward in NAFTA and future US models.

[55] This was only after the Polish "Law on Copyrights and Rights Related of February 4, 1994" was passed; by then, Solidarity had been in power for years.

[56] Vandevelde 1993b: 657–8. Interpretation corroborated in Kinnear and Hansen 2005.

[57] Neither Canada nor Mexico was an ICSID member, which may have been a sticking point in negotiations if these enforcement clauses had not been created and tested with the Poland treaty.

Argentine Domestic Political Context and Relationship with US

In 1989, the Argentine economy was in severe recession and suffering runaway inflation. In May 1989 alone, the currency lost half its value. In this month, Carlos Menem was elected President. Less than two weeks after the election, riots erupted in Rosario and Cordoba over food shortages and other consequences of hyperinflation. The riots spread, a state of emergency was declared, and power was transferred to Menem five months early. Menem and his government began to implement dramatic stabilization and reform policies, in the belief that privatization and liberalization would introduce discipline and hard foreign currency into the Argentine economy, which would bring down inflation.[58]

Menem cultivated good relations with then-US President George H. W. Bush. Menem believed American support could help Argentina regain credibility with financial markets and international institutions;[59] American support could serve as cover for (or as a scapegoat for) unpopular austerity policies;[60] and American firms could provide much-needed new foreign investment. Menem advertised how attractive his radical reforms were for investors: "We shall privatize the State-owned entities. We have opened the doors to private capital, including from abroad, without limitations and under the same conditions as with domestic capital. There will be full repatriation of earnings. We are solving some of our problems."[61] These are many of the substantive provisions in a US investment treaty. The Bush administration wanted to reinforce and reward these reforms, as with Poland. Bush argued: "we need a rapid round of bilateral talks because the efforts Argentina is making are tremendous."[62] Bilateral negotiations, and the BIT they produced, were even better for Menem politically than previous forms of US support, which had included public statements, "quiet work" (a diplomatic euphemism for influence in Argentina's favor at the World Bank),[63] and OPIC programs. For Menem, the BIT was a tangible representation of increased investment and therefore harsh policies could be framed as a trade-off: we make tough reforms in order to receive investment.

There was one problem: arbitration. Argentina was the intellectual home of the Calvo Doctrine and on the international stage had long been a symbolic stronghold of opposition to investor–state arbitration—in Argentina, investor–state

[58] Levitsky (1998) notes Menem and his Peronist administration were able to implement a set of neoliberal reforms that run counter to traditional Peronism, without losing the Party's base. Levitsky and Way (1998) compare this with the experience of Solidarity in Poland.

[59] Memcon between President Bush and Carlos Menem, October 1, 1990. US BPL.

[60] Telcon between President Bush and Carlos Menem, March 1, 1990. US BPL.

[61] Memcon between President Bush and Carlos Menem, September 27, 1989. US BPL.

[62] Memcon between President Bush and Carlos Menem, September 27, 1989. US BPL.

[63] See Secretary of State James Baker's words, in the Memcon between President Bush and Carlos Menem, October 1, 1990. US BPL.

arbitration had more salience, and a more direct resonance with concepts like independence and equality than in almost any other country. Even Menem's administration, which had not hesitated to make radical changes to the Argentine economy, did not believe they could overturn opposition to investor–state arbitration. It was clear months before negotiations began that access to arbitration was the defining issue of the negotiation. In December 1990, the Argentine Foreign Minister announced that his government desired a BIT. The American Ambassador to Argentina responded:

> We can have a [bilateral investment] treaty any time if we solve one problem—the "fork in the road." We believe that our investors must be able to make a choice at the beginning of an investment dispute of whether to seek redress in local courts or through international arbitration.[64]

The Ambassador's message was clear: unless you grant our investors direct access to arbitration, there will be no BIT. The Argentine minister replied only, "we need to convince our legislature on that."[65]

Desire for a US BIT was strong enough that the Menem administration was willing to upturn Argentina's position on arbitration. Within six months of that exchange, in May 1991, Argentina signed the ICSID Convention. The US–Argentina BIT was signed five months later. Argentina did not deposit its instrument of ratification for the ICSID Convention until October 19, 1992. The BIT came into force the next day.

Reasons the US Administration Sought a BIT with Argentina

There were three reasons the US sought a BIT with Argentina: to reinforce the reform process and secure advantages for American firms, to establish Argentina as a model for the rest of the region, and because of the symbolic importance of Argentina agreeing to investor–state arbitration.

The US administration believed that a BIT would lend Menem support and lock in his reform policies. There was also a sense that the treaty would help US firms take advantage of the lucrative investment opportunities created by large-scale privatization. Testifying to the Senate, a top negotiator said: "Argentina is engaged in the most comprehensive privatization program in its history and is implementing other wide-ranging market reforms as well. The BIT can help support these moves and get our companies in on the ground floor."[66] US negotiators saw the BIT with Argentina as a stepping stone toward other arguments. In 1993, the USTR summed up the approach well:

[64] Ambassador Terrence Todman, in response to Foreign Minister Domingo Cavallo. Quoted in Memcon between President Bush and Carlos Menem, December 5, 1990. US BPL.

[65] Memcon between President Bush and Carlos Menem, December 5, 1990. US BPL.

[66] Testimony of Daniel Tarullo in the Hearing before the Committee on Foreign Relations of the United States Senate, September 10, 1993. US Treaty Doc 103–2.

> Every effort should be made to create "stepping stones" that eventually lead to free trade agreements with other Latin American countries... We are prepared, for example, to pursue bilateral investment treaties and bilateral intellectual property agreements... All of these efforts should be seen as "stepping stones" toward the larger goal of hemispheric free trade.[67]

The shared ideological ground between the Bush and Menem administrations made Argentina an ideal first partner for the US strategy of negotiating high-standard agreements and then using them as precedents.

The symbolic importance of Argentina accepting investor–state arbitration was recognized. In the Senate hearings, a US negotiator explained how the BIT equaled Argentina formally giving up the Calvo Clause:

> One item of particular interest in the Argentine BIT is that, like many Latin American countries, Argentina has long subscribed to the so-called Calvo Doctrine which requires that foreign investors submit disputes arising in a country to that country's local courts. This treaty contains an absolute right to international arbitration of investment disputes and thereby removes US investors from the restrictive operation of the Calvo Doctrine. Such a precedent with Argentina has already helped pave the way for similar agreements with other Latin American countries.[68]

Interestingly, American investors and industry groups appear to have been far more interested in access to arbitration with regard to Argentina than ever before. In a letter endorsing the US–Argentina BIT, the United States Council for International Business wrote: "[we particularly want to note the treaty's] establishment of agreed dispute settlement procedures, allowing investors to bring disputes directly to binding third-party arbitration. This is the most valuable of the BIT provisions for promoting investor confidence."[69] This interest may reflect timing: the Argentina BIT overlapped with the NAFTA negotiations, which drew industry attention to investor–state arbitration.

Direct access to arbitration was an important concession for Argentina to make. Vandevelde argues that "Argentina agreed to the inclusion of an investor-to-state dispute provision without any substantive concessions from the United States."[70] I argue that the US did make a substantive concession—intellectual property rights. Presumably, based on comments Bush made to Menem about the importance of intellectual property, the US would have liked

[67] Remarks by Michael Kantor, USTR, before the Council of the Americas Washington conference, May 4, 1993. Clinton Presidential Library.

[68] Testimony of Daniel Tarullo in the Hearing before the Committee on Foreign Relations of the United States Senate, September 10, 1993. US Treaty Doc 103–2.

[69] Statement of the United States Council for International Business, Hearing before the Committee on Foreign Relations United States Senate, September 10, 1993. US Treaty Doc 103–2.

[70] Vandevelde 1993(b): 691.

to include intellectual property provisions in the BIT. The US may have used the fact that they removed intellectual property from the negotiations as a source of leverage. Notably, the US administration had included intellectual property in the BITs with Bulgaria, Romania, and Kazakhstan, which were all submitted alongside the Argentine BIT to the Senate.[71]

For US negotiators, it was important for Argentina to make clear that they were departing from the Calvo Clause both by joining ICSID and by inserting new language into the treaty. The negotiation of the Argentina BIT, Vandevelde observed, "occasioned a marked revision of the investor-to-State dispute provision."[72] As with the Poland negotiations, US practice evolved ahead of the model treaty: changes made for Argentina were then integrated into the US model treaty (the 1992 version). The changes reduced or eliminated sources of ambiguity that could be used to deny or limit direct access to arbitration.

ICSID MEMBERSHIP AS A PREREQUISITE FOR AN INVESTMENT TREATY

ICSID membership mattered in the Polish and Argentine negotiations. Yet this does not demonstrate that ICSID membership mattered in all US negotiations: in fact, the importance of ICSID membership for the US government changed over time and by negotiating partner.

Membership in ICSID has never been an across-the-board prerequisite for a BIT with the US. In many situations where the US government could have insisted its negotiating partner join ICSID, it did not. For instance, the US signed a BIT with Grenada three years after the American military intervention there. The BIT negotiations reportedly took under an hour and the Grenada BIT is identical to the US model.[73] Grenada was not in a position to resist US pressure—yet Grenada did not join ICSID before the treaty came into force. US officials may have thought access to an international tribunal unimportant with Grenada—where they could reasonably expect a quiet phone call to straighten out any dispute. By this logic, then, the negotiations in which ICSID membership was important to American officials are those with governments of greater mettle.

This change in US officials' attitudes toward ICSID membership corresponds to a broader change in the American treaty program in the late 1980s.

[71] Hearing before the Committee on Foreign Relations United States Senate, September 10, 1993. US Treaty Doc 103–2.

[72] Vandevelde 1993(b): 642.

[73] Vandevelde 1992: 38.

The US government began to negotiate with larger economies and more politically significant countries. As an official put it in 1990:

> I think the BIT program has received something of a shot in the arm in the past two years with the change in Eastern Europe and with the President's Enterprise for the Americas Initiative; that the countries we are negotiating with are, in general, larger economies and have a greater political significance than the earlier round of negotiations we did for investment treaties. We are very pleased with that.[74]

This change was also noted by other officials. As former US official Kenneth Vandevelde observed, "over the course of ten years of negotiations [1982–92], there has been a gradual but clearly discernible shift in the ideology underlying the BITs."[75] During the initial drafting process and early negotiations, investment treaties were not conceived of as political tools. The Assistant Legal Adviser during the drafting process, Scott Gudgeon, wrote: "as an initiative proposed by international legal specialists within the US Government, the BIT program was originally endowed with primarily legal policy concerns."[76] Then, as the 1980s progressed, the end of the Cold War and the debt crisis created new opportunities, and new purposes, for US BITs. An existing institution was put to new purposes, without changes in its form; this is conversion in action. For the American government, BITs increasingly become instruments of foreign policy because they provided a convenient way of locking in domestic reforms and cementing closer relations with countries that had not previously been allies.

As US BITs were imbued with greater political significance, access to ISDS, and in particular membership in ICSID, took on a new meaning and importance—but only in negotiations with certain countries. In my reading, the available evidence suggests that the Argentine, Russian, and Turkish BITs may have been conditional on these countries joining ICSID.[77] Having recently become acting Russian Prime Minister, Yegor Gaidar signed the ICSID Convention in person at the World Bank on June 16, 1992. The next day, June 17, 1992, Gaidar signed the United States–Russia BIT in person in Washington.[78]

[74] Secretary McAllister speaking in the Hearing before the Committee on Foreign Relations of the United States Senate, September 18, 1990. US Treaty Doc 101–18.

[75] Vandevelde 1993(a): 168. Vandevelde also worked in the Office of the Legal Adviser in the US State Department, from 1982 to 1988, and was involved both in drafting model texts and in actual negotiations.

[76] Gudgeon 1986: 111. Gudgeon was Assistant Legal Adviser, State Department, 1982–4.

[77] The possibility of ICSID membership being a prerequisite for these treaties was confirmed in off-the-record interviews.

[78] It is possible that the Russian government was keen to tie its own hands and burnish its credibility. The evidence that I have does not rule out such an explanation, but off-the-record interviews (which I have been unable to verify with official written evidence available at this time) suggest US pressure, or, as one interviewee put it, that Gaidar was "dragged to ICSID kicking and screaming."

The US Senate quickly held hearings and recommended ratification, but the Russian Duma did not support ratification. With the BIT off the table, Russia never ratified the ICSID Convention. The actions of the Turkish government also suggest reluctance to join ICSID and that the Turkish government was closely watching the US Senate to see if they needed to ratify ICSID or not. The Turkish government signed the ICSID Convention in 1987 but did not ratify until the BIT had progressed through the US Senate two years later. Turkey joined ICSID with a long, unusual notification that reads like an attempt to undo the act of ratification:

> I also have the honour to hereby notify, pursuant to Article 25 (4) . . . that only the disputes arising directly out of investment activities which have obtained necessary permission, in conformity with the relevant legislation of the Republic of Turkey on foreign capital, and that have effectively started shall be subject to the jurisdiction of the Center. However, the disputes, related to the property and real rights upon the real estates are totally under the jurisdiction of the Turkish courts and therefore shall not be submitted to jurisdiction of the Centre.[79]

Turkey never filed its implementing legislation with ICSID,[80] and in 1998, Turkey filed another notification to ensure the Turkish government was not liable for actions by the Turkish Electricity Generation and Transmission Corporation (TEAŞ) or Petroleum Pipeline Corporation (BOTAŞ).[81]

If the Turkish government was so reluctant to join ICSID—and given how strongly the Turkish government expressed its opposition to the idea of investor–state arbitration throughout the 1960s and 1970s—why did the government reverse its position in the late 1980s? Pressure from the US likely plays an important role, but so does domestic politics. In the 1980s, a powerful Prime Minister, Turgot Ozal, implemented far-reaching structural reforms in Turkey, including a series of measures to liberalize foreign investment.[82] By the late 1980s, Ozal's party was struggling to hold power, especially after rival political parties, which had been banned after a 1980 coup, were able to participate again.[83] Ozal's reforms were divisive, inflation was high, and he needed to bolster his support. For Ozal, a BIT was a tangible way to link his reforms to increased investment and give his policies the imprimatur of the US government. Given the earlier measures to liberalize foreign investment, Turkey did not need to make many concessions to get a US BIT—but one

[79] ICSID/8-D. Turkish negotiators did not seem to have been aware at the time, but a notification is not legally the same as an exception (Parra 2013), so Turkey's notification holds no legal weight.

[80] ICSID/8-F.

[81] ICSID/8-C. These notifications likely relate to the Ceyhan pipeline, and may have been a pre-emptive step taken specifically to prevent action by Armenian-American groups.

[82] Onis and Webb 1994: 134. [83] Onis and Webb 1994: 165.

concession that Ozal needed to make was direct access to arbitration for US investors and ICSID membership.

In the Argentina–US, Russia–US, and Turkey–US negotiations, ICSID membership was reimaged in ways that ICSID's founders in the early 1960s had likely not anticipated. The role of investor–state arbitration within these three treaties was to lock in domestic liberalization reforms with international law, by definition limiting the policy options available to a government. Have treaties like these, when coupled with expansive interpretations, unduly restricted the ability of governments to act when, for instance, confronting an economic emergency or facing public health or environmental issues? Chapter eight evaluates how governments have begun to rethink their answer to this question in the last two decades.

CONCLUSION

When circumstances change, the reasons for investment treaties and the purposes of ISDS within those treaties change too. This chapter identified four characteristics of American treaties that have changed over time: the desirability of investors having standing; the relationship between investment treaties and additional investment; the use of investment treaties to reward and lock in liberalization; and a requirement to ratify the ICSID Convention. The investor–state arbitration provisions written in the first American model treaties in the late 1970s were put to new purposes, as administrations changed and as external political challenges changed. These provisions went from being unimportant, for instance, in negotiations with Grenada or Panama, to being the crux of the negotiations, as they were in negotiations with Argentina. Over time, the purposes that US officials ascribed to investor–state arbitration in US treaties changed substantially. If this conversion occurred in the American treaty program, corresponding changes over time are likely to have occurred in other treaty programs too.

8

Why is Exit So Hard? Positive Feedback and Institutional Persistence

The previous chapter examined American government decisions on the road to NAFTA. This brief chapter probes government decisions in the period after NAFTA came into force in 1994, as more governments found themselves respondents in investment arbitration. This chapter does not retell the developments that have occurred since 1994 in investor–state arbitration, since extensive scholarship on treaty developments and cases from this era exists. Instead, this chapter focuses narrowly on the feedback processes that have stabilized investor–state arbitration and have made it difficult for governments to exit.

Conventional theories assume that when international institutions no longer serve the interests of states, governments change those institutions or exit them. In this vein, Simmons observes that investment treaties have "underdelivered investment and served up an unexpectedly large wave of litigation,"[1] and argues that "states are beginning to resist and renegotiate the rules that seem increasingly to threaten their sovereignty."[2] Yet the only evidence of resistance that she cites is an uptick in annulment proceedings at ICSID, most of which was driven by Argentina.[3] That is remarkably little resistance; it is debatable if annulment proceedings even constitute an expression of dissatisfaction with investor–state arbitration overall. Even more remarkably, when states do renegotiate, "most renegotiations either leave ISDS provisions unchanged or render them more investor-friendly."[4] In the most systematic review of recent investment treaties, Alschner finds that "contrary to prior anecdotal and empirical evidence, investment claims do not lead to systematic treaty design changes. Most innovation

[1] Simmons 2014: 13. [2] Simmons 2014: 14.

[3] At that point, Argentina had filed eight annulments, double the number of the second-highest government (Egypt), but since then, the number of annulment proceedings has grown. This could be due to changing legal strategies or law firms advising annulment; it is not a clear indicator of exit.

[4] Broude, Haftel, and Thompson 2017: 2–3.

attributed to investment claims actually pre-dates them."[5] If arbitration has underdelivered investment and served up costly litigation instead, why have governments been slow to change or exit the system? Why do institutions persist, even when they generate unintended consequences for the states that created them?

Institutional persistence, even when institutions generate unintended consequences, is expected to be relatively common in historical institutionalist explanations. Historical institutionalist theory emphasizes that when positive feedback processes operate, they enhance the stability of institutions, making exit more difficult. The primary positive feedback process that I argue operated here is the creation of a non-state constituency, made of law firms, investors, and related interest groups, with an interest in the investor–state arbitration. Over time, new policies or institutions can create constituencies, and these constituencies can develop preferences and resist change. Setup, interaction, and cognitive effects may additionally enhance the stability of an institution. Actors make more and more commitments because of positive feedback, gradually building deeper, more stable foundations for the institution. In addition to creating a constituency with an interest in investor–state arbitration, feedback processes for other actors—including government officials—have generated decentralized commitments that make exit difficult. The decentralized structure of these commitments has led to competitive dynamics that serve to stabilize investor–state arbitration still further.

The first section of this chapter discusses the possible actions that governments can take to exit or reshape investor–state arbitration. To date, governments have engaged in remarkably little exit: only a small fraction of the investment treaties, contracts, and domestic laws that give access to investor–state arbitration have been affected by exit or renegotiation to make access to investor–state arbitration more restrictive. Additionally, some of the steps governments have taken toward exit have been ineffective or have been thwarted by partner countries or tribunals. Exiting from investor–state arbitration is difficult, and the legal complexity of exit is exacerbated by political, bureaucratic, and perceived reputational obstacles to exit. The second section explores how positive feedback has created a new constituency of law firms and investors with an interest in arbitration and therefore has led to a new politics of ISDS. The third section discusses other types of positive feedback that have helped to stabilize and develop a dense web of commitments enshrining investor–state arbitration. The fourth section observes that over time, as more actors became involved in investor–state arbitration, competitive dynamics emerged: competition between law firms, arbitration organizations, and even jurisdictions hoping to host arbitrations makes exit and reform

[5] Alschner forthcoming.

more difficult. The barriers to exit may be highest for capacity-constrained states—a reality picked up in the concluding chapter.

VARIETIES OF EXIT

When a government denounces the ICSID Convention, it does not exit from investor–state arbitration. Denouncing the ICSID Convention does little to insulate governments from future claims; claims against that government could still be brought to any other arbitration venue, including the ICSID Additional Facility. The example of Bolivia illustrates the complexities of exit. Bolivia denounced the ICSID Convention in 2007 after a few cases, including the particularly controversial *Aguas del Tunari* case.[6] This denunciation had symbolic value that mattered for domestic politics, but it did not affect the likelihood or possibility of investor-state cases being brought against Bolivia. There are two reasons for this: the New York Convention and the second consent. First, the New York Convention substitutes for the ICSID Convention with regard to enforcement.[7] If governments were serious about exiting investor–state arbitration, they would denounce the New York Convention too, but to date no government has done so. Second, denouncing the ICSID Convention does nothing to the consent to investor–state arbitration in venues other than ICSID. For instance, the Bolivia–UK investment treaty provides investors with access to ICSID, the ICSID Additional Facility, the ICC, and if six months elapse without agreement on where to arbitrate, a default submission to ad hoc arbitration under the UNCITRAL Arbitration Rules.[8] This treaty was not renegotiated and remains in force, and Bolivia has faced at least three claims under this Bolivia–UK treaty since denouncing the ICSID Convention.[9] If the Bolivian government's aim was to avoid new claims, then denouncing the ICSID Convention was ineffective.

[6] For a legal summary, see De Gramont 2006; for a summary of the controversy, see Finnegan 2002.

[7] Although there is an important difference: awards rendered under the ICSID Convention have automatic enforcement, whereas enforcement through the New York Convention relies more on national courts in the seat of the arbitration (which may be unpredictable, such as the Hague District Court overturning the Yukos award).

[8] Article 8, UK–Bolivia Investment Promotion and Protection Agreement (1988, came into force 1990).

[9] There are likely to be more recent cases against Bolivia that are not publicly available, but the three known claims (according to the Investment Treaty Arbitration Law website, as of May 2017) under the UK treaty are: *South American Silver Limited v Bolivia*, UNCITRAL, PCA Case No. 2013–15; *Guaracachi America, Inc. and Rurelec PLC v The Plurinational State of Bolivia*, UNCITRAL, PCA Case No. 2011–17; and *Guaracachi America, Inc. and Rurelec PLC v The Plurinational State of Bolivia*, UNCITRAL, PCA Case No. 2011–17. Bolivia has also faced claims under other treaties.

If governments aim to prevent foreign investors from being able to bring claims against them, then governments need to remove consent from domestic laws, contracts, and treaties. Removing consent from each of these three types of instruments requires a different process and brings with it different challenges.

There are approximately forty governments in the world that provide investors with direct access to investor–state arbitration in their domestic law.[10] Rewriting domestic law to remove access to arbitration may seem straightforward to external observers, but officials actually contemplating it likely perceive obstacles. To begin with, all of the governments with access to investor–state arbitration in their domestic law are capacity-constrained and low income. Government officials, especially in capacity-constrained governments, face many competing pressures for their time. Writing and passing new domestic legislation requires the use of valuable political capital and time, and new legislation to remove access to arbitration is not inherently high-priority: it is a relatively technical change and an arbitration case is a relatively low-probability risk. Officials within the Finance Ministry, Treasury, or Investment Promotion Agency might be hesitant to remove access, especially since doing so goes against the guidance of the World Bank.[11] In addition to internal opponents of the reform, cautioning or threatening statements might be issued by foreign investor groups or the economic attachés of foreign embassies, statements which might, for instance, suggest that foreign investment inflows will drop if the proposed change comes into effect.[12] This sort of fear-mongering can occur even if, as happens to be the case, World Bank loan approval in no way depends on governments providing access to investor–state arbitration and the decision-making of potential or actual foreign investors is unlikely to be influenced by the presence or absence of access to ISDS in domestic law.[13] As a result of these challenges, the only governments that have removed access to investor–state arbitration from their domestic law have done so in the wake of cases.[14] It is likely that a case brings attention to these provisions and creates a greater awareness of their potency within the government.

Governments can also remove consent to investor–state arbitration in contracts with foreign investors. Most contracts are confidential, and therefore it is not possible to gather systematic information about the extent to which

[10] UNCTAD (2016: 10) report that twenty-six laws provide explicit consent and eleven are unclear, which means that if a case were brought, an arbitration tribunal would decide if they had jurisdiction under the law or not.

[11] The World Bank Guidelines on the Treatment of Foreign Direct Investment have included access to ICSID arbitration since they were promulgated in 1992. For details, see Shihata 1993.

[12] Mossallam 2015.

[13] If access to ISDS is decisive for a particular investor, the government always has the option to negotiate a contract providing for ISDS with that investor individually.

[14] This matches the logic articulated by Poulsen and Aisbett (2013) for treaty claims.

governments have renegotiated, terminated existing contracts, or not negotiated new contracts with investor–state arbitration. For government officials, the obstacles to renegotiating contracts are different from those to rewriting domestic law. To begin with, a government may have dozens or even hundreds of contracts in force. Several different agencies of the national government and many different state, territory, or local governments may all have contracts with foreign investors in force. The transaction costs to renegotiating all these agreements might be immense. Governments may not believe it is a good use of time and resources to do so: contracts are less likely to include language as vague and open to expansion as treaties, and officials may believe the potential liabilities they face in a contract-based case are smaller. In addition, officials may be extremely hesitant to tamper with an existing relationship with a foreign investor.

Governments have many options with regard to removing or renegotiating access to arbitration provided in investment treaties. If their treaty partner is willing to cooperate with them then a government can issue a joint interpretive statement, renegotiate while the existing treaty remains in force, renegotiate after letting the treaty expire, mutually terminate without an explicit agreement to extinguish the sunset clause, or mutually terminate with an explicit agreement to extinguish the sunset clause. If their treaty partner is not willing to cooperate then governments can issue a unilateral interpretive statement, let the treaty expire and inform their treaty partner they will not renew, or terminate the treaty. In all these options, the sunset clause will operate. There are also many intermediate options; the discussion here is only a simplified summary of the options, many of which generate complex legal questions, discussed at length by legal scholars.[15]

Some governments have over a hundred treaties in force, and they would need to consider those options with regard to each treaty. The bilateral political relationship affects renegotiation too. A government may be hesitant to ask another government about renegotiation in case that introduces tensions or affects the bilateral relationship. Alternatively, a government may deny another government's request to renegotiate. Third, as discussed below, economic attachés or other embassy officials do not have the same incentive to renegotiate treaties as they do to negotiate them in the first place—renegotiation is a much less alluring prospect. In addition, treaty renegotiation may attract the attention of foreign investor groups or other "investment protection advocates," who are likely to lobby against removing access to ISDS.

[15] Lavopa, Barreiros, and Bruno 2013; Voon, Mitchell, and Munro 2014; Gordon and Pohl 2015; Voon and Mitchell 2016.

Table 8.1. How Governments Could Exit Investor–State Arbitration[16]

	Type of Exit	Examples
Unilateral Actions	Rewrite domestic law (to remove consent)	Egypt, Tunisia, El Salvador
	Renegotiate or terminate contracts	Unknown (contracts are private)
Unilateral Actions toward Multilateral Treaties	Withdraw from multilateral treaty	Italy (from the Energy Charter Treaty)
	Withdraw from the ICSID Convention	Bolivia, Venezuela, Ecuador
	Withdraw from the New York Convention	None
Unilateral Actions toward Bilateral Treaties	Make an Interpretive Statement	Switzerland in *SGS v Pakistan* case
	Let treaties expire	South Africa, Indonesia
	Withdraw from treaties before expiry	Ecuador, Bolivia
Mutual Actions toward Bilateral Treaties	Make a Joint Interpretive Statement	US, Canada, Mexico (as NAFTA parties)
	Renegotiate treaties	Germany, the Netherlands (many others)
	Let treaties expire and then renegotiate	India, for instance India–EU
	Mutually terminate	Czech Republic, Italy, Ireland (intra-EU)

These various modes of exiting investor–state arbitration are summarized in Table 8.1 above. The table includes all possible modes of exit, even when no example of a state pursuing this course of exit exists yet. Additionally, governments may pursue any combination of these actions that they believe suit their interests.

Table 8.1 shows the many options available in theory to governments to exit investor–state arbitration. The reality is that most governments most of the time do not use these options. The examples listed in the table are the exceptions to the rule that governments do not exit their commitment to investor–state arbitration, even when officials within the government believe investor–state arbitration does not serve their interests. Why? The next section articulates factors that militate against exit.

[16] Thorough discussions of the complex consequences of each of these actions as well as more examples and more detailed examples can be found in Gordon and Pohl (2015), Voon and Mitchell (2016), and the *Investment Arbitration Reporter*.

THE NEW POLITICS OF INVESTOR–STATE ARBITRATION

Institutions, once created, have the potential to create a new politics through the creation of new constituencies. Farrell and Newman show how this operates with regard to international regulatory politics.[17] I argue that the same mechanism operated during the rise of investor–state arbitration. When the ICSID Convention came into force in 1966, the practice of international law was profoundly different, and in particular, many of the transnational law firms that play an outsize role in investor–state arbitration today barely existed. Law firms were almost entirely absent from the creation of the ICSID Convention. Today, however, law firms and private legal practitioners are central to investor–state arbitration; through decades of positive feedback, a constituency has grown with an interest in investor–state arbitration. This constituency has expanded to include new roles, such as "quantum" experts that specialize in estimating damages and third-party funders searching for potentially winning cases.

Investor–state arbitration is a prestigious and lucrative field of practice. The potential fees in investor-state cases have grown over time as the field has come to be dominated by "large law firms that mobilise teams of lawyers using expensive litigation techniques borrowed from corporate litigation practices."[18] Available evidence suggests a law firm receives around $10 million in fees from an average investor–state arbitration.[19] Larger cases command larger fees: Russia was ordered to pay $60 million for the claimant's legal fees in the Yukos case, approximately 75 percent of the claimant's total legal fees, which exceeded $80 million.[20] This figure includes only work related to the arbitration itself, but the same firm is representing the client in enforcement proceedings in the Netherlands, France, and Belgium, as well as proceedings begun in Germany, India, the UK, and the US.[21] The head of the majority shareholder group vowed "a lifetime of litigation,"[22] which, even if the shareholders have many defeats along the way, will be lucrative, steady work for law firms. Looking at the awards underestimates the revenues that law firms get from tasks related to investor–state arbitration that are unlikely to be reported in eventual arbitral awards. The overarching point is: firms are rewarded financially and in terms of prestige when they act as counsel in an investor–state case. This positive feedback creates a strong incentive for them

[17] Farrell and Newman 2010. [18] OECD 2012: 19.

[19] Comprehensive evidence on legal fees is not available, but in 2011, the OECD Secretariat surveyed 143 available awards (sixty-two of which provided no information about the parties' legal expenses), and found costs "averaged over 8 million" (Gaukrodger and Gordon 2012: 19). They note other sources suggesting "ISDS costs have skyrocketed in recent years."

[20] *Yukos Universal Limited (Isle of Man) v Russian Federation* (Award 2014): 577.

[21] Shearman & Sterling 2017. [22] Goldhaber 2010.

to seek out new cases. Aggressive pursuit of this incentive has been one driver of the exponential caseload growth in investor–state arbitration.

As the caseload grows and as expansive new interpretations are successful and then repeated in several decisions, the right to investor–state arbitration is stabilized. Once a right is created, and perhaps more importantly, known to motivated and talented lawyers, it becomes difficult to remove or limit that right. Unlike in 1976, when only 15 percent of in-house counsel in Fortune 1000 firms were "familiar with" ICSID,[23] today it is likely that a higher proportion of in-house counsel are aware of investor–state arbitration.[24] Many law firms have built practices that include investor–state arbitration, and these practices must find cases in order to sustain themselves. The density of law firms active in investor–state arbitration is a change from previous decades, when investor–state arbitration was dominated by a handful of firms with one firm, Coudert Brothers, acing in almost half the ICSID cases during the 1980s.[25] As these actors have strengthened their capacity to act in investor–state arbitration, they have also stabilized the institution and made it more difficult to change or exit.

SETUP, INTERACTION, AND COGNITIVE EFFECTS OF INVESTOR–STATE ARBITRATION

The positive feedback effects for law firms are relatively straightforward: by bringing cases, and especially by winning cases, law firms and other private actors develop into a constituency with a strong interest in the maintenance of investor–state arbitration. There are also other feedback effects at work for other actors, notably government officials. Feedback effects for government officials are more complex, and only brief examples will be introduced here, which illustrate setup, interaction, and cognitive effects of investor–state arbitration.[26]

Setup costs occur when an institution, once created, sets in motion processes that encourage its continuance and discourage change.[27] Here I argue that government officials have relatively strong incentives to negotiate investment

[23] Ryans and Baker (1976: 70) asked, "Are you familiar with the Convention on the Settlement of Investment Disputes?" Apart from the 15 percent of respondents that were familiar with it, 81 percent reported that they were not and the rest did not give an answer.

[24] However, Yackee (2010) found that many in-house legal counsel in American multinationals are not familiar with investment treaties.

[25] Parra 2017: 124.

[26] Elaborated in the section on 'Gradual Institutional Development', Chapter one of this volume.

[27] Zürn (2016: 205–15) and elaborated in Chapter one.

treaties initially, but little or no corresponding incentive to seek renegotiation. Officials get positive feedback from negotiating investment treaties: it can serve as a tangible marker of accomplishment during their tenure as ambassador or in another office, it is an indicator of good relations between two governments, and it may also please other audiences, such as their own firms, foreign firms, or even international organizations.[28]

Renegotiation, on the other hand, may sound to officials like a technical task with little upside that poses a risk of creating tensions with the treaty partner. Additionally, the treaty partner might refuse to negotiate, or officials, especially from capacity-constrained governments, may be conscious of their country or government's reputation and not want to take any action that gives the impression that they are disregarding their commitments under international law. These hurdles do not make it impossible to renegotiate; rather, they mean that it takes something notable—a large, visible claim, for instance—for governments to overcome the setup costs and pursue renegotiation.

Another aspect of setup costs is that positive feedback accrues to officials in the ministry responsible for negotiating treaties, while it is often officials in a different ministry that are left to respond to cases and pay awards. The officials that negotiate treaties may not even be informed when their country becomes a respondent. This is more likely in capacity-constrained countries, but occurs elsewhere. In one European country, for instance, the officials responsible for investment treaty arbitration, if they had the power to do so, would cease treaty negotiation and let their existing treaties expire, but these expert officials have almost no communication with officials in the ministry that negotiates investment treaties. That ministry is still exploring further negotiations, for reasons that "have little to do with the content of the treaties."[29] Updating treaty content or learning based on previous cases, as seen in the US practice, is the exception.[30] This absence of learning is even more prevalent when countries use outside counsel. In these instances, the negative feedback of losing cases may not have much impact on officials; the ministry that signs investment treaties may be even less affected by feedback from cases than from the positive feedback they receive from signing new treaties.

Interaction effects occur when configurations of complementary institutions are built; when institutions have interlocking qualities, it can help to sustain and stabilize all the components. A major interaction effect is the relationship between bilateral investment treaties and investor–state arbitration: if this interaction had not occurred then investor–state arbitration would

[28] Poulsen (2015) discusses the rewards that officials receive in much greater detail.

[29] Interview with country official. The division between "negotiating ministry" and "respondent ministry" emerged in several interviews with officials from different regions.

[30] On US learning, see Menaker (2004).

look very different today. Here I use two smaller developments to illustrate interaction effects in investor–state arbitration: the ICSID Additional Facility and appointing authority. Both of these developments seemed minor when they emerged, but over time they were tied into other institutional developments and became important in spreading investor–state arbitration.

When the ICSID Additional Facility came into being in the late 1970s, its framers were certainly not anticipating NAFTA. Yet this interaction between the ICSID Additional Facility and NAFTA (and other treaties) has enhanced the stability of investor–state arbitration. When the Additional Facility was initially proposed, a core purpose was to help governments renegotiate outdated concession contracts: Broches suggested that ICSID's mandate be broadened so it could administer fact-finding proceedings, which would be useful "in connection with the renegotiation by parties of investment agreements."[31] During the subsequent year, the contract renegotiation element was dropped from the proposal.[32] The Additional Facility was also initially proposed as temporary, but has become permanent, and has enabled governments that are not ICSID member states, like Mexico and Canada (until 2013), to provide access to the Additional Facility in their treaties and become parties in arbitrations organized by ICSID. These interactions have stabilized investor–state arbitration.

Appointing authority is another seemingly small development, but it has enabled more interaction between arbitral organizations and states that had opposed the ICSID Convention; over time these interactions have stabilized investor–state arbitration. Appointing authority has old roots in arbitration, but first appeared in investor–state arbitration in the 1970 ICSID Annual Report, which explained that parties could designate the Secretary General as appointing authority, even if the arbitration was not held under the auspices of ICSID.[33] The impact of appointing authority took decades to develop, but it slowly, and with substantial help from the UNCITRAL Arbitration Rules,[34] brought countries that had opposed the ICSID Convention into the realm of ICSID arbitration. Writing as Secretary General in 1991, Shihata pointed out:

[31] ICSID Tenth Annual Meeting: Annex.

[32] Yet Parra (2012: 142) notes, "Broches was and would remain ardently in favor of such renegotiation where necessary to restore the economic equilibrium of long-term agreements in light of changed circumstances." See also Broches (1974 [1995]: 519), in which he discusses inequitable agreements.

[33] ICSID Fourth Annual Report: 5. Echoing the advance consent advocacy explored in Chapter six, the Report even suggested that parties "consult with the Centre before concluding such agreements and submit at least a draft of the disputes settlement procedure to it for comment" (Fourth Annual Report: 5). Parra (2012: 151) notes that the Report cited the ICJ as a precedent. The ICJ Statute does not mention appointing authority, but the President of the ICJ had long acted in this capacity.

[34] Article 6 of the UNCITRAL Arbitration Rules creates a need for an appointing authority. The UNCITRAL Rules were first released in 1976.

"A notable example of this [appointing authority] may be found in several recent guarantee agreements executed by Brazil, which is not a member of ICSID, in respect of loans to Brazilian public entities by a national of Canada [a Canadian bank], which is not a member of ICSID either."[35] Appointing authority also provided a useful way for arbitration organizations other than ICSID to acquaint themselves with potential customers. The PCA became a popular choice for appointing authority, and even issued model clauses specific to the UNCITRAL Arbitration Rules. ICSID did not issue model clauses but made its advisory services available and became a common choice for appointing authority.[36] Appointing authority provided another interaction between treaties and arbitration, which stabilized and helped investor–state arbitration grow wider and more diffuse.

Cognitive effects occur when actors adapt their mindsets, expectations, and behavior in response to an institution; actors become accustomed to the existence of an institution. There are many potential cognitive effects that could be identified in the rise of investor–state arbitration, but here I focus on sunset clauses, also known as survival clauses, an aspect of investor–state arbitration that actors have become accustomed to and carry forward, even where their original purpose does not hold. Sunset clauses appear in most investment treaties, and they extend the treaty's provisions if the treaty is terminated. For instance, when Indonesia terminated its treaty with the Netherlands on July 30, 2015, the government did so knowing that the treaty protections would remain in force until July 30, 2030, due to a fifteen-year sunset clause in the treaty.

Sunset clauses do not appear in any other field of international law. These clauses appeared in the first German and Swiss investment treaties, and then, like many provisions, have been copied in hundreds of investment treaties. The initial justification, as expressed by one of the officials responsible for drafting the first Swiss treaty, was that sunset clauses were important for investors making long-term, capital-intense investments. In 1962, this official explained that: "With regard to underdeveloped countries, which are chiefly interested in long-term investments, this protective period [extending protection for fifteen years after termination] may be a very important consideration because it provides inducement for investors to make long-term investments despite the political risks involved."[37] For this logic to work, it is necessary to assume that potential investors scour the text of the relevant treaty for sunset clauses before investing. Even in Switzerland at that time, when investor groups were comparatively well informed by their government about treaty provisions, this was a strong assumption. With the passage of time and in

[35] Shihata 1991: 297, footnote 34. See also Delaume 1983: 13. [36] Parra 2012: 152.

[37] "Protection of Investments in International Law, by Dr. E. Diez, Head of the Legal Service of the Swiss Foreign Office," US Government translation of a lecture delivered (in German) before the Swiss Society of International Law, Berne, November 24, 1962. CH C.41.124.5.2.

other countries, the likely validity of this assumption has become weaker. It is extremely unlikely that many investors consider sunset clauses in an investment treaty before they invest.

More importantly, it is not clear what proportion of the investment covered by investment treaties today is "long-term" or resembles the type of investment this official believed was in the interest of "underdeveloped countries." Yet there is no countervailing obligation that an investor must meet to be covered by a sunset clause: today any investor, no matter how short term their investment, is automatically extended the privileges of a sunset clause. Sunset clauses are likely not relevant for the vast majority of foreign investments made today. Yet they persist.

Cognitive effects have perpetuated a belief that investment treaties, alone out of the instruments of international law, need sunset clauses. Where conventional accounts would expect a widespread move away from sunset clauses given their outdated justification, potential to be costly for governments, and limited benefits, only a few countries, recently and hesitantly, have adjusted their approach to sunset clauses. The European Commission has taken several actions, notably initiating infringement proceedings against five member states over the termination of intra-EU BITs,[38] which have prompted discussions about how governments can extinguish sunset clauses as part of their actions to terminate a treaty mutually.[39] The 2015 Indian Model treaty lowered sunset clauses to five years[40] and flipped the presumption of renewal, letting the treaty lapse automatically after ten years, unless the parties agree in writing to renew it.[41] This is the exception to the general rule that sunset clauses persist: for instance, the US and Colombian model BITs have ten-year sunset clauses[42] while Canada and Norway provide fifteen years.[43] There is a strong cognitive effect that sunset clauses are needed. Cognitive effects, interaction effects and setup costs have all served to stabilize and expand investor–state arbitration.

COMPETITIVE DYNAMICS THAT FURTHER STABILIZE INVESTOR–STATE ARBITRATION

There is another dynamic generated by previous developments and their positive feedback that further stabilizes investor–state arbitration: competition.

[38] Discussed in Dahlquist, Lenk, and Rönnelid (2016).
[39] Voon, Mitchell, and Munro 2014; Harrison (2012).
[40] Article 38.3 of the India model BIT (2015).
[41] Article 38.2 of the India model BIT (2015).
[42] Article 22.3 of the US model BIT. Article XIII:3 of the Colombia model BIT.
[43] Article 42.4 of the Canada model BIT; Article 34.2 of the Norway model BIT.

In this section, I suggest that competition between arbitration secretariats and competition between jurisdictions—in addition to competition between law firms—serves to stabilize the institution. The decentralized structure of investor–state arbitration, where treaties or contracts usually give potential claimants and their counsel choices about where to take their cases, generates competition between arbitration organizations and jurisdictions.

Many investment treaties provide a menu of options for investor–state arbitration, enabling claimants to choose between a list of arbitration organizations. ICSID, PCA, ICC, SCC, Singapore International Arbitration Centre, the London Court of International Arbitration, and a number of other centers can administer investor–state arbitrations. ICSID and the PCA are interstate organizations, while the others are private organizations. Governments are not their "principals." Furthermore, insofar as organizations seek to have cases filed with them, they are likely to be responsive to the actors bringing cases, mainly investors and their counsel. An arbitral organization can market itself as, for instance, cheaper, faster, or less transparent, in order to convince a party (or their counsel) to file a claim there instead of with other organizations that are eligible to administer the same case. As a recent survey of commercial and investor–state arbitration practitioners noted, "an institution's reputation and recognition is essential to its commercial appeal. Respondents will select an institution because of its reputation and their previous experiences of that institution."[44] Arbitration organizations can also compete or market themselves at the moment of treaty drafting: an organization has a better chance of being selected if they appear in treaty text.

Competitive dynamics are also at play between jurisdictions looking to host arbitrations.[45] Jurisdictions can be the seat of the arbitration and they can be the venue: the "seat" determines which national laws and courts have supervisory jurisdiction, while the "venue" is the physical location. The seat and venue may not be the same, and an arbitration may have more than one venue. The five "most preferred and widely used seats" for commercial and investor–state arbitration are London, Paris, Hong Kong, Singapore, and Geneva.[46] There are reasons why jurisdictions would compete to be the seat or the venue: both could potentially be lucrative for a city or country. This leads governments to update or modify regulations to make themselves arbitration-friendly. For instance, a recent article in the Global Arbitration Review touts the reforms Saudi Arabia is making to become an arbitration-friendly jurisdiction:

> Saudi Arabia was the first country in the Arab world to adopt a comprehensive arbitration law in 1983, recognising the need for fast, effective commercial

[44] White and Case 2015: 2.
[45] I thank Maxim Usynin for bringing this to my attention.
[46] White and Case 2015: 2.

> dispute resolution. Now, says Majed Al Rasheed of the Saudi Centre for Commercial Arbitration, developments in the law and regulations are transforming the jurisdiction into one that is truly arbitration-friendly.[47]

Much of this competition between jurisdictions is to lure commercial arbitration cases, which are more numerous, but it also affects, and stabilizes, investor–state arbitration.

Competitive dynamics and perceptions of competition are exacerbated by the lack of a deliberative hub in investor–state arbitration. Competition without a multilateral place for monitoring makes it more difficult for governments to be informed or exert control. The lack of a geographical hub in which to share information or coordinate reform likely affects capacity-constrained states most. While officials from OECD states meet regularly to discuss investment issues in Paris, non-OECD states have largely lacked a consistent, regular place to meet and discuss.[48] This has several consequences. One with particular relevance in investment is that standing multilateral deliberations, even if they are just consultative, create opportunities for better monitoring, capacity-building, and potentially reform. The ICSID Administrative Council, which has the same one-state, one-vote system as the UN General Assembly, has a limited mandate and meetings have often been poorly attended. Paradoxically, while the absence of a multilateral, deliberative hub has stymied monitoring and capacity-building, the competitive dynamics that exist instead have stabilized and led to the expansion of investor–state arbitration.

CONCLUSION

Governments have done little to exit investor–state arbitration, despite many officials and observers believing that it has underdelivered investment and served up costly litigation instead. This brief chapter sets out the range of actions that governments can take to exit or renegotiate the access that they have provided to investor–state arbitration. Exiting from investor–state arbitration is difficult legally and technically—exiting and renegotiating raise thorny legal questions.

Yet the legal complexities of exit are not the only reason why governments have not exited or renegotiated in large numbers. This chapter identifies several ways in which feedback processes have made it more difficult for governments to exit or change investor–state arbitration. Through positive

47 “Saudi Strides,” April 11 2017.

48 With the exception of the UN Centre on Transnational Corporations from 1974 to 1993 (Sauvant 2015).

feedback in the form of revenue and prestige, a constituency of law firms, investors, and interest groups has developed that has expanded and stabilized the institution of investor–state arbitration. Additional positive feedback is generated by setup, interaction, and cognitive effects, all of which have operated to stabilize investor–state arbitration.

Governments do not inherit blank slates: their ability to make reforms or change course is limited by previous decisions. Even when some officials within a government would like to renegotiate or rescind access to investor–state arbitration, they face obstacles to making those changes. Those obstacles or challenges include: ministries pursuing different priorities, bureaucratic obstacles to dealing with low-probability risks, the high transaction costs of renegotiating hundreds of treaties and contracts, reputational fear that they will be perceived as disregarding international legal obligations, and a lack of bilateral bargaining power. Some of these obstacles may be more serious in capacity-constrained countries: for instance, reputational concerns may not affect the European Commission, but may paralyze a small ministry in a poor country. All of these factors can impede a government's exit or renegotiation of the access to investor–state arbitration that it has provided, even when some officials within the government would like to renegotiate or rescind that access. These obstacles, and a well-resourced non-state constituency, are some of the reasons why exit is hard and institutions persist even when they generate unintended consequences for the states that created them.

Conclusion

The introduction posed one central question. What explains the rise of investor–state arbitration? Subsequent chapters probed the incremental process by which a proposal that British officials called "rather a strange idea on the Bank's part"[1] became contemporary investor–state arbitration. The institution of investor–state arbitration had a centralized start inside the World Bank, where the ICSID Convention emerged and where the idea to insert access to arbitration into investment treaties originated. Despite these centralized origins, investor–state arbitration has never had just one purpose. It was not the product of foreign investors demanding standing and a new way to resolve disputes: in fact, there was little interest from investors for decades. Similarly, officials from capital-exporting governments in the 1960s did not believe investor–state arbitration was the best way to protect investment, nor an effective way to facilitate additional investment, nor the most direct way to develop international investment law. Yet over time and for different audiences, investor–state arbitration would be imbued with all these purposes as well as new ones, for instance, being a way to lock in liberalization reforms, or more recently, being a way to enforce labor standards or corporate social responsibility norms. Investor–state arbitration has always been an amalgam, a multipurpose composite that various actors—state and non-state actors alike—have reinvented and repurposed.

Do any of this book's findings provide lessons that are relevant for contemporary officials? Officials dealing with investor–state arbitration today operate in a maelstrom of controversy, with the institution embodying the worst fears of those concerned about runaway globalization. As the introduction mentioned, even actors generally in favor of globalization scorn investor–state arbitration: the European Trade Commissioner called ISDS "the most toxic acronym in Europe"[2] and *The Economist* described it as a way to

[1] Note from Stuart Milner-Barry, February 1, 1962, subject: "Arbitration Centre." UK T 312/251.

[2] See introduction; Commission Cecilia Malmström said this in Washington DC (Palmer 2015) and at the European Parliament (Ardhe 2015).

"convince the public that international trade agreements are a way to let multinational companies get rich at the expense of ordinary people."[3] The odds seem stacked against the survival of investor–state arbitration. Yet one of the overarching lessons from this book is that institutions persist. Even when their initial rationale has largely disappeared and even when they generate unintended consequences, there are reasons to believe actors will pursue transformative institutional change gradually, for instance through layering or conversion, instead of exit. Investor–state arbitration may change, and is changing, but is unlikely to disappear anytime soon.

Another feature of institutional persistence is that previous developments constrain and enable what can emerge in the present: this is especially evident with regard to the private–public tension in investor–state arbitration. All of the visions outlined for investor–state arbitration's future define themselves in terms of the clash between public and private paradigms—a clash created by a small group of drafters over fifty years ago. As Chapter four mentioned, the earliest versions of the ICSID Convention emerged in a drafting committee of the American Bar Association; the experts in this committee consciously blended public international law (for instance, drawing from the Statute of the ICJ) and private law (for instance, drawing from the ICC Rules on Conciliation and Arbitration). This hybrid vision created intersections and tensions that have animated scholarly debates for years.[4] The terms of today's debate, in which many propose to pull investor–state arbitration in a more "public" direction, were set by developments that occurred decades ago.

A public investment court is not a new idea. Before he created ICSID, Aron Broches recognized that a permanent "public" court would deliver more consistent jurisprudence and better legal outcomes. He believed the political foundations for such a court were absent. Speaking in 1962, he told an audience of lawyers:

> You will also note that I envisage arbitral tribunals as composed on an ad hoc basis, rather than a standing tribunal with fixed membership. It is sometimes argued in favor of the latter that it would permit the gradual development of a body of case law by a group, in essence a court, which would have continuity. But this advantage would be outweighed by far by the political complications involved in determining the composition of such a tribunal. In my own view these complications might well prove an insurmountable obstacle.[5]

[3] *The Economist* 2014.

[4] Alvarez 2011, 2016; De Brabandere 2014; Douglas 2003; Kulick 2012; Maupin 2013; Mills 2011; Montt 2009; Roberts 2010, 2013, 2015, 2015; Schill 2009(b); Thompson 2011; Tienhaara 2009; Vadi 2016; Van Harten 2007.

[5] "The Need for a Permanent Arbitral Tribunal" Address by A. Broches, June 13, 1962. WB Folder 1651418.

Over fifty years later, Broches may still be right: international legal bodies rest on political foundations, and governments may not be ready to make the required compromises and sacrifices. Creating a court requires negotiated agreement on substantive law, extensive investment in building capacity and facilitating compliance, as well as reckoning with equality—deciding if foreigners and citizens should be equal before the law, or if foreigners need special rights. In the remainder of this chapter, I outline public and private ideal types and elaborate on the political decisions required for the public vision to be realized. Since governments are unlikely to make the compromises necessary for a "public" vision to be fully realized, I argue a "private" system may, paradoxically, be the best way to serve public interests.

THE "FULLY PUBLIC" VISION OF THE FUTURE

The fullest "public" vision for investor–state arbitration involves a hierarchical legal system along the lines of the Court of Justice of the EU (CJEU).[6] In this vision, investor–state arbitration or an investment court system is best conceptualized as a means of judicial review.[7] There would be judicial dialogue between constitutional courts and the supranational body, as in the CJEU, and a preliminary reference procedure, as in the CJEU. While the CJEU is an alluring model for rectifying what many perceive as the inconsistencies and untenable outcomes of investor–state arbitration, the vision of transforming investor–state arbitration into the CJEU papers over fundamental differences between these two legal systems. Here I enumerate three.

1. Agreement on Substantive Law

The CJEU interprets European Union law, which developed from founding treaties. There is no comparable agreement in investment law. To suggest the 1962 OECD Draft as a founding document overlooks the reality that at no point could even a small group of states with similar investment protection interests agree to support the Draft: the OECD could not even pass a *non-binding* resolution endorsing the principles of the Draft unanimously.

[6] Schill (2017) argues investor–state arbitration should "draw inspiration" from the relationship between constitutional courts and the CJEU. This is a step further than his earlier scholarship, but a logical progression from it.

[7] Schill (2009b: 10–17) argues we should see ISDS as a form of judicial, administrative, or constitutional review.

Historically, at the center of investor–state arbitration's rise is a studied avoidance of specifying which law, or whose law, would apply. Of the proposal to create ICSID, Broches wrote: "The proposals are modest in the sense of being limited to procedure and because of their optional nature. But I have no doubt that their adoption would constitute a significant step forward toward the establishment of the Rule of Law in international investment."[8] Which or whose rule of law would the proposal help establish? The proposal and its framers were careful not to specify. Experts, governments, and civil society campaigners today ask questions in a context that Broches and other framers of ICSID could not have anticipated. Yet more often than not, they ask the same question that hounded ICSID's framers: what law, whose law, should govern international investment? In 1969, Schwarzenberger argued that ICSID's lack of substance leads right back to debates about substance: "In a circuitous way, the IBRD Convention on Investment Disputes of 1965 led back to the issue the draftsmen of the IBRD Convention had tried hard to evade: the substantive rules of international law governing the protection of foreign property."[9] Investor–state arbitration is a flexible system of dispute resolution that can be appended to any substantive rules. Formally, it does not have any founding treaties or substantive principles. Foreign investment is intrusive; it has always raised sensitive questions about domestic policy autonomy and always will. The difficulty of reaching negotiated agreement on substantive investment principles to serve as foundations for a multilateral, public system is not to be underestimated.

2. Extensive Capacity Building and Compliance Support

There is an extensive and well-funded institutional apparatus to increase states' ability to comply with European Union law. The EU uses both cooperative and coercive measures to improve states' capacity and incentives for compliance. Enforcement and management are two logics of compliance: the first argues that compliance problems are best remedied through sanctions, while the latter emphasizes that non-compliance often results from capacity limitations and rule ambiguity. The CJEU system combines these logics into a ladder of steps that facilitate compliance with EU law: first there is preventative capacity building and rule clarification; second, forms of monitoring that enhance the transparency of state behavior and expose violators; third, a legal system that further clarifies existing rules; and deterrent sanctions as a final measure.[10]

Investor–state arbitration, in contrast, has only enforcement—and enforcement that can be unpredictable and inconsistent, with cases on similar facts

[8] Broches [1963] 1995: 163.
[9] Schwarzenberger 1969: 153.
[10] Tallberg 2003: 143.

reaching opposite conclusions.[11] Historically, there has been no capacity building, no rule clarification, and no monitoring that enhances the transparency of state behavior. For these reasons, with the current institutional design, claims that investor–state arbitration contributes to "the rule of law" are hollow. Investor–state arbitration has always been separate from other World Bank efforts to improve the rule of law.[12] Investor–state arbitration was not created to strengthen local courts; it was created to enable foreign investors to avoid them. Massoud shows how authoritarian regimes benefit from embracing international arbitration, because it ensures that foreign investment disputes are resolved outside of domestic purview, obviating the need for nondemocratic states to create independent courts.[13] Arbitration subverts the development of domestic legal institutions and domestic rule of law.[14]

The prerequisites of a "public" system include agreement on substantive law as well as resources devoted to building capacity and supporting compliance. History suggests little grounds for optimism on this point: the UN Centre on Transnational Corporations, the first and likely most effective provider of technical assistance on legal issues related to foreign investment, was unceremoniously extinguished by the US and UK governments.[15]

3. Equality

All individuals have equal procedural rights before the CJEU. The same is not true of investor–state arbitration: the premise of investor–state arbitration is that foreigners have a procedural right that citizens do not have. As Lowe observes, "the consequence is plain and inescapable. BITs give foreign investors wider rights than nationals possess."[16]

To move toward a full "public law" system, then, all governments would need to provide access to investor–state arbitration in their domestic law. Today, roughly forty of the poorest countries in the world provide foreigners, and only foreigners, with access to investor–state arbitration in their domestic law. Would wealthier countries, for instance the US and Germany, agree to provide foreigners—and only foreigners—with direct access to arbitration in their domestic law? This would mean that citizens or companies with dual nationality have access to arbitration, but citizens or companies without dual

11 Waibel 2007. 12 Carothers 2006. 13 Massoud 2014.

14 Recent cases involving denial of justice claims are a partial refutation of this assertion, but they are atypical.

15 Sauvant 2015: 53–9.

16 Lowe 2007: 49. This statement, and any discussion of equality, brings us back to the Calvo Doctrine, which is, at its core, about equality before the law (Montt 2009). Here again, Wälde's (1996) observation that traditional capital-exporters like the US and Germany adhere to the Calvo Doctrine when they are respondents is still relevant.

nationality do not.[17] Or would these governments agree to expand access so that their own citizens as well as foreigners would have direct access to international arbitration?[18] It is difficult to imagine the American or German government agreeing to either of these situations. Yet these are the kind of concessions that underlie the CJEU, and would be required in order for equality to exist in investor–state arbitration.

The challenges inherent in moving toward a "fully public" system should not be underestimated. A system like the CJEU requires agreement—negotiated agreement, in founding treaties—on substantive law. It requires member states to be willing to commit substantial resources to capacity building and other steps that facilitate compliance and support local institutions, including courts. This is a profoundly different logic to investor–state arbitration, which was created to enable particular actors to avoid local courts. Perhaps the most vexing is equality. Should foreigners and citizens have equal procedural rights? For investment law to become a fully public system, governments must reckon with this question.

THE "FULLY PRIVATE" VISION OF THE FUTURE

The opposing vision is investor–state arbitration moving toward a fully "private" system, by which I mean no longer providing consent in investment treaties or domestic law. While not as much has been written exploring this direction of travel, there are reasons to believe that public interest concerns could be ameliorated by a move in this direction, without imperiling investment protection. Here I advance three benefits of this move.

1. More Predictable, Limited Liability

The most fundamental change of moving toward a private system is for investor–state arbitration to be removed from investment treaties and domestic law. Access to investor–state arbitration could be provided, as it was before Broches and ICSID, in contracts between investors and states. Moving to a contract-based system is not the same as doing away with the procedural right to arbitration: if a particular investor were concerned about access to arbitration, then they could secure this access in a contract with the government.

[17] Defining who is "foreign" enough has long been a vexing question; Parra (2017: 52–3) summarizes the "considerable debate" on this topic at the consultative conferences.

[18] It is, of course, common for governments like the US or Germany (or subnational entities) to be respondents in their own courts over property claims or other investment-related issues.

Moving to contract-based arbitration enables governments to make their potential liability more predictable. It also gives states and investors the opportunity to reach a more complete contract and provide more specific guidance to arbitrators, if a dispute arises and does go to arbitration. International actors could still play a useful role building capacity and sharing best practices in contract negotiation and renegotiation. Additionally, while moving to a contract-based system is commonly associated with a move toward confidentiality and away from transparency, this need not be the case. Governments can decide to submit their contracts to international or national repositories or otherwise make them publicly available, perhaps with names redacted.[19] Contracts by themselves are not necessarily confidential, nor are contract-based arbitrations necessarily more confidential than treaty-based arbitrations.

2. Better Defining Political Risks

A core rationale for investor–state arbitration is that foreigners need a special procedural right because they face additional, political risks that nationals do not face. Arbitration is not the only, nor necessarily the best way for investors to manage political risks, however. Here again, the way governments helped their investors manage political risks before Broches and ICSID suggest a different way forward. As Chapter three mentioned, the early German and Swiss investment treaties set out substantive standards, and then provided for dispute resolution through political risk insurance.

Political risk insurance has continued operating in parallel to investor–state arbitration, and provides an alternative way to identify state behaviors that deserve compensation. What if international law—for instance the Fair and Equitable Treatment provision—were defined by the actions that capital-exporting governments are willing to compensate their investors for in a political risk insurance claim? It is a provocative but revealing question: the political risk insurance written by capital-exporting governments considers a much smaller range of behaviors worthy of compensation than most arbitral tribunals.

3. Selecting More Appropriate Institutional Designs

Historically, governments provided consent to investment dispute resolution retrospectively, after a dispute arose. In certain situations, retrospective consent may lead to more appropriate institutional design. A common way for

[19] For instance, www.resourcecontracts.org already provides a repository of publicly available investment contracts and is funded in part by the World Bank.

investment disputes to arise is for many claims to emerge out of one situation, for instance, Argentina during their economic emergency, Spain's renewables legislation, Russia's invasion of Crimea, or civil conflict in Libya. Investment arbitration is suboptimal for this situation: the outcomes it generates (and the size of awards) will likely be inconsistent, even when cases present virtually identical facts. These inconsistent awards create a costly domestic political nightmare for the respondent government. Other institutional designs are far better suited to this situation: a claims commission, for instance, could be constituted that would likely generate more consistent decisions, more consistent compensation amounts, and more orderly payment of awards.

INSTITUTIONAL PERSISTENCE

The public and private visions outlined in this section are ideal types, and relatively radical changes to contemporary investor–state arbitration are required for either of these visions to be realized. This book shows that radical changes are rare. Existing structures endure, even if slowly, over time, they are put to new purposes or transformed through layering. Far more likely than radical revisions to investor–state arbitration are more incremental changes, perhaps in the form of carve-outs, interpretive committees, or transparency provisions. These accumulating incremental changes also intersect with larger proposals, like an investment court system, and changing external factors, such as the increasing reciprocity of investment flows. Change does not necessarily undermine institutional stability, however. The rise of investor–state arbitration occurred over several decades, generating processes that have expanded, stabilized, and transformed the institution. Even though investor–state arbitration has generated unintended consequences for governments, it is likely to persist.

Archives

Note: Every archival document cited in the book is available (where copyright permits) as a PDF in the Qualitative Data Repository (https://qdr.syr.edu/). Search for the title of this book in the Repository, then the documents are available as PDFs, sorted by the chapter in which they were cited.

AVL: Axis Victims League

Box 2 (3/9): Publication by various institutions and organizations on restitution matters. 1942–66. https://archive.org/details/axisvictimsleague.

CH: Bundesarchiv Bern (Swiss Federal Archive)

C.41.124.5.1. Übereinkommen zur Beilegung von Investitionsstreitigkeiten zwischen Staaten und Angehörigen anderer Staaten. Weltbank. Multilateraler Investitionsschutz. (Agreement to Mediation of Investment Disputes between States and Citizens of other States. World Bank. Multilateral Investment Protection). Split into 1964–7 and 1968–70.

C.41.124.5.2. Multilateraler Investitionsschutz (Multilateral Investment Protection).

C.41.124.5.3Investitionsschutz Industrie-Holding (Investment Protection Holding Company).1961–3.

DE: Bundesarchiv Koblenz (German Federal Archive)

B102/130141Behandlung von Kapitalanlagen in ausländischen Staaten, insbesondere bilaterale Vereinbarungen u. Landesgesetze (Treatment of Investment in Foreign Countries, Especially Bilateral Agreements). 1956–65.

B102/27082: Schutz privater Vermögensrechte im Ausland; Grundentwurf Investitionsschutzabkommen (Protection of Private Investments Abroad; Blueprint of an Investment Protection Agreement). 1958–60.

B102/47640: Errichtung eines internationalen Garantieinstituts für Kapitalanlagen im Ausland (Foundation of an International Guarantee Institute for Capital Investments Abroad). 1960–2.

B102/48464: Vermittlungs- u. Schiedsgerichtstätigkeit der Weltbank (Mediation and Arbitration Efforts of the World Bank). 1961–3.

IFZ: Institut für Zeitgeschichte (Institute for Contemporary History), Munich

135/45. Bestand: Heinz Krekeler, Signatur: ED 135, Bandnummer: 45, Titel: Deutsche Botschaft Washington, III, 1953–4.

NZ: National Archives of New Zealand

NZ 241 International Relations – Topics – Convention on the Settlement of Investment Disputes. 1970–85. Archives Reference Number ABVP W5218 7410, Record Number LEG 19-5-15, Box 241.

UK: National Archives of the United Kingdom, FCO (Foreign and Commonwealth Office)

FCO 48/145 World Bank convention on the settlement of investments disputes.

FCO 69/689 FRG's Investment Promotion and Protection Agreements.

FCO 69/740 Anglo-Swiss Investment Talks.

FCO 69/658 Investment Promotion and Protection Agreements: UK Policy and Proposed Agreements.

FCO 69/667 International Centre for the Settlement of Investment Disputes (ICSID).

FCO 69/671 Anglo-French Investment Talks.

FCO 69/662 Investment Promotion and Protection: Whitehall Meetings.

FCO 69/711 US Investment Promotion and Protection Agreement Policy.

UK T (Treasury)

T 236/5429 Proposed International Convention for the Protection of Foreign Investors.

T 236/5430-1 1958 Proposed International Convention for Protection of Foreign Investors.

T 236/5436 Proposed International Convention for Foreign Investors: Draft Convention prepared by Sir Hartley Shawcross and Other Lawyers.

T 312/1498 Papers leading up to the Investment Disputes Bill ratifying the International Bank for Reconstruction and Development convention for the settlement of investment disputes.

T 312/545 The Setting Up Under the IBRD Auspices of An Arbitration Centre for the Settlement of Investment Disputes (1962–3).

T 312/251 The Setting Up Under the IBRD Auspices of An Arbitration Centre for the Settlement of Investment Disputes, 27.06.61–10.04.62.

US: United States National Archives (US)

State Department (The National Archives at College Park, Maryland)

US 595219 Box 2. OECD Convention 61–64 and Investment Insurance. RG 59, Series: Records Relating to Economic Matters, 1953–75, Archives Identifier 595219.

US 595219 Box 4. OECD Convention 66–67. RG 59, Series: Records Relating to Economic Matters, 1953–75, Archives Identifier 595219.

US 595219 Box 11. DAC-9 Working Party on Private Investment 1968. RG 59, Series: Records Relating to Economic Matters, 1953–75, Archives Identifier 595219.

US 595219 Box 13. Foreign Property Convention. RG 59, Series: Records Relating to Economic Matters, 1953–75, Archives Identifier 595219.

US 2788553. Box 1 and Box 2. Records Relating to the Bilateral Investment Treaty, 1977–83. RG59, Series: Office of the Legal Advisor, Office of the Assistant Legal Advisor for African Affairs, Archives Identifier US 2788553.

Senate Committee on Foreign Relations (Center for Legislative Archives, Washington D.C.)

LA Bill S.3498. Legislative Bill Files of the Committee on Foreign Relations during the 89th Congress. RG 46, Series: Committee Papers, 1817–2011, Chapter 10: Records of the Committee on Foreign Relations, 1816–1988 [1947–68, 80th–90th Congress]. Archives Identifier 16893608.

US BPL: George Herbert Walker Bush Presidential Library

All "Memcons and Telcons" are available by date and name of participant here: https://bush41library.tamu.edu/archives/memcons-telcons.

US CPL: William Jefferson Clinton Presidential Library

Kantor Remarks ("History of USTR—Speeches & Testimony of Ambassador Kantor, 1993 [6],") https://clinton.presidentiallibraries.us/items/show/5752.

History of the US Department of the Treasury during the Clinton Administration, 1993–2001: https://clinton.presidentiallibraries.us/items/show/5345.

US FBI: Federal Bureau of Investigation

"Abs, Hermann J." RG 65, Series: FBI Records Declassified under the War Crimes Disclosure Acts, Class 105, File 056532, Section 001, Box 167. Note: Abs also has a Central Intelligence Agency (CIA) file, which was not consulted but has also been declassified as part of the Nazi War Crimes Interagency Working Group.

US TPL: Harry S. Truman Presidential Library

All available by name of document, in "The Oil Crisis in Iran, 1951–1953" collection here: https://www.trumanlibrary.org/whistlestop/study_collections/iran/index.php.

WB: World Bank Group Archives

Folder 1651418 – Broches, M. Aron – Articles and Speeches (1951–82) – Volume 1. http://pubdocs.worldbank.org/pubdocs/publicdoc/2014/5/162881399487976375/wbgarchives-1651418.pdf.

Folder 1651419 – Broches, M. Aron - Articles and Speeches (1951–82) – Volume 2. http://pubdocs.worldbank.org/pubdocs/publicdoc/2014/5/786671399487976649/wbgarchives-1651419.pdf.

Folder 1651420 – Broches, M. Aron – Articles and Speeches (1951–82) – Volume 3. http://pubdocs.worldbank.org/pubdocs/publicdoc/2014/5/173621399487976904/wbgarchives-1651420.pdf.

Folder 30171148 – President George D. Woods Speeches – 1964. (Not available online.)

Special Note on Archive Material from ICSID

Many ICSID documents (Annual Reports as well as ICSID/5, ICSID/6, ICSID/8C, D, and F) are now available from the Secretariat's website: https://icsid.worldbank.org/en/.

“Opening Remarks” and “Addresses” to the Annual Meetings of the Administrative Council, and “Press Releases” from these meetings are not available on the ICSID website. These documents can be accessed in many law libraries, as they were mailed with the Annual Reports for many years. Unless otherwise cited, I accessed these documents through personal collections or through the Bodleian Library, University of Oxford.

References

Abbott, Kenneth, Robert Keohane, Andrew Moravcsik, Anne-Marie Slaughter, and Duncan Snidal. 2000. "The Concept of Legalization." *International Organization* 54 (3): 17–35.

Abdelrehim, Neveen Talaat Hassan. 2010. "Oil Nationalisation and Managerial Disclosure: The Case of Anglo-Iranian Oil Company, 1933–1951." PhD diss., University of York.

Abs, Hermann. 1957. "The Safety of Capital." In *Private Investment: The Key to International Industrial Development; A Report of the San Francisco Conference, October 14–18, 1957*, edited by James Daniel. New York: McGraw-Hill.

Abs, Hermann. 1991. "How I Joined Deutsche Bank." Lecture held on the occasion of the Public Inaugural Meeting of the Historical Association of Deutsche Bank, Frankfurt am Main, June 12. http://www.bankgeschichte.de/en/docs/Abs_Vortrag_englisch(1).pdf.

Aisbett, Emma. 2009. "Bilateral Investment Treaties and Foreign Direct Investment: Correlation Versus Causation." In *The Effects of Treaties on Foreign Direct Investment*, edited by Karl Sauvant and Lisa Sachs. Oxford: Oxford University Press.

Allee, Todd, and Andrew Lugg. 2016. "Who Wrote the Rules for the Trans-Pacific Partnership?" *Research and Politics* July–September: 1–9.

Allee, Todd, and Clint Peinhardt. 2010. "Delegating Differences: Bilateral Investment Treaties and Bargaining over Dispute Resolution Provisions." *International Studies Quarterly* 54 (1): 1–26.

Allee, Todd, and Clint Peinhardt. 2011. "Contingent Credibility: The Impact of Investment Treaty Violations on Foreign Direct Investment." *International Organization* 65 (3): 401–32.

Allee, Todd, and Clint Peinhardt. 2014. "Evaluating Three Explanations for the Design of Bilateral Investment Treaties." *World Politics* 66 (1): 47–87.

Alschner, Wolfgang. Forthcoming. "The Impact of Investment Arbitration on Investment Treaty Design: Myth Versus Reality." *Yale Journal of International Law.*

Alter, Karen, Larry Helfer, and Jacqueline McAllister. 2013. "A New International Human Rights Court for West Africa: The ECOWAS Community Court of Justice." *American Journal of International Law* 107 (4): 737–79.

Alter, Karen, and Sophie Meunier. 2009. "The Politics of International Regime Complexity." *Perspectives on Politics* 7 (1): 13–24.

Alvarez, José E. 2011. *The Public International Law Regime Governing International Investment.* Leiden: Brill.

Alvarez, José E. 2016. "'Beware: Boundary Crossings'—A Critical Appraisal of Public Law Approaches to International Investment Law." *Journal of World Investment & Trade* 17 (2): 171–228.

Aminzade, Ronald. 2013. *Race, Nation, and Citizenship in Post-Colonial Africa: The Case of Tanzania.* Cambridge: Cambridge University Press.

Anghie, Antony. 2004. *Imperialism, Sovereignty, and the Making of International Law*. Cambridge: Cambridge University Press.

Ardhe, Christian. 2015. "Transatlantic Partnership: Why We Need It." *Svenskt Näringsliv*, February 5. http://www.svensktnaringsliv.se/english/transatlantic-partnership-why-we-need-it_609926.html.

Barnett, Michael, and Liv Coleman. 2005. "Designing Police: Interpol and the Study of Change in International Organizations." *International Studies Quarterly* 49 (4): 593–620.

Barnett, Michael, and Martha Finnemore. 1999. "The Politics, Power, and Pathologies of International Organizations." *International Organization* 53 (4): 699–732.

Barnett, Michael, and Martha Finnemore. 2004. *Rules for the World: International Organizations in Global Politics*. London: Cornell University Press.

Bauer, Michael, and Jörn Ege. 2016. "Bureaucratic Autonomy of International Organizations' Secretariats." *Journal of European Public Policy* 23 (7): 1019–37.

Beach, Derek. 2004. "The Unseen Hand in Treaty Reform Negotiations: The Role and Influence of the Council Secretariat." *Journal of European Public Policy* 11 (3): 408–39.

Bell, Bernard. 1990. Oral History, interview by John Lewis, Richard Webb, and Devesh Kapur. November 21. World Bank History Project, Brookings Institution.

Berge, Tarald Laudal, and Øyvind Stiansen. 2016. "Negotiating BITs with Models: The Power of Expertise." PluriCourts Research Paper No. 16–13.

Biermann, Frank, and Bernd Siebenhüner. 2009. "The Role and Relevance of International Bureaucracies: Setting the Stage." In *Managers of Global Change: The Influence of International Environmental Bureaucracies*, edited by Frank Biermann and Bernd Siebenhüner. Cambridge, MA: MIT Press.

Bonchiş, Claudia. 2015. "Victoraş Micula, moştenitorul imperiului European Drinks, i-a şocat pe turiştii de la malul mării. Şi-a folosit avionul pe post de trambulină (Victoras Micula, European Drinks empire heir, shocks tourists by using the seafront as trampoline)." August 18. *Adevarul* http://adevarul.ro/locale/oradea/victoras-micula-mostenitorul-imperiului-european-drinks-i-a-socat-turistii-malul-marii-Si-a-folosit-avionul-post-trambulina-1_55d378f0f5eaafab2cb33bb4/index.html.

Borchard, Edwin. 1929. "Responsibility of States for Damage Done in Their Territory to the Person or Property of Foreigners." *American Journal of International Law* (Special Supplement 23): 133–239.

Brandon, Michael. 1960. "Recent Measures to Improve the International Investment Climate." *Journal of Public Law* (9): 125–32.

Braithwaite, John, and Peter Drahos. 2000. *Global Business Regulation*. Cambridge: Cambridge University Press.

Broches, Aron. [1959] 1995. "International Legal Aspects of the Operations of the World Bank. Recueil des Cours." In *Selected Essays: World Bank, ICSID, and Other Subjects of Public and Private International Law*, edited by Aron Broches. London: Martinus Nijhoff.

Broches, Aron. [1963] 1995. "Settlement of Investment Disputes. Address to the World Conference on World Peace through Law." In *Selected Essays: World Bank, ICSID, and Other Subjects of Public and Private International Law*, edited by Aron Broches. London: Martinus Nijhoff.

Broches, Aron. [1966] 1995. "The Convention on the Settlement of Investment Disputes: Some Observations on Jurisdiction." In *Selected Essays: World Bank, ICSID, and Other Subjects of Public and Private International Law*, edited by Aron Broches. London: Martinus Nijhoff.

Broches, Aron. [1972] 1995. "The Convention on the Settlement of Investment Disputes between States and Nationals of Other States." In *Selected Essays: World Bank, ICSID, and Other Subjects of Public and Private International Law*, edited by Aron Broches. London: Martinus Nijhoff.

Broches, Aron. [1973] 1995. "The Dimension of Development. Statement at the First Session of the Centenary Celebration of the International Law Association, Brussels, 30 August 1973." In *Selected Essays: World Bank, ICSID, and Other Subjects of Public and Private International Law*, edited by Aron Broches. London: Martinus Nijhoff.

Broches, Aron. [1974] 1995. "Multi-National Corporations in World Development. Address to the Council on Religion and International Affairs." In *Selected Essays: World Bank, ICSID, and Other Subjects of Public and Private International Law*, edited by Aron Broches. London: Martinus Nijhoff.

Broches, Aron. [1982] 1995. "Bilateral Investment Protection Treaties and Arbitration of Investment Disputes." In *Selected Essays: World Bank, ICSID, and Other Subjects of Public and Private International Law*, edited by Aron Broches. London: Martinus Nijhoff.

Broches, Aron. 1984. Oral History, interview by Robert Asher. April 18. World Bank/IFC Archives, Oral History Program.

Broches, Aron. 1984. Oral History, interview by Robert Asher. May 23. World Bank/IFC Archives, Oral History Program.

Broches, Aron. 1985. Oral History, interview by Robert Oliver. November 7. World Bank/IFC Archives, Oral History Program.

Broches, Aron. 1990. Oral History, interview by John Lewis, Richard Webb, and Devesh Kapur. October 20. World Bank/IFC Archives, Oral History Program.

Broude, Tomer, Yoram Haftel, and Alexander Thompson. 2017. "Legitimation Through Renegotiation: Do States Seek More Regulatory Space in Their BITs?" Hebrew University of Jerusalem Legal Research Paper 17–1.

Brownlie, Ian. 1979. *Principles of Public International Law*. Third Edition. Oxford: Clarendon Press.

Brown, Robert. 2010. "Measuring Delegation." *The Review of International Organizations* 5 (2): 141–75.

Brown Weiss, Edith. 2002. "A Tribute to Paul Szasz." *Cornell International Law Journal* 35: 465–9.

Büthe, Tim, and Walter Mattli. 2011. *The New Global Rulers: The Privatization of Regulation in the World Economy*. Princeton: Princeton University Press.

Büthe, Tim, and Helen Milner. 2008. "The Politics of Foreign Direct Investment into Developing Countries: Increasing FDI through International Trade Agreements?" *American Journal of Political Science* 52 (4): 741–62.

Büthe, Tim, and Helen Milner. 2014. "Foreign Direct Investment and Institutional Diversity in Trade Agreements: Credibility, Commitment, and Economic Flows in the Developing World, 1971–2007." *World Politics* 66 (1): 88–122.

Campbell, Andrea Louise. 2003. *When Policies Make Citizens: Senior Political Activism and the American Welfare State*. Princeton: Princeton University Press.

Capoccia, Giovanni. 2016. "When Do Institutions Bite? Historical Institutionalism and the Politics of Institutional Change." *Comparative Political Studies* 49 (8): 1095–127.

Capoccia, Giovanni, and R. Daniel Kelemen. 2007. "The Study of Critical Junctures: Theory, Narrative and Counterfactuals in Historical Institutionalism." *World Politics* (59): 341–69.

Carothers, Thomas. 2006. *Promoting the Rule of Law Abroad: In Search of Knowledge*. Washington DC: Carnegie Endowment for International Peace.

Chayes, Abram, and Antonia Handler Chayes. 1995. *The New Sovereignty: Compliance with International Regulatory Agreements*. Cambridge, MA: Harvard University Press.

Chernykh, Yuliya. Forthcoming. "The Gust of Wind: The Unknown Role of Sir Elihu Lauterpacht in the Drafting of the Abs-Shawcross Draft Convention." In *International Investment Law and History*, edited by Rainer Hofmann, Stephan Schill, Christian Tams. Cheltenham: Edward Elgar.

Chilton, Adam. 2016. "The Political Motivations of the United States' Bilateral Investment Treaty Program." *Review of International Political Economy* 23 (4): 614–42.

Chwieroth, Jeffrey. 2007. "Neoliberal Economists and Capital Account Liberalization in Emerging Markets." *International Organization* 61 (2): 443–63.

Colen, Liesbeth, Damiaan Persyn, and Andrea Guariso. 2016. "Bilateral Investment Treaties and FDI: Does the Sector Matter?" *World Development* 83: 193–206.

Collier, John, and Vaughan Lowe. 1999. *The Settlement of Disputes in International Law: Institutions and Procedures*. Oxford: Oxford University Press.

Collier, Ruth Berins, and David Collier. 1991. *Shaping the Political Arena: Critical Junctures, the Labor Movement, and Regime Dynamics in Latin America*. Princeton: Princeton University Press.

"Comments: New Approach to US Enforcement of International Arbitration Awards 1968." *Duke Law Journal* 2: 258–82.

Commission, Jeffrey. 2007. "Precedent in Investment Treaty Arbitration: A Citation Analysis of a Developing Jurisprudence." *Journal of International Arbitration* 24 (2): 129–58.

Correa, Carlos. 2000. *Intellectual Property Rights, the WTO and Developing Countries: the TRIPs Agreement and Policy*. London: Zed Books and Third World Network.

Côté, Christine. 2014. "A chilling effect? The Impact of International Investment Agreements on National Regulatory Autonomy in the Areas of Health, Safety and the Environment." PhD diss., London School of Economics.

Crawford, James. 2004. Preface. In *Imperialism, Sovereignty, and the Making of International Law*, by Antony Anghie. Cambridge: Cambridge University Press.

Czichon, Eberhard. 1995. *Die Bank und die Macht. Hermann Josef Abs, die Deutsche Bank und die Politik*. Cologne: Papyrossa.

Dahlquist, Joel, Hannes Lenk, and Love Rönnelid. 2016. "The Infringement Proceedings Over Intra-EU Investment Treaties—An Analysis of the Case Against Sweden." *Swedish Institute for European Policy Studies: European Policy Analysis*, Issue 2016:4epa.

Deal, Michael. 1978. "United States Dependence on Caribbean Bauxite and the Formation of the International Bauxite Association." *Maryland Journal of International Law* 4 (1): 68–76.

De Brabandere, Eric. 2014. *Investment Treaty Arbitration as Public International Law.* Cambridge: Cambridge University Press.

De Gramont, Alexandre. 2006. "After the Water War: The Battle for Jurisdiction in Aguas Del Tunari, S.A. v Republic of Bolivia." *Transnational Dispute Management* 3 (5): 1–41.

Delaume, Georges. 1983. "The ICSID and the Banker." *International Financial Law Review* 2: 9–12.

Delaume, Georges. 2004. Oral History, interview by Robert Grathwol. May 10 and 17. World Bank Group Archives, Oral History Program.

Dezalay, Yves, and Bryant Garth. 1996. *Dealing in Virtue: Transnational Commercial Arbitration and the Construction of a Transnational Legal Order.* Chicago: University of Chicago Press.

Dolzer, Rudolf, and Yun-I Kim. 2013. "Germany." In *Commentaries on Selected Model Investment Treaties*, edited by Chester Brown. Oxford: Oxford University Press.

Dolzer, Rudolf, and Margerte Stevens. 1995. *Bilateral Investment Treaties.* The Hague: Martinus Nijhoff.

Douglas, Zachary. 2003. "The Hybrid Foundations of Investment Treaty Arbitration." *British Yearbook of International Law* (74): 151–289.

Drago, Luis. 1907. "State Loans in their Relation to International Policy." *American Journal of International Law* 1: 692–726.

Elkins, Zachary, Andrew Guzman, and Beth Simmons. 2006. "Competing for Capital: The Diffusion of Bilateral Investment Treaties, 1960–2000." *International Organization* 60 (4): 811–46.

Elm, Mostafa. 1992. *Oil, Power, and Principle: Iran's Oil Nationalization and Its Aftermath.* Syracuse, NY: Syracuse University Press.

Falleti, Tulia, and Julia Lynch. 2009. "Context and Causal Mechanisms in Political Analysis." *Comparative Political Studies* 42 (9): 1143–66.

Farrell, Henry, and Abraham Newman. 2010. "Making Global Markets: Historical Institutionalism in International Political Economy." *Review of International Political Economy* 17 (4): 609–38.

Fauchald, Ole Kristian. 2008. "The Legal Reasoning of ICSID Tribunals—an Empirical Analysis." *European Journal of International Law* 19 (2): 301–64.

Fearon, James. 1991. "Counterfactuals and Hypothesis Testing in Political Science." *World Politics* 43 (2): 169–95.

Finnegan, William. 2002. "Leasing the Rain." *The New Yorker.* April 8. http://www.newyorker.com/magazine/2002/04/08/leasing-the-rain.

Finnemore, Martha. 1993. "International Organizations as Teachers of Norms: The United Nations Educational, Scientific, and Cultural Organization and Science Policy." *International Organization* 47 (4): 565–97.

Fioretos, Orfeo. 2011. "Historical Institutionalism in International Relations." *International Organization* 65 (2): 367–99.

Fioretos, Orfeo. 2017. "Institutions and Time in International Relations." In *International Politics and Institutions in Time*, edited by Orfeo Fioretos. Oxford: Oxford University Press.

Fioretos, Orfeo, ed. 2017. *International Politics and Institutions in Time*. Oxford: Oxford University Press.

Fioretos, Orfeo, Tulia Falleti, and Adam Sheingate. 2016. "Historical Institutionalism in Political Science." In *The Oxford Handbook of Historical Institutionalism*, edited by Orfeo Fioretos, Tulia Falleti, and Adam Sheingate. Oxford: Oxford University Press.

Ford, Alan. 1954. *The Anglo-Iranian Oil Dispute, 1951–1952*. Los Angeles: University of California Press.

Franck, Susan. 2007. "Foreign Direct Investment, Investment Treaty Arbitration and the Rule of Law." *McGeorge Global Business and Development Law Journal* 19: 337–68.

Franck, Susan, Anne van Aaken, James Freda, Chris Guthrie, and Jeffrey Rachlinski. 2017. "Inside the Arbitrator's Mind." *Emory Law Journal* 66: 1117–77.

Gall, Lothar. 2005. *Der Bankier Hermann Josef Abs. Eine Biographie*. München: Beck.

Gallagher, Kevin. 2010. "Policy Space to Prevent and Mitigate Financial Crises in Trade and Investment Agreements." G-24 Discussion Paper Series. No. 58.

Garner, Robert. 1961. Oral History, interview by Robert Oliver. July 19. Oral History Research Office, Columbia University.

Gaukrodger, David, and Kathryn Gordon. 2012. "Investor-State Dispute Settlement: A Scoping Paper for the Investment Policy Community." OECD Working Papers on International Investment 2012/03.

George, Alexander, and Andrew Bennett. 2005. *Case Studies and Theory Development in the Social Sciences*. London: MIT Press.

Gertz, Geoffrey. 2016. "Commercial Diplomacy and Investment Protection: American Diplomatic Interventions to Protect US Assets Overseas Since 1990." DPhil diss., University of Oxford.

Goldhaber, Michael. 2010. "A Lifetime of Litigation—The Fall of Yukos." *Legal Week*. July 9.

Gordon, Kathryn, and Joachim Pohl. 2015. "Investment Treaties Over Time—Treaty Practice and Interpretation in a Changing World." OECD Working Papers on International Investment 2015/02.

Graves, Harold. 1973. "The Bank as International Mediator." In *World Bank Since Bretton Woods*, edited by Mason, Edward, and Robert Asher. Washington DC: Brookings Institute Press.

Gudgeon, K Scott. 1986. "United States Bilateral Investment Treaties: Comments on Their Origin, Purposes, and General Treatment Standards." *Berkeley Journal of International Law* 4 (1): 105–35.

Guillaume, Gilbert. 2011. "The Use of Precedent by International Judges and Arbitrators." *Journal of International Dispute Settlement* 2 (1): 5–23.

Guzman, Andrew. 1998. "Why LDCs Sign Treaties That Hurt Them: Explaining the Popularity of Bilateral Investment Treaties." *Virginia Journal of International Law* 38: 639–88.

Gwin, Catherine. 1997. "US Relations with the World Bank, 1945–1992." In *The World Bank: Its First Half Century*, edited by Devesh Kapur, John Lewis, and Richard Webb. Washington DC: Brookings Institution Press.

Gwynn, Maria. 2016. *Power in the International Investment Framework*. Basingstoke: Palgrave Macmillan.

Hacker, Jacob. 2004. "Privatizing Risk Without Privatizing the Welfare State: The Hidden Politics of Social Policy Retrenchment in the United States." *American Political Science Review* 98: 243–62.

Hacker, Jacob, and Paul Pierson. 2014. "After the 'Master Theory': Downs, Schattschneider, and the Rebirth of Policy-Focused Analysis." *Perspectives on Politics* 12(3): 643–62.

Hacker, Jacob, Paul Pierson, and Kathleen Thelen. 2015. "Drift and Conversion: Hidden Faces of Institutional Change." In *Advances in Comparative-Historical Analysis*, edited by James Mahoney and Kathleen Thelen. Cambridge: Cambridge University Press.

Haftel, Yoram. 2010. "Ratification Counts: US Investment Treaties and FDI Flows into Developing Countries." *The Review of International Political Economy* 17 (2): 348–77.

Haftel, Yoram, and Alexander Thompson. Forthcoming. "When Do States Renegotiate Investment Agreements? The Impact of Arbitration." *The Review of International Organizations*.

Hale, Thomas. 2015. *Between Interests and Law: The Politics of Commercial Disputes Under Public and Private Authority*. Cambridge: Cambridge University Press.

Hale, Thomas, David Held, and Kevin Young. 2013. *Gridlock: Why Global is Failing When We Need It Most*. Cambridge: Polity.

Hall, Peter. 2010. "Historical Institutionalism in Rationalist and Sociological Perspective." In *Explaining Institutional Change: Ambiguity, Agency, and Power*, edited by James Mahoney and Kathleen Thelen. Cambridge: Cambridge University Press.

Hallward-Driemeier, Mary. 2003. "Do Bilateral Investment Treaties Attract Foreign Direct Investment? Only a Bit . . . and They Could Bite." World Bank Development Research Group Policy Research Working Paper. Washington, DC.

Hanrieder, Tine, and Michael Zürn. 2017. "Reactive Sequences in Global Health Governance." In *International Politics and Institutions in Time*, edited by Orfeo Fioretos. Oxford: Oxford University Press.

Haralz, Jonas. 1997. "The International Finance Corporation." In *The World Bank: Its First Half Century*, edited by Devesh Kapur, John Lewis, and Richard Webb. Washington DC: Brookings Institute Press.

Harrison, James. 2012. "The Life and Death of BITs: Legal Issues Concerning Survival Clauses and the Termination of Investment Treaties." *Journal of World Investment & Trade* (13): 928–50.

Helleiner, Eric. 2014. *Forgotten Foundations of Bretton Woods: International Development and the Making of the Postwar Order*. Ithaca: Cornell University Press.

Hershey, Amos. 1907. "The Calvo and Drago Doctrines." *American Journal of International Law* 1: 26–45.

Higgins, Rosalyn. 1994. *Problems and Process: International Law and How We Use It*. Oxford: Clarendon Press.

Hogan, Frances. 1969. "The Hickenlooper Amendments: Peru's Seizure of International Petroleum Company as a Test Case." *Boston College Law Review* 11: 77–89.

Hood, Miriam. 1983. *Gunboat Diplomacy, 1895–1905: Great Power Pressure in Venezuela*. Second Edition. London: Allen and Unwin.

Hudson, Manley. 1930. "The First Conference for the Codification of International Law." *American Journal of International Law* 24: 447–66.

ICC. 1949. "International Code of Fair Treatment for Foreign Investments, drawn up by the ICC's Committees on Foreign Investments and Foreign Establishments." Reproduced in *International Investment Instruments: A Compendium*. Volume III, compiled by UNCTAD. UN Sales No E.96.II.A.11.

ICSID. 1970. *History of the Convention: Documents Concerning the Origin and the Formulation of the Convention in English* (Volume I and II, Parts 1 and 2). Washington DC: ICSID.

ICSID. 2016. "The ICSID Caseload—Statistics." Issue 2016–2. Washington DC: ICSID.

IDA. 1966. "1965–1966 Annual Report World Bank and IDA." Washington DC: World Bank.

Ikenberry, G John. 1992. "A World Economy Restored: Expert Consensus and the Anglo-American Postwar Settlement." *International Organization* 46 (1): 289–321.

ILA. 1948. "Draft Statutes of the Arbitral Tribunal for Foreign Investment and of the Foreign Investments Court." Reproduced in *International Investment Instruments: A Compendium. Volume III*, compiled by UNCTAD. UN Sales No E.96.II.A.11.

Iliff, William. 1961. Oral History, interview by Robert Oliver. August 12 and 16. Oral History Research Office, Columbia University.

Institutul National de Statistica. 2017. "Earnings—since 1991, the monthly series." http://www.insse.ro/cms/en/content/earnings-1991-monthly-series.

James, Harold. 2001. *The Deutsche Bank and the Nazi Economic War against the Jews: The Expropriation of Jewish-Owned Property*. Cambridge: Cambridge University Press.

Jandhyala, Srividya, Witold Henisz and Edward Mansfield. 2011. "Three Waves of BITs: The Global Diffusion of Foreign Investment Policy." *Journal of Conflict Resolution* 55 (6): 1047–73.

Jinnah, Sikina. 2010. "Overlap Management in the World Trade Organization: Secretariat Influence on Environmental Politics." *Global Environmental Politics* 10 (2): 54–79.

Jinnah, Sikina. 2014. *Post-Treaty Politics: Secretariat Influence in Global Environmental Politics*. Cambridge, MA: MIT Press.

Jinnah, Sikina, and Abby Lindsay. 2015. "Secretariat Influence on Overlap Management Politics in North America: NAFTA and the Commission for Environmental Cooperation." *Review of Policy Research* 32 (1): 124–45.

Johnson, Tana. 2014. *Organizational Progeny: Why Governments are Losing Control over the Proliferating Structures of Global Governance*. Oxford: Oxford University Press.

Joods Monument. 2017. "Abraham Broches and His Family." Added April 7, 2016. https://www.joodsmonument.nl/en/page/496255/abraham-broches-and-his-family.

Johnson, Simon, and Marzena Kowalska. 1994. "Poland: The Political Economy of Shock Therapy." In *Voting for Reform: Democracy, Political Liberalization, and Economic Adjustment*, edited by Stephan Haggard. Washington DC: World Bank Publications.

Jones, Geoffrey. 2005. *Multinationals and Global Capitalism: From the Nineteenth to the Twenty-first Century*. Oxford: Oxford University Press.

Jupille, Joseph, Walter Mattli, and Duncan Snidal. 2013. *Institutional Choice and Global Commerce*. Cambridge: Cambridge University Press.

Kapur, Devesh, John Lewis, and Richard Webb. 1997. *The World Bank: Its First Half Century, Vol I and II*. Washington DC: Brookings Institute Press.

Kellow, Aynsley, and Peter Carroll. 2013. "Exploring the Impact of International Civil Servants: The Case of the OECD." *International Journal of Public Administration* 35 (7): 482–91.

Keohane, Robert. 2017. "Observations on the Promise and Pitfalls of Historical Institutionalism in International Relations." In *International Politics and Institutions in Time*, edited by Orfeo Fioretos. Oxford: Oxford University Press.

Keohane, Robert, Andrew Moravcsik, and Anne-Marie Slaughter. 2000. "Legalized Dispute Resolution: Interstate and Transnational." *International Organization* 54 (3): 457–88.

Kerner, Andrew. 2014. "What We Talk About When We Talk About Foreign Investment." *International Studies Quarterly* 58 (4): 804–15.

King, Gary, Robert Keohane, and Sidney Verba. 1994. *Designing Social Inquiry: Scientific Inference in Qualitative Research*. Princeton: Princeton University Press.

Kinnear, Meg, Geraldine Fischer, Jara Minguez Almeida, Luisa Fernanda Torres, and Mairée Uran Bidegain. 2015. *Building International Investment Law: The First 50 Years of ICSID*. The Hague: Kluwer Law International.

Kinnear, Meg, and Robin Hansen. 2005. "The Influence of NAFTA Chapter 11 in the BIT Landscape." *UC Davis Journal of International Law and Policy* 12 (1): 101–19.

Kleinheisterkamp, Jan. 2012. "European Policy Space in International Investment Law." *ICSID Review* 27 (2): 416–31.

Kopper, Hilmar. 1997. "The World Bank's European Funding." In *The World Bank: Its First Half Century*, Vol II, edited by Devesh Kapur, John Lewis, and Richard Webb. Washington DC: Brookings Institute Press.

Koremenos, Barbara. 2016. *The Continent of International Law: Explaining Agreement Design*. Cambridge: Cambridge University Press.

Kulick, Andreas. 2012. *Global Public Interest in International Investment Law*. Cambridge: Cambridge University Press.

LaFeber, Walter. 1993. "Thomas C. Mann and the Devolution of Latin American Policy: From the Good Neighbor to Military Intervention." In *Behind the Throne: Servants of Power to Imperial Presidents, 1898–1968*, edited by Thomas McCormick and Walter LaFeber. Madison: University of Wisconsin Press.

Langford, Malcolm, and Daniel Behn. Forthcoming. "Managing Backlash: The Evolving Investment Treaty Arbitrator?" *European Journal of International Law*.

Lauterpacht, Elihu. 2008. Oral History (Second Interview), interview by Lesley Dingle. Squire Law Library, University of Cambridge.

Lauterpacht, Elihu. 2009. Foreword. In *The ICSID Convention: A Commentary*, by Christoph Schreuer. Cambridge: Cambridge University Press.

Lavopa, Federico, Lucas Barreiros, and Victoria Bruno. 2013. "How to Kill a BIT and Not Die Trying: Legal and Political Challenges of Denouncing or Renegotiating Bilateral Investment Treaties." *Journal of International Economic Law* 16 (4): 869–91.

Lebow, Richard Ned. 2000. "Contingency, Catalysts, and International System Change." *Political Science Quarterly* 115 (4): 591–616.

Levitsky, Steven. 1998. "Crisis, Party Adaptation and Regime Stability in Argentina: The Case of Peronism, 1989–1995." *Party Politics* (4): 445–70.

Levitsky, Steven, and Lucan Way. 1998. "Between a Shock and a Hard Place: the Dynamics of Labor-Backed Adjustment in Poland and Argentina." *Comparative Politics* 30 (2): 171–92.

Lindblad, J. Thomas. 2011. "The Economic Decolonisation of Indonesia: a Bird's-eye View." *Journal of Indonesian Social Sciences and Humanities* 4: 1–20.

Lindblom, Charles. 1959. "The Science of 'Muddling Through'." *Public Administration Review* 19: 79–88.

Lindblom, Charles. 1979. "Still Muddling, Not Yet Through." *Public Administration Review* 39: 517–26.

Linos, Katerina, and Tom Pegram. 2016. "The Language of Compromise in International Agreements." *International Organization* 70 (3): 587–621.

Lipson, Charles. 1985. *Standing Guard: Protecting Foreign Capital in the Nineteenth and Twentieth Centuries*. Berkeley: University of California Press.

Lowe, Vaughan. 2007. "Changing Dimensions of International Investment Law." Oxford Legal Studies Research Paper No.4/2007.

Lowenfeld, Andreas. 2003. "Investment Agreements and International Law." *Columbia Journal of Transnational Law* 42 (1): 123–31.

Maddison, Angus. 1995. *Monitoring the World Economy 1820–1992*. Paris: OECD.

Mahoney, James, and Kathleen Thelen, eds. 2009. *Explaining Institutional Change: Ambiguity, Agency, and Power*. Cambridge: Cambridge University Press.

Mahoney, James, and Kathleen Thelen, eds. 2015. *Advances in Comparative-Historical Analysis*. Cambridge: Cambridge University Press.

Manger, Mark, and Clint Peinhardt. Forthcoming. "Learning and the Precision of International Investment Agreements." *International Interactions.*

Mansfield, Edward, and Helen Milner. 2012. *Vetoes, Vetoes, and the Political Economy of International Trade Agreements*. Princeton: Princeton University Press.

Marcussen, Martin, and Jarle Trondal. 2011. "The OECD Civil Servant: Caught Between Scylla and Charybdis." *Review of International Political Economy* (5): 592–621.

Mason, Edward, and Robert Asher. 1973. *The World Bank Since Bretton Woods.* Washington DC: Brookings Institute Press.

Massoud, Mark Fathi. 2014. "International Arbitration and Judicial Politics in Authoritarian States." *Law & Social Inquiry* 39 (1): 1–30.

Maupin, Julie. 2013. "Public and Private in International Investment Law: An Integrated Systems Approach." *Virginia Journal of International Law* (54): 367–435.

Maurer, Noel. 2011. "The Empire Struck Back: Sanctions and Compensation in the Mexican Oil Expropriation of 1938." *Journal of Economic History* 71 (3): 590–615.

Maurer, Noel. 2013. *The Empire Trap: The Rise and Fall of U.S. Intervention to Protect American Property Overseas, 1893–2013*. Princeton: Princeton University Press.

Menaker, Andrea. 2004. "Benefiting from Experience: Developments in the United States' Most Recent Investment Agreements." *UC Davis Journal of International Law and Policy* 12: 121–9.

Mettler, Suzanne. 2005. *Soldiers to Citizens: The G.I. Bill and the Making of the Greatest Generation*. New York: Oxford University Press.

Miles, Kate. 2013. *The Origins of International Investment Law: Empire, Environment, and the Safeguarding of Capital*. Cambridge: Cambridge University Press.

Miller, Arthur. 1959. "Protection of Private Foreign Investment by Multilateral Convention." *American Journal of International Law* 53 (2): 371–8.

Mills, Alex. 2011. "Antinomies of Public and Private at the Foundations of International Investment Law and Arbitration." *Journal of International Economic Law* 14 (2): 469–503.

Milner, Helen. 1997. *Interests, Institutions, and Information: Domestic Politics and International Relations*. Princeton: Princeton University Press.

Minhas, Shahryar. 2016. "Learning from Incredible Commitments: Evolution and Impact of Bilateral Investment Treaties." PhD diss., Duke University.

Mitchell, Andrew, and Elizabeth Sheargold. 2015. "Protecting the Autonomy of States to Enact Tobacco Control Measures under Trade and Investment Agreements." *Tobacco Control* (24):e147–53.

Montt, Santiago. 2009. *State Liability in Investment Treaty Arbitration: Global Constitutional and Administrative Law in the BIT Generation*. Oxford: Hart Publishing.

Moravcsik, Andrew. 1997. "Taking Preferences Seriously: A Liberal Theory of International Politics." *International Organization* 51 (4):513–53.

Moravcsik, Andrew. 1999. "A New Statecraft? Supranational Entrepreneurs and International Cooperation." *International Organization* 53 (2): 267–306.

Mortenson, Julian Davis. 2010. "The Meaning of 'Investment': ICSID's *Travaux* and the Domain of International Investment Law." *Harvard International Law Journal* 51 (1): 257–318.

Moschella, Manuela, and Eleni Tsingou. 2013. "Introduction: The Financial Crisis and the Politics of Reform: Explaining Incremental Change." In *Great Expectations, Slow Transformations: Incremental Change in Post-Crisis Regulation*, edited by Manuela Moschella and Eleni Tsingou. Colchester: ECPR Press.

Mossallam, Mohammad. 2015. "Process Matters—South Africa's Experience Exiting Its BITs." Global Economic Governance Programme Working Paper 2015/97.

Murrell, Peter. 1993. "What is Shock Therapy? What Did It Do in Poland and Russia?" *Post-Soviet Affairs* 9 (2): 111–40.

Neumayer, Eric, and Laura Spess. 2005. "Do Bilateral Investment Treaties Increase Foreign Direct Investment to Developing Countries?" *World Development* 33 (10): 1567–85.

Newcombe, Andrew, and Lluis Paradell. 2009. *Law and Practice of Investment Treaties: Standards of Treatment*. The Hague: Kluwer Law International.

Nwogugu, E.I. 1965. *The Legal Problems of Foreign Investment in Developing Countries.* Manchester: Manchester University Press.

OECD. 2012. "Investor-state dispute settlement public consultation: 16 May–9 July 2012." Investment Division. http://www.oecd.org/daf/inv/internationalinvestmentagreements/50291642.pdf.

O'Keefe, Patrick. 1980. "The International Centre for Settlement of Investment Disputes." In *The Year Book of World Affairs 1980, Volume 34,* edited by George Keeton and Georg Schwarzenberger. London: Stevens & Sons.

Oliver, Robert. 1975. *International Economic Co-operation and the World Bank.* London: Macmillan.

Oliver, Robert. 1995. *George Woods and the World Bank.* London: Lynne Rienner.

Onis, Ziya, and Steven Webb. 1994. "Turkey: Democratization and Adjustment from Above." In *Voting for Reform: Democracy, Political Liberalization, and Economic Adjustment,* edited by Stephan Haggard. Washington DC: World Bank Publications.

OPIC. 2017. "Claims and Arbitral Awards." https://www.opic.gov/who-we-are/transparency/claims-and-arbitral-awards.

Palier, Bruno. 2005. "Change: French Social Policy in the 1990s." In *Beyond Continuity: Institutional Change in Advanced Political Economies,* edited by Wolfgang Streeck and Kathleen Thelen. Oxford: Oxford University Press.

Palmer, Doug. 2015. "Malmström's Washington Agenda." *Politico.* May 4. http://www.politico.eu/article/malmstroms-washington-agenda.

Paparinskis, Martins. 2010. "Limits of Depoliticisation in Contemporary Investor-State Arbitration." In *Select Proceedings of the European Society of International Law,* edited by James Crawford and Sarah Nouwen. Oxford: Hart.

Parra, Antonio. 2012. *The ICSID Convention: A History.* Oxford: Oxford University Press.

Parra, Antonio. 2013. "Participation in the ICSID Convention." *ICSID Review* 28: 169–78.

Parra, Antonio. 2015. "'Black's Bank' and the Settlement of Investment Disputes." In *Practising Virtue: Inside International Arbitration,* edited by David Caron, Stephan Schill, Abby Cohen Smutny, and Epaminontas Triantafilou. Oxford: Oxford University Press.

Parra, Antonio. 2016. "Remembering Aron Broches." October 14, 2016. Oxford University Press, Investment Claims. http://oxia.ouplaw.com/page/icsid-aron-broches.

Parra, Antonio. 2017. *The ICSID Convention: A History.* Second Edition. Oxford: Oxford University Press.

Patashnik, Eric. 2008. *Reforms at Risk: What Happens After Major Policy Reforms are Enacted.* Princeton: Princeton University Press.

Patashnik, Eric, and Julian Zelizer. 2013. "The Struggle to Remake Politics: Liberal Reform and the Limits of Policy Feedback in the Contemporary American State." *Perspectives on Politics* 11 (4): 1071–87.

Paulsson, Jan. 1995. "Arbitration Without Privity." *ICSID Review* 10 (2): 232–57.

Pauwelyn, Joost. 2014. "At the Edge of Chaos? Foreign Investment Law as a Complex Adaptive System, How It Emerged and How It Can Be Reformed." *ICSID Review* 29 (2): 372–418.

Peinhardt, Clint, and Rachel Wellhausen. 2016. "Withdrawing from Investment Treaties but Protecting Investment." *Global Policy* 7: 571–6.

Pierson, Paul. 1996. "The Path to European Integration: A Historical Institutionalist Analysis." *Comparative Political Studies* 29 (2): 123–63.

Pierson, Paul. 2004. *Politics in Time: History, Institutions, and Social Analysis*. Princeton: Princeton University Press.

Pinchis-Paulsen, Mona. 2014. "The Ancestry of 'Equitable Treatment' in Trade: Lessons from the League of Nations During the Inter-War Period." *Journal of World Investment & Trade* 15 (1): 13–72.

Pinchis-Paulsen, Mona. Forthcoming. "The Devil is in the Details: Using Historical Methodology to Investigate 'Fair and' 'Equitable Treatment' Clauses in Post-War United States' Commercial Treaties." In *International Investment Law and History*, edited by Rainer Hofmann, Stephan Schill, and Christian Tams. Cheltenham: Edward Elgar.

Platt, D.C.M. 1968(a). "Economic Factors in British Policy during the 'New Imperialism'." *Past and Present* (39, April): 120–38.

Platt, D.C.M. 1968(b). *Finance, Trade, Politics in British Foreign Policy 1815–1914*. Oxford: Clarendon Press.

Pollack, Mark. 2003. *The Engines of European Integration: Delegation, Agency, and Agenda Setting in the EU*. Oxford: Oxford University Press.

Posner, Elliot. 2005. "Sources of Institutional Change: The Supranational Origins of Europe's New Stock Markets." *World Politics* 58 (1): 1–40.

Potestà, Michele. 2011. "The Interpretation of Consent to ICSID Arbitration Contained in Domestic Investment Laws." *Arbitration International* 27 (2): 149–70.

Poulsen, Lauge Skovgaard. 2015. *Bounded Rationality and Economic Diplomacy: The Politics of Investment Treaties in Developing Countries*. Cambridge: Cambridge University Press.

Poulsen, Lauge Skovgaard, and Emma Aisbett. 2013. "When the Claim Hits: Bilateral Investment Treaties and Bounded Rational Learning." *World Politics* 65 (2): 273–313.

Prud'homme, Hector. 1985. Oral History, interview by John Muir. May 2. World Bank/IFC Archives, Oral History Program.

Puig, Sergio. 2013. "Emergence and Dynamism in International Organizations: ICSID, Investor-State Arbitration, and International Investment Law." *Georgetown Journal of International Law* 44 (2): 531–608.

Puig, Sergio. 2014(a). "No Right Without A Remedy: Foundations of Investor-State Arbitration." In *The Foundations of International Investment Law*, edited by Zachary Douglas, Joost Pauwelyn, and Jorge Vinuales. Oxford: Oxford University Press.

Puig, Sergio. 2014(b). "Social Capital in the Arbitration Market." *European Journal of International Law* 25 (2): 387–424.

Raustiala, Kal, and David Victor. 2004. "The Regime Complex for Plant Genetic Resources." *International Organization* 58: 277–309.

Reissner, H.G. 1967. "The Merchant Bankers" *Association of Jewish Refugees in Great Britain (AJR) Information*, June. http://www.ajr.org.uk/journalpdf/1967_june.pdf.

Rixen, Thomas. 2011. "From Double Tax Avoidance to Tax Competition: Explaining the Institutional Trajectory of International Tax Governance." *Review of International Political Economy* 18 (2): 197–227.

Rixen, Thomas, Lora Anne Viola, and Michael Zürn, eds. 2016. *Historical Institutionalism and International Relations: Explaining Institutional Development in World Politics*. Oxford University Press.

Roberts, Anthea. 2010. "Power and Persuasion in Investment Treaty Interpretation: the Dual Role of States." *American Journal of International Law* 104 (2): 179–225.

Roberts, Anthea. 2013. "Clash of Paradigms: Actors and Analogies Shaping the Investment Treaty System." *American Journal of International Law* 107 (1): 45–94.

Roberts, Anthea. 2015. "Triangular Treaties: The Extent and Limits of Investment Treaty Rights." *Harvard Journal of International Law* 56 (2): 353–417.

Rose-Ackerman, Susan, and Jennifer Tobin. 2005. "Foreign Direct Investment and the Business Environment in Developing Countries: The Impact of Bilateral Investment Treaties." Yale Law and Economics Research Paper Number 293.

Ryans, John, and James Baker. 1976. "The International Centre for Settlement of Investment Disputes (ICSID)." *Journal of World Trade Law* 10: 65–79.

Salacuse, Jeswald, and Nicolas Sullivan. 2005. "Do BITs Really Work? An Evaluation of Bilateral Investment Treaties and their Grand Bargain." *Harvard International Law Journal* 46: 67–130.

"Saudi Strides." 2017. *Global Arbitration Review* April 11. http://globalarbitrationreview.com/article/1139222/saudi-strides.

Sauvant, Karl. 2015. "The Negotiations of the United Nations Code of Conduct on Transnational Corporations: Experience and Lessons Learned." *The Journal of World Investment & Trade* 16: 11–87.

Schachter, Oscar. 1996. "New Custom: Power, Opinio Juris, and Contrary Practice." In *Theory of International Law at the Threshold of the 21st Century*, edited by Jerzy Makarczyk. The Hague: Kluwer Law International.

Schickler, Eric. 2001. *Disjointed Pluralism: Institutional Innovation and the Development of the U.S. Congress*. Princeton: Princeton University Press.

Schill, Stephan. 2009(a). *The Multilateralization of International Investment Law*. Cambridge: Cambridge University Press.

Schill, Stephan. 2009(b). "International Investment Law and Comparative Public Law—An Introduction." In *International Investment Law and Comparative Public Law*, edited by Stephan Schill. Cambridge: Cambridge University Press.

Schill, Stephan. 2017. "The Constitutional Frontiers of International Economic Law." *EJIL: Talk!* March 9. https://www.ejiltalk.org/the-constitutional-frontiers-of-international-economic-law/.

Schlandt, Jakob. 2013. "15 Juristen gegen die Demokratie" (15 Jurists Against Democracy) *Frankfurter Rundschau* March 23. http://www.fr-online.de/wirtschaft/vattenfall-15-juristen-gegen-die-demokratie,1472780,22189216.html.

Schmidt, John. 1976. "Arbitration Under the Auspices of the International Centre for Settlement of Investment Disputes (ICSID): Implications of the Decision on Jurisdiction in Alcoa Minerals of Jamaica, Inc v Government of Jamaica." *Harvard International Law Journal* 17: 90–109.

Schreuer, Christoph. 2001. *The ICSID Convention: A Commentary*. Cambridge: Cambridge University Press.
Schreuer, Christoph, Loretta Malintoppi, August Reinisch, and Anthony Sinclair. 2009. *The ICSID Convention: A Commentary*. Second Edition. Cambridge: Cambridge University Press.
Schrijver, Nico, and Vid Prislan. 2013. "Netherlands." In *Commentaries on Selected Model Investment Treaties*, edited by Chester Brown. Oxford: Oxford University Press.
Schwarzenberger, Georg. 1969. *Foreign Investments and International Law*. London: Stevens & Sons.
Shea, Donald. 1955. *The Calvo Clause: A Problem of Inter-American and International Law and Diplomacy*. Minneapolis: University of Minnesota Press.
Shearman & Sterling 2017. "Yukos: Largest Arbitral Award Ever." Accessed May 14 2017. http://www.shearman.com/en/services/practices/international-arbitration/yukos-arbitral-award.
Shihata, Ibrahim F.I. 1986. "Towards a Greater Depoliticization of Investment Disputes: The Roles of ICSID and MIGA." *ICSID Review* 1 (1): 1–25.
Shihata, Ibrahim F.I. 1991. *The World Bank in a Changing World: Selected Essays*. Compiled and edited by Franziska Tschofen and Antonio Parra. Dordrecht, NL: Martinus Nijhoff.
Shihata, Ibrahim F.I. 1993. *Legal Treatment of Foreign Investment: the World Bank Guidelines*. London: Martinus Nijhoff.
Shoup, Laurence, and William Minter. 2004. *Imperial Brain Trust: The Council on Foreign Relations and United States Foreign Policy*. New York: Monthly Review Press.
Simmons, Beth. 2014. "Bargaining Over BITs, Arbitrating Awards: The Regime for Protection and Promotion of International Investment." *World Politics* 66 (1): 12–46.
Skocpol, Theda. 1992. *Protecting Soldiers and Mothers: The Political Origins of Social Policy in the United States*. Cambridge, MA: Belknap Press.
Slater, Dan, and Erica Simmons. 2010. "Informative Regress: Critical Antecedents in Comparative Politics." *Comparative Political Studies* 43 (7): 886–917.
Soifer, Hillel David. 2012. "The Causal Logic of Critical Junctures." *Comparative Political Studies* 45 (12): 1572–97.
Sornarajah, M. 2004. *The International Law on Foreign Investment*. Second Edition. Cambridge: Cambridge University Press.
Soule, George, David Efron, and Norman Hess, under the supervision of Alvin Hansen. 1945. *Latin America in the Future World*. New York: Farrar and Rinehart, for The National Planning Association.
Spears, Suzanne. 2010. "The Quest for Policy Space in a New Generation of International Investment Agreements." *Journal of International Economic Law* 13 (4): 1037–75.
Streeck, Wolfgang, and Kathleen Thelen, eds. 2005. *Beyond Continuity: Institutional Change in Advanced Political Economies*. Oxford: Oxford University Press.
Szasz, Paul. 1970. "The Investment Disputes Convention and Latin America." *Virginia Journal of International Law* 11: 256–65.

Szasz, Paul. 1988. Oral History, interviewer and date of recording unknown. Accessed in the Cornell Law School Heritage Project: http://scholarship.law.cornell.edu/lawschool_heritage/34.

Tallberg, Jonas. 2003. *European Governance and Supranational Institutions: Making States Comply*. London: Routledge.

Tallberg, Jonas. 2010. "The Power of the Chair: Formal Leadership in International Cooperation." *International Studies Quarterly* 54 (1): 241–65.

Taylor, Telford. 1949. "Final Report to the Secretary of the Army on the Nuremberg War Crimes Trials under Control Council Law No. 10." Washington DC: US Library of Congress. https://www.loc.gov/rr/frd/Military_Law/pdf/NT_final-report.pdf.

Tetlock, Philip, and Aaron Belkin. 1996. "Counterfactual Thought Experiments in World Politics: Logical, Methodological, and Psychological Perspectives." In *Counterfactual Thought Experiments in World Politics: Logical, Methodological, and Psychological Perspectives*, edited by Philip Tetlock and Aaron Belkin. Princeton: Princeton University Press.

Thelen, Kathleen. 2004. *How Institutions Evolve: The Political Economy of Skills in Germany, Britain, the United States, and Japan*. Cambridge: Cambridge University Press.

Thomas, J. Christopher. 2017. "Dispute Settlement: An Appellate Mechanism for Investment Treaty Disputes?" United Nations Audiovisual Library of International Law, International Economic Law.

Thompson, Grahame. 2011. *The Constitutionalization of the Global Corporate Sphere?* Oxford: Oxford University Press.

Tienhaara, Kyla. 2009. *The Expropriation of Environmental Governance: Protecting Foreign Investors at the Expense of Public Policy*. Cambridge: Cambridge University Press.

Time Magazine. 1967. "West Germany: Two Sprecher for One." June 16.

The Economist. 2014. "The Arbitration Game." October 11.

Toye, John, and Richard Toye. 2004. *The UN and Global Political Economy: Trade, Finance, and Development*. Bloomington: Indiana University Press.

Toye, Richard. 2003. "Developing Multilateralism: The Havana Charter and the Fight for the International Trade Organization, 1947–1948." *The International History Review XXV* (2): 253–305.

UNCTAD. 1964. "Final Act and Report of the First United National Conference on Trade and Development." March 23–June 16, 1964. E/CONF.46/141, Vol 1.

UNCTAD. 1996. *International Investment Instruments: A Compendium*. Volume III, Regional Integration, Bilateral and Non-governmental Instruments. UN Sales No E.96.II.A.11.

UNCTAD. 2016. IIA Mapping Project. As of December 1, 2016. http://investmentpolicyhub.unctad.org/IIA/mappedContent.

Vadi, Valentina. 2016. *Analogies in International Investment Law and Arbitration*. Cambridge: Cambridge University Press.

Van Den Berg, Albert Jan. 1981. *The New York Arbitration Convention of 1958*. The Hague: Kluwer Law.

Vandevelde, Kenneth. 1992. *United States Investment Treaties: Policy and Practice.* Boston: Kluwer Law and Taxation.
Vandevelde, Kenneth. 1993(a). "Of Politics and Markets: The Shifting Ideology of the BITs." *International Tax and Business Law* 11 (2): 159–86.
Vandevelde, Kenneth. 1993(b). "US Bilateral Investment Treaties: The Second Wave." *Michigan Journal of International Law* 14: 621–704.
Vandevelde, Kenneth. 2010. *Bilateral Investment Treaties: History, Policy, and Interpretation.* Oxford: Oxford University Press.
Van Genugten, Willem, and Michael Scharf. 2007. Foreword. In *Criminal Jurisdiction 100 Years after the 1907 Hague Peace Conference.* The Hague: TMC Asser Press.
Van Harten, Gus. 2007. *Investment Treaty Arbitration and Public Law.* Oxford: Oxford University Press.
Van Harten, Gus. 2013. *Sovereign Choices and Sovereign Constraints.* Oxford: Oxford University Press.
Vaubel, Roland. 2006. "Principal-Agent Problems in International Organizations." *The Review of International Organizations* 1 (2): 125–38.
Voon, Tania, and Andrew Mitchell. 2016. "Denunciation, Termination and Survival: The Interplay of Treaty Law and International Investment Law." *ICSID Review* 31 (2): 413–33.
Voon, Tania, Andrew Mitchell, and James Munro. 2014. "Parting Ways: The Impact of Investor Rights on Mutual Termination of Investment Treaties." *ICSID Review* 29 (2): 451–73.
Waibel, Michael. 2007. "Two Worlds of Necessity in ICSID Arbitration: CMS and LG&E." *Leiden Journal of International Law* 20 (3): 637–48.
Waibel, Michael. 2011. *Sovereign Defaults Before International Courts and Tribunals.* Cambridge: Cambridge University Press.
Waibel, Michael, and Yanhei Wu. 2012. "Are Arbitrators Political?" Draft accessible here: https://www.researchgate.net/publication/256023521_Are_Arbitrators_Political.
Wälde, Thomas. 1996. "Investment Arbitration under the Energy Charter Treaty—From Dispute Settlement to Treaty Implementation." *Arbitration International* 12 (4): 429–66.
Weaver, Catherine. 2008. *Hypocrisy Trap: The World Bank and the Poverty of Reform.* Princeton: Princeton University Press.
Weir, Margaret. 2006. "When Does Politics Create Policy? The Organizational Politics of Change." In *Rethinking Political Institutions: The Art of the State* edited by Ian Shapiro, Stephen Skowronek, and Daniel Galvin. New York: New York University Press.
Weller, Patrick, and Yi-Chong Xu. 2010. "Agents of Influence: Country Directors at the World Bank." *Public Administration* 88: 211–31.
Wellhausen, Rachel. 2015. *The Shield of Nationality: When Governments Break Contracts with Foreign Firms.* Cambridge: Cambridge University Press.
Wells, Louis, and Rafiq Ahmed. 2007. *Making Foreign Investment Safe: Property Rights and National Sovereignty.* New York: Oxford University Press.
White & Case. 2015. "International Arbitration Survey: Improvements and Innovations in International Arbitration." Conducted with Queen Mary University of London. http://www.arbitration.qmul.ac.uk/docs/164761.pdf.

Note: WikiLeaks Cables Relating to Jamaican Bauxite Mining are in Chronological Order

WikiLeaks cable ID: 1973STATE206992_b from October 19, 1973. "OPIC- Release of Church Sub-Committee Report" https://www.WikiLeaks.org/plusd/cables/1973STATE206992_b.html.

WikiLeaks cable ID: 1973KINGST03921_b from November 17, 1973. "Governments to Open Discussions with Aluminum Companies" https://www.WikiLeaks.org/plusd/cables/1973KINGST03921_b.html.

WikiLeaks cable ID: 1973STATE250610_b from December 27, 1973. "Bauxite Commission and GOJ Bauxite Policies" https://www.WikiLeaks.org/plusd/cables/1973STATE250610_b.html.

WikiLeaks ID: 1974KINGST00054_b from January 5, 1974. "Bauxite Negotiations Sitrep 1" Declassified June 30, 2005. https://www.WikiLeaks.org/plusd/cables/1974KINGST00054_b.html.

WikiLeaks cable ID: 1974KINGST00069_b from January 7, 1974. "Bauxite Negotiations Sitrep 3" Declassified June 30, 2005. http://www.WikiLeaks.org/plusd/cables/1974KINGST00069_b.html.

WikiLeaks ID: 1974STATE083254_b from April 24, 1974. "Bauxite Negotiations" https://www.WikiLeaks.org/plusd/cables/1974STATE083254_b.html.

WikiLeaks cable ID: 1974KINGST01492_b from April 26, 1974. "Bauxite Negotiations Sitrep 32: Eyeball to Eyeball" https://www.WikiLeaks.org/plusd/cables/1974KINGST01495_b.html.

WikiLeaks cable ID: 1974KINGST01495_b from April 27, 1974. "Bauxite Negotiations Sitrep 34: Confrontation Hanging Fire" https://www.WikiLeaks.org/plusd/cables/1974KINGST01495_b.html.

WikiLeaks cable ID: 1974KINGST01706_b from May 15, 1974. "Bauxite Negotiations Sitrep #48" https://www.WikiLeaks.org/plusd/cables/1974KINGST01706_b.html.

WikiLeaks cable ID: 1974KINGST01772_b from May 21, 1974. "Bauxite Sitrep 58: Looking Backward and Forward" https://www.WikiLeaks.org/plusd/cables/1974KINGST01772_b.html.

WikiLeaks ID: 1974STATE158129_b from July 22, 1974. "Alcoa's Second Quarter Profits Soar" https://www.WikiLeaks.org/plusd/cables/1974STATE158129_b.html.

WikiLeaks cable: 1974KINGST02613_b from July 29, 1974. "Bauxite and Aid Education Loan" https://www.WikiLeaks.org/plusd/cables/1974KINGST02613_b.html.

WikiLeaks ID: 1974STATE194229_b from September 4, 1974. "USG Position on IBRD Loan for Jamaican Airport Development" https://www.WikiLeaks.org/plusd/cables/1974STATE194229_b.html.

WikiLeaks ID: 1975KINGST02242_b from June 11, 1975. "Bauxite Negotiations Make Haste Slowly" https://www.WikiLeaks.org/plusd/cables/1975KINGST02242_b.html.

WikiLeaks ID: 1975KINGST02414_b from June 24, 1975. "Alcoa to Start Talks with GoJ" https://www.WikiLeaks.org/plusd/cables/1975KINGST02414_b.html.

Wilber, Donald. 1954. Overthrow of Premier Mossadeq of Iran: November 1952–August 1953. CIA, Clandestine Services History, declassified 2000. http://www2.gwu.edu/~nsarchiv/NSAEBB/NSAEBB28/1-Orig.pdf.

Woods, Ngaire. 2006. *The Globalizers: the IMF, the World Bank, and their borrowers.* London: Cornell University Press.

World Bank. 1964. Annual Meetings of the Boards of Governors, Tokyo, September 7–11. http://documents.worldbank.org/curated/en/591861468167659630/pdf/534000BR0board10Box345609B01PUBLIC1.pdf.

World Bank. 2014. Voting Powers: Allocation of Votes by Organization. http://www.worldbank.org/en/about/leadership/votingpowers World Bank Corporate Secretariat. 2014. Voting Power of Executive Directors. Data as of August 29, 2014. http://siteresources.worldbank.org/BODINT/Resources/278027-1215524804501/IBRDEDsVotingTable.pdf.

World Nuclear Association. 2017. "Nuclear Power in Sweden" http://www.world-nuclear.org/information-library/country-profiles/countries-o-s/sweden.aspx.

Xu, Yi-Chong, and Patrick Weller. 2008. "'To Be, But Not to Be Seen': Exploring the Impact of International Civil Servants." *Public Administration* 86: 35–51.

Yackee, Jason. 2007. "Do BITs Really Work? Revisiting the Empirical Link Between Investment Treaties and Foreign Direct Investment." University of Wisconsin Legal Studies Research Paper Number 1054.

Yackee, Jason. 2008. "*Pacta Sunt Servanda* and State Promises to Foreign Investors Before Bilateral Investment Treaties: Myth and Reality." *Fordham International Law Journal* 32 (5): 1550–613.

Yackee, Jason. 2010. "Do Bilateral Investment Treaties Promote Foreign Direct Investment? Some Hints from Alternative Evidence." *Virginia Journal of International Law* 51 (2): 397–442.

Young, Oran. 1989. "The Politics of International Regime Formation: Managing Natural Resources and the Environment." *International Organization* 43 (3): 349–75.

Zürn, Michael. 2016. "Historical Institutionalism and International Relations—Strange Bedfellows?" In *Historical Institutionalism and International Relations: Explaining Institutional Development in World Politics*, edited by Thomas Rixen, Thomas, Lora Anne Viola, and Michael Zurn. Oxford: Oxford University Press.

Index